THE
SHATTERED SILENCE

THE
SHATTERED SILENCE

The Eli Cohen Affair

by

Zwy Aldouby and Jerrold Ballinger

COWARD, McCANN & GEOGHEGAN, INC.

New York

THIRD PRINTING

Library of Congress Catalog Card Number: 73-81016

Printed in the United States of America

For Sofia and Ilan

Contents

Illustrations follow page 246.

ACKNOWLEDGMENTS

The people to whom we are indebted are many, and it would be impossible to name them all. We owe a great debt of gratitude to our editor, Patricia Brehaut Soliman, for her guidance, invaluable advice, and saintly patience. She has taken a personal interest in seeing us through this book and was good enough to help us with the manuscript and to offer much valuable criticism. We must also acknowledge a very heavy debt of gratitude to our fellow newspapermen Jacques Lacoste, Larry O'Donnell and Miguel Angel Alvarez Roig, who have helped us conduct the investigations in Beirut, Damascus and Buenos Aires, without whose help this book could not have been adequately written. We wish to express our thanks to Dr. Bruno Piterman, John G. Diefenbaker, MP Maurice Orbach and MK Moshe Sneh for answering our extensive queries. We also acknowledge the generous assistance of Mrs. Huysmans for allowing us to use the documents concerning the intervention of her late husband, Belgian Minister of State Camille Huysmans, in behalf of Eli Cohen. Our gratitude goes to Dr. Strothmann of the Bonn Foreign Ministry, MB Eugen Selbmann and especially State Attorney Lorenz Rupp for their invaluable assistance.

Special thanks must go to Batonnier Paul Arrighi and Maîtres Jean Talandier and Adrian Wolters, without whose aid we would not have been able to proceed with our project. For much helpful advice we must thank Murad Semach, Baruch Sachs, Baruch Mizrachi and Shlomo Cohen-Sidon. We also found invaluable the information supplied by Roger Baldwin, Sean MacBride, Victor Feather, Eugene Descamps, and we especially appreciated the aid of Dr. Oscar Karbach and Mrs. Ella Maier of the World Jewish Congress.

For his editorial guidance we would particularly like to thank Russel Nevins, who has worked on the book almost from its inception, offering invaluable suggestions. Our gratitude also goes to Adriawa Evans for her devotion and extracurricular typing.

Last but not least we would like to thank Bill Cohen for his patience, devotion and support throughout the writing stage and Leonard Shearer for the much helpful advice he has given us. To all these and to the many others who must remain anonymous for obvious reasons we express our sincere gratitude.

Book One
The Capture

1
The Raid

Damascus was nearly deserted before dawn on the rainy Sunday morning of January 24, 1965. Abu Rummaneh, the luxurious residential sector that scales Mount Kassiun to the north, lay silent, its streetlamps haloed in mist. Only a band of dogs which had sneaked into the city from the Ghuta oasis roamed the quarter noisily, pawing for food in the mounds of garbage stacked along the alleys.

General Staff Headquarters, the normally bustling fortresslike complex off Abu Rummaneh Boulevard, was unusually still. The green, white and black Syrian tricolor drooped in the rain, floating limply over the main building. The sentries huddled in their towers to protect themselves from the cold western wind that blew out of Lebanon, and the MP's assigned to patrol the narrow path behind the barbed wire took refuge in the guardhouse. The immobile tanks guarding the entrance gave the scene the air of a desolate battlefield, gloomy and abandoned in the floodlights that constantly scoured the compound.

The neon cross on the Armenian church had just flickered out when the stillness was broken by a small motorcade of dappled olive military trucks and staff cars painted with tan desert colors approaching the gates from inside the compound. The leading car, a chauffeur-driven Moskwich bearing no identification other than two tiny banners attached to its front fenders stopped momentarily at the outer checkpoint. A military policeman rushed out of the sentry box, glanced at the two officers seated in the back and, after recognizing the trim figure of the chief of military intelligence, hurried forward to lift the barrier.

Akid Ahmad Suidani, the colonel who headed Syria's Second Bureau, seemed visibly disturbed as he spoke, softly but rapidly, to his chief of Internal Security. *Mukadem* Azziz Maaruf, a short, chunky lieutenant colonel with dark hair thinning in front, deep black eyes and bushy eyebrows slightly drawn, listened impassively as his superior carefully described the difficulties of the operation ahead. But when he was praised for his performance during the preparatory stage, his expression betrayed a trace of self-satisfaction. Colonel Suidani abruptly interrupted his monologue to answer the sentry's salute and perfunctorily waved the driver to move on.

The convoy sped down Abu Rummaneh Boulevard in the direction of Parliament. At street corners, soldier-watchmen in heavy boots and long overcoats continued to doze lazily over their rifles, undisturbed by the sudden passing of troops. They were startled out of their stupor only when the motorcade stopped short a few hundred yards away, within view of the Palace of Guests. A contingent of counterintelligence agents carrying Samoval submachine guns and more than a dozen plainclothesmen with no visible weapons jumped from the cars and gathered on the sidewalk around a thin-faced young major. Adnan Tawara, head of the Palestine Department in the Internal Security Services, issued last-minute instructions. He then walked over to a group of officers commanding heavily armed elite troops who were waiting patiently in the curbed trucks and gave orders to set up roadblocks around the General Staff compound and dispatch patrols to the nearby area between the Yazid and Tara rivers. Within minutes, a detachment of red-capped military police bolstered by squads of commandos in camouflaged fatigues threw a tight cordon around eight city blocks. Tawara later assigned another unit to seal off vital roads, detour traffic, prevent the trams and buses from making their regular stops, and keep early risers away from the neighborhood.

While the troops were taking up their positions, the major's jeep drew up behind Suidani's limousine now parked with lights off alongside the main roadblock. Tawara made his report, and the two conferred briefly, but their conversation was constantly interrupted by a stream of radio messages coming over the transmitter-receiver strapped onto the jeep's rear seat. After answering a torrent of questions from roadblock commanders who sought clarification about the deployment, the two proceeded to make a final strategy review.

By the time all units had assumed their positions a chilly breeze had parted the mist. The city lamps finally won their battle against darkness. Only a few sounds rang faintly from the nearby Kurdish Quarter: the lonely bray of a donkey and the barking of hungry dogs. It was close to 6:24 A.M., and a freight train leaving for Beirut chugged out of the Hidjaz railway terminal with furious puffs and sharp whistles. The sounds of early morning heralded by the crow of roosters were now echoed by a chorus of cries from the Old City; the cries of sherbet sellers calling early risers to refresh their hearts reverberated from the Citadel. The traffic noises intensified, and the smell of cheap gasoline invaded the jasmine-scented morning.

As the gray light cleared, Tawara sought his superior's permission to begin the operation. Suidani, however, preferred to wait a while longer. The colonel stressed the importance of raiding apartment No. 8 in the four-story white-stone building at precisely five minutes past seven. At that moment the deep voice of a muezzin summoning his faithful to prayer came over a loudspeaker from a nearby minaret. The long-drawn cry of *Allah akbar. Ashhad an la ilah illa-llah* rose in splinters of sad refrain, falling tremulously away. A muffled answer chimed in from the hundreds of mosques all over the city.

Suidani studied his watch. The time was forty-five minutes past six. The two officers held a whispered conference, and the major signaled his men to deploy. A phalanx of detectives and counterespionage agents spread out, moving slowly in pairs, down Chahabander Street toward the building which stood across from the General Staff Headquarters, not far from the private residence of the president of the republic, General Amin al-Hafez. As they approached the house, a detective on stakeout signaled that all was quiet. Tawara carefully positioned his men: A number of plainclothesmen took cover behind the trees flanking the street; others hid in nearby doorways or in the pockets of shadow around the house. They covered the entrance, the backyard and all four corners of the building. The rest stood a few hundred yards away ready to storm the house at a sign from Major Tawara.

Besides Suidani, Tawara and a few select officers of the counterespionage service, only Brigadier Mazid al-Hindi, chief of the Internal Security Services, the general in charge of the military police and the heads of the secret police were aware of the raiding party's ultimate objective: the arrest of a Baath Party official so highly placed in the Syrian government that practically no state secret was beyond his reach. Yet by sheer happenstance, Suidani's counterintelligence bureau had discovered that the man, whose credentials as a loyal Syrian had seemed impeccable, was very probably working from within to undermine the nation's security. What the bureau could not determine was his real identity and the nation for which he was working. The unexpected discovery had triggered an elaborate and painstaking investigation producing some clues, but equally as many dead ends. The only certainty was that the apartment was occupied by Kamal Amin Taabet, a handsome thirty-nine-year-old bachelor, who owned a thriving import-export firm specializing in Damascene furniture, tapestries and *objets d'art*. According to public records, he had been born in Lebanon to Syrian parents, who emigrated first to Egypt and then to Argentina. Taabet had arrived from Buenos Aires in January, 1962. He quickly became a member of the Damascus *haut monde*, and many a socialite had succumbed to his charm. But despite his social successes, Taabet had gracefully eluded the traps of both designing mothers and eligible daughters.

A committed Marxist and fiery patriot, Taabet had enrolled in the Arab Socialist Baath Party shortly before it came to power in 1963. Like all militants, he underwent a routine loyalty check, but his background received no more than peripheral attention from the Second Bureau. Discreet inquiries at Baath headquarters further revealed that in the course of the last two years he had befriended high-ranking Army officers and government officials, among them Secretary General Michel Aflak, former Premier Salah al-Bitar and President Amin al-Hafez, none of whom ever had reason to question his dedication to Arab Socialism. Taabet was a member of the National Revolutionary Council, and, at the suggestion of Hafez, had been appointed to the party's executive bodies. Two weeks before, his name had been put forward by council members for the post of Minister of Information in an upcoming Cabinet realignment. Taabet had visited the highly restricted Syrian-Israeli border area several times in the company of senior Syrian and Egyptian officials, and Suidani also learned that several influential officers in the military faction of the Baath had suggested that the Argentinean émigré be appointed Deputy Minister of Defense. His candidacy was scheduled to be discussed at a special meeting of the NRC on the first Tuesday in February.

As soon as he had read these first reports, Suidani ordered Taabet's telephone tapped and his apartment placed under constant surveillance. The bureau also shadowed him around the clock, concentrating on a vigilant observation of his relationship with the Baath higher-ups. "From the moment I saw the list of those who knew him," Suidani later said, "I suspected Taabet was involved in actions inimical to the nation's security." One whose name he could not reveal, "but who was known for his influence in the highest echelons of Damascus," particularly puzzled Suidani. But the investigation was not centered only on Taabet. Most of his contacts were scrupulously screened. "We investigated all those who were in the habit of visiting him," Suidani recounted. "But from the very beginning, we encountered many difficulties, partly because of the extreme care with which Taabet acted. He employed no maid, cleaned his own apartment and washed his own clothes . . . We also found that . . . he had an agreed signal for certain visitors. He opened the door only after a prearranged series of rings."[1]

The wearisome trailing nevertheless paid dividends, and counterespionage agents soon accumulated a fairly comprehensive file on Taabet's contacts. Those he seemed closely involved with were quietly arrested in the hope that they might yield useful information about his activities. As arbitrary arrests of party activists were commonplace, the disappearance of some of his friends was not expected to arouse Taabet's suspicion. Yet from all the hours of questioning, the bureau did not glean a single piece of information that might lead to the discovery of Taabet's true identity.

On Friday, January 22, Suidani, Maaruf and Tawara met in the first of two conferences to discuss tactics. The counterespionage officers urged the postponement of any precipitous action for at least forty-eight hours to allow their agents to track down more of Taabet's contacts. Suidani, however, favored an immediate move, arguing that a surprise raid might enable them to capture evidence that would identify Taabet's home base. At the second conference on Saturday, the three agreed to extend the surveillance for two more days. One team of detectives disguised as road workers would watch the apartment house; another contingent would follow visitors, while a third remained ready to apprehend Taabet himself. Suidani sought approval of this scheme from Defense Minister Mamdouh Jaber, but his plan was flatly vetoed. The complex procedure would accomplish nothing, the minister said, and ordered Taabet's immediate seizure.[2]

Major Tawara, who was assigned to organize the raid, carefully coordinated the operation in conjunction with the military and civilian police and scheduled it for the following morning. "We set the hour for breaking into the apartment at seven A.M.," Suidani remembered, "with the intention of finding him in bed. We wanted to prevent him from defending himself or trying to commit suicide by jumping from the fourth floor. Three men were assigned to storm his room, while a fourth was to subdue him in bed."[3] A note of Hollywood-style dramatics was included in the instructions given those assigned to open the apartment door. Should the lockpick fail, they were to break the door down with their bodies or shoot its hinges off with submachine guns.

At 7:02 the mixed contingent led by Suidani and Tawara moved closer into position around the apartment building, and at four minutes past the hour agents descended on the house from all points. At a signal from Tawara one of the officers opened the front door, startling an elderly man clad in pajamas, who was standing in the hall with a flashlight in his hand. The neighbor, a tenant on the first floor, had come out to investigate the strange noises, but the raiders gave him no chance to satisfy his curiosity. A large palm covered his mouth, while five men armed with submachine guns raced up the stairs to the fourth floor.

It took one of the detectives only seconds to force the door. The others passed him and rushed through the apartment. When the bedroom door flew open, Taabet looked up in disbelief. He was sitting by a miniature transmitter, its tubes still glowing, his fist on the Morse key. He had started transmitting one hour earlier that morning and was as shocked as Suidani, who later said, "Taabet surprised us. He was awake and awaiting a message." The stunned Taabet made no attempt to reach for the gun lying on the night table but instead grabbed a flask of acid that lay nearby and threw it on his codes and ciphers. His next reaction was to protest indignantly at the armed intrusion and to insist that he was an Arab immigrant from Argentina whose hobby was operating a shortwave radio. A plainclothesman, who had pinned back Taabet's arms, showed no intention of being convinced. His pistol pointed directly at the back of the suspect's neck, the trigger finger beginning to tighten. Taabet did not resist and stood perfectly still as the arrest was made.

One of the newly arrived detectives was able to retrieve some of the documents from the acid solution with the barrel of his gun. Tawara and Suidani were rewarded for their timing. Among the documents was "a piece of paper on which Taabet had written a coded message he had just finished transmitting," Suidani related. "It ended with the words 'will give supplementary information concerning.' "[4] In a metal cylinder lying open on the floor, they also found several sheets containing clear-language messages about upcoming major political changes in the Baath that Taabet had had no time to encode.

The counterintelligence officers ransacked the eight-room apartment. Every corner was carefully examined; the tile floors were lifted, walls were broken, and the luxurious furniture was systematically taken apart. The bathroom revealed a photo laboratory and the kitchen floor a second transmitter, two bars of Yardley soap filled with *plastique*, several rolls of microfilm, a book of addresses and Taabet's checkbooks and entire commercial correspondence with firms in Switzerland, Belgium and Germany. When asked about the explosives, Taabet denied they were to be used for sabotage and claimed they had been intended to destroy the two transmitters. But Suidani's bewilderment reached a peak, he later confided, when his agents uncovered a movie camera equipped with infrared film and a tape recorder built into the wall of the green guest room—a setup—in the best German espionage tradition.*

Guarded by two detectives, Taabet stood near a desk in the study, focusing his entire attention on the intruders. Using a moment when they were inattentive, he slowly extracted a cyanide pill from a drawer behind him. The instant he felt the capsule between his fingers, Taabet attempted to throw it into his mouth. One of the policemen shouted a warning, and both jumped him; they managed to retrieve the poison after a short struggle.

*At the close of the last century, William Stieber, the police director of Kaiser Wilhelm I, established in Berlin a "Green House" where a select few who possessed many secrets of state could seek erotic entertainment. In the house provisions were made for the practice of observing every imaginable form of indulgence, including secret listening holes and double mirrors through which Stieber's agents could watch their prominent guests. A green "Salon Kitty," the counterpart of Stieber's house in World War II, also in Berlin, was a creation of Hitler's evil genius, SS Police and Intelligence Chief General Reinhard Heydrich. Concealed behind double walls, exotic furnishings and subdued lights, microphones, cameras and tape recorders had been installed by the Nazis to trap SS higher-ups in their most intimate and unguarded moments.

Taabet was handcuffed and forced into a chair facing Suidani. *"Shkun anta?* [Who are you?]" the colonel asked harshly.
"What is your real name?" Without waiting for an answer, he
demanded, "Who do you work for? Who sent you to spy on
us?" Taabet replied matter-of-factly that he was an Arab from
Argentina who had been asked by a compatriot in Buenos Aires
to send and receive messages in code that he did not understand. "I have never wanted to know their real contents," he
said simply. "I agreed to work merely as a radio operator for
large amounts of money." He had always met his employers in
Switzerland, Taabet explained, but was totally unaware of their
identity. While he was still talking, a detective handed the
colonel three notebooks with codes discovered in a metal con-
tainer hidden in an arm of one of the sofas. Suidani asked
ironically how he had found a secret formula for coding and
decoding without knowing the actual meaning of the message.
Taabet had nothing further to say.[5]

Major Tawara then asked for his belt, tie and shoelaces and
instructed the two plainclothesmen to bring the prisoner to the
barracks of the 72nd Armored Division at the Hamadieh base.
He was to be placed under heavy guard until the interrogators
took charge. Taabet was pushed into a police van, and before
his bewildered neighbors could collect themselves, the entire
party was racing off.

The guard on duty at the jail of the 72nd Armored Division
unlocked the heavy iron door at the end of the corridor and
stepped aside to allow a captain to enter. The narrow solitary-
confinement cell was dark and humid, and the officer could
barely distinguish the figure sitting on the concrete floor in the
corner. He ordered the man to rise and follow him up the stairs
to the commandant's office on the second floor, where Suidani
and Tawara were already waiting in the company of Inspector
Suleiman Sarraj, director of the High Police Committee.

Before Taabet could accept the chair he was offered, the
door opened, and Lieutenant General Amin al-Hafez entered
with an entourage of five. The two officers saluted, while the

inspector deferentially retreated. The president, conveniently forgetful of his previous relationship with Taabet, began questioning him as if they were now meeting for the first time. He demanded to know to whom the prisoner had been sending the messages and what type of information he had transmitted. "At first," Hafez would recall, "we thought that he was in fact an Arab . . . who had been recruited by the Israeli intelligence services in Argentina and planted in Syria. But when I looked into his eyes, I had my doubts as to his Arab identity." Cautiously, Hafez began to question Taabet about Moslem customs. The prisoner was confused. The president abruptly ordered him to recite a passage from the Fatha, the first chapter of the Koran. Taabet began to declaim the prayer but faltered at the end of a few phrases. He attempted to explain his uncertainty by telling the president that he did not remember the Scriptures because he had left the Middle East when he was only a boy. Hafez was not satisfied. He pressed Taabet for more details "about our religion," but the prisoner preferred to remain silent. "That was when I realized my doubts were justified," the president remembered. "He was not an Arab." Turning to Suidani, Hafez snapped, "I think he is a Jew—an Israeli agent! " To a Lebanese newsman he later boasted, "It was not the first time in my life that I recognized a Jewish spy . . . I have a certain experience in such interrogations."

The president instructed Tawara to press his inquiry in a new direction and stop at nothing, even torture, to make Taabet talk. He wanted to know exactly what information the agent had communicated and to what enemy. He then left for the nearby Officers' Club to await the outcome of the interrogation. Two hours later, when Suidani informed him that Taabet was stubbornly maintaining his initial story, the president returned to the commandant's office only to hear the prisoner repeat time and again the same answers. "His clumsy attempts to deny espionage intent were somewhat pathetic," Hafez would later remark. "But then one clings to any straw in a fight for one's life. . . . He ultimately resigned himself to the inevitable."[6] The president signaled Tawara to resume third-degree methods and was about to leave when Taabet suddenly spoke, "There will be no need for that," he said in a steady voice. "I am an Israeli operative employed by the Mosad Haelion Lemodiin Ubitachon.* My name is Eliahu ben Shaul Cohen, and I live with my wife and three children in Bat Yam, near Tel Aviv. All I will add is that I have operated in the best interest of my country."[7] The officers in the room stood silent. Red with anger, Hafez stepped forward and slapped the prisoner on the face. Then, without a word, he left hurriedly, followed by his entourage.

The following morning Eliahu Cohen was again summoned to the interrogration room. He barely had time to sit on the only available chair when Suidani entered, smiling effusively. During the interrogation, the colonel suggested that Eli could improve his situation by agreeing to send false information over the captured transmitter. If he chose to collaborate, Suidani promised to save his life; in the event he declined, the bureau would still use a double. Eli readily agreed but added that "the Center would never fall into such a predictable, obvious trap." The colonel was surprised at his willingness to cooperate and warned that the slightest digression from the prescribed message would mean immediate death. Eli assured him that he would radio only what was ordered.

Moments later the prisoner was led into another office, where his miniature transmitter lay ready. Shortly before eight a technician, who was to monitor the broadcast, handed him an already-coded message. Conscious of Suidani's pistol pointed at his head, Eli started sending without checking its contents. The Arab operator nodded affirmatively at the colonel's inquiring look. The transmission was clear.

After Eli had ended, they all sat silently waiting for a reply. Only seconds passed before Tel Aviv's signal came over the Phillips radio connected to the miniature transmitter. Suidani smiled triumphantly as his operator dashed down the numbers, deciphered them and handed him the message. In addition to

*The Supreme Agency for Intelligence and Security, Israel's equivalent of the CIA.

the standard acknowledgment, it read: "Yesterday's information unclear. Please repeat." Suidani nodded, and Eli took the key. The colonel now watched his every move, glancing occasionally at his subordinate. The Center ok'd but insisted that reception was bad and ordered Eli to transmit again that same evening at eight.

Suidani was radiant. Tel Aviv suspected nothing; his plan had worked. He had made contact with the control station in Israel, opening an information channel into the Mosad. Eli, in turn, realized that he had succeeded in warning the Mosad, which was obviously playing for time. During the three years he had worked in Damascus the last line of every message he had radioed was always garbled. A coherent text was the pre-arranged signal that he had been arrested.[8]

In the evening Eli again transmitted a clear, straight message. After he had finished there was silence. When a similar attempt failed again the following day, Suidani understood that the game was lost and ordered his technician to radio a final message, this time not from Operative 88:

To Levi Eshkol and the Chief of the Israeli Intelligence Services: Kamal and his friends are now our guests in Damascus. We are waiting for you to send us their friends. Will inform you later of their fate. Colonel Ahmad Suidani, Chief of Military Intelligence, for the Syrian Counterespionage Service.[9]

Book Two
The Man

2
The Haret

While the Kamal Amin Taabet case was becoming a volatile political issue in Damascus, the arrest of Eli Cohen on charges of espionage had created an air of bafflement in Bat Yam, Israel. Relatives, friends and neighbors grew even more incredulous as the details of Eli's mission began to seep out. No one close to the Cohens in the Ramat Yosef suburb had suspected that the charming but rather reserved civil servant could possibly have been leading a double life. Indeed, many who had known Eli in Israel would later say that he seemed to have been one of the least likely recruits for espionage. He was considered a quiet, hardworking government employee, an exemplary husband and a devoted father—from all appearances, a stable, uncomplicated man with no outward contradictions. His major pleasures were swimming, hiking or watching the Saturday soccer matches. He had no particular interest in music or art. He drank little, never gambled and so completely avoided discussions of local or foreign affairs that his friends could not recall where he stood on any issue.

Eli's placid temperament belied the romantic image of the intelligence agent and disguised a character more enigmatic than anyone had imagined. He was also endowed with most uncommon abilities which particularly suited him to serve in the Mosad. "He had a surplus," one of his superiors later said, "of every quality we were looking for." Eli possessed exceptional powers of retention, a superior knowledge of electronics, an unusual affinity for languages and, above all, a sense of mission molded by a harsh, often dangerous early life.

Eliahu Cohen was born on December 16, 1924, in Alexandria, Egypt, the son of an impoverished shopkeeper, who, like thousands of Jews and Christians, had emigrated from the predominantly Moslem vilayet of Aleppo, Syria, toward the end of 1914. Shaul Cohen had chosen the relative security of life in Egypt because of his precarious existence in Greater Syria, then a part of the Ottoman Empire. At the turn of the century, government under the regime of the Sultan of all Ottomans and Caliph of the Arabs, Abdul Hamid II, and his successor, Muhammad V, was rapacious, venal and slipshod. The vast majority of the Jews in Asia Minor lived in misery but were nevertheless mercilessly taxed. Administrative extortion reached a scale and scope unknown elsewhere, and corruption, a common practice, pervaded the state. The lives of both the Arabs and the minorities were dependent on the cruel whims of the pashas. Scores were arbitrarily imprisoned, executed or deported to remote parts of the empire. The rigors of Turkish hegemony did not slacken, even after the revolution of the Young Turks and the substitution for the sultan's rule of that of the Committee of Union and Progress. "Justice was a matter of bribes," a historian of the era observed, "property a matter of favor and life a matter of luck."

For most of his young life, Shaul had lived in this perilous atmosphere marked by the ever-present threat of military tribunals and firing squads. When he grew older, he began wishing for opportunities and rewards greater than his homeland could offer. As a number of his relatives had settled in the flourishing Jewish community of Alexandria, he resolved to emigrate to Egypt.

The ship that brought Shaul to Egypt docked in the Eastern Harbor of Alexandria only a few weeks before the outbreak of World War I. The young Syrian émigré found Alexandria

feverishly preparing to thwart a threatened Turko-German invasion from bases in Palestine. The local British garrison was
organizing the city's defense, and the population was readying
itself for a long struggle. Citizens were busy stockpiling provisions, reinforcing defenses left from the Napoleonic Wars or
digging new trenches. But the feared siege never materialized,
and Alexandrians were spared the hardships of war. Their allies,
however, subjected them to four years of humiliating treatment
and arrogant condescension that created a burning resentment
which would endure until the last British soldier left Egypt.

For a short time, while looking for work, Shaul stayed with
his relatives. The letters of introduction he carried from Aleppo
soon helped him secure employment in a tie atelier owned by a
wealthy Jewish merchant. In the years of prosperity that followed the Treaty of Versailles, Shaul struck out on his own,
opening a small fabric and tie shop centrally located in the
Haret al-Yahud, the Jewish Quarter. Before long, he gave up all
but a sentimental attachment to his homeland. He still talked
with nostalgia about Aleppo and never lost his Syrian accent
but easily assimilated into the ranks of the community's middle
class and came to consider himself for all purposes an Egyptian.
Shaul was unable, though, to acquire Egyptian citizenship and,
like all immigrants, was forced to remain stateless.[1]

As soon as he had established firm roots, his relatives began
encouraging him to find a suitable wife. They proposed many
matches, but he tactfully dodged their overtures. Then, one
day, he met Sofie. She was also from Aleppo and had come to
Egypt only shortly before him. They were married after a brief
courtship in a traditional ceremony. Lacking enough money for
larger quarters, the couple stayed in a modest apartment until
the birth of their daughter Odette, then moved to larger quarters in the Passage Duak, not far from the store. In the following years, Shaul's business prospered, and he began making
yearly trips to Paris, where be bought natural silks for the
workshop. "Shaul made ties for all the rich Arabs," his wife
would later boast. "We lived very well, and I even had a
maid."[2]

*   *   *

Sofie gave birth to Eliahu, their first son, two years after the British had abolished the protectorate and recognized Egypt as a quasi-independent country. Under the new rule, the Jewish community continued to enjoy complete freedom of worship, and as always, religion took precedence over nationality. Eli was raised to understand that he was first a Jew, then an Egyptian. His father had told him at a very young age that being a Jew was something deeply important. As the boy grew older, Shaul taught him the laws and customs and commanded him to practice these rites faithfully. He reared Eli in the dogmatic and other-worldly oriented Jewish tradition, exposing him early to Hebrew, the Bible, Sabbath, festivals—the vast complex of Jewish heritage.

The family rituals and the Orthodox climate of the ghetto in which Eli was raised did much to reinforce his God-consciousness. He said his daily prayers without fail and eagerly anticipated the Sabbath eve celebrations. While his brothers were mainly intent on spending the seventh day savoring the rich food and enjoying the songs and leisure, Eli scrupulously followed the exercises prescribed by the Orthodox ritual, honoring all commandments and prohibitions. "He was the most religious of us all," his brother Maurice later recalled. "He never rode the tram on Saturdays, nor did he touch or kindle fire, handle money, write or work."[3]

In later years Eli would accompany his father to the synagogue and pray with the men. At thirteen, the day of his Bar Mitzvah, he was given a white silk prayer shawl and allowed to mount the platform for the first time to answer the call to the Torah. In the weeks to come, he gave himself without reservation to the contemplation of God.

From then on, Eli mourned and fasted with the grown-ups on the Ninth of Av for the destruction of the Temple and on the Seventeenth of Tamuz for the breach in the walls of Jerusalem. Each Yom Kippur, at the end of a two-week period of repentance, mutual forgiveness and supplication which marked the Days of Awe, he took his place by his father in the first row at the synagogue. "He used to participate in the services from the opening Kol Nidre prayer and until the last call of the shofar sounded," a friend of the family remembered. "He sat there for the whole day without a word of complaint and refused to leave even for a breath of fresh air." [4] He followed the rabbi retelling the ordeal of the martyrs who died for the Torah and for Zion and listened raptly to the cantor singing the story of Jonah who attempted to flee from the Lord, sitting spellbound until the shofar yielded a tremulous staccato marking the end of the Day of Atonement.

The enthusiasm with which Eli took part in these religious ceremonies and his obvious intelligence prompted his father to enroll him in the school sponsored by the local synagogue, whose curriculum placed the strongest emphasis on a thorough knowledge of the Hebrew language. Eli's quickness to learn gained him entrance into the École Maimonides, the community's elementary school, at the age of six—a year earlier than usual. When the time came to graduate, the French program taught there was changed to Arabic, and Eli had to prepare for two final examinations. His performance was considerably higher than average, and at ten, he was ready for the Lycée.

The Cohens were now determined that their eldest son continue his education and encouraged him to enter the competition for a partial scholarship at the Lycée Français. Eli passed the tests without difficulty, and his father gladly supplemented the grant.

During the years at the Lycée, self-improvement was Eli's preoccupation. While his fellow students played soccer during recess, he retired with a book to a corner of the yard or remained inside the classroom solving equations. Complex problems fascinated him, and he spent most of his time on mathematics. He also made special efforts in languages, often staying up until dawn to memorize the French and Arabic grammar or study Greek, Italian, German or English.

At first, the withdrawn youth with the dreamy eyes was not particularly popular at school. But as shy and lonely as he was,

Eli sometimes joined the games of pirates the children played on the reefs that protect the shallow Anfuchi Bay—a sanctuary which real pirates had once used. After each masquerade as a seagoing outlaw, he would return home at night soaked and disheveled. But his desire for solitude (he preferred most of all to swim or fish in the waters of the Ancient Harbor) and the scholastic honors he won caused both envy and resentment among the children, who teased him unmercifully until they came to recognize his selflessness. Eli considered the ease with which he learned as a gift to be shared and was always ready to help them with their assignments. "He spent hours helping me with my homework," David Crudo, one of his classmates recalled, "and never left before he was certain that I understood everything."[5]

Fellow students were not the only ones to seek Eli out. For a small fee, he taught French to Arab adults his teachers recommended. But since the meager income from private lessons was not enough for books and hobbies, Eli decided to search for a better-paying position. He finally found work in a relative's dress shop, work that denied him most of the fun of adolescence. "He never attended class outings and rarely went to the movies," a friend remembered.

The few free moments he found were dedicated to the Nationalist Movement for a Free Egypt, a school society which most Christian, Moslem and some Jewish students attended with the active encouragement of their liberal Egyptian teachers. Eli considered himself a patriot whose religious beliefs did not preclude national allegiance. During the last years of high school he became a member of the Lycée's Committee for Egyptian Freedom, on which students of the three faiths were represented, and often participated in anti-British street demonstrations. "I have seen him surrounded by fellow students," recalled one of his friends, "cheering, waving and shouting, 'Egypt to the Egyptians!' like any other Arab nationalist."[6] Realizing the dangers anti-British demonstrations could offer to his fellow Jewish students, Eli always went through classes ahead of time warning the children and urging them to go home.[7]

Despite the enthusiasm of the young, most of the adults hesitated to commit themselves as Egyptian Jewry was torn by the controversy over whether to back the occupation forces or side with the Arabs. In Alexandria, the question of loyalty was even more perplexing because Joseph de Picciotto, a strong opponent of the British, occupied the presidency of the Jewish community.

Eli's nationalism met with approval from some relatives and friends, yet those closest to home did not freely condone his stand. The Cohens were skeptical about their son's public display of political conviction but never attempted to restrain him.

Between classes and the dress shop, Eli had little time of his own. What free hours he did find were spent roaming through the historic ruins and ancient quarters of Alexandria, photographing the remains of Roman and Hellenic culture and the seething life around him with the Kodak box camera he had received on his Bar Mitzvah. The photos he developed and printed were proudly presented as gifts to friends and relatives.

Among the few hobbies Eli could afford was a picture collection of weapons. He had become interested in firearms during the war and kept a record of the latest innovations by pasting newspaper and magazine clippings in large scrapbooks. Warplanes fired his enthusiasm. Articles and photos on aircraft covered the entire wall behind his bed. He learned to distinguish between Messerschmitts, Savoyas, and Spitfires by watching the dog fights overhead as the Axis rained bombs on the city. Identifying automobiles was another pastime. Leaning over the balcony above the Passage Duak, Eli would dictate the make, year and color of passing cars and trucks to one of his brothers and later test his memory by recalling the data on the list.[8] It was a game he had devised after acquiring mnemonic skill from the endless practice of retaining passages from the Talmud.

Weekends and holidays were devoted to helping Odette with their brothers and sisters. Eli often took the children to the royal Montazah Palace to play in the rose gardens or among the old cannon on the terrace of the Selemlik, the men's quarters,

by the huge sun dial. There were also outings to the zoo,
excursions to the Anfuchi Pier for carefree afternoons of swimming in the Mediterranean and visits to the lush Municipal
Nuzha Gardens, where a military orchestra played every Friday.
Occasionally, they picnicked near the Mariut Lake or in the
pine woods above Abukir Bay. Sometimes the youngsters went
for a ride in the circular tram along the New Quai to watch the
boat builders at work by the Eastern Harbor. A special treat was
the jaunt in a creaky, open horse-drawn carriage along the
Mahmudieh Canal to the Cotton Exchange of Minet al-Bassal,
where they skidded in the streets slippery with fluff or sat by
the round fountainhead watching the donkey carts carrying
cotton to the piers.

As he grew older, Eli began to wander alone from the *haret*
more frequently. He now relished hunting down the best bargains from among the wares offered by the Greek, Armenian
and Italian merchants who owned most of the small shops in
the city and thus came to know well the ebullient, money-mind-
ed Levantine Alexandrians. His encounters in the business section with Allied military personnel were not as enjoyable, yet
far more enlightening. The impertinent questions pleasure-seek-
ing soldiers often asked local youngsters forced Eli to quickly
learn the evasive replies which neither revealed anything nor
gave offense.

Eli's parents were determined that he develop a strong feeling
of pride in his heritage, an attachment to his people and loyalty
to the demands of God. They wanted him thoroughly inocu-
lated with the serum of Jewish learning which had proved so
efficacious in withstanding the dangers of assimilation. Eli thus
enrolled at the Midrasha Rambam, a school for advanced Talmudic learning, directed by the chief rabbi of Alexandria,
Moshe Ventura. The rabbi at once recognized Eli's exceptionally
retentive mind. He painstakingly guided him word by word,
sentence by sentence, through passages of the Talmud. Eli was
quick to grasp the complexities of the sacred books and, before
long, could read the Rashi commentary and the critical and

explanatory notes freely. He became the leading participant in discussions about the ritual and legal codes of the Shulhan Aruch, the mystic teachings of the Kabbalah, which originated in Alexandria, and the interpretations of the Zohar.

It was not long before tales of his precocity spread through the quarter. Classmates at the Midrasha reported that he could recite the entire hymn of *Nishmat Kol Khai* and knew the Sayings of the Fathers by heart. He was said to absorb whole chapters from the Gemara, and when the rabbi would test him by starting a sentence, Eli easily completed the passage. None of his friends was therefore surprised when the rabbi elevated the youth from *matmid* (devoted student) to *iluy*, the honor given the pupil with the greatest aptitude.

In later years, Rabbi Ventura entrusted Eli with the instruction of the younger children and eventually had him take over the class. Hoping his prize student would one day succeed him not only at the Midrasha but also as the head of the congregation, the rabbi tried to convince Eli to follow in his footsteps. "Your son has a good head," he once told Sofie Cohen. "He can be anything he wishes, even a rabbi." Ventura repeatedly pleaded that Eli continue rabbinical studies at the seminary on the Greek island of Rhodes and even promised to persuade the community to raise the necessary funds.[9] Eli tactfully rejected the proposal. He had already made a decision to pursue secular studies at Faruk University in Alexandria.

In June, 1941, as the German panzer divisions of Field Marshal Erwin Rommel were pouring over the Egyptian frontier, the remnants of the British Eighth Army received the order to withdraw toward the desert railway station at al-Alamein. The new front line was now only 60 miles west of Alexandria. In the city, the British began burning documents and preparing to sabotage their own installations. Allied headquarters evacuated English women and children to Palestine and the Sudan. Many non-Arabs were impatiently waiting to follow the Allies into exile, but in the Jewish Quarter life went on as usual. Candidates for graduation were in the midst of their final exams. Eli had to meet a taxing schedule, running from one school to the other, in spite of the Italian air raids, until his last baccalaureate test at the Lycée and finals exams at the Midrasha were completed.

Aside from the air attacks, which had done little damage, the war had not directly affected Eli's life, although there were clearly discernible signs of change all around him. Rommel's victories in the Libyan Desert had stirred a latent pro-Axis feeling among the Arabs, and sympathy for the Third Reich only heightened the rampant Egyptian nationalism. The declaration of the Nazi propaganda machine that "Egypt is for the Egyptians" had been hailed by both the royal house and the ruling Wafd Party. Germanophile officers, who regarded Rommel's arrival as a prelude to the liberation of Egypt by the Axis, actively plotted rebellion. Pro-Nazi groups began exploiting the citizens' irritation aroused by the food shortage, the state of siege and the military camp atmosphere, agitating to turn spontaneous street outbursts into explosive anti-British demonstrations. Encouraged by their successes, the fascist Green Shirts of the Young Egypt organization, the Blue Shirts of the conservative Wafd Party and the ultranationalist Moslem Brotherhood were already planning a victory parade for the triumphant Wehrmacht. Anticipating its arrival, they urged the people to fashion German and Italian flags for the day of liberation. But overeager students would not wait and swarmed the streets of Alexandria and Cairo to assail the British with cries of *Hiza Faruk fawk rasak, ya George* [Faruk's foot on your head, King George] and shouts of *Ila'l amam, ya Rommel* [Forward, Rommel] . . . We are your soldiers.

The Jewish community feared not only the Axis advance, but the jubilant reaction of militant Arabs. A Nazi takeover, they were convinced, would lead to a massacre or, at best, mass deportations, with little or no interference from the Arab populace. Unable to flee Egypt because the British would not allow them to emigrate to Palestine, they became the Allies' staunchest supporters. Their hopes were not misplaced. Rommel's defeat in August, 1942, and the final departure of his ravaged forces from North Africa almost a year later, saved them from certain genocide.

It had taken Eli quite a long time to comprehend the strange Moslem world around him, but he eventually felt at ease in the Oriental atmosphere. He came to understand the fatalism of the worshipers of Allah, and the Shaban and Bairam festivals preceding and following the annual Ramadan fast no longer seemed a mystery to him. He enjoyed milling with the crowds during the processions when the Holy Carpet returned from Mecca. But, above all, Eli relished the Sham en-Nessim spring festival that fell on the Coptic Orthodox Easter when both Moslem and Christian Alexandrians were joined by their Jewish neighbors in picnicking on the banks of the Nile. Most of the Arabs he met were impoverished artisans, store owners, servants or peddlars whose level of existence was far below anything he had seen in the *karet*. Hunger was no rarity in Moslem quarters, and Eli realized the extent of the people's desperation when he saw boys his own age searching through refuse for something edible or imitating the beggars who displayed missing arms and legs, invoking the name of Allah to shame passersby into giving them a piaster.

Only rarely did Eli have an opportunity to glimpse the wealthy, the pashas and the beys, the princes and the princesses, who usually escorted King Faruk and Queen Farida (The Only One) on their visits to Alexandria to take up residence at the Ras al-Tin Palace or set up court for the summer at the Montazah Palace.

Eli had first seen a royal cortege when he was twelve. The then Crown Prince Faruk had just returned from the Woolwich Military Academy in England on board the *Viceroy of India* to assume the throne on the death of his father, Fuad I. Along with the tens of thousands lining the streets to greet the future king, Eli and his brothers hailed the tall, slim young prince as he rode down the Rue de France to the Bab al-Jedid railway station. "Eli later admitted having been among those who shouted, 'Long live Faruk, King of the Faithful,'" a childhood friend recalled. He even conceded feeling a swell of pride as he listened to a military band playing the national anthem over the thunder of a hundred cannon and watched the young prince salute the green banner with half crescent and three stars before departing for Cairo to be crowned.[10]

His romantic attitude toward the crown and the aristocracy of 200 families who ruled Egypt soon shifted to a more somber view. The king's eccentric behavior had already become the talk of the city. Alexandrians were shocked by Faruk's monumental appetite, reckless drinking and obsessive gambling, his frenetic night life and the openness of his sexual escapades. The king's reputation was further tarnished by an apparent indifference toward the plight of the poor. On one occasion he had ordered ping-pong balls dropped by plane on a nearby village bearing the message that they could be redeemed for a bag of candy he later actually presented. It was Faruk's peculiar way of easing the burdens of the fellaheen.

Eli began to speak out indignantly against the extravagances of the rich. While ship-watching from the cape dominating the Eastern Harbor, he had seen many an uninhibited party given by the king for his courtesans aboard the royal yachts *Fakhr al-Behar* or *Mahroussa*. Together with his friend Baruch Mizrachi, he would look on resentfully at the endless procession of turbaned Nubian servants, in richly embroidered jackets and dark silk pantaloons, who carried delicacy-laden trays from the Ras al-Tin Palace to the boat. At a time when half the population existed on bread, onions and black tea, it struck Eli as a dangerous incongruity.

When Franklin Roosevelt visited Alexandria before the wartime Cairo Conference and held a reception on board the cruiser *Quincy* for Faruk, Emperor Haile Selassie of Ethiopia and the Saudi Arabian monarch, Ibn Saud, Eli and Mizrachi joined onlookers at the quai and watched King Saud and his flamboyant entourage arrive aboard an American destroyer with a royal party of forty-eight and a sizable flock of sheep. Scorning cabins, the desert potentate, Mizrachi recalled, had a tent rigged to a gun turret, furnished it with gilded chairs and Persian rugs

and held court in full splendor, with food tasters, slaves, concubines and wives.[11] For weeks afterward, Eli would not cease to
talk about the wastefulness and unreality of such an opulent
life-style.

As one who did not entirely believe in a preordained future,
Eli could hardly accept the abysmal gap between the classes. He
was ready to rebel against the unjust conditions, yet looking
realistically at the tangled issues, he recognized he could do
little as a Jew and felt only growing despair. There was first,
though, the increasing hostility toward his own people to be
overcome. The struggle for a Jewish homeland in Palestine,
which had intensified at the war's end, and its repercussions on
the community in Alexandria would ultimately cause Eli's
loyalty to Egypt to be profoundly shaken.

After the war had moved back to Europe, Britain's security
apparatus in the Middle East again turned its full attention to
the struggle in Palestine as the three Jewish undergrounds renewed their efforts to forge an independent Jewish state. Until
the threat of a German invasion had collapsed, an uneasy lull existed between the antagonists. Many Palestinian Jews had enlisted
in the British Army, and a Jewish Brigade was formed to fight the
Nazis on the western front. The Haganah, the clandestine military
arm of the Jewish Agency, a conglomerate of leftist Zionist parties, had placed itself at the disposal of the Mandate authorities.
The Irgun Zevai Leumi, the secret army organization of the Zionist Revolutionist movement, had maintained a self-imposed truce
and halted all operations against the British administration. Only
the Lokhamei Herut Israel, or Lechi, a terrorist group commonly
known as the Stern Gang, had actively continued resistance.

When hostilities in Palestine were rekindled, bitterness and
resentment, dammed up by years of restraint, broke through in
a wave of violence. Police stations were again bombed, officers
shot in the streets, banks held up and arms hijacked. Seeking to
regain a tight rein on the Mandate, the high commissioner, Sir
Harold MacMichael, retaliated swiftly. The Palestine police imprisoned hundreds of suspected dissidents and imposed house

arrests, curfews and fines. Scores were exiled to Mauritius and Eritrea; those caught rebelling openly were hanged.

Long before the homeland in Palestine had become a tangible reality for Eli, it had lived in his historical and religious imagination as Eretz Israel—a land that was once a kingdom and would be again when the Messiah came to lead the Jews back to the Holy Land. Indeed, it was a conviction rooted in Jewish tradition from the lechayims offered to the homeland on each holiday and the fervent prayers for rain in Palestine on the Festival of Booths to the parting words of "Next year in Jerusalem," which worshipers uttered every Passover. The incantations were repeated by the older Jews with the fatalistic acceptance of God's will; they believed that for mortals the distance to be traveled between dream and reality was potentially limitless. But the young did not consider the struggle occurring several hundred miles to the northwest irrelevant to their own destiny. Eli's father too thought it inevitable and proper: The older generation had struggled to keep Judaism alive; *their sons and daughters would now make the dream of Israel come true.*

During the new wave of repression in Palestine, the majority of Egyptian Jewry was not overly sympathetic with Zionist aims in the Holy Land. Those who had prospered during the war feared jeopardizing their wealth and security by supporting the cause. The investigations conducted by British Field Security into the activities of local Zionists only increased their anxiety. As a consequence, leading Jews in commerce and the professions and Cairo's chief rabbi, the old and nearly blind Haim Nahum Pasha, were almost all outspokenly anti-Zionist. On one occasion, when a Haganah agent, Ruth Klieger, approached the industrialist Cattaui Pasha, president of the community in Cairo, and asked him to help finance illegal emigration to Palestine, he responded by threatening to set his dogs on her. The less influential and the poor became either equally hostile or indifferent.[12]   Individuals and organizations backing the movement could do little but support it silently.

Both the Zionists and their opponents were shaken, however, when the drama of the Palestine conflict was unexpectedly played out on Egyptian soil. In the morning of November 7, 1944, Eli opened the *Bourse Egyptienne* and saw the passport photos of two young Palestinian Jews underneath the headline ACCUSED OF MURDER. The day before, Eliahu Beit Zuri and Eliahu Hakim had fatally wounded Lord Moyne, the former colonial secretary and newly appointed minister of state for the Middle East, as he left his Cairo villa in the Zamalek district. The Egyptian police seized them only minutes after the shots were fired. At the Bab al-Halk Prison, Eli learned, the two had confessed to membership in the Lechi underground and freely admitted plotting the assassination. "I never saw two cap-tured men who looked less beaten than these brave, arrogant, brutal, heartless young fanatics," wrote the British Field Security chief in Cairo.¹³ Later that evening, following an emergency operation by King Faruk's physician, Lord Moyne died.

The murder first caused a storm of indignation among Egyptian Moslems, Christians and Jews and hindered local Zionist activities. But the defiant appearance of the accused in the courtroom, made all the more compelling by their youth, had a strong countereffect on the community. At one of the sessions, drowning out protests from the judges, Beit Zuri delivered a two-hour political tirade, accusing the British in Palestine of carrying out a policy detrimental to the interests of the Jewish people. "If we have turned to the gun," he thundered at one point, "it is because we were forced to do it. When we found that every other effort would not help, we understood that the only way to fight a rule based on violence is to use violence."

Zuri's defiance figured prominently in Egyptian press re-ports and caused a widespread feeling of respect among the Arabs. The same Moslem students who had celebrated Rommel marched through Cairo chanting, "Free the Moyne slayers." Even though the demonstrations were largely spurred by anti-British feeling, the admiration for the courage the Palestinians had exhibited was obviously sincere and forced many Egyptian Jews to reconsider their own views about Zionism.

But as everyone assumed, the support Zuri and Hakim received in Moslem quarters and their dramatic stand in court did little to move the judges. After a week of deliberations, the five-man tribunal sentenced them to death. The Grand Mufti of Egypt confirmed the decision with the words from the Koran "Who kills shall be killed." Two months later, on March 22, the youths proudly mounted the gallows. Refusing to wear the black hood, they died singing the "Hatikvah," the Hebrew song of hope.[14] The unyielding conviction of the two Eliahus strongly affected Eli. Their martyrdom, he later admitted, would bring him much closer to the Zionist cause.

Alexandria's Jewish leaders, who now harbored the hope that their countrymen would come to accept the idea of double loyalties, actively promoted the cause of Zionism among both the rich and the poor members of the community. Religious acts were given new meaning by the struggle for a Jewish homeland, the movement's blue and white flag flew over the Jewish school where the offices of the Zionist Federation of Egypt were located, and evening classes in Hebrew were offered at the synagogue—first by Palestinian soldiers serving in the British forces, then by three teacher-emissaries from Eretz Israel. But the wealthier supporters were mainly "salon Zionists" who devoted their energies to cocktail parties and plush receptions for visiting heads of the Jewish Agency in Palestine. They considered themselves *engagé* by buying a subscription to the local Zionist *Tribune Juive* or by patronizing the Tel Aviv Habimah Theater and Philharmonic Orchestra whenever they toured in Egypt.

The activists advocated a more militant attitude. When their demands fell on deaf ears, they turned their efforts to organizing the poor. One of them, Moshe Ben Asher—a Polish immigrant—opened a Zionist club in the *haret* and started a farm for local young people on the city's outskirts. When the Zofim (Scouts) organization in Palestine sent Rafael Ricanati to found a branch in Egypt, Ben Asher helped him recruit members from the Maccabi sports club and geared both societies toward Zionism.[15]

While still in high school, Eli had enrolled in the Maccabi together with his brothers. He was active on the soccer team and soon became an athletic instructor for the younger members. Although he spent much time at the Maccabi, Eli showed an increasing interest in the local chapter of the politically oriented Hachalutz Hazair (Young Pioneers), a youth group of the labor movement in Palestine, which he later joined. As an avid reader of the *Tribune Juive*, he never missed the lectures its fiery editor, Jacob Rabin, gave at Hachalutz meetings. Eli not only absorbed the Zionist teachings of such elder leaders, but was introduced to Marx and Engels, the theory of communal life in the kibbutz and the struggle of the Haganah for the creation of a Jewish state.

Before long Eli became a political instructor in Hachalutz and started devoting his full energies to indoctrinating the young, who came to respect both his talks and the friendly attitude he adopted on hikes, sports events, summer camp or nights around the fire. In the Hachalutz he was also initiated into the Zionist struggle. Like all Young Pioneers, he served as courier and guide to Palestinian emissaries who selected immigrants and channeled refugees from Europe.[16] It was in this clandestine world that he first learned to obey without asking questions and to fulfill orders without hesitation.

At Maccabi and Hachalutz functions, Eli met Samuel Azar, who had been several years behind him at the *Lycée*. Sami shared Eli's own genuine concern for Egypt and a burning enthusiasm for the creation of a Jewish homeland in Palestine. His commitment to the cause impressed Eli deeply, and although he was five years his junior, the two became close friends. Samuel Bakhour Azar was the son of a rabbi who had emigrated from Turkey at about the time Shaul Cohen had arrived in Egypt. But disabled by a tram accident, his father had been forced to work as a tailor, and their family of five relied heavily on the aid of Sami's mother, who earned a meager salary as a seamstress. Sami, always the first in his class, was a scholarship student and had skipped a few levels in junior high school. He was already an accomplished painter and sculptor at thirteen when Ricanati recruited him for the Maccabi; his sister was the first to join the scouts.

The imaginative, cheerful young Azar became a popular instructor in the pioneer movement, and his influence during Eli's formative political period was to be considerable.[17] For much of the next turbulent decade, the two were to be almost inseparable—a friendship that deepened as the conflict in Palestine came to alter the lives of the Jews in Egypt. The bitter struggle, which was now intensifying, would lead them both into the militant fields of illegal immigration and espionage—a labyrinth from which there would be no exit.

3
Operation Goshen

The chilling news spread relentlessly from one family to another in the Jewish Quarter of Alexandria: Thirty-five miles away; in the *haret* of Cairo, a pogrom had been unleashed by Moslems incited by recent events in the Palestinian conflict. Mobs had put the torch to the *haret*, burning down a synagogue and desecrating twenty-seven Torah scrolls; the community's hospital, soup kitchen, home for the aged, shelter for transients, as well as the quarters of the Art Society, had been totally destroyed. Fear that the rampage would spark a local wave of terror gripped the ghetto. The Cohens and their neighbors bolted their doors and braced for the worst.

The reports from Cairo on that second day in November, 1945, stunned Eli, although he was hardly unaware of the slender barrier holding back a potential avalanche of hatred against the Jews. The last years of the World War had been free of pogroms, owing largely to the conscientious efforts of the British commandant of the city police, who had prevented pro-Axis agitators and extreme nationalists from venting their anti-British frustrations on Alexandria's Jews. Even after the Zionist presence in Palestine became a rallying cry for pan-Arabism throughout Egypt, calm had prevailed. Eli had felt no uneasiness about openly participating in Zionist activities, despite the intensification of extremist propaganda from the revivalist Moslem Brotherhood, which now blamed the Jews for all the country's ills. He continued to have faith in Egyptian justice and dismissed the ultranationalist propaganda as empty rhetoric.

His optimism would not last long. Campus violence at Al Gizeh University, capped by a massacre of students, a leftist-inspired general strike and marches on the British embassy in Cairo were finally climaxed by worker riots in Alexandria. For the first time, Eli experienced the terror of a clash with seething mobs whose impotence against the city police had turned them on the Jews.

Earlier in the fall, after passing exhaustive preliminary exams, Eli and a classmate at the Lycée, Murad Semach, enrolled as students of electrical engineering at Faruk I University in Alexandria. They were the only two Jewish students admitted in 1946 to the preparatory curriculum of the School of Engineering. The Arab professors made no effort to disguise their hostility to the Jews, and except for the Copts and liberal Moslems, the politically active undergraduates, many of them Brotherhood members, were no less antagonistic. This bleak academic climate, plus the demanding job Eli held at the Richard Mizrachi import-export. firm, made serious study a grueling task.

During this period, British troops were preparing to withdraw from the city, and students frequently declared strikes so they could actively harass the soldiers into a faster departure. "Eli was always among them," recalled Semach, "shouted 'El-Galaa, [Evacuation],' just as hard as they were."[1] Soon the strikes were being called so often that classes at the university were almost discontinued, and Eli had to complete his studies at home. But he still managed to pass the exams and enrolled for his first-year engineering program.

When negotiations for a withdrawal of all British troops from the delta to the canal zone broke down a year later, Jews were victimized during sporadic outbreaks in the large cities. An uncontrollable mob rioted on the Feast of Muled al-Nabi, the anniversary of the Prophet Muhammad, which fell on February 2, 1947. But a week later Eli and a group of friends who had pledged strong support for the fight against the British, stood in the midst of a sullen crowd, watching the Union Jack over the Mustapha Pasha barracks lowered after sixty-four years. His mood and that of the other spectators were ones of great joy as they watched a face-saving parade marking the evacuation of the last British soldier from Alexandria.[2]

Eli's attempt to enlist in the Army at the beginning of 1947 was fully in character with his avowed patriotism. Rather than avoid conscription by paying a proscribed sum expected from young Jews who were unwelcome in the service, Eli faced a recruiting officer, only to be promptly declared ineligible on the grounds of questionable loyalty.[3] The rejection came as no surprise, considering the burgeoning anti-Jewish feeling. This contagion was stronger among Arab businessmen who resented the Jews' wealth and legendary commercial skill but objected, in fact, much more to the import of Palestinian goods, often cheaper than and far superior to their own, than to the creation of a Jewish national home in Palestine.

The powerful Moslem Brotherhood, which preached Arab superiority and moral regeneration, was quick to exploit the resentment. Proclaiming that the nonbelievers—the British and the Jews—exerted a corrupting influence, it successfully manipulated the emotions of the middle class, as it had done before with the poor and the hungry. In mosques and at rallies Brotherhood kadis preached violence against the foreigners; their leader, the Supreme Guide Hassan al-Banna, harangued his more than half million followers into a xenophobic frenzy. "We will not confine our fight to the elimination of the Jews," he repeatedly cried. "All the Occident, every wearer of the hat, is our mortal enemy." Rich in quotations from the Koran, his sermons claimed to restore self-respect, yet appealed to the basest instincts. The Brethren readily obeyed the call for a jihad (holy war) against the infidels. Throughout 1947 the Nile Valley Liberation Society, a front for the Brotherhood, prepared for a terrorist campaign: Its agents cached large quantities of arms and ammunition, recruited volunteers and formed Liberation Battalions. The attacks finally began in broad winter daylight with the killing of Jews and British soldiers and the bombing of homes of unfriendly politicians. Since Brotherhood partisans held offices in high places, few of the culprits were brought to justice. Such was the power of the Brotherhood that the throne did not dare interfere, the political police looked the other way, and military intelligence refused to take seriously the reports that extremist officers in the Army trained and supplied the Brethren.

The Brotherhood's onslaught against the Jews spurred Eli to enlist in the Committee Guards, a vigilante group formed over much opposition from the rich and influential.[4] The Guards mounted a protective belt around the community, and when riots erupted again in the capital on August 22 and were echoed by unruly demonstrations in Alexandria, the Jews were finally ready.

Yet Eli understood that these disorders would be only the beginning, if the United Nations' General Assembly, then determining the future of Palestine, voted to divide the Mandate into Arab and Jewish states. When the partition resolution was passed at a stormy session on November 29, his fears were realized. The six Arab delegations rejected the plan, which gave the 678,000 Palestinian Jews 5 percent of the land—much of it desert—while consigning 1,269,000 Arabs to the remainder, and stalked out in protest. Within hours, anti-Semitic outbursts flared in Syria, pogroms erupted in Iran, and hundreds were butchered in Aden and Bahrein. On the same day, the political police raided Jewish homes and hotels in Cairo and Alexandria, arresting many of their occupants.

"That morning in November," Semach recounted, "we arrived at the university without knowing that a general strike against the resolution had been called. Some of our Christian friends advised us to return home. They suggested that we avoid classes until the situation cooled off. Eli was furious. He challenged the Moslems to chase him out if they dared. He could not believe that they would do that to him, who only a year earlier had marched with them demanding the withdrawal of British troops from Egypt. . . . I must confess that I was afraid. Eli was one against a hundred. I tried to convince him to leave, but only when our Christian friends intervened did he reluctantly decide to depart."[5]

After that, because of increased harassment, Eli was forced to pursue his studies at home. With the assistance of several Christian friends, who provided the lesson plan, and the guidance of two Jewish instructors, whom the faculty had not dared to dismiss, Eli readied himself for the final examinations. The dean of the Faculty of Engineering gave him and the nine other Jewish students permission to take the tests, in spite of their lack of attendance. To avoid clashes with the extremists, they were placed under police protection and examined separately.[6] Although Eli passed all the tests, intensified student unrest would prevent him from attending second-year courses.

The government had encouraged the employment of bullying tactics against the Jews of Egypt in the belief that the Palestinian Arabs and their allies in neighboring countries would deal handily with the Jewish settlers. Faruk and fellow members of the Arab League never envisioned that the poorly armed, small Yishuv (settlement) in Palestine would be capable of defending itself even against unseasoned troops. Contingency plans they had formulated at a secret conference in the Lebanese summer resort of Inshias, in the event the partition plan was accepted, were drawn up under the assumptions that Tel Aviv and Jerusalem would be occupied with little difficulty and that victory would be quick and total.

Arab bands in Palestine had meanwhile rallied around the Grand Mufti of Jerusalem, Hadj Amin al-Husseini, who sounded the war cry for the Islamic faithful, preaching: "Who votes for death will not die; who seeks death will receive the gift of life." The Arab League pledged support to the cause and helped recruit 8,000 volunteers to aid the Palestinian irregulars. (The Egyptians, for their part, armed 3,000 Moslem Brethren.) But the new army was rife with dissension, the result of suspicion, rivalry and ancient prejudices. The Egyptians, Druzes, Syrians and Iraqis had little in common but their hatred of

Zionism. The league had also grievously miscalculated the depths of the Zionists' fighting spirit. When the Brotherhood battalions attacked from the south on the day after the UN partition vote, they encountered fierce resistance and had to be reorganized by regular officers hurriedly dispatched from Cairo into the field.

This measure was still far from enough to turn the tide. The Jewish undergrounds counterattacked; the Brethren were repulsed at the key settlement of Kfar Darom, despite artillery support and their numerical superiority. This setback and the losses on the other fronts came as a rude awakening to Egyptian leaders. The masses, however, were unaware of the truth; most news from the front had been first filtered through the fine sieve of Arab optimism. But the foreign press, which Eli read closely, did not foster any illusions.

On Friday, May 14, 1948, anticipating a pogrom, the Jews of Egypt barricaded themselves in their homes. That morning, Shaul Cohen had tuned in early to the BBC frequency, as the entire family gathered expectantly around the radio to hear a live broadcast of the final moments of British rule in Palestine. Within minutes of 9 A.M., after reviewing a guard of honor in the Jerusalem Government House, the high commissioner, Sir Alan Cunningham, climbed into his black, bulletproof Daimler to the sounds of a Scottish funeral dirge and, leaving the Highlanders' wailing pipes behind, sped to the airport, where he boarded an RAF transport plane for Haifa. At a second ceremony in the northern port he officially ended with a short speech thirty-four years of British rule and sailed with the last contingent for Cyprus.

Shortly afterward, at 4 P.M., the chairman of the Jewish Agency, David Ben-Gurion, mounted a podium in the Tel Aviv Museum to the applause of Zionist leaders and members of the provisional government. Standing under a portrait of the father of Zionism, Theodor Herzl, the "Old Man" undramatically read the declaration of independence proclaiming Israel a state. Less than eight hours after the ceremony and exactly twenty-seven minutes before the dissolution of the Mandate, the General

Assembly at Lake Success passed the proposal for the partition of Palestine. As Eli and his family listened to the historic words, they felt a growing awareness that the events taking place far from the *haret* would someday alter their lives.

The UN action was greeted in Cairo with demoniac rage. Arab League delegates, who for twelve days had discussed the gloomy outcome of the undeclared war, decided to send regular army units into Palestine. As member states were told to prepare for all-out war, a spokesman outlined three justifications for the Arab call to arms: the belief in glorious death as a road to paradise, the opportunities it offered for plunder and the love of slaughter for its own sake. The coming struggle with the Zionists, he predicted, "will be a war of extermination . . . which shall be spoken of like the Mongol massacres and the Crusades."

The Egyptian High Command, fully supported by the Cabinet and Parliament, was reluctant to risk a military adventure with its ill-prepared army, but the king waved aside the generals' fears and ordered his troops "to help establish security and tranquillity in Palestine." The polling day, May 15, at 5 A.M. the league's 25,000-strong Regular and Irregular Forces for the Liberation of Palestine, a conglomerate of armies from Egypt, Transjordan, Iraq, Syria and Lebanon, supported by Saudi Arabian and Yemeni units, launched a massive invasion of Palestine. The Egyptian forces opened the jihad against the Jews with a Spitfire raid on Tel Aviv while its army of 10,000—three battalions supported by armor, artillery and air power—rolled into the undefended Negev desert.

Egypt's official entry into the war was the signal for the start of a full-scale campaign of retribution against the country's Jews. While troops poured into Palestine, squads of political police, armed with special warrants, entered Alexandria's *haret* at dawn, searching homes, synagogues and community buildings for arms, radio transmitters and Zionist literature. Hundreds of younger residents suspected of Zionist activities were rounded up and held in the community's schools, where interrogation teams sought futilely to obtain confessions of espionage—a capital offense. The guilt of 141 suspects, including 26 women, was at last established arbitrarily. By executive order of the military governor, they were interned at Abukir, a former British Air Force base in the nearby Libyan Desert. Relatives of the Cohen family were among those arrested;[7] yet, for reasons unknown, Eli was spared detention.

Although Jewish leaders had emphatically proclaimed their opposition to Zionism many times in the past, all the *harets* were indiscriminately raided in the coming weeks, and some 2,000 were seized and questioned by the political police. The leadership hurried to reaffirm its national allegiance. Cairo's chief rabbi, Haim Nahum, pleaded that all "stand up and defend our country against the Zionists" and urged his flock to contribute to the Egyptian Soldiers' Chest and the Relief Fund for Arab Refugees. In a vain attempt to prove their patriotism, the Jews of Alexandria donated 80,000 pounds to the Army and an equal sum for Arab refugees.

But the pledges of support did not deter the government from carrying out a policy of repression against the "Zionist allies" in Egypt which made previous anti-Jewish episodes pale by comparison. The *haret* was placed under curfew; all meetings, including those of community and synagogue boards, had to be reported to the authorities so that official observers could be present; and the various organizations were required to submit their membership lists to the Ministry of the Interior for scrutiny. Maintaining that the Jews exercised excessive control over finance, commerce and industry and constituted a disproportionately large percentage of officeworkers, the government now enforced a previously passed Company Law which decreed that 75 percent of salaried employees and 90 percent of all laborers had to be Egyptian nationals. The most devastating sanction ordered the confiscation of private and business assets of those interned or under police surveillance; a levy of 10 percent of the property's value was made to defray the costs of administering the funds. Nor was there an easy avenue of escape. A special decree prohibited Jews from leaving the country without an exit visa, while the amount of money, securities or jewelry which could be taken out was drastically limited.

The Zionists of Alexandria accepted the repressive measures with resignation and prayed for their brothers in Israel; many of the elders placed their hopes in a rapid end to the war. Their optimism was kindled by the first dispatches of victory which indicated that the conflict would not last long. On the surface, the facts appeared to substantiate the press accounts. The main arm of the Egyptian expeditionary force had marched triumphantly into Arab-held cities in the southern Negev and seized control of the highways and large areas in the desert. But after capturing a kibbutz and encircling a number of other settlements, the Egyptians had been brought to a standstill in the northern Negev. With their supply lines and inexperienced troops overtaxed by their own successes, they readily agreed to a twenty-eight-day cease-fire offered by the Swedish mediator, Count Folke Bernadotte.

The unexpected lull proved a crucial boon to the Israelis. The three undergrounds were merged into Zahal (the Israel Defense Forces), and the new army was reorganized into separate land, air and sea commands. Before hostilities erupted again, Zahal could field a partially equipped 60,000-man army, several artillery pieces, some improvised tanks and armored cars, and a few planes. The Egyptian command in the interim had boosted its Army to 18,000 men, practically exhausting Cairo's military capacity. Eli had watched a parade of the fresh contingents before they left for the Israeli front. "Their departure raised our first doubts about stories of Egyptian successes," one of his friends later remarked. "If they were ready to enter Tel Aviv, as they claimed, why throw such massive reinforcements into the thick of the fighting? "[8] The Army explained its decision nearly to double the expeditionary force by announcing a forthcoming offensive, but the Jews, who had access to the foreign press and listened to European and Israeli stations, were by now discussing the military situation with justified skepticism.

The growing doubts about the war were not shared by them

alone. The unexpected halt in the fighting after only a month
bewildered the Arab populace, which had been inundated with
radio bulletins proclaiming brilliant victories and depicting King
Faruk, sporting a beret and field marshal's baton, as a heroic
military leader. The public was also inflamed by a virulent
propaganda barrage against the "Zionist bandits" in Palestine
and stories describing Israeli atrocities. Ugly omens appeared.
Anti-Jewishness, masquerading as anti-Zionism, grew respec-
table, and cafés in Alexandria displayed signs reading JEWS
AND DOGS NOT ADMITTED. But when it became obvious
that there would be no swift victory, Moslems vented their
growing rage on the *harets*. Twelve houses in Cairo occupied by
Jews of the Karaite sect were blown up, killing twenty and
injuring forty-one. The authorities remained numb to the violence. Hospitals refused aid; police and firemen obstructed the
rescue work. The quarter was invaded by marauding Arabs, who
dragged Jews from streetcars, buses and taxis, then beat and
robbed them while the city police stood watching.

By the end of the first week in July the impatient Egyptians
broke the cease-fire with a two-pronged attack on agricultural
settlements, but the Israelis managed to thwart the offensive.
The Royal Egyptian Air Force angrily retaliated with the first
raid in history on Jerusalem. The ten-day war that followed
produced an unbroken string of Israeli triumphs.

During this second round, the Jews of Alexandria and Cairo
endured the most harrowing episodes of mob violence. On
Friday the sixteenth a wing of Flying Fortresses purchased by
the Israeli Air Force in South Africa carried out their first
mission while flying over Cairo on their way to Israel. Shortly
after sunset, just as the Ramadan fast had ended, the B-17's
swooped over the Abdin Palace, dropping four bombs which
missed the target wildly. Since the alarm failed to sound until
after the raid had started, residents of the densely populated
area were trapped in their homes. Dozens of buildings were
demolished and a large number of civilians killed. When word
spread that the Jews had rained bombs on the capital, hundreds
stormed past the soldiers posted to protect the *haret* but were

repulsed by the Committee Guards. The city police arrived three hours later only to join the mob in a frenzy of murder and pillaging.

The press rationalized the violence on the following day by accusing Egyptian Jews of signaling the enemy aircraft to their targets. Without notice, 200 wealthy Jewish families living near the palace were evicted from their homes, their possessions hauled off in trucks or piled in the street and offered for sale. The government provoked further reprisals with a simulated defense—replete with sirens, blackouts and antiaircraft fire— against nonexistent Israeli planes. The reaction was fierce. Bombs shattered the city's two largest department stores, both owned by Jews, killing 3, injuring 17 and damaging 500 surrounding shops. Later that summer, homes and businesses were rocked by other blasts which the authorities alleged had been caused by air raids and explosions of hidden arms caches. The Moslem Brotherhood exploited the terrorist climate by operating a protection racket in the *harets*, forcing shopkeepers and café owners to pay for the privilege of not having their premises damaged. The extortionists were of little help. As the summer went on, property worth millions was burned, while the number of dead reached 250.

On July 19 a second truce went into effect, yet both Israelis and Egyptians continued operations on a limited scale, out of sight of the United Nations Truce Commission. Only after the war resumed in October did Zahal take the initiative and, in a thrust south, lay open the road to the Negev. By the time King Faruk had appointed a new commander of the expeditionary forces, the Israelis had overrun the desert, throwing his army back into the Sinai Peninsula. The Egyptian High Command had no choice but to agree to a third cease-fire on October 22.

The collapse of their army came as a traumatic revelation to the politicians, who charged betrayals and sellouts. But despite the military humiliation, Egypt refused to negotiate an armistice, for neither the government nor the throne could risk an admission of defeat. The Israeli General Staff thus readied the *coup de grâce*. In two successive December offensives, Zahal crossed the border into Egypt; before the year had ended, the fate of the Egyptian Army was irrevocably sealed. This time the British intervened and pressed for a cease-fire, threatening to employ their own troops to force their will. On December 29, fearing a break in relations or an open war with Great Britain, Ben-Gurion accepted a truce and ordered the evacuation of the Sinai Peninsula.

The Egyptian Army's debacle during the last offensive had by now become strikingly apparent, as wounded soldiers and officers on leave returned from the front. Next to the propaganda accounts of decisive victories over the Zionists, the truth caused intense disillusionment with every symbol of authority. Unrest mushroomed: The Cairo police chief was murdered while battling rioting medical students at Fuad al-Awal University; Prime Minister Nokrashy Pasha was shot and killed in the elevator of the Interior Ministry; and not long after, Moslem Brotherhood bullets struck down the governor of Cairo. In an attempt to check the wave of terror, the government ordered the Brethren dissolved.

A newly appointed Cabinet was in a near panic. When the Israelis renewed their offensive on January 3, 1949, by attacking the southern tip of the Gaza enclave, the palace finally realized that the inevitable surrender would topple the government and breed anarchy. Four days later, Cairo accepted a permanent cease-fire and agreed to negotiate an armistice. After forty-three days of talks with the Israelis, the Egyptian delegation entered the ballroom of the Hôtel des Roses on the Greek island of Rhodes to sign the agreement which allowed them to retain the Gaza enclave but forced their relinquishment of the entire Negev—a defeat which even the most well-oiled propaganda machine could not disguise. Faruk's power remained unchallenged, but a wave of reaction against his corrupt regime swept the cities.

The crushing defeat inevitably brought new reprisals against the Jews, always convenient mob scapegoats. "Not a day passes without . . . murders in Cairo and Alexandria, or the dynamiting of homes and stores," wrote a correspondent for the *Cyprus*

Mail. "There is little to choose between the street mobs and the police with respect to lawlessness and brutality." The *haret* in Alexandria, once a relatively safe harbor, was now engulfed by fear. Shaul Cohen, who a generation before had sought refuge from persecution, was forced to uproot himself again. When the government announced in 1949 that it would grant exit visas to Jews on the condition that they not return, the Cohens decided to leave for Israel via France with their two daughters. The six boys would temporarily remain behind. "Don't worry," Eli reassured his mother before departure, "I'll be there within a month."[9] Sofie Cohen was to wait seven years before seeing him again.

Eli's decision to remain in Egypt was made largely for practical reasons. By the time his four younger brothers emigrated in 1950, leaving only Maurice behind, he had resumed his second-year studies at the university. To achieve his ambition of earning a degree in electronics would have been exceedingly difficult in Israel without an adequate knowledge of modern Hebrew. He could therefore only hope that as the bitter memory of the war in Palestine faded, student turmoil would subside. His expectations were to be short-lived. Life at the university inevitably reflected the tensions and despair gripping the lower and middle classes. The British still occupied the canal zone, and the searing wounds caused by the war with Israel showed no signs of healing.

Socially and economically, the country was crumbling by the end of 1951. A staggering birthrate brought 1,200 new mouths to feed each day in a nation whose population density was among the highest in the world—1,500 fellaheen were cramped into each square mile along the banks of the Nile—and only 2.5 percent of the land was under cultivation. During the year, the average annual income stood virtually frozen at $75, while the cost of living soared by 22 points. Added to this catalogue of miseries, the production of the economy's mainstay, wheat and cotton, had fallen off drastically. Even the once loyal fellaheen no longer believed that the king was more concerned about their fate than the fleshy pleasures he now openly pursued. Eli had often seen him enter through the back door of the al-Mussa Hospital overlooking the Mediterranean, where he had installed a love nest (in addition to those in the ten palaces he owned) of seventeen sumptuously furnished rooms on the top floor. Faruk's only major concession to the masses was his avowal of hatred for the British, made largely to satisfy the Moslem Brotherhood. Ironically, this ersatz passion, meant to unite the people behind the throne, would help bring about his downfall.

After Anglo-Egyptian negotiations over the evacuation of the canal zone had collapsed, the new premier, Nahas Pasha, annulled a fifteen-year treaty and launched the "Battle of the Canal" by ordering a general boycott of the British garrison; the crippling economic siege was coupled with devastating raids by guerrilla bands. In reprisal, the British fought back with heavy artillery and tanks, leveling entire villages. In January, 1952, after the Buluk Nizam (Egyptian Auxiliary Police) overran a military depot at Tal al-Kebir, the British stormed their canal zone headquarters at Ismailia. Six hours later, when the white flag was raised, 80 policemen had been killed, scores lay wounded, and more than 1,000 were hauled off to prison. The next morning, a day which would come to be known as Black Saturday, the Buluk Nizam and bands of extremists marched in protest on the Abdin Palace, chanting, "Death to the British" and "Kill the Jews." In the orgy of revenge that followed, Eli and Azar were savagely set upon and beaten while trying together with other Committee Guards to protect the Jews in the *haret* from the angry mob. [10] Only by nightfall, with 26 dead, famed landmarks and 400 buildings gutted by fire, 12,000 homeless and $70,000,000 in damage, did the king finally declare martial law and order the Army into Cairo.

In the aftermath of Black Saturday, Nahas Pasha was sacrificed as a salve to the British. For the next five months the king kept the government in a continuing state of crisis as he shuffled a quickly changing succession of prime ministers. But his autocratic methods backfired. On July 23, a junta of twelve army officers under Colonel Muhammad Naguib seized the vital centers of government and communications in Cairo. The king, who was spending the summer at the Ras al-Tin Palace in Alexandria, at first did not grasp the seriousness of the officers' intentions but, when presented with a list of stringent demands, began to comprehend that his throne was in jeopardy. He hastily withdrew more than $2,000,000 from the royal account in the Misr Bank, siphoned another £1,000,000 from the treasury against his allowance, and had all the gold in the palace crated and made ready for departure. Three days after the start of the coup Faruk capitulated to the demands of the Revolutionary Council and in a face-saving gesture abdicated in favor of his first son, Ahmad Fuad, Crown Prince Said.

In the early evening of July 26, Eli stood watch on the Corniche with thousands of Alexandrians as the king, his 290 pounds swathed in the uniform of a grand admiral of the fleet, emerged from the palace with Queen Narriman and their entourage. The crowd looked on silently as a band played the national anthem and the green flag was lowered, folded and presented to the monarch. Faruk embraced Premier Ali Maher and the American ambassador and walked up the gangplank with head high. At 5:45 P.M. the *Mahroussa*, laden with his treasure, steamed out of the harbor, carrying the royal family into permanent exile.

The king's ouster was not mourned by the majority of Egyptians, particularly the Jews, who believed his overthrow would herald the birth of a government at last concerned with the people's welfare. But while Colonel Naguib promisingly announced dramatic plans to alleviate some of the country's chronic problems, the security services, now headed by officers who had not forgotten their humiliation in Palestine, initiated an anti-Zionist campaign. In the wave of arrests following the coup, Eli was picked up on suspicion of engaging in Zionist activities.

The capricious arrest made a profound impression on Eli, who still considered himself a loyal Egyptian and was thought of as such by many of his Arab friends. Although released shortly and without charges from the Governorate Prison inside the grounds of the city police headquarters where he had been held, Eli was far from safe.[11] On his return to Faruk University, he had to bear the stigma of a troublemaker. While he was gone, a chronic lack of professors and politicization of the campus had disrupted classes, causing standards to drop sharply. Eli managed nonetheless to prepare himself for the final tests. But his professors, who had learned of his arrest, refused to give him passing grades, despite his above-average work. In addition, Eli had to endure continued harassment from members of the student revolutionary guard, who spent more time battering the few remaining Jewish students than demonstrating against the British.[12] The following year Eli was forced to withdraw from the university entirely.

Looking for work was no easy undertaking. At twenty-four, as a Jew, he could find employment only in the few Jewish businesses left open. The only respite from the unrelieved burdens was the time he spent with a rich, somewhat older widow who owned a millinery shop on Missala Street.[13] After months of searching, he was finally hired as an accountant for a lumber company. But when an acquaintance, Abraham Clark, proposed that he manage his dress store, Eli readily accepted. A close friendship developed between the two. Clark, who was married to a Greek girl of the Christian faith, introduced Eli to her sister Maria. "He became very fond of her," recalled his friend Murad Semach. "She was a ravishing, ebullient young girl, and Eli seemed extremely happy. He always talked about her and went nowhere without her. His friends never missed the opportunity to tease him about Maria, but that did not make him angry; on the contrary, it pleased him."[14]

The romance with Maria did not quell the anguished concern he felt for his people. By now his vision of a more democratic system, drastic social reform and an end to corruption had faded. He was angered by both the regime's repressive measures against political opponents and its discriminatory policy toward the Jews. He saw no other solution for the hardships of the community but mass exodus and began actively aiding illegal emigration to Europe and Israel.

Eli was not unfamiliar with the clandestine operations of the Mossad le-Alya Bet, (Class B Immigration Agency) which organized illegal transports to Palestine. As a member of the Hachalutz he had often acted as courier for the organization. But the nature of the underground activities had changed markedly since before the war when escape from Arab countries and entry into Palestine had been fraught with peril. At the war's start Moshe Ben Asher had organized the first transports from Alexandria which sailed along the Egyptian coast to Palestine. Later Jewish servicemen in the British Army had helped Egyptian Jewesses to emigrate by means of fictitious marriages. By mid-1943 David Hameiri, a wiry *kibbutznik* from Ashdot Yaakov who oversaw emigration from Arab countries for the Mossad, formed an Egyptian branch and put at its head a dark-haired, tough-looking Haganah agent named Ruth Klieger, who had gained renown as an organizer for the labor movement. But Cairo's wealthy Jews refused even to listen to Ruth; she fared better, however, in Alexandria. Some of the most influential members of the community helped her enlist young Zionists and non-Jewish sympathizers into a Mossad network which smuggled small transports of local emigrants and European refugees on foot, by camel, car or train through Gaza to kibbutzim in the northern Negev. One of her trusted collaborators, Albert Schwika, directed the effort from his stationery store in the marketplace of Alexandria. Despite the difficulties created by the British consular authorities, he supplied emigrants with temporary passports acquired with the complicity of Egyptian officials and transit visas to Europe. Many Young Pioneers left for Israel to join the Haganah before Schwika was shot in a Tel Aviv street during a curfew while on a debriefing trip to Palestine.

After V-E Day Mossad operations were taken over by Levi Avrahami, a third-generation sabra, who, under the cover of a

British captain, had fulfilled similar missions in other Arab countries. As the official immigration quota for Palestine had been limited to 1,500 refugees a month, transports from Europe and North Africa were now routed to Tel Aviv by Avrahami's men. Eli had often delivered messages and guided Jews to Avrahami's headquarters, a two-story villa on the outskirts of Alexandria which served as a health resort for Allied soldiers but was in fact a center for Haganah activities in the area.[15] But with the outbreak of hostilities in 1948, operations virtually ground to a halt, and only after the Mossad's official dissolution in 1950 were contacts taken over by the Israeli intelligence services. Emigration from Egypt, now code-named Operation Goshen, was conducted with the aid of the Jewish Agency under the watchful eye of Cheil Modiin, Israel's Military Intelligence Corps.

As soon as the British occupation had ended, the Egyptians dropped many of their restrictions covering emigration, mainly because they wished to prevent the development of a Jewish fifth column in the event of renewed hostilities with Israel. But Jews who wished to leave the country with more than a bare minimum of funds and possessions still faced major obstacles. To ease their passage, Zionists were instructed by Jewish Agency emissaries to set up the Gruenberg Tourist Office in Cairo's central Immobilia Building with a branch in Alexandria. Through these travel agencies emigrants could obtain the vital documents—exit and police permits, income tax releases, passports or *laissez-passers*, transit visas to Italy or France and fictitious visas to South America. As soon as they reached Marseilles, Naples or Genoa, the emigrants were placed in transit camps and, after medical clearance, sailed for Israel.[16] The complex procedure, of course, required close contacts with Egyptian officials, some of whom could be persuaded to cooperate for a price.

Eli was most helpful in this crucial phase of the operation. He spent long hours in cafés along Hurieh Street and the nightclubs of the glittering Attarine Quarter entertaining frontier police officers and customs and passport control aides whom he wined, dined and bribed to overlook regulations. He also cemented

relations with the French, German, Italian and British vice-
consuls, who were prepared to provide transit visas for extra
payment.[17]

During the period he was building his network of connections, Eli was summoned to the home of his friend Sami Azar, a
frequent contact on emigration matters. Azar asked him to rent
a room not too close to the center of the city which could be
used as a meeting place for a "Zionist discussion group." Eli
required no explanation. Only after he had found and rented
suitable quarters did he ask Sami about the group's activities.[18]
This time Azar admitted that the room was to be used as headquarters for a cell of local Zionists gathering military, political
and economic data for the Israeli intelligence services. On
another occasion, while the two discussed emigration problems,
Azar urged Eli to join the group, but he was already too heavily
committed and gave no definite answer.

Two years earlier, in 1951, Colonel Benyamin Gibli, commander of Israel's military intelligence corps, Cheil Modiin, had
called together the department heads at his office in Tel Aviv-
Jaffa to discuss intelligence gathering in Egypt. Among the suggested operational plans was the formation of a new espionage
network to expand the scope of the existing apparatus. The
groundwork had been laid as early as 1944 when the Political
Department of the Jewish Agency had set up a listening post in
Cairo under the guise of a service club for Palestinian soldiers.
Ruth Klieger later recruited local Zionists to assist agents of the
Shai Sherut Yediot, the Information Service of the Haganah
high command, in general intelligence gathering about the British and the Arabs. Her successor, Levi Avrahami, further developed the network to include not only political and military
espionage, but sabotage and arms acquisitions.

Shortly before the 1948 conflict, some agents were forced to
abandon Egypt; others were recalled and reassigned. Left behind were lone operatives, who worked in the major cities or
within the British military establishment, and networks recruited from among the ethnic and religious minorities—Copts,

Greeks, Armenians and Italians. Shortly after the invasion, Tel Aviv instructed the former Mossad operative, Dr. Victor Saadi, a physician who worked at the Hôpital Israelite in Cairo, to organize an espionage ring with Jews who had escaped imprisonment. Saadi was able to recruit a small number of Zionists who were still well placed and maintained excellent relations with Egyptian officials. His group, code named *Beyahad* (Together), gathered political and military intelligence, advised community leaders on immigration matters, reactivated contacts with both Jews and Arabs who had helped the Haganah in illegal immigration.[19]

A wide variety of information was beamed to Modiin in Tel Aviv. The Israelis even infiltrated the expeditionary force with agents disguised as Arab civilians who worked at military bases. Field Security, military intelligence, the counterespionage agency and the political police failed to expose any important rings during the war, allowing Modiin to work undisturbed until the armistice was signed.

While Saadi's organization continued to operate, the number of agents increased steadily. Shortly after the 1952 coup, Modiin planted Captain Max Bennet, one of its most efficient operatives, in Cairo. Bennet, the son of a Jewish father and Catholic mother, was a native of Cologne, Germany. He had emigrated to Palestine with his parents at the age of sixteen, after Hitler had been appointed Reich chancellor. Bennet studied electrical engineering and joined the Haganah underground at an early age. In the Second World War he had served with the RAF and during the Palestine conflict became a transport officer in an infantry battalion. Bennet had planned to make the Air Force his career, but his Aryan appearance and knowledge of German, plus the fact that he was only half Jewish and not circumcised, attracted the attention of Modiin recruiters, and as soon as the war ended, he was transferred and trained for covert operations.

Bennet was first sent to establish a cover in England, where he acquired British citizenship as a Russian émigré under his real name. While in London, he met Jean, the daughter of a wealthy

British family; they were married after a short courtship, and a
son, Midan, was born a year later. On his first assignment, Bennet was sent to Teheran, where he established a cover as a shop
owner dealing in Persian rugs, while directing illegal emigration
to Israel through Syria and Lebanon. He later entered Iraq as
the representative of a British commercial firm for which he
opened branches throughout the country. From headquarters in
Baghdad Bennet gathered military and political information and
conducted acts of sabotage. When his identity was uncovered by
the Iraqi security services, he escaped to Jordan and returned to
Israel.

Modiin sent him next to establish a cover in Germany, where
he acquired citizenship under the alias Emil Witbein and worked
under the direction of Major Avraham Dar, a young sabra of
Yemenite descent, who would not soon forget his subordinate's
abilities. As a new cover, Bennet found employment with a firm
that manufactured artificial limbs and, in 1952, gained easy
entry into Cairo as the company's representative. He negotiated
a contract with the Egyptian Army for the supply of artificial
limbs and as a result met General Naguib, who at the time was
also chairman of the War Veterans Organization. Naguib was
strongly impressed by Bennet's concern for the wounded in the
Palestine War, and within a short time the Israeli became a
frequent guest at the general's house. Through Naguib and his
staff, Bennet met many influential officers, developing excellent
sources of information.[20] Colonel Gibli nonetheless found the
current operation in Egypt less than sufficient for the country's
security needs and, following lengthy deliberations, instructed
Dar to oversee recruitment of a new network composed of
militant Zionists which would remain dormant until the time
was ripe for its activation. Several days after this conference
Modiin radioed Dr. Saadi that an emissary named John Darling
would soon arrive from Tel Aviv. The agent was none other than
Dar himself.

Major Dar arrived in Cairo in the late summer and checked in
at a luxury hotel in the Zamalek district. Carrying a British

passport under his alias, he registered as the representative of a Manchester electrical appliance manufacturer. He immediately contacted Saadi, and the two met twenty-four hours later in a tearoom by the Nile. After the doctor briefed him about conditions in Cairo, Dar explained Tel Aviv's need for a new network. He suggested that Saadi recruit a small number of dedicated Zionists who were in a position to gather intelligence and would later be willing to undergo training in Israel.

The person who could best carry out such a task, Saadi believed, was a twenty-four-year-old socialite and Olympic athlete of Turkish-Yugoslav parentage named Victorine Ninio, who worked for a British import-export firm specializing in typewriters. Besides the esteem she enjoyed in Zionist circles, Victorine still had friends in high society; as a member of the Lido Club in the Heliopolis suburb where she was known as Marcelle, Victorine was on friendly terms with many young Egyptian officers and civilians well connected with the junta.

At Dar's request, Saadi arranged a meeting with Victorine at a café near the Nasr Cinema. He was anxious to determine her motives for wanting to help Israel and asked her many personal questions. The girl talked about her life with quiet ease and finally convinced him of her devotion to the Jewish cause. After the interview, Dar agreed with Saadi that Victorine would make an ideal recruiting officer and instructed him to ask her to seek out potential candidates.

At a second meeting, Victorine came prepared with an impressive list of young Zionists. To direct the Cairo unit, she proposed a Tunisian citizen, Dr. Moïse Lieto Marzouk, the twenty-eight-year-old son of a wealthy pharmacist and Karaite Jew, who had gone to medical school with Saadi and practiced surgery at the Hôpital Israelite in the capital. Others in the Cairo group included Eli Jacob Naim, a twenty-two-year-old clerk at the Schwartz Company; Caesar Josef Cohen, an employee of the Zilkha Bank; Meir Samuel Meyuhas, a commercial agent; and Meir Josef Zaafran, a twenty-six-year-old architect. Victor Moïse Levi, a salesman, was chosen as head of the Alexandria cell. He was later replaced by Eli's close friend

Samuel Azar, who would serve only in a nominal capacity, allowing Levi to take active charge. The members assigned to his unit were all twenty-one years old: among them were Philippe Herman Nathanson, an assistant broker at the Bourse, and Robert Nissim Dassa, a clerk.

Dar rented a villa in the Zamalek district, bought a new Chevrolet, and during the following two months shuttled between Cairo and Alexandria instructing the young operatives in basic information-gathering techniques. One outcome of his work was a growing attachment to Victorine; as the days went on, the vibrant young woman came to mean more and more to Dar—a relationship that would ultimately mar his judgment of espionage matters.

Although initial assignments undertaken by the members of the two cells resulted in little of substance, the major was convinced that the network would eventually become highly productive. At the beginning of 1952, after leaving Victorine with a contingency fund of 1,000 Egyptian pounds, he flew to Europe and returned to Tel Aviv.[21]

The network was continuing to increase its efficiency in the coming months when Dar radioed Saadi requesting that five members be sent to Tel Aviv for basic intelligence training. Although Azar and a number of others declined for various personal reasons to make the journey, Levi, Marzouk, Dassa and Nathanson were enlisted. The fifth member was Eli, who had finally been convinced by Azar to join the network.[22] His friend had heatedly contended that the growing evidence of anti-Jewish feeling in the government raised the specter of fierce reprisals against both Zionists and non-Zionist members of the community in the event of another major war. He also pointed out that with the last of Eli's family safe in Israel—Maurice had left in 1951—he need not fear that his activities would endanger those closest to him. Besides, his contacts with officials in passport control and on the border could prove invaluable. These arguments, along with his respect and trust for Sami, had shattered Eli's remaining resistance.

Saadi told the five to take their yearly vacations and booked their passage to Marseilles. Marzouk sailed first in the company of a patient he was supposedly taking to France for medical treatment—a plot necessitated by Egypt's watchful eye on travel by physicians, lest they leave the country and never return. He met Dar in Paris and after a short debriefing was confined to his hotel room until departure. A week later Dar exchanged his Egyptian documents for an Israeli passport and supplied a ticket for a Zim liner to Haifa. Levi arrived a short while afterward, followed by Dassa, Nathanson and Eli.

In the port city, they were each met by a Modiin liaison officer, escorted through customs, then driven to an intelligence school in Jaffa. For the next three months a female sergeant named Rachel and a young sabra called Gideon supervised their training. They underwent courses in radio transmission, coding, employment of invisible inks, photography, topography, demolition and general intelligence gathering.[23] Three months later Modiin prepared to return them to Egypt. They would later be given tangible evidence of their new status when two transmitters, ciphers and explosives were smuggled into Egypt and delivered to Victorine.

Before Marzouk and Levi left Israel, Dar briefed them at length about their mission. He explained that a Modiin officer would arrive shortly to take charge of the group; they were to obey his every order without hesitation and carry out all actions and assignments he would require. While the five were still training, Gibli had decided to assign Max Bennet the task of overseeing the network's activities. Although Bennet normally operated alone, he had acquired invaluable experience while dealing with Persian and Iraqi Zionists; just as important was the fact that he was an Israeli, aloof from the pressures and entanglements of the local community. Bennet, who had left Egypt shortly before the fall of General Naguib after supplying Tel Aviv with detailed information about the struggle for power in the revolutionary junta, was in Germany awaiting orders. Dar was to brief him about his new mission and supply the necessary paraphernalia for the network.

When Bennet heard that he would have to work with a group of relative amateurs led by inexperienced ringleaders who knew one another intimately, he rebelled. But headquarters emphasized the importance attached to the development of this source of information and ordered him to oversee the network. Bennet was a soldier and had no choice but to obey. Toward the end of 1953, confident that his cover was flawless, he returned to Cairo with his wife and son as consultant for Cairo Motors, the Anglo-Egyptian agency of the Ford Motor Company, rented a spacious villa in the Zamalek district and first called on old friends; he was warmly welcomed back to the Gezira Sporting Club and the inner circle of junta supporters. "Witbein was an expert in transportation," a high-ranking officer later testified. "His advice was sought by all."

As soon as he had established himself, Bennet made contact with Victorine and handed her the two transmitters he had brought for the network. He later met Marzouk and Azar for a short conversation and he relayed a six-word message from Dar: "I want you to obey him." Bennet finally ordered that contact be made only through Victorine. "We asked no questions," Azar later recalled, "and we never saw him again."[24]

Throughout the remainder of the year, under Bennet's supervision, the two groups achieved such remarkable successes in military, political and economic espionage that the Israelis were often better informed about the activities of the junta than many high-ranking officials in the Egyptian government. Yet the most dramatic and fateful mission of the network was still to come.

4
Sabotage in Alexandria

Modiin commander Benyamin Gibli was far from the least of those concerned over recent reports relayed by the Cairo network about the steps the junta had taken to strengthen the armed forces and support fedayeen raids into Israel. In the light of the somber evaluations his analysts supplied, Gibli was unable to share the views of Premier Moshe Sharet and his moderate-dominated Cabinet that the government of Colonel Gamal Abdul Nasser, who had assumed the chairmanship of the Revolutionary Council from Naguib at the beginning of 1954, favored a peaceful solution of the conflict with Israel.

The bellicose statements of the new Egyptian leadership and the intensification of skirmishes along Israel's southern border, though disquieting, did not disturb Gibli as much as what seemed to be a potentially devastating policy shift in London. A sale of aircraft to the Egyptian Air Force coupled with an agreement over the Sudan had set the stage for a Suez withdrawal. The probability of an immediate accord over the evacuation of the canal zone, without a guarantee of Israeli rights, thus heightened his fears that the waterway would be irrevocably closed to Israeli shipping, and the bases in the Nile Delta, which the British had stocked with huge caches of arms, would fall into Egyptian hands.

The portents from Washington appeared even darker. There was ample evidence of a pro-Egyptian drift in the Middle

Eastern policy of the Eisenhower administration. Secretary of
State John Foster Dulles had been seeking the friendship of
Arab leaders for the past two years by proposing the resettle-
ment of Palestinian refugees in Israel and the internationaliza-
tion of Jerusalem. His aides in the State Department, who held
high hopes that Egypt would become the cornerstone of a
Western-oriented regional alliance, had promised Nasser not
only moral backing but the same military and economic aid the
United States had given Saudi Arabia and member-states of the
Baghdad Pact, Iraq, Turkey and Iran. And as a token of good
faith, Washington allowed Cairo to purchase strategic materials
in the United States.

The potentially dangerous foreign policy moves made by
England and the United States had a devastating impact on
Israeli intelligence circles. Few members of the General Staff
found any solace in the placating statement issued by Whitehall
and Foggy Bottom which attempted to reassure Israel that the
two governments intended to maintain an impartial friendship
with both Arabs and Jews. Churchill's dramatic assertion "I am
a Zionist" and London's pledge to block any aggression against
Israel did little to dispel their fears that England would give in
to virtually every demand made by Nasser over the canal issue,
making a peaceful settlement with Egypt after a withdrawal from
the Suez an impossibility. They were just as skeptical about
American assurances that the reciprocal coziness between Washington and the junta, with broad hints of an arms agreement
and a place for Egypt in a pro-Western regional alliance, would
not harm Israel.

Colonel Gibli, unlike some of his civilian colleagues in the
intelligence community, scorned diplomatic overtures and considered secret political operations as the only way to alter the
pro-Arab trend in Western policies. Gibli's superiors, Defense
Minister Pinchas Lavon and Chief of Staff Lieutenant General
Moshe Dayan, though mutually antagonistic, supported his position. They both seemed determined to follow the same bellicose
policy toward the Arabs that Ben-Gurion had advocated before
he resigned to tend sheep and meditate at Sde Boker in the

remote Negev desert. But Lavon was at loggerheads with Sharet and most Cabinet members; he was also snubbed by many of his subordinates. And to add to his isolation, he was being denied access to sources of information other than Modiin. (The newly created Mosad, which came under the jurisdiction of the prime minister, was at the time in the process of taking over the duties of foreign intelligence gathering.) Lavon thus hesitated to adopt a more aggressive attitude toward covert operations in Egypt. In May, after discussing the situation with Gibli, Lavon rejected his propositions to employ networks of young Zionists in sabotage; he promised, though, to discuss the matter again at a later date. [1]

Gibli saw no point in waiting. As an aspirant to the post of chief of staff, he realized that a successful secret operation which would tip the balance in favor of Israel could also further his own ends. If the sabotage acts attained their goal, he would have no difficulty in receiving Lavon's approval and the blessings of even the most skeptical moderates in Sharet's Cabinet. And he could then personally claim the credit. In case of failure, the only ones to be blamed would be his subordinates. Thus strengthened by his own ambition and sure of Dayan's backing (he was also said to have won the blessing of Ben-Gurion), Gibli decided to ignore Lavon's equivocation and act on his own. [2]

Once he had made his decision, the colonel entrusted the mission of activating the network to the Special Operations Department code-named Unit 131. Its chief was Lieutenant Colonel Mordechai "Motke" Ben Zur, a former field intelligence officer of the Harel Brigade and lieutenant colonel in the reserves. Ben Zur, who had often proved himself in the field, was most eager to undertake covert operations abroad. [3] The Cairo sabotage plan was, therefore, received with gratitude and enthusiasm.

In the first week of June, after a routine conference of department heads, Gibli asked Ben Zur to remain behind. Reviewing the progress of intelligence gathering in Egypt, the colonel praised the proficiency of the Cairo and Alexandria rings; the intelligence reports they had provided far exceeded initial expectations. On the negative side, clashes of personality within the network had caused needless friction—a problem that Bennet as a lone operative was unable to resolve. Marzouk's strongly independent stance also ruffled the Center. Nonetheless, Gibli felt that by now the two cells had acquired enough experience to broaden the scope of their activities and were ready for the new phase of their overall mission: the sabotage of American and British installations in Egypt. The terrorist acts, Gibli explained, aimed at bringing about a rupture in relations between Cairo and the Western powers, would be made to appear the work of Communists or ultranationalists. He then instructed Ben Zur to ready the unit for action in July. When Gibli had concluded, Ben Zur understood that authorization for the operation had apparently been given by either Lavon or Dayan.[4]

In order not to endanger Bennet's primary mission of military intelligence gathering by assigning him to reconcile private feuds, Ben Zur selected Lieutenant Colonel Avri, his former superior in the Harel Brigade and now an experienced Modiin operative, to oversee the operation. The twenty-nine-year-old agent had successfully carried out several missions in Egypt as Waffen SS officer Paul Frank, a cover he had established in West Germany. While in Cairo, he had cultivated close friendships with the commander of the Navy, the military intelligence chief, Interior Minister Zakharieh Muhieddin, the Grand Mufti of Jerusalem and the chief German military adviser.[5] Ben Zur was therefore convinced that under Avri's supervision, the risks involved in the network's new and far more dangerous undertakings would be greatly minimized.

After a series of conferences at Modiin Headquarters, Avri was ordered to fly to France, where Ben Zur would await him for a briefing. The chief of special operations arrived in Paris at the beginning of June. At a café in St. Germain des Pres, Ben Zur presented Avri with the final plan conceived by headquarters. Along with the leaders of the two rings, Avri would have full responsibility for every aspect of the operation. Further instructions, Ben Zur explained, would be broadcast in code on Kol Israel's daily *How to Cook* program. At the second meeting in Paris, Ben Zur gave Avri the order to initiate the bombings.[6]

Upon his return to Egypt on June 30, Avri found the network in turmoil. Marzouk was no longer participating in its activities, and the Cairo ring was practically dissolved; Azar was incapacitated by personal problems, and Eli, traveling for his firm, could not operate the transmitter he was assigned. As Victorine was of greater aid to Bennet, Avri would not involve her in the sabotage operation. He decided to deal only with the Alexandria ring and contacted Nathanson, who had proved the network's most militant operative. Avri summoned him and Levi to a secret meeting in Cairo where he outlined their assignments. But when Avri disclosed that their men would have to carry out acts of sabotage intended to isolate Egypt from the West, they both made no effort to conceal their displeasure. At a later meeting Dassa contended that the bombings of public buildings would inevitably cause death or injury to many innocent civilians; he felt no hatred for ordinary citizens who were not responsible for government policy and saw no reason why they should suffer. Azar was no less opposed. He told Avri flatly that he could not in good conscience comply. Faced with their intransigence, Avri first attempted persuasion but failing to find convincing arguments, finally resorted to threats and warned that such insubordination might force him to "take extreme measures."

When the sabotage order was passed down to the others, it was received with equal foreboding. Eli reacted with resentment and anger for the first time since joining the Zionist underground. The Modiin command unquestionably had to consider the security of Israel before its operatives' feelings; yet to Eli, the intelligence officers in Tel Aviv seemed incapable of understanding that not every Arab was an enemy and that to risk harming civilians was anathema to Jews who had spent their lives in Egypt. He was not irrevocably committed to destroying everything Egyptian; certainly he did not consider himself a saboteur capable of carrying out any mission regardless of the consequences. For his friends, Levi, Nathanson and Dassa, however, the order carried the full weight of authority. Having trained in Israel, they considered themselves under the same obligation as Israeli soldiers. Their eventual decision to fulfill the assignment, whatever the cost to their consciences, was sufficient reason for Azar to take part in the bombings. The damage inflicted to morale, nonetheless, would never be repaired.

At a joint conference the following morning, Avri discussed with Levi the targets where incendiary devices and time bombs were to be planted. The operation, they agreed, would be divided into two phases: the ring would first sabotage public buildings, then place diversionary bombs in U.S. and British installations. Levi, Nathanson, Dassa and Azar would plant the bombs, while Eli would maintain contact with Tel Aviv. The men would run only the minimum risk, as their actions would inevitably be blamed on extremist forces.

Later in the afternoon, Eli and his group were summoned to the apartment headquarters on Ramleh Square, where Levi showed two training films on the preparation and use of explosives which Modiin had sent from Tel Aviv and Dassa demonstrated how to conceal phosphorus incendiary devices in eyeglass cases and how to wire time bombs into boxes of Vim detergent. It took Eli and his friends only hours to refresh their memories.

Two days after his arrival, Avri was able to radio headquarters. Tel Aviv acknowledged and gave the green light. Modiin Headquarters ordered to start the bombings in exactly forty-eight hours and culminate them on the second anniversary of the coup, a likely date for anti-Nasser agitation.

On Thursday, July 1, Avri took an unprecedented step by meeting personally with all four Alexandrians, Levi, Nathanson, Dassa and Azar, and issuing final instructions. He was well aware, he told them, that they had misgivings about sabotage, but the orders received from Tel Aviv were categorical: American and British property had to be damaged in order to create tension with the two countries. Such action might enable dissident Members of Parliament in Britain to prevent an agreement for the evacuation of the Suez bases and could sway American public opinion against the arming of Egypt. But above all, Avri stressed, the havoc they created would be blamed on the Communists, Green Shirts or Moslem Brethren, discrediting the military regime as unpopular, unstable and unworthy of Western aid. He then proceeded to outline the steps of the mission: The group would place the bombs in main post offices, railroad stations, movie theaters, British and American consulates and libraries of the United States Information Service.[7]

The first phase of the operation was carried out within a twelve-day period. On Friday, July 2, fire bombs dropped into three parcel post mailboxes destroyed the mailing room at the General Post Office on Place Ismail in Alexandria, injuring several clerks.[8] Tuesday morning, the fourteenth, Dassa and Azar arrived at the USIS library in Cairo's Liberation Square shortly before closing time. "Under the pretext of doing research," Azar would recall, "we placed the explosives between the shelves." Later in the evening a blast shook the library. But a number of homemade devices they placed in the baggage department of the main railway station caused only minor damage. That same evening, an explosion caused by a bomb Levi and Nathanson had planted at the USIS office on Ramleh Boulevard in Alexandria rocked its library. Hysteria mounted in both cities, as sirens wailed through the streets with increasing frequency. No public place was considered immune. The chief of the political police had no evidence that any of the extremist groups were involved, but as the press clamored for action, hundreds of known agitators from both left and the right were rounded up and imprisoned.

The Alexandria group again went into action in the third week of July. On the afternoon of the twenty-third, Cairo patrons of the Rivoli and Radio cinemas discovered two devices placed by Dassa and Azar which a bomb squad dismantled minutes before they were to explode. At the same time, a blaze set by Levi was extinguished in the Alexandria Lido theater.

By Friday evening, police reinforced by army units were
deployed throughout Egypt in full force. The Alexandria Criminal Investigation Department assigned its plainclothesmen to
watch every public building in the city. Captain Hassan Zaki
al-Manawi from the Atarine Police Station took up his post near
the Rio Cinema early that evening. He was standing in front of
the box office eyeing the crowd when he suddenly heard cries
for help and saw a young man, his jacket ablaze, run from the
theater. The inspector wrestled him to the pavement, attempting to smother the flames. In the struggle, an eyeglass case fell
from the man's pocket, scattering a black powder onto the
sidewalk. After helping him to his feet, al-Manawi instinctively
examined the spilled substance: he immediately recognized the
basic ingredients used in homemade incendiary devices. The
young man, who identified himself as Philippe Nathanson, insisted that he was not badly hurt, but al-Manawi refused to let
him go. An escort of black-bereted city policemen rushed him
to the nearby Government Hospital, where a Bickford fuze and
incriminating papers were found in his possession. Later questioned at the Manshieh Police Station, Nathanson denied any
connection with the bombings. A quick search of his apartment,
however, led to the discovery of compromising letters "about a
man called 'Paul,' who seemed to be an important person," plus
photos of Dassa and Levi. A more thorough search uncovered a
darkroom with negatives of bridges and military installations
and a secret cache with two boxes of explosives, a number of
homemade bombs and seven microfilms containing chemical
formulae for the preparation of *plastique*.

Samir Darwish, head of the Alexandria CID, who had taken
over the preliminary investigation, at once realized that he
possessed the first clue in the "July mystery bombings" and
confronted the prisoner with the evidence. Nathanson radically
changed his story, now stubbornly insisting he was a Communist under instructions to carry out random acts of terror
against the regime. He withstood the torture, but in the morning, when Darwish told him that his mother was being held on
suspicion of collaboration, Nathanson broke down and made a

complete confession, naming his accomplices by their code names and identifying "Pierre" (Levi), who had participated with him in the bombings. [9]

Levi had been just as unsuccessful in his last mission as had "Henri" (Nathanson). He had attempted to bomb the Metro Cinema in Alexandria but, unable to obtain a ticket because of a "Woman-Only" matinee, had decided to postpone the operation. Later that evening, when he heard rumors of Nathanson's arrest, he quickly disposed of the bomb in a nearby canal and decided to wait until morning before seeking instructions from Avri. Levi unsuccessfully attempted to reach Azar by phone and went to a debriefing appointment he had with Avri instead. After reassuring the confused and frightened young man, the Israeli operative suggested they meet again the following day in Alexandria. He hoped by then to be able to assess the situation and plan the next move. Levi was on his way home when the police detained him. He would soon succumb to his interrogators and reveal the identity of "Roger," his co conspirator Dassa.

Dassa, who had planted a bomb in the Cairo Cinema the night of Nathanson's arrest, had stayed overnight in the capital and had taken an early morning train home, unaware of the arrests. A team of detectives picked up the stunned Dassa at the Alexandria railway terminal and whisked him to the Mashieh Station, where he was subjected to intensive grilling by Darwish. Dassa denied all knowledge of the bombings but, when confronted with Nathanson and Levi, who had already acknowledged involvement, confirmed his and "Jacques' " (Azar's) participation.[10]

Meanwhile, Azar had called Dassa's home to get a report on his actions in the capital and learned of the arrests from his parents. When he read in the morning papers about the Rio Cinema incident, he rushed to see Avri at a prearranged meeting place. Azar arrived on Rue des Banques badly shaken. Disregarding security procedures, he made no effort to avoid an open conversation. He told Avri of the arrests and insisted that it was imperative something be done before the police swooped down on those who were still free. Avri refused to choose an immediate course of action and icily ordered him to return home and find out more details. Azar reluctantly obeyed.

At a second meeting the following day, Azar was in a state of panic. He told Avri what he knew and was ordered to aid in an attempt to destroy any evidence left at the apartment-headquarters. They both rushed to Ramleh Square, entered the apartment through a window, and hurriedly removed documents, transmitters and explosives. Avri gave Azar the bulky material and told him to destroy it; he only took with him a tiny, expensive radio. Their timing could not have been more propitious. As they were leaving, the police arrived in force.

At the third meeting a week after the arrests, Avri attempted to convince Azar to leave the country with him. Azar refused, arguing that he could not abandon his mother. Avri decided to give him one more chance to change his mind and set up a fourth and last meeting. Forty-eight hours later, taking the necessary precautions, he arrived at the prearranged place ahead of time and was getting ready to approach the street corner when he saw a police detail arrive. Moments afterward, Azar was led from a prison van and stationed at the meeting place to await his contact. Avri calmly left the premises. [11]

In the meantime, while Azar was being led to the station, Eli stopped at a café on his way home from the office. He sat sipping coffee when a police detective he knew well came by the table to tell him about the arrest of "a local Zionist who had been involved in the recent bombings." Eli managed to feign shock that a Jew had been implicated and after a short exchange left the café hurriedly. He went straight to the apartment he had rented for the group in the hope of destroying anything which might be used as evidence but found the building already surrounded by police. [12] Strangely enough, no one of the arrested would ever mention the ring's wireless operator, "Alex" (Eli's code name).

CID interrogators, reinforced by General Security agents, questioned Azar day and night. As they had found in his possession the material Avri had ordered him to destroy, he had finally acknowledged his part in the bombings and mentioned having recently met "Robert" (Avri), whom he knew under the alias Paul Frank, and confessed that he was to contact him again within a few days. It was from Azar that the police also wrenched the names of Zaafran and Meyuhas. Their arrest would lead to the capture of the last members of the no longer operational Cairo ring—Naim, Cohen, and Marzouk. When Zaafran was asked whether he knew the "Paul" mentioned in the letters found in Nathanson's apartment, he simply said: "Sure, that is the cover name used by Dr. Marzouk."

Though well aware of the roundups in Cairo and Alexandria, Marzouk had gone to work at the hospital where he was seized by a force of CID detectives and counterespionage agents of the Mukhabarat (General Security Service). During his initial interrogation, Marzouk revealed some details of the Zionist apparatus. The apartment-headquarters in Alexandria, he admitted, "was not meant to be used only for radio transmissions but also as a meeting place for Israeli intelligence officers who periodically came to Egypt for inspection . . . " One of them, Marzouk claimed, was in Cairo at that moment, but he could not lead the police to him since he had always made contact through "Claude" (Ninio), the liaison between the network's two rings and the center in Israel.[13] The name of Victorine-Marcelle had been previously mentioned by the other suspects, and a warrant for her arrest was immediately issued.

The usually well-informed Victorine-Marcelle learned of the arrests only by chance. She tried to contact Bennet by means of a message she left at the prearranged "drop," but when he did not appear at the meeting by late Monday afternoon, she considered it too dangerous to remain in the city any longer. Taking a leave of absence from work under the pretext of attending her sick mother, she quietly left Alexandria. But her anxiety did not go unnoticed. Shortly after she had left the office, the Cairo police received an anonymous phone call from one of her colleagues who had grown resentful of Victorine's fame and social contacts and had become suspicious of her behavior. By the time detectives burst into her apartment she was already gone. The police, nonetheless, found much more than they had expected: The body of a young man later identified as a fellow operative was hanging from a beam of the bathroom ceiling. [14]

Detectives subsequently traced Victorine to a resort near Alexandria and broke into her room just as she tried to leap from a window. Confronted with the disclosures of her fellow conspirators, she finally admitted her role in the network but denied knowing the exact whereabouts of Max Bennet; she actually knew only the license number of his car. But, Victorine had once carelessly approached Bennet while he was in the company of intelligence officials, one of whom recalled the encounter. The information from these two sources, though minimal, was sufficient to trace Bennet. The police checked with all the doormen in the Zamalek district until they found Bennet's blue Chevrolet. After a search revealed a radio transmitter in the oil tank, they set up an ambush in Bennet's garage and caught him red-handed while he attempted to contact Tel Aviv. [15]

As the police inexorably closed in, Avri, having lost radio contact with the center, sent an open telegram to a contact in Germany—"Pierre [Levi's code name] gone bankrupt. Staying on to save investment"—and signed his son's name. The cable was forwarded to Tel Aviv by regular mail. Forty-eight hours later, Modiin Headquarters ordered Bennet to leave Cairo. He nevertheless only felt secure enough to send out his family, while he stayed on.

Unaware of the network's confessions, Avri attempted to confuse the police by continuing the bombings himself. He blew up a refinery near Cairo and threw hand grenades from a passing car into the entrance of a military base in the canal zone. But after Azar's arrest, he concluded that it was too late to arrange for the escape of men who were still free, particularly since Modiin had failed to supply the forged documents promised for such an emergency. He calculated that his own arrest would cause far more damage to Israeli intelligence than his abandonment of the network. It was vital, therefore, that he leave Egypt. Fearing that the police would seal off the borders, he decided against using a planned escape route through Libya. He sold his car and took a Lufthansa flight to Munich.[16]

Aside from Avri, Saadi, along with a number of unidentified members of the network, managed to elude the police. Two weeks after Nathanson's arrest, eleven of the operatives were in custody.

Eli had been implicated in the case by the documents found in Azar's apartment and was seized shortly after the first arrests along with 150 Cairenes and Alexandrian Jews, all of whom had Zionist records and were known to be on friendly terms with members of the network. Brought before a team of interrogators headed by the military attorney, Amin Abdul Ala, Eli was subjected to an interminable staccato of questions. As doggedly as his inquisitors tried to pry a confession, Eli disclaimed having any knowledge of the ring and its operations. Ala was still unwilling to chance his release and had him transferred to the Siwa desert prison near the Libyan border where enemies of the regime of all persuasions were herded together in abject misery and denied contact with the outside world. After four months of periodic questioning, the military attorney failed to find even the slightest link between Eli and the accused and grudgingly ordered his release along with twenty other suspects. [17]

After the preliminary investigation had been closed by the Cairo and Alexandria CID and the General Security Services, the eleven saboteurs were transferred to the Army Detention Center in Cairo and handed over to the Military Investigation Branch. Isolated and denied access to counsel, they were questioned for forty-three days and nights. They all acknowledged Zionist affiliation but were still unwilling to cooperate in spite of the incriminating evidence the police had found in their possession. (CID counterespionage agents, who had searched the network's seven apartments in Cairo and Alexandria, had discovered a wealth of "professional paraphernalia"—documents, maps, photographs, microfilms, copies of correspondence with Modiin fronts in Europe, miniature tape recorders, explosives and even an automatic leaflet distributor. Particularly puzzling was the number of radio transmitters. Although only three had been operated by Bennet, the Cairo and the Alexandria rings, the security services claimed to have found six more concealed in jam jars, auto oil tanks and even a Bible.) The prisoners' contempt for collaboration was further demonstrated when Victorine made a second attempt at suicide. On August 11, while waiting for the interrogator to arrive, she heard a knock on the door. As the guard got up to answer, she leaped, and, in a swift move, jumped through the window. Her act proved futile; she had fallen only one floor and suffered a broken leg and minor injuries. "The Zionist agents would rather have died than harm Israeli intelligence by divulging its secrets," later remarked one of the military attorneys while testifying about the prisoners' spirit.

To achieve a breakthrough, the Military Investigation Branch decided that more extreme measures were in order. Torture and intimidation were ultimately used on Bennet, Ninio, Marzouk [18] and Azar to pressure them into signing a prepared confession. This excruciating method proved successful. All eleven succumbed to their inquisitors.

Radio Damascus was the first to announce the arrests of the "Zionist gang which threatened the internal security of Egypt and was undermining Anglo-Egyptian talks." But the official statement about the case was made only on October 6, over Radio Cairo by Interior Minister Zakharieh Muhieddin. The police investigation, he announced, had been completed with the confessions of the accused, and he was now able to reveal "Israel's plot to spread sedition and unrest in Egypt." The objective of the bombings, Muhieddin disclosed, had been "to worsen relations between Egypt on the one hand and Britain and the United States on the other." It had also been convincingly established, he added, that Jews living in Egypt had been forced to work for the ring in spite of their desire to remain loyal to the government. The press hastened to publicize the minister's assertion. "All the Jews of Egypt should follow closely the upcoming spy trial and repeat the story to their children a hundred times," urged the daily *al-Mussawar.* "They would thus see that Israel only wants to make them betray the country that had treated them so generously." [19]

As the opening of the trial approached, there were other portents besides Muhieddin's clear assumption of guilt which clouded the fate of the defendants. Israeli-Egyptian relations had been further strained over an incident sparked by the Anglo-Egyptian Canal Zone agreement signed by a jubilant Nasser in Cairo on July 27, 1954. Sharet, who feared Egypt would close the door to any future diplomatic efforts to keep the Suez open for Israeli shipping, decided to test Nasser's intentions. On September 28 the 500-ton *Bat Galim* flying the white and blue Star of David steamed into the canal with a crew of ten and a cargo of meat and plywood from Massawa. The Port Said authorities arrested the sailors and sequestered the ship and its cargo.

In addition to its problems with Israel, the junta was beset by domestic strife. Nasser had reacted to attacks on the regime by lashing back at his enemies with arbitrary arrests and purge trials of dissidents conveniently labeled "Communists led and run by Zionists." Yet the more Nasser sought to stifle the opposition, the more vocal it became. The Moslem Brotherhood, combining skillful propaganda with carefully staged riots, launched an all-out war against the premier. The new supreme guide, Hassan al-Hodeibi, plotted a coup, signaled by Nasser's assassination, in which every Cabinet minister and 160 revolutionary officers were marked for death. By the final week of October the virulence had reached a climax. As Nasser mounted the podium in Alexandria's Muhammad Ali Square to address a wildly enthusiastic crowd of more than 200,000, a young member of the Brotherhood's ultramilitant Secret Wing raced forward, firing eight shots at close range. Inexplicably, the bullets missed their target. The organization was again dissolved, and arrests reached the 1,000 mark. "We must finish once and for all with those who use arms and violence," declared Nasser's minister of state. "We have decided not to allow these reptiles to crawl among us again." Significantly, the same apocalyptic rhetoric was used by the Cairo press in referring to the accused Zionists. The trial, proclaimed *al-Gumhuriya*, would show the world that "Egypt wants only to cleanse her territory of spies and traitors in the same way she wanted to cleanse it of reactionaries, agents of imperialism and corruptors."

The court-martial opened in Cairo on Saturday, December 11, 1954, against an unprecedented backdrop of violence and repression. Eli arrived at the Court of Appeals, a massive three-story structure of ocher stone located in the heart of the Old City, shortly before the gavel was pounded at 9:30 A.M. He was well aware that his presence might arouse the suspicions of the authorities and the curiosity of his friends on trial, who no doubt felt uncertain and abandoned. Yet he believed it was vital to prove to those with whom he had shared so much in the last two years that they had not been deserted.

Towered over by two dozen red-fezzed blue-uniformed policemen, the eleven defendants were led into a dingy, deteriorating chamber, where a high dock covered with steel mesh and encircled by a spiked balustrade had been erected. Each took his place in the dock between two guards. Victorine alone was assigned a space in the second row behind the bench of the defense. The five members of the Supreme Military Tribunal, presided over by Brigadier Muhammad Fuad al-Digwi, sat behind a long table under a huge inscription: "He Who Has to Judge Shall Judge Rightly." In a box to their right, four military prosecutors shuffled briefs, while behind the partition in the front row a battery of eight Egyptian defense attorneys and their French, British and German colleagues, who had been denied the right to plead, conferred in tense whispers. The Quai d'Orsay had assigned two *maîtres* to represent Marzouk, who held Tunisian citizenship; Bonn had sent a lawyer to defend Bennet, a West German subject; and his wife had retained the services of a British barrister. The press box was filled to capacity. Among the seventy spectators crowding the courtroom were three diplomatic observers and a representative of the World Jewish Congress; at least 10 percent of those present, a witness later recalled, were political police officers. Only close relatives of the accused had been allowed to attend, after having been warned not to talk to the defendants or even to look at them.

The proceedings, held in accordance with Ottoman military law, were opened by a court officer who read the names of the thirteen accused—Dar and Avri were being tried in absentia—and paused only briefly before listing in a disembodied voice the members of the Supreme Military Tribunal, only one of which had passed his bar examinations. As soon as he had finished, Marzouk's attorney, Maître Ahmad Rushdi, a former minister of justice and chairman of the Egyptian Bar Association who had been retained by the French government, defiantly requested an adjournment. The police, he explained, had refused him permission to consult his client before the trial, and the prosecution had failed to present him with Marzouk's dossier. He was still unaware of the charges brought against his client. The senior prosecutor blandly told the court that the indictment had not been distributed to any of the defense counsels simply because there were not enough copies available. General Digwi was apparently not concerned by the staggering handicaps under which the counsel for the defense labored. He did not find the omission at all worrisome and told the *maître* that he would have to obtain his knowledge of the case in court.

During the exchange, the eleven defendants sat impassively in the dock. Nor did any of them show any sign of emotion when the general prosecutor began reading the indictment. "The accused," he stated with pathos, "were engaged in collecting and disseminating information calculated to assist an enemy country and create a state of disturbance and public unrest, endangering the safety of Egypt." They were charged either collectively or separately on counts of criminal conspiracy, espionage for Israel, the manufacture and possession of explosives and incendiary devices and the carrying out of acts of sabotage. After a short recess, the prosecutor demanded the death penalty for all thirteen. When he had ended, each of the defendants softly pleaded "not guilty."

Before the first session was closed, Eli listened with growing depression as Nathanson, the government's star witness, attempted to absolve himself of all responsibility for the bombings. Nathanson boasted to have foiled the "Zionist plot to destroy cinemas and public buildings" by setting himself ablaze in front of the Rio Cinema. His participation in the earlier bombings, he insisted, had come only after Avri threatened to inform the authorities of his voyage to Israel.

For most of the next two weeks, Eli commuted to Cairo almost daily. He sat in the courtroom as the prosecution produced seventeen witnesses, the majority of them police officers, in its effort to prove the guilt of those involved in "monstrous crimes against Egypt." After only forty-eight hours of such statements, Dassa, Levi, Azar and Nathanson changed their strategy and confessed the accusation, claiming that they had been misled. They ignored the real aims of those who directed them and had never wanted to act against Egypt.

When the court resumed its deliberations in the second week of the court-martial, the assistant prosecutor requested permission to make an announcement. A hush fell over the room as he informed the court that Max Bennet, scheduled to testify that Tuesday morning, had committed suicide in his cell the previous night. Bennet, an inquiry instituted by the court later revealed, had been under close surveillance before his death for having attempted to bribe a guard to smuggle potassium cyanide into his cell. He had nevertheless managed to convince another to exchange a razor blade for a half chicken he had received in a package from the British consulate. By the time he was found lying on the floor Bennet had already lost too much blood. He weakly asked for water and died. He left a note asking that a tree be planted in his memory and urging his wife to marry again. [20] "Bennet died by his own hand," editorialized a Cairo daily, "when he learned that Egypt is the grave of Zionists and Zionism."

Bennet's death deepened Eli's gloom. The captain's refusal to place himself at the mercy of the tribunal seemed to underscore the apparent willingness of the others to collaborate in the hope of obtaining lenient sentences.

After another recess, the tribunal moved to Alexandria for an on-the-spot examination of the "bomb factory" and sabotage sites. It also witnessed Nathanson and Levi demonstrate how they had slipped explosives into an airmail letter box. The co-operativeness of the accused was in keeping with the strategy of the defense attorneys who planned to show that their clients were only pawns in a plot over which they had no control. "They were children who did not know what they were doing," the counsel for several of the defendants asserted. "They played with fire and it burned them. . . . These boys should be lashed and sent home. They fell easy prey to adventures and even blackmail." Some of the accused attempted to reinforce his explanation, claiming that they had ignored the real aims of those who directed them. "I am no Zionist," bluntly stated Nathanson. "Israel doesn't interest me." Azar admitted that the bombings were intended "to harm relations between Egypt and the United States, particularly at the time of negotiations for economic aid to Egypt." He told the court: "I tried to break away, but I couldn't." When General Digwi asked if he believed that Egyptian Jews were proud of his actions, Azar replied sadly, "I think they must all be very sorry . . . I never meant to betray Egypt. I threw an incendiary device into the sea rather than harm innocent people in my country."

Eli was at first disappointed by Marzouk's testimony, which he regarded, no doubt somewhat self-righteously, as an abject attempt to avoid any responsibility for his actions. The doctor had been quick to assert that "John Darling deceived us. I re-fused to cooperate as soon as I found out he had other motives in mind." But Marzouk's contention clearly indicated the cyni-cal attitude he had decided to adopt. The network, he insisted, had been formed to help end the tension between Egypt and the Jews; indeed, he never realized that he was spying for Israel "until the words were used by the prosecutor." He similarly disclaimed having acted as the head of the Cairo ring and, revis-ing a previous confession, denied all charges of military espi-onage. The other defendants also struck an ingenuous pose. "I have confessed to everything I have done," Levi said on the stand. "But I want the court to know that I took the whole affair as fun. I am an Egyptian before I am a Jew, and at no time did I think I was causing harm to Egypt, my country. I will never live or die as an enemy of Egypt." Dassa simply stated: "I never knew the real purpose of the group. I was only seventeen."

It remained for Victorine to display what Eli considered an honorable defiance before the tribunal. Her attorney, Maître Barsum Salama, accused the police of having "tortured, beaten and forced her to talk under pressure"—a charge never investigated or denied by the court—and asserted that she "had merely accepted financial help from John Darling to help her mother who was dying of cancer." Yet Victorine made no effort to gain the court's sympathy. Asked a number of times about her relationship with Darling, she repeatedly replied: "I have nothing to say." President Digwi interjected: "What do you mean you have nothing to say?"

Victorine:	It means I don't want to reply to this question.
Digwi:	Meaning, you know the answer but you don't want to reply?
Victorine:	Yes.
Digwi:	Why don't you want to reply to this question?
Victorine:	I just don't want to.[21]

On January 6, 1955, after the final summations by the prosecution and the defense, the tribunal recessed to consider the verdicts. Three weeks later, on the morning of the twenty-seventh, the court reconvened for five minutes to pass sentence. The courtroom was packed full, with police, foreign correspondents, diplomats and TV crews. The relatives of the accused were absent; only the father of Dassa sat alone on a bench in the center. A mood of optimism could almost be felt among the press gathered expectantly in a corner. The period between the trial and the announcement of the verdict had been regarded as unprecedented and seemed to offer some hope for the defendants. It was exactly noon when the judge advocate, Colonel Ibrahim Sami, took the president's chair and, turning to face the accused, studied them for a moment before speaking. He refrained from reading the sixty-page verdict and merely called out the sentences. Marzouk was the first to be named. He rose, then stiffened and leaned heavily against the dock upon hearing that he had been condemned to death by hanging. Sami Azar, his eyes glazing, listened stonily to the same sentence before collapsing. The colonel slowly read the other sentences: Victor Moïse Levi and Philippe Herman Nathanson, life imprisonment; Victorine Ninio and Robert Nissim Dassa fifteen years; and Meir Josef Zaafran and Meir Samuel Meyuhas, seven years—all at hard labor. Eli Jacob Naim and Caesar Josef Cohen were acquitted. Marzouk coolly congratulated the two. "After sentence was passed," remembered one of the accused, "he approached me, gripped my hand and uttered *'mabruk'* [good luck]." None of the other prisoners reacted when the colonel announced that the sentences had already been approved by President Nasser as military governor of Cairo, although this sudden change in procedure curtailed the defense's efforts, virtually eliminating any chance of appeal.22   Five months of numbing solitary confinement had resigned them to their fate.

The death sentences were received with cries of outrage. Foreign observers who had attended the trial characterized the court's decision as a "vindictive judgment" and charged that the verdict had been motivated by "external and internal political reasons." They had mainly been given to show the Arab League, then meeting in Cairo, that the regime could be tough not only with Moslem Brotherhood leaders, who had been executed earlier, but also with the Jews.

Last-minute appeals by Britain, France and the Vatican went unheeded. The United States, which considered the verdicts "an internal Egyptian matter," remained officially indifferent to the situation. Pleas for clemency by the families of the condemned were also ineffective. Marzouk's mother and one of Azar's sisters kept a vigil each day in front of Nasser's home in the hope of seeing the rais (chief) and asking for mercy. But even the chief rabbi of Egypt, who had always had access to Nasser, twice requested an audience and found that his influence was unavailing.

The government carried out its retribution on Monday, January 31, against the two men who had, ironically, sought at first to prevent the bombings but had been caught in a web of conflicting loyalties and emotions. News that they would die in the morning was spread through the *harets*, and at dawn, Eli joined a crowd of 200 gathered in front of the Bab-al-Halek Prison. At 8 A.M. Marzouk, handcuffed and manacled, was led to the gallows, between two warders. He wore a black shirt, bright-red trousers and a purple cap—the garish uniform of the condemned. Upon reaching the scaffold, the indictment and verdict were read to him by a high-ranking Egyptian officer: "His face was frozen," the Karaite Rabbi Baruch Salah later said, "as if the words were not directed to him." After the *hacham* had prayed in Hebrew, Marzouk asked as a last wish to be buried near his father. The hangman moved forward with hood and rope. Ten minutes later Marzouk was officially pronounced dead. A half hour passed before another detail of guards brought Azar from his cell. He prayed and received comfort from Rabbi Haim Matri. "Azar refused a last request," Rabbi Matri remembered, "but he was much more emotional than Marzouk, and tears came to his eyes when he said the *Vidui*." He repeatedly uttered, "God, forgive me," before the trap was sprung.[23] Outside the prison gates, Eli saw the black flag hoisted.

The execution and imprisonment of the eleven Zionist operatives only spurred the efforts of the Political Police to snuff out any remnants of what they called a Jewish fifth column, and the country's remaining 45,000 Jews were particularly vulnerable to charges of subversion. Throughout 1955, all Jews lived under the constant threat of standing trial for espionage and Communist-Zionist activities. But while Zionists were still the prime target of the Political Police, it soon became apparent that every Jew would be made to feel Nasser's wrath. The government was no longer bothering to make much of a distinction between loyal citizens and those actively supporting Israel.

Whenever Eli opened the semi-official *al-Ahram* he came across editorials illustrated with vilifying cartoons which only the publications of the Third Reich could match in venom and irresponsibility. Accounts of "outrage against Arabs in Occupied Palestine" appeared next to articles accusing Jewish businessmen, physicians and community officials of espionage, sabotage and speculation. In trams and buses, at street corners and railway stations, Eli was accosted by youths who distributed anti-Jewish tracts of the Islamic Congress. Even the evening radio programs were dominated by commentators who gave vent to anti-Jewish sentiments and guest lecturers who cited the peril Judaism posed to Islam. Sooner or later, however, promised the official fortnightly *al-Gumhuriya*, "world Jewry would be exterminated as the Nazis did earlier." The government's publishing houses printed similar tirades, and Alexandrian bookstores were stocked with ragged displays of anti-Jewish propaganda and cheap novels. Indoctrinating schoolchildren to hate was officially made part of the curriculum. Ministerial memorandums instructed all teachers, including Jews, to enlighten their pupils about "the bitter enemy of Islam and the Arabs—Israel." "Instill in the heart of the youths a hatred of Israel," the directive urged, "as we are doing with the armed forces."

The new policy embittered Eli. "I saw him lose his temper for the first time," Baruch Mizrachi recalled, "when he heard that his relatives' children would have to face such lies and slander."[24] The Ministry of Education also ordered Jewish schools to admit Moslems so they would be able further to "exert pressure upon the other pupils." Until then there had been no ban on Hebrew, and the community schools in Alexandria taught the 650 remaining children a full curriculum of Judaic learning. But 120 Jewish homes were suddenly searched for Hebrew literature, and a group of youths were whisked to jail for violating a pledge not to learn the language. Zionist activists ordered their followers to destroy any compromising material.

Eli himself visited the homes of relatives and friends urging them to dispose of prayer books in order to avoid arbitrary accusations of Zionism. Every jeweler in Alexandria was notified that the manufacture of Star of David charms or medallions bearing Hebrew characters was strictly prohibited. Girls were stopped in the street and ordered to remove their necklaces; those who refused were arrested. Alarmed by the danger such practices represented to Jewish culture, the chief rabbi appealed to Nasser. To deny the use of Hebrew signs, he claimed, struck at the very roots of the religion. His pleas were to no avail.

The new persecution also affected the country's other minorities. Many of Eli's Coptic and Catholic friends had expressed uneasiness at the Muhammadanization drive. Some openly complained of discrimination, particularly from the Islamic clergy, and the systematic exclusion from public office. Conscious of the danger of violence, they prepared to emigrate. The Copts and Catholics who knew of Eli's good connections with the police and emigration officials asked him for aid. He helped many leave, often using the facilities of the illegal Zionist apparatus. But while Armenians, French and British, Maltese Cypriots and Lebanese sailed en masse, many Jews still preferred to stay and face the uncertainties of the future.

Eli led a campaign of persuasion, arguing in favor of the necessity to flee the inevitable pogroms. As a result, the young willingly registered for aliyah (immigration), but Eli encountered stiff resistance among the older people, who were reluctant to give up their comfortable surroundings for the difficulties of readjustment abroad.[25] Yet the cruel vagaries of history would shortly end whatever freedom of choice still remained.

After the 1956 conflict, angered by its second defeat, Cairo lost no time in waging another campaign of retribution against the Jews. This time, however, a new and particularly sinister element was introduced; the program of repression would be supervised by former Nazi officials. During the Sinai campaign a number of Egyptian vehicles had been spotted bearing swastikas, and Arabic translations of Hitler's *Mein Kampf* were found in the knapsacks of dead and captured soldiers. With the fall of the Reich, former Nazis who had first fled to Spain and South America in fear of war crimes trials discovered that the Middle East offered greater advantages. By 1948 large numbers had arrived in Egypt, and many were soon holding executive positions in the government.

It was no coincidence that many of the 6,250 Arabized Germans living in Egypt had been entrusted with the maintenance of internal security. The majority held powerful posts in the State Security Cadre (SSC), an outgrowth of the Royal Security Services, which had been patterned by the junta after the SS. Its 70,000-man force, officially described as "the backbone of Egypt's protective apparatus against the aggressive elements of Zionism and imperialism," fell under the jurisdiction of Interior Minister Zakharieh Muhieddin but was directed by Lieutenant Colonel Ali al-Nasher, the former Leopold Gleim, who had commanded the Leibstandarte Hitler, the Führer's personal guard, and later had headed the Gestapo office in Warsaw.

Gleim's Political Department was directed by Colonel Ibn Salem, the former Bernhard Bender, who had served on the personal staff of SS Reichsführer Heinrich Himmler. On orders of Interior Minister Muhieddin, Bender had prepared a secret report entitled "The Final Solution of the Jewish-Zionist Problem Within Territories of Sovereign Egypt," which the ministry of the Interior implemented on January 26, 1956. As a result, broader powers were given to Bender's Jewish Section (formerly the Zionist Police) which now maintained close surveillance on the *harets*. An up-to-date dossier was kept on each Jewish family, and all incoming and outgoing mail was censored and photostated. Detectives of the Political Department carried out mass arrests, conducted interrogations in special centers established at Cairo's Maadi Police Station and on board the freighter *Marinaio Rosso* anchored at Alexandria, helped prepare indictments, and oversaw internment camps. The methods employed were strikingly reminiscent of another era. Arrests took place at dawn; prisoners were classified into A, B, and C categories; suspects were held for long periods without being charged; and hostages were seized whenever the Israelis threatened retaliatory border operations.

A Prisons Section within the PD was headed by Munir Gamal, the former SS Colonel Joachim Dämling, of the Düsseldorf

Gestapo. His vast experience in the martial arts was not over-looked when Bender ordered the creation of concentration camps for Jews and political opponents of the junta. Dämling established model camps in the Heliopolis Fortress, the al-Gizeh Barracks in Cairo, the Mustafa Hanun Pasha camp near al-Mazza and the Burg al-Arab Center near Alexandria. The grimmest of all was a fifth camp at the Samara Barracks in the Libyan Desert, 135 miles southwest of Cairo, where Eli had spent almost four months in 1954. Gleim's Economic Department, a unit modeled after the SS Wirtschaftsamt, had a Registration Section which kept meticulous records of all property owned by Egyptian Jews and made certain that those leaving the country signed waivers renouncing all claims to possessions left behind. Their belongings were then confiscated and either held by the Purchase Section or auctioned off to Moslems at the Sales Center in the al-Damara Hall. Nothing was spared to ensure that the Jews did not breach monetary regulations: The Finance Ministry's Bureau of Foreign Revenue kept a staff solely devoted to preventing tax fraud by Jewish businessmen, and a team of twenty inspectors worked in Switzerland under various covers, checking on evasions of capital and gathering information on number accounts held by Egyptian Jews.

For the Jews of Egypt the living nightmare of the Third Reich had been a remote and largely unfelt horror. But Eli and the more informed members of the community saw Nasser's willingness to place a host of notorious Nazis in command of an apparatus designed largely to suppress the Jews as auguring a new and diabolic policy. The immediate evidence, in any case, seemed to support his pessimism. Even before the fighting ended in the canal zone, scores were arrested in the *harets,* and the leaders of all the communities were held in prison without trial. In Alexandria's Jewish Quarter police raided some 900 homes at random, seizing one member from each family as a hostage to discourage Israeli reprisals. A collective form of house arrest was imposed. Electric and phone services were discontinued. When the ban was eventually lifted, Jews found they could not meet in public places or patronize restaurants and cafés. Every possible measure was undertaken to cripple and destroy the community. With the exception of an order to close the majority of the synagogues, which the police claimed were being used to disseminate Zionist propaganda, the government found no need to justify its acts. In short order, schools were summarily shut and hospitals commandeered by the Army. No Jew, however influential, was safe. Government decrees debarred all attorneys and revoked the licenses of physicians and engineers. Unskilled workers were summarily dismissed, and plans were announced for the sale of all Jewish-owned firms and banks to Egyptian nationals.

The process of sequestration even affected Jews with little or no property. When Eli was ordered to give up his apartment to Palestinian refugees, he had little choice but to leave. Yet as a token act of defiance, he refused to remove his belongings and gave the key to a young couple in the same building for safekeeping. Nor was he sufficiently intimidated to consider ending his work in illegal emigration. Now, more than ever, skilled operatives were needed to assist the thousands of Jews who flocked to the community centers seeking a means of escape. The government had made certain that those wishing to leave enjoyed pitifully few rights. No money could be transferred out of the country; even those who held visas were permitted to take with them only 20 Egyptian pounds. Eli was kept busy using his contacts to assure that the émigrés might escape with at least adequate means to begin a new life.

As the days passed, life in Egypt became more precarious. Nasser's minister of religion ordered a decree read in every mosque which held all Jews responsible for the acts of Egypt's enemies and ordered their immediate expulsion. But even this final decree did not mean an end of the campaign of harassment. The number of Jews arrested surged even higher. Those who escaped detention were not overlooked. Lines in front of passport offices grew longer as entire families, clutching deportation orders, were herded from one official to another and granted exit visas only after signing a pledge of no-return.

Within a three-month period the authorities peremptorily forced 10,000 Jews to depart.

Eli could not elude the government's efficiently run expulsion machinery for long. In the early hours of a rain-swept morning in the last week of November, his sleep was broken by a pounding on the door of the unfurnished room he had managed to find after much difficulty. Unlatching the chain, he faced two sullen officers of the SSC, who proceeded to make an exhaustive and fruitless search of the apartment before driving him, without explanation, to the Manshieh Police Station on Muhammad Ali Square. The inspector on duty told him that he was under arrest but specified no charges. He was then thrown into a fetid cell, overcrowded with anxious, perspiring suspects, and, a half hour later, transferred to the Hadra Jail. For the next several days, Eli passed the hours speculating with the other prisoners about their fate. The guesses ranged from immediate expulsion to execution. There was still no clue to the government's intentions when an order of transfer arrived, and Eli was taken in handcuffs to an Army detention center in the Menashe Schools on Rue Sultan Hussein.

He was relieved of his personal effects and led to a dark cubicle quartering twenty men. For three days there was no food. The prisoners lay on their cots drained of energy, rising only to crawl over the motionless bodies of the others on their twice-daily visits to the toilet. Exercise was forbidden. Whatever freedom they had once enjoyed seemed to have been a tormenting illusion. Ironically, the center was not far from Cromer Park, where Eli had played as a child.

One afternoon, as he was lying sleeplessly on his bed, a guard called his name from the doorway. Within the hour, the soldier told him, he would be transferred to the ship *Marinaio Rosso*. Eli accepted the news with the stony demeanor he had learned to present to the police, but his anxiety deepened. The ship's reputation among Jews as a "floating hell" was not exaggerated. A former Italian cargo vessel docked permanently in the Eastern Harbor, it had been converted into an eighty-cell prison designed for cases of special interest. A bugging center in the radio room monitored all conversation between prisoners; third-degree methods were used on those reluctant to talk in a miniature torture chamber on a lower deck. Yet after two harsh experiences under similar circumstances, Eli was prepared for another ruthless grilling about his contacts with Zionists and his work in illegal emigration. He was kept aboard the *Marinaio Rosso*, though, only a number of days. When his turn came to be released, his interrogators told him that he would shortly receive papers ordering his expulsion from Egypt.[26]

As soon as they arrived in the mail, Eli applied to the Ministry of the Interior for a two-month delay. The request seemed to have the opposite effect. Almost immediately, he was sent a notice to report to the Passport Bureau with two photographs. It was the start of a series of Kafkaesque encounters with Egyptian bureaucracy. "I was received by an extremely corpulent official, who was quietly sipping coffee," he later wrote a friend. "The small sign on his desk read: MAJOR MUHAMMAD. I did not know him. But I couldn't help reflecting that, despite the hatred of the English, the officers fell over backward to imitate them. They adopted British military ranks, uniforms, even their faults." The major produced Eli's file from a stock of dossiers on his desk and began asking questions so irrelevant that he felt obliged to explain they had been drawn up by a higher official in Cairo. At the conclusion of the interview, the officer requested that Eli sign a standard document relinquishing his property and the right to return to Egypt. Before leaving, Eli decided "to take advantage of his apparent good humor" and asked whether he could return to inquire about the extension. The major's mood altered. He replied curtly that another visit to the bureau would be useless and instructed Eli "to remain where you are and wait for notification from Cairo."

On Christmas Eve, the major suddenly appeared at Eli's apartment, demanding to know why he had not been back to the bureau. Eli was nonplussed. He countered laughingly that this was exactly what he had been told not to do. The major merely frowned and asked whether he had a passport. Eli handed him the document and was abruptly told to come to the office after Christmas, when "we will make all the necessary arrangements for your departure."

Forty-eight hours later Eli was directed to the desk of a slight, sour-looking official who sat listening intently to Oum Kalthum, Egypt's most popular female vocalist. Major Muhammad stood behind him but gave no sign of recognition. The official switched off the radio and slowly opened a dossier. "Cairo has granted your request for a postponement," he announced dryly. The extension, he added, would be for a period of twenty days. Eli asked whether the additional time started that day, and the official replied without a hint of mockery that the postponement had begun from the date his request was submitted and had therefore already expired. Major Muhammad eyed Eli coldly before speaking: "Take the first available ship," he snapped and left the room. Whatever reluctance Eli felt about leaving Egypt had passed. "I felt decidedly lighter after receiving the final order," he wrote. "Since the Anglo-French invasion, I had practically become useless."[27]

The following day Eli took a taxi to the Eastern Harbor. He carried one suitcase, 20 Egyptian pounds and among other papers a *laissez-passer* stamped "not valid for return to Egypt." He boarded the Egyptian liner *Misr*, which had been charted by the International Red Cross to carry 967 refugees. That same evening the ship docked in Naples, where a Jewish Agency official assigned him a room in a small hotel by the railroad station. Several days later he left by train for Genoa, where he boarded a ship that would take him to Israel.

5
Nadia

The Italian steamer *Fellipe Grimoni*, carrying several hundred emigrants from Egypt, docked in the port of Haifa near noon, on February 12, 1957. A group of health and immigration officials, who had boarded the ship at sea, settled in the main lounge and proceeded to check the tourists' papers.

While the agonizingly slow process of disembarkation continued, Eli joined the other passengers on the upper deck, jostling for a view of the city. He looked disinterestedly at the people on the pier who waved and exchanged shouts with their relatives. He knew that no one was there to meet him; the sudden departure from Alexandria had made it impossible to send word of his arrival. A feeling of loneliness overwhelmed him, heightened by the uncertainty of where his mother and father lived. The sole means of contact he had with the family was the faded address of his younger brother Maurice.

Until he could go ashore, Eli witnessed with mounting emotion the scenes of joy, the tears and the prayers which marked this return to Zion. When his turn came, he clutched his single suitcase and took his place in the long lines that formed in the enormous, drab building which served as a warehouse, customs and immigration center. Officious personnel of the Sochnut (Jewish Agency), posted at various stations, questioned the newcomers. The lengthy interviews were followed by countless tedious questionnaires. Eli was at last issued a *teudat ole* (immigrant's identity card), which automatically entitled him to Israeli citizenship.

When asked where he planned to live, Eli explained that he intended to join his brother in Tel Aviv. To his inquiries about employment, he was given brief advice and told that the Association of Egyptian Jews would supply additional information. A blue-uniformed traffic policeman finally guided him outside, where Sochnut officials directed the immigrants to buses bound for the cities and the kibbutzim.

On the pier fellow passengers were still enacting joyful reconciliations. Eli was watching the scene somewhat dispiritedly when he suddenly heard a man's voice call his name. Turning around, he recognized an old friend of his father's from Alexandria. He remembered the man, whom he had not seen in more than fifteen years, only as Peretz. In the rush of talk that followed, Eli learned that his brother Maurice had since moved to Ramat Gan, near Tel Aviv, and that his parents had bought a new apartment and now lived in Bat Yam, south of the city. Before the two parted, Peretz, who knew the Egyptians had stripped the émigrés of almost all their possessions, pressed several pounds into Eli's hand and promised to visit him soon.[1]

Heavy raindrops had just begun to splatter across the rooftops of Ramat Gan as Eli arrived at his brother's apartment on Haroe Street. He knocked on the door only to find no one home. Eli had to wait only a short while before the wife of Maurice arrived; she would let him into the house only after he had properly identified himself. When Maurice returned from work, he stared uncomprehendingly before recognizing the young man. Without a word, the two fell into each other's arms. Once inside the house, Eli found his brother relatively unaffected by the years. He learned that Maurice's life had undergone only conventional changes: He had married an Iraqi girl, worked as a postal clerk in Tel Aviv, and was settled happily in the suburbs. Maurice, who had not seen Eli for almost six years, noticed that the passage of time had taken more than its usual toll on his elder brother. Anxious to learn the reasons, he questioned him about his last years in Alexandria. Eli knew that the only news the family had received in the last seven years were oral messages conveyed by Jewish deportees—writing to Israel was considered an act of espionage punishable by death—and attempted to relate his life in Egypt. Speaking without emotion, he mentioned having been imprisoned for abetting illegal emigration but seemed otherwise reluctant to discuss the past. Maurice understood and did not press for details.

He told Eli that Sarah lived nearby and Odette was happily married to a Pazgaz official named Carmona. As soon as Eli learned that his elder sister had a telephone, he hastened to call her. Odette neither recognized his voice nor believed it was really him until he recounted intimate details of their childhood days in Alexandria.[2] With Eli so near, Odette refused to postpone their reunion and had him promise to come to her house that same night.

Eli feared the shock of a sudden phone call might upset his mother and father and suggested that he see them at once. He at first refused to let his brother accompany him and insisted upon traveling alone to Bat Yam. Maurice reluctantly gave detailed directions, took Eli to the local terminal, then joined him at the last minute. The two had to walk only a few hundred yards from the Ramat Yosef station to the three-story cooperative apartment building on Cairo Martyrs Street in a suburb of curving beaches and white concrete homes built on the sand dunes of the Mediterranean where their parents lived. When Eli stood before the house, he noticed a young boy who looked vaguely familiar and inquired in French whether Shaul Cohen was home. But before the boy could reply, a woman standing on a second-floor balcony shouted, "Abraham, who is this man? " Eli answered her in Arabic. The woman gasped, then began to weep and ran into the street to embrace her eldest son.[3]

That Friday night, at the family reunion, the Cohens' small apartment was crowded with children and grandchildren. At dinner, they all sat watching intently as their mother, now in her early sixties, shielded her eyes and intoned the traditional blessing. Her coal-black hair streaked with gray glittered in the light. Her sad face and eyes that never smiled had remained unchanged. Eli helped his father read from the Bible, while the others, who had grown less conservative, politely waited for the prayers to end. After Shaul had blessed the bread and passed a slice to everyone at the table, he chanted the kiddush over the wine; Eli answered with a somber "Amen," and all raised their glasses to praise "God who has kept us in life and preserved us and brought us to this day." There had been no compromise in Eli's orthodoxy. He still obeyed every law, ate only kosher foods, and faithfully observed the Sabbath.

Friends and relatives arrived after dinner for a homecoming party the Cohens were giving on the roof. In the course of the evening, Eli discovered that he shared the same feeling Maurice, Odette and his mother had at first so innocently expressed. He was, in some ways, a stranger. Except for the eleven-year-old Abraham, all his brothers and sisters were married and had charted their own lives in Israel's demanding environment. The youngsters he once protected were now veterans of the Sinai campaign; they had taken new names—Ezra, Zion, Efraim—and his parents, who still spoke Syrian Arabic with an Aleppo accent, constantly mixed the language with Hebrew words. The entire family seemed to relish the freedom of the new surroundings. Life in Egypt had been almost entirely forgotten.

Eli was at once elated and bewildered by the vitality, clamor and bustle of life in Tel Aviv. Cars and buses huffed and honked, pouring in from the suburbs; shoppers filled the sidewalks of Ben Yehuda, King George and Allenby streets. The city, home of a philharmonic orchestra, an opera, forty-nine cinemas, a dozen theaters and ninety banks, was beset by almost every municipal problem—pollution, traffic congestion, flight to the suburbs and juvenile crime. Evening strollers in the neon glitter of Dizengoff Street, youngsters in dual exhaust sportscars, espresso cafés and nightclubs featuring striptease artists raised Tel Aviv to the ranks of a Mediterranean playground. But beyond this glittering façade, Eli recognized the harsh discipline of a people who lived within range of Arab guns and worked six days a week, reclaiming desert, planting parks and forests, building new settlements and nursing a new Jewish pride.

The real, everyday Israel was a far cry from the Jewish land of dream and prayer. The new society was less religiously inclined and more fiercely nationalistic. Eli at first did not grasp the ever-growing desire of the sabras and the old immigrants to break with the Jewish past which they had come to associate with an obscurantist religion and a history of alienation and helplessness. They were impatient with tales of the Diaspora and preferred to identify, not with world Jewry, but with the ancient Hebrews. They chose as their heroes not those who revolted against the Nazis in Warsaw and Auschwitz, but the soldiers of the Masada garrison who committed suicide rather than surrender to the legions of Rome.

Born in violence, Israel had bred a generation of men and women who had become tough and resilient from living in the shadow of annihilation. Eli came to admire their sense of destiny and moral fervor. He respected their inventiveness and natural flair for improvisation but resented their self-conscious hauteur—an attitude in which he saw much of the provincial naïvete that he had left behind.

The Israeli tended to look down on the Oriental Jew, who, in his view, had preserved a sense of frustration and rootlessness. He resented the stream of new arrivals from Arab countries and the rapid Levantinism of Israel. Although many Egyptian Jews had Zionist backgrounds like Eli and possessed skills vital for the growth of the economy, they were still privately snubbed, and indeed some had begun wondering whether it had been wise to leave the temporary haven they had found in Europe after expulsion from Egypt. This climate of discrimination Eli sensed—more fancied than real—was a subtle one, but nonetheless there.

In the months to come, Eli lived with his parents, sharing the family's second bedroom with Abraham, and assumed the responsibilities of the eldest son, much as he had done years earlier in Alexandria. He tutored Abraham, who had just entered the Bat Yam Municipal High School, helped him with mathematics and languages, and soon became his closest companion. But the soft-spoken youth with small eyes and a thin, long face enjoyed the games Eli taught him much more. At the 1957 Independence Day parade, while waiting for the mechanized units to pass, Eli wagered the boy that he could recall the serial numbers of every tank and armored car in the column. Abraham made a list of more than 100 vehicles, the numbers of which Eli repeated without error.[4] This and similar feats helped turn Abraham into a willing partner for the memory exercises Eli himself had enjoyed as a child.

Eli's attachment to Abraham did not prevent him from socializing often with his younger brothers and sisters. His easy accessibility brought him the adoration of his nieces and nephews. He spent hours romping about the floor with the babies, telling bedtime tales to the youngsters and playing chess and checkers with the elder ones. He would sit back and look on tolerantly as they pondered every move with much giggling. Eli fed those who refused to eat, coaxing them with funny stories, and once even climbed into the bathtub fully clothed when the children balked at bathing. He never refused to take them to a matinee, the beach or the amusement park in Jaffa. Before long *Hadod* Eli (Uncle Eli) became the children's favorite relative.

He rarely found time, however, to visit friends from Alexandria, but did frequent some local cafés and, on Saturdays, went to a soccer match or saw an occasional movie in Tel Aviv. The search for employment was his major preoccupation. Eli realized that without a college degree there was little hope of finding work in electrical engineering. He had entertained the thought of being able to continue his studies at the Technion, the Institute of Technology in Haifa, for, like many of his classmates at Faruk University who had been forced to leave college before graduation, he was eligible for a loan which would cover his tuition, room and board. His Hebrew, however, was judged inadequate, and an adviser recommended that he enter an *ulpan*, a Hebrew school for adults. When Eli discovered that entrance examinations would be given only at the beginning of the next academic year, he chose to postpone his plans and find work. His fluency in other languages prompted him to look for a position as a translator, all the while spending hours studying Hebrew. Never during this period was he approached by nor did he contact Israeli intelligence. Obviously wishing to forget the past, he guarded the secrets of his last years in Egypt "like a safe, which no one in the family could open."[5] At thirty-three, he at last wanted to build a peaceful new life.

It was not long before Eli realized that in a country where multilinguists were common, a knowledge of seven languages did not necessarily assure him a good position. The jobless weeks passed quickly without a solution in sight. He was beginning to grow restless when a former university classmate suggested he contact the Association of Egyptian Immigrants. Eli had no great hopes of finding work there, but to his amazement, he found that Abraham Sirmano, an old friend and schoolmate from Alexandria, headed the organization. Sirmano knew of Eli's involvement in illegal immigration and suggested that he consider working for intelligence. Eli reluctantly agreed, and the association referred him to an "import-export" company on Allenby Street which, he was told, had an opening for a translator.

Several days later an elderly secretary showed Eli into an austere third-floor office above Hertzl Street where a husky Army captain of about thirty received him warmly. There was nothing about the surroundings to cause suspicion, but the moment the officer requested that he translate an article from the Egyptian daily *al-Ahram*, Eli understood that the firm was a front for intelligence activities. The captain seemed satisfied with the results and promised to notify him of a decision within weeks. The same day, he wrote to his superiors strongly recommending the applicant. Eli was immediately subjected to a thorough security check, the results of which were submitted to the personnel department of the Shin Beth (General Security

Service). A civilian interviewed him once more—this time in a café—and he was subsequently offered a post at 170 Israeli pounds ($55) a month in one of the research departments of the counterespionage agency. Eli began commuting to Tel Aviv-Jaffa, where he worked in a well-guarded compound, translating and evaluating the Arab press. His three co-workers were Jews from Egypt and Iraq whose knowledge of Hebrew was far greater than his own. The department heads, an Army captain named "Shimshon" and a civilian called "Israel," did not rate his translations highly and tactfully suggested a transfer to the archives.[6]

The new job was not to last long. An abrupt reorganization forced Eli to leave. Having meanwhile joined the Histadrut Labor Federation, he was now entitled to seek work at union employment centers. He spent the coming weeks standing in lines and accepted whatever temporary positions became available: A gas company hired him for a brief term; other odd jobs followed in development centers such as Kiryat Gat, Beer Yaakov and Ashkelon. While continuing to hunt for permanent employment, he enrolled in bookkeeping and marketing courses offered by the Ministry of Labor and completely immersed himself in his studies.[7] He easily acquired the government diploma and, with the recommendation of a childhood friend, found a position with Hamashbir Hamercazi, the nationwide chain of co-operative food stores. Initially, he was assigned to the company's accounting department at headquarters on Salame Street in downtown Tel Aviv but was quickly promoted to accountant inspector and began traveling throughout the country, auditing records of outlying stores.

As always, Eli was slow in making friends. No one in the office knew him intimately, and more than one co-worker would later remember his extreme reserve. Most spoke highly of him, recalling his ironic sense of humor and genuine cooperativeness. Company officials were quick to single out his apparent ambition and exceptional energy. Yet despite his seeming involvement in the firm, many had felt at the time that he would not stay with Hamashbir for long. "We assumed he would move on to something more challenging," explained one of his former colleagues. "He was too bright to remain a clerk his entire life."[8]

Though the intuition about Eli's future would prove correct, there was nothing in his daily routine to indicate that he was dissatisfied. Secure in his position, he lacked—or so those closest to him maintained—only a wife and family. "All his younger brothers were already married," his mother explained, "and we wanted him to do the same . . . but Eli had always been shy with women."[9] Relatives and friends often found opportunities to introduce him to girls they considered likely matches, but Eli would smilingly shake his head at the hints or outright proposals that he marry.

An encounter in the spring of 1959 changed his skeptical outlook. At a Friday night party in Maurice's apartment, Eli's sister-in-law introduced him to Nadia, a friend she thought especially suitable for him. To everyone's astonishment, Eli showed an unusual interest in the tall, pleasant girl with brown eyes and short-cropped black hair. (He later admitted having liked her from the very first moment.) "We were surprised," Maurice later said. "Eli was always gallant with women but had never been serious about them."[10] In the ensuing conversation, he learned that the twenty-seven-year-old Iraqi-born girl was also a new immigrant. She had belonged to a *hachshara* (youth group) in Kibbutz Nir David but, finding it difficult to adapt to kibbutz life, had returned to live with her parents. She later completed a nursing course in Tel Aviv and, at the time Eli met her, was working on a late shift at the Hadassah hospital.

Nadia was fascinated by Eli and told him bluntly that she was anxious to see him again. Within days, he began courting her in earnest. In the months to come there was little time to be together besides weekends. They would often rendezvous on Friday evenings in a Tel Aviv café, go to the movies or attend a private party in the home of a mutual friend. On most Saturdays, Eli would wait for Nadia in front of the Rama Cinema in Ramat Gan, from which they walked to the nearby Yarkon

River to row or watch the passing boats and talk of the past. Nadia's open and effusive manner charmed Eli. Yet when she first asked him about his life in Egypt, he was not responsive. One night, though, for no apparent reason, he began to speak about Azar and the hanging, choosing his words as carefully as he made his moves on the chessboard. On other weekends they climbed to the Masada or strolled along the beaches of Caesarea and Herzliya. It was on these shores of the Mediterranean that Nadia told a somewhat startled Eli that he was going to marry her.

In the course of a few weeks Nadia brought Eli home to meet her family. Awhile later Eli introduced her to his parents. Knowing that she would be severely judged, Nadia was terrified. But Eli's mother later solemnly assured him that he had made an excellent choice. Despite different origins and social backgrounds—still an important factor among new immigrants—both families came to accept the betrothal. With their parents' aid and combined savings, the young couple made a down payment on a two-room cooperative apartment on Hatchia Street in Bat Yam. Until the house was completed, they would have no choice but to live in cramped quarters with Eli's mother and father.

In August, 1959, after a brief courtship, the two were married in a modest Sephardic ceremony in Tel Aviv. Having won a trip to Eilat in a raffle, they decided to spend their honeymoon on the banks of the Red Sea. The trip to the tiny port at the bottom of the Negev cone was a rather harrowing experience. The Eged bus and escort of command cars reached Eilat after a twelve-hour journey through the desert on a dirt road which no private car would brave alone. Their accommodations at the Hotel Sinai were unexpectedly comfortable, and the newlyweds set out to explore the southern frontier town. They observed the underwater coral formations, fished in the transparent deeps, and walked the hills and wadis along the border.

Eli, by now charged with the unwavering optimism common to all sabras, was enchanted with what he saw and discussed the possibility of moving to Eilat with Nadia. He enthusiastically tried to convince her that frontier life held many advantages.

Eilat was an Eldorado for the young; with the liberation of the Gulf of Aqaba, East African trade had become lucrative, and the boom port's population had jumped to 1,800. Skeptically, Nadia pointed to the inconveniences of hot weather, icy desert winds, an acute shortage of water and the absence of hospitals.[11] She would not listen even when Eli laughingly assured her that the town council was obliged to pay for a return flight and hotel bill for every expectant mother so she might have her baby in civilization.

A number of days after Eli returned to the office, the receptionist informed him that a visitor was on his way up. Minutes later a man approached his desk and introduced himself as Captain Zalman, adding pleasantly, "The last name is unimportant. I am from the Ministry of Defense." Eli offered him a seat and listened somewhat amazed to his explanation: The captain told him that he had been referred by Sirmano, "who spoke highly of your abilities," and proceeded, without formalities, to offer him a post with the ministry. Over coffee, at a small restaurant nearby, Zalman elaborated and asked whether Eli would consider an interesting, responsible position which required extensive traveling to Europe, South America and perhaps, even Arab countries. It was a rather demanding job, the captain conceded, but paid almost twice his current salary. Before Eli could respond, he bluntly admitted being an intelligence officer. The service, he said, was continually seeking capable men. His superiors were familiar with Eli's past and had, in fact, been observing him for some time. They were convinced that he was suited for espionage work. Politely, but firmly, Eli rejected the offer. He told the captain that he had recently married and did not wish to leave the country. Zalman appeared disappointed, but did not pursue the subject; he requested only that Eli avoid mentioning their conversation to anyone.[12]

Eli felt no guilt at his refusal. For the first time since his youth, the life he led was remarkably stable and comfortable. He could at last indulge in reading and self-analysis, browse through the immense collection in the public library and borrow books by the score. He discovered the stirring poetry of Haim Nachman Bialik and Shaul Tshernichovsky, who glorified the ancient rebels of Israel, and studied Achad Haam, Pinsker and philosophers who spoke of the ultimate redemption. Encouraged by Nadia, he took up oil painting and artistic photography. His passion for the sea again awakened, and he often sailed with his brother Ephraim on a friend's boat along the Tel Aviv seashore or took part in coastal races with the Zevulun sailing club. He used the rest of his free time to keep up with new developments in electronics through texts and magazines, in the hope that he would eventually obtain his degree.

Captain Zalman saw Eli on several other occasions but failed to persuade him. In the meantime, Nadia, who was expecting a baby, left her job. Eli was forced to work overtime in order to compensate for the lost income. It was during this period that Zalman approached him again, this time with the generous offer of a high civil service rating with a salary of 350 pounds a month.* "The service will train you for six months," he said. "If dissatisfied, you are free to resign."[13] When the captain finished, Eli hesitated but once again demurred.

Four weeks after this last conversation, Eli received a note from his superior at Hamashbir, stating that the company was planning a reorganization which compelled the management to cut back its staff. A number of recently hired employees were to be released; Eli was given a month's notice. The new circumstances made him reconsider Zalman's proposal. "I felt bad sitting home," Eli later said, "and watching my wife go to work every morning and return exhausted in the evening."[14] When the captain contacted him again, Eli agreed to volunteer for espionage work in the field. †

*Field operatives are paid according to fixed scales and receive the same salaries as middle-echelon government officials. The director of the services earns some 1,600 pounds a month ($535); an agent's minimum salary does not exceed a third of that amount. Unlike their counterparts in other countries, Israeli operatives do not receive additional income for hazardous duty.

†The sudden loss of his job, so soon after what appeared to be a final rebuff to Zalman, was said not to have been coincidental. The Mosad, one source noted, had used similar tactics when other recruiting measures failed. The Mosad later unofficially denied having caused Eli's dismissal, pointing out that the large number of employees at Hamashbir had been discharged at the time.

At Zalman's urging, he told Nadia that he had accepted a position with Mishlachat Hakniot (Buying Mission) of the Defense Ministry and would have to undergo a training program which might take a number of months. He then added that she would not be permitted by regulations to phone or visit him at work. Since such orientation programs were common in the civil service, Nadia did not press him for details. "He told me that he had been appointed a government salesman and would have to make frequent trips to Europe," she later recalled; "he did not want to discuss his new position, so I asked no more questions."[15]

6
The Apartment off Allenby Street

Eli had to meet Zalman on the first day of training in a café on the corner of Rothschild Boulevard and Allenby Street. After an exchange of shaloms, the two walked silently along Allenby in the direction of Mugrabi Plaza. Zalman led Eli down a side street in the heart of the business district, into a residential building and up a stairway to a third-floor apartment that the Mosad had rented. He was to live there for the next four months, while mastering the rudiments of intelligence operation.

Zalman first introduced Eli to a man named Yitzhak, who would directly supervise the classes. As soon as Zalman had left, Yitzhak presented the new student to Asher, a sabotage instructor whose Arabic, Eli noted, was unmistakably Syrian. They all sat for a while considering several aliases for him before finally choosing his old *nom de guerre*, Alex. Yitzhak eventually began the briefing. Eli would be restricted to the apartment. He would be allowed walks after dark, but always in the company of one of the men. "It might seem to you more like the life of a prisoner," Yitzhak concluded, "but we have to take these precautions for security reasons."

During the next five days the mornings were devoted to discussions on current political and military issues in the Middle East, particularly those concerning the United Arab Republic, on which Yitzhak was an authority. On the afternoon of the sixth day a husky middle-aged man arrived and was introduced to Eli as Gideon, his radio instructor. Without a comment, Gideon unpacked a Morse practice set and asked Eli to send a series of dots, dashes. Eli transmitted a perfect combination of both. At the end of the test, Eli asked how much practice he would need to reacquire proficiency. Gideon smiled. "Write the alphabet as many times as you can in one minute; then multiply the letters by three and translate them all into code. The result is the average number of dots and dashes which must be sent and received per minute before one can be a good radio operator."

Gideon was astonished by the speed with which his student mastered the Morse alphabet. Eli worked on the relatively simple two-toned exercises first, rapidly progressing to the more difficult three-toned signals. By the end of only a few lessons he could easily handle those with four or more tones. Gideon also demonstrated the various rhythms with which one could more readily remember the letters; eventually Eli came to send and receive forty to sixty letters per minute. A more difficult phase of the communications course was the study of coding methods and the use of reverse processes for decoding. Eli was also given instruction in the operation of a newly developed miniature wireless and transmitted twice daily with an unknown operator at the Mosad headquarters.

The monastic routine in the apartment never varied: early rise, breakfast, training, lunch, training, dinner, training and night walk. It did seem more the life of a recluse than an agent. "I felt like a lost man living with lost men," Eli later remarked, although at the time he never complained. While his radio course continued, he mastered the techniques of sabotage. Asher taught him how to make explosives with simple chemicals which could be purchased in any pharmacy. He produced thermites from potassium chlorate of nitrate combined with sugar which burned at 3,000 degrees and demonstrated ways to prepare simple dynamite from potassium chlorate and oil. The lessons reminded Eli of his friends' attempts to produce incendiary devices and homemade bombs in Alexandria. He was amazed, though, at the ease with which Asher constructed time bombs by linking two wires from the hands of a wristwatch to a battery which, in turn, was attached to a burning mixture, gelignite or *plastique*. Setting the device for a period up to twelve hours—longer times required a seven- or fourteen-day alarm clock—the mechanism was detonated as the hands crossed during a prespecified revolution. The acid trick was much simpler. The lid of an ordinary bottle filled with sulfuric acid was pierced and a piece of cardboard inserted into the opening; the strip dissolved within two hours, permitting the liquid to flow toward the compound and activate the detonator and the charge.

The radio and sabotage curriculum completed, Yitzhak eased the restrictions and permitted Eli to move about more freely. There was still no indication, however, that he would be allowed to go home on leave, and an order soon arrived for him to join a demolition training course at an Army base in the south. Combat veterans taught him how to place and camouflage contact charges, blow up trains and destroy bridges. After scoring among the first in the class, Eli was sent back to his home unit.

Training was further broadened to include Army field intelligence techniques, topography, and the gathering, recording and analysis of secret information. Revolver target practice was held almost daily. Eli also became adept at identifying Arab and Soviet military insignia and grew familiar with a wide range of aircraft, armor, artillery and personal weapons. After returning to the apartment, he studied lockpicking, the use of modern espionage equipment and the myriad ways of building *slikim* (caches) and concealing equipment and microfilm.

Still another Mosad instructor demonstrated the employment of invisible inks. First rubbing both sides of a piece of high-grade paper with dry cotton for approximately twenty minutes, he placed it vertically on a glass surface and lightly printed a note with the aid of a matchstick dipped in a special solution. The paper was then turned horizontally and used for a standard letter which was either typed or written. (The party receiving the concealed message had to process it by machine or chemicals.) To master the use of invisible inks, Eli wrote practice letters each day and received comments on his errors until the Mosad specialist was satisfied with his performance.[1]

Yitzhak next introduced a number of exercises to simulate conditions an agent might encounter in the field. In the course of a surveillance exercise, he ordered Eli to proceed to a nearby newsstand and, while buying a paper, identify the agent who had been trailing him, without giving any indication that he knew he was being watched. Back at the apartment, his observations were verified by a film and photographs which another team had made.[2] In the coming weeks, Eli also traded roles; he trailed unsuspecting agents himself and perfected the skill of losing pursuers in a crowd.

When Mosad officials asked Yitzhak to evaluate his student's performance to date, he gave them an excellent report. Eli was considered ready for a final test: He would have only ten days to establish a convincing new identity. Carrying the French passport of an Egyptian Jew who had emigrated to Africa and was now living in France, Eli would travel to Jerusalem and, speaking only French and Arabic, make friends who could later verify his cover. Eli boarded a train for the one-hour ride to the capital, checked into a small hotel, and began exploring the city, quickly becoming acquainted with a number of unsuspecting Jerusalemites. To these casual acquaintances Eli explained that he had come for a brief visit before settling in Israel. He also managed to make more important contacts. Among others, he dined with a Ministry of Justice official and discussed the transfer of funds from France with a local banker.[3]

At the end of the exercise, on the eve of the Jewish New Year, Eli returned to Tel Aviv and was given a short leave, which he and Nadia spent with Ephraim, now a member of Kibbutz Revivim in the Negev. Upon his return, Eli was told that he had been constantly observed by a team of agents in Jerusalem; their reports indicated he had successfully carried out his assignment. After the debriefing, Yitzhak sent him for three days of physical, psychological and psychotechnical examinations. "When you return," he promised, "we'll discuss the details of your first mission."

*   *   *

While undergoing extensive training, Eli had come into contact with various departments of the Supreme Agency for Intelligence and Security. The personnel he talked to were guardedly
cooperative; he was given only the information essential for his
ultimate mission. But these conversations and his own observations enabled him to piece together an overall picture of the
service's aims, functions and organization.

The Mosad, which took its name from the illegal immigration
organization of the Jewish Agency, had been created in 1953
from a core of administrators and field operatives in the Political Department of the Foreign Ministry to collect intelligence
abroad on countries hostile to Israel. The service frequently
exchanged experts and often combined operations with the
other four intelligence and counterespionage services, especially
Modiin and the Research Department of the Foreign Ministry.
The head of the Mosad also presided over the Central Committee of the Security Services composed of the directors which
coordinated the five services.* He held the title of *memune*
(literally "The Man in Charge"), had final responsibility for all
agencies, and reported directly to the prime minister. His identity was considered a state secret; his name would be released
only after he left the civil service.

---

*The present-day structure of Israel's intelligence community emerged in 1953.
Data on Arab political and military developments which provide the basis for
immediate and long-range strategic planning and policy decisions are collected and
analyzed by Cheil Modiin, or Chaman, the Army Intelligence Corps. Open sources
and classified reports on Arab political activities are compiled and studied by the
Machleka Medinit, the Research Department of the Foreign Ministry. Internal security operations and the gathering of information on enemy agents inside Israel are
carried out by the Sherut Bitachon Klali, or Shin Beth, the General Security Service.
Counterespionage within the Arab community is conducted by the Agaf Letafkidim
Meiuchadim, the Special Investigations Division of the Israel Police, which also acts as
a legal arm of the Shin Beth. Intelligence on all foreign countries is collected abroad
by the Mosad Elion Lemodiin Ubitachon, the Supreme Agency for Intelligence and
Security, created in 1953 from a core of administrators and field operatives in the
Research Department. The agencies are coordinated by the Veada Merkazit Lesheru-
tei Habitachon, the Central Committee of Security Services, composed of the five
directors. Each Veada member is accountable to a subcommittee of Cabinet ministers
which, in turn, is overseen by the Knesset Foreign Affairs and Security Committee.

The Mosad chief, Iser Harel, about whom Eli had heard much during the latter part of his schooling, was a diminutive (five feet two) balding man, known to his associates as Little Iser. Born Iser Halpern in 1912 in Vitebsk, Russia, he emigrated with his family to Latvia after the Bolshevik Revolution to escape a wave of persecution against the Jews. The youth, who came from a middle-class background, joined the leftist Zionist Poalei Zion organization and, influenced by its teachings, emigrated to Palestine in 1929. Halpern was sixteen years old when he arrived in Kibbutz Shfaim near Herzliya with one suitcase and a concealed pistol. For the next thirteen years he packed oranges and worked on irrigation projects. Eventually, he joined the Haganah, married, and became the father of a daughter. In 1942 Iser took the Hebrew name Harel and enlisted in the Notrim, the Jewish Auxiliary Police. His attitude toward the British, however, was less than submissive; he was dismissed after refusing to apologize for striking a British superior who had made an anti-Semitic remark. Harel afterward devoted his entire energies to the Haganah and became a full-time Shai agent. The head of the Haganah's Information Service, David Shaltiel, was so impressed with his energy and analytical abilities that he placed Harel in charge of the Interior Security Department, where he was first noticed by David Ben-Gurion, then head of the Jewish Agency, and by Israel Galili, the commander of the Haganah. The changes Harel instituted won him the higher post of Shai commander for the Tel Aviv region. In the wake of the first Arab-Israeli war, he was entrusted with the creation of the Shin Beth and later the formation of the Mosad, of which he became the director. After he was appointed *memune* of all services, Harel gained the reputation of a loyal and considerate chief, who spared no effort to protect his operatives and extricate them from difficult situations. Under his guidance, the Mosad gained international prestige, which he saw as fully justified. "If intelligence is a battle of wits," Harel would remark, "then Israel is second to none in the world."[4]

In an effort to achieve this high level of performance, Eli learned, operatives were taught the newest security and espio-

nage techniques in special courses. The agents who graduate
from intelligence institutions were joined by scores of professionals from seemingly unrelated fields. The number of administrative personnel, security officers, domestic agents and over-
seas operatives was unusually small—several thousand—and the
total operating budget minuscule compared with the $4 billion
estimated to be spent annually on intelligence by the United
States.

Like many of its counterparts, the Mosad recruited on the
basis of ability and devotion to country. It attempted, as far as
possible, to avoid employing the James Bond type. "We don't
want adventurers or heroes in our service," Iser Harel, Israel's
first *memune*, once remarked. "Neither do we want volunteers,
such as those who contact us frequently and offer their services.
Our rule is: We choose the man, investigate him and, if found
adequate, offer him a job. . . . We want our men to be honest,
devoted, loyal and patriotic," Harel explained. "In other words,
we want them human. . . . Modesty, frugality and, above all, absolute secrecy . . . are essential to our efficiency. Men who have
trouble in keeping anonymous and are inclined to disclose that
they are engaged in secret activities have to leave us quickly."[5]

Female agents were also employed in covert operations and
often surpassed male operatives. Strict rules, though, were
observed, "lest the use of women involve immoral conduct."
"Sex," Harel claimed, "was not employed in our ranks to
achieve objectives."[6] The *memune*'s somewhat puritanical attitude was in keeping with the pretentious high-mindedness
which characterizes Israel's intelligence community. The Mosad,
however, was known to have employed Arabs, Germans and
many other nationals, both male and female, who operated
without restrictions, using sex, assassination, kidnapping and
blackmail as levers for information.

As Eli's training entered the final stages, Syria became the
focal point of his studies. A syllabus of books, films, documents
and intelligence reports that the Mosad provided guided him
through the maze of political, military, economic and social

background material which he had to absorb in order to strengthen his cover. Syria was considered by the Israelis the most unpredictable among their dangerous neighbors. Her modern history had been characterized by chronic instability, the result of irreconcilable political factions and a host of contradictions inherent in the country itself. Along with constantly shifting loyalties and a succession of short-lived regimes, these conditions had produced a climate which made the Syrian government a likely target for infiltration.

Much of the national malaise could be traced back to World War II, when the Allies fought successfully to prevent the use of Syria as a base for Axis operations. General de Gaulle, who emerged as leader of the Free French Forces, reluctantly recognized Syria as an independent country in 1943 and appointed Taj al-Din its first president. The French concession, however, failed to satisfy Syrian nationalists, who increased their pressure for the election of legislative bodies. Further agitation eventually established Shukri al-Kuwatli as president of the republic and compelled the French to withdraw all controls. Two years later Syria received full diplomatic recognition from the United States and the Soviet Union. On February 24, 1945, it finally entered the war on the side of the Allies, thus gaining entrance to the United Nations.

The withdrawal of the last French units was completed by 1946. In the forthcoming elections the appointment of President al-Kuwatli was confirmed. One of the new regime's first acts was to press for Arab unity. When Israel was established, inter-Arab talks took on overtones of hysteria. Twenty-seven thousand Syrian volunteers, reinforced by Army units, overran Palestine's northern border but fought with a singular lack of success. Although Syria did not suffer a major setback, the common Arab defeat also became her own.

The 1948 war served as a catalyst to bring the Army to power and make Syria the first Arab state to turn to military dictatorship. Embittered by the fiasco in Palestine and weary of rampant corruption in the old regime, a cabal of Syrian officers emerged in 1949 to assume control. At the end of March, Chief of Staff Brigadier Husni al-Zaim seized power in a bloodless coup; he invested himself with the rank of marshal and began planning social reforms. But before a few weeks had passed, there was hardly a person left in Syria whom Zaim had not antagonized. Devoid of popular support, his rule degenerated into open dictatorship. "Give me five years," he pleaded with his comrades-in-arms, "and I'll make Syria as prosperous and enlightened as Switzerland." They gave him less than five months. In mid-August, Brigadier Sami al-Hinawi marched into Damascus, threw Zaim in jail and, denouncing his "viciousness, lawlessness and disregard for national tradition," ordered his execution.

For two months, Hinawi and a Supreme War Council ruled with a civilian front presided over by the elder statesman Hashem al-Atasi. But when the president embarked upon a union with Iraq, an Army faction headed by Colonel Adib al-Shishakli came out in violent opposition to the merger. In mid-December, for the third time in three-quarters of a year, the Army rebelled. Shishakli charged Hinawi with treason and expelled him to Beirut, where he was later shot in revenge for Zaim's execution.

The new military ruler allowed Atasi to remain president but controlled the government from behind the scenes. Fearing a change in the country's political complexion after the adoption of a liberal constitution, Shishakli engineered a second coup in November, 1951, and for the next two years ruled with an iron fist. By 1953, any pretense of democracy was discarded, and Shishakli assumed the posts of both president and prime minister.

As the harshness of military rule intensified, politicians along with the Army began plotting rebellion. In February, 1954, a Provisional Military Council of three high-ranking officers representing different political parties led the insurrection which toppled Shishakli and forced him to flee to Brazil, where he later died at the hand of an assassin. In an unprecedented move, the putschists handed over the reins of government to the politicians. After new elections, Kuwatli returned from

Egyptian exile and assumed the presidency. During the following four years, parliamentary rule and freedom of the press and of association were never achieved. A parliamentary regime existed in theory, but in practice Syria was still ruled by a junta under Chief of Staff General Shawkat Shukeir. This situation produced endless conspiracies, constant disorders and a succession of unstable Cabinets.

Following the trend set by the Shishakli dictatorship of moving Syria further toward the Soviet bloc, the two-time president intensified his overtures to the USSR. Kuwatli's effort to obtain economic and military support succeeded beyond expectations. In 1955, Damascus received substantial shipments of arms from the Russians; trade agreements were signed with Moscow and Peking; and two years later, the president returned from the Soviet Union with a pledge of $570,000,000 in aid.

While a Soviet-Syrian axis was being forged, raids and counterraids intensified along the border with Israel. Emplacements in the Golan Heights shelled the kibbutzim in the northern Galilee, while Zahal retaliated with commando operations, taking prisoners and killing scores of soldiers and civilians. The humiliated Syrians would get their revenge only when Egypt nationalized the Suez Canal, an act which Damascus regarded as a crippling blow to the Israeli economy. Nasser's daring action sparked enthusiastic demonstrations throughout Syria—the largest in the Middle East. But despite the clamor, Kuwatli's administration sent no troops into battle to help the Egyptians at the outbreak of the Sinai campaign in October, 1956.

The issue of Arab unity had meanwhile not diminished in both capitals. Ever since independence, Syria had been the target of her rival neighbors. Damascus, "the heart of the Arab nation," was both the prize and battleground of inter-Arab feuds among Iraq, Jordan, Egypt and Saudi Arabia. Such outside pressures were reflected in the fragmentation of Syria's internal political structures. Most politicians did not believe in the durability and territorial integrity of their country. They saw political salvation in terms of an alliance or union and were committed to one or another Arab camp. Kuwatli, who had spent a comfortable exile in Egypt and was a fervent admirer of Nasser, deftly maneuvered for a union with the rais. He had the backing of the influential Socialist-nationalist Baath, whose leadership hoped that Nasser would help them gain power they had been unable to win at the ballot box. To forestall any anti-union moves from opponents in the Army, Egyptian troops were allowed to enter Syrian soil. The consummation of the act was but a short step away.

After less than three weeks of negotiations, the United Arab Republic of Egypt and Syria, "the first step toward a single Arab nation of 60 million," was proclaimed with widespread jubilation in February, 1958, with Nasser as president and Kuwatli as one of four vice-presidents. The UAR was divided into two regions—Northern (Syria) and Southern (Egypt)—governed by a central Cabinet of twenty Egyptians and fourteen Syrians. (Many of the posts were held jointly by a minister from each region.) Several days after the announcement was made, Nasser presented a seventeen-point program to adoring throngs in Damascus. One stipulated that the armies of both nations would be placed under a dual command and based on each other's territory.

The hastily concluded union was no ideal solution to Syria's problems. Though apparently pro-Nasser, the 4,500,000 Levantine-Syrians were separated by much more than 150 miles of sea and the state of Israel from their 26,000,000 African-Egyptian brothers. They had, in fact, little in common except the Arabic language. Fiercely individualistic and historically ungovernable, the Syrians were as distinctive from the Egyptians, traditionally amenable to central authority, as the Vietnamese were from the Chinese. Nasser's rule thus bore from the outset the mark of improvisation and uncertainty. The Syrians were given no sense of participation in the running of their own affairs. Government was conceived in terms of keeping order rather than as a constructive experiment harnessing Syrian talents and enthusiasm for the union. A partyless police state thus emerged in the Northern Region.

The political vacuum left by a ban on all parties could hardly be filled by Nasser's National Union, and strains began to show not long after the UAR's much-heralded birth. A deepening economic crisis worsened by a three-year drought only intensified anti-Egyptian feelings, which soon found open and undisguised expression; production had dropped off steadily; exports had dwindled while imports climbed steeply; the trade deficit increased, the rate of taxation skyrocketed, and gold and hard currency reserves plummeted; imports from abroad were forbidden, and the Syrian market was flooded by a steady stream of cheap Egyptian goods. Harsh nationalization laws affecting private companies finally brought discontent to an unprecedented peak. These unpopular nationalization and centralization measures antagonized the majority of the population. The landowners and the powerful business community recoiled at the drastic land reforms and Socialistic programs that Nasser sought to impose from Cairo.

The feeling of discontent was by no means confined to industrial, commercial and farming circles. The ethnic and religious minorities, upon whose communal rights of internal autonomy the Egyptians had infringed by imposing an Arabization program, had their own grudges against the regime. The rais had also antagonized the civil servants and the politicians, among them the Baathites, by hoarding most of the executive power in the union. He further alienated the Syrian Army by assigning Egyptian officers, who were less than sensitive to Syrian pride, to the Northern Region. The result of these difficulties, Nasser would later lament, was "three and a half years of endless troubles."

Toward the end of fall, Eli underwent a last phase of orientation, which unexpectedly proved the most trying. Yitzhak had arranged for lodgings in Nazareth, where a Moslem kadi was to tutor him privately in the Koran. His teacher, Sheik Muhammad Soliman, had been told that the pupil was specializing in Oriental studies at Jerusalem University and needed outside instruction. Under the sheik's tutelage, Eli attempted to learn the five

daily prayers of Islam and the customs for holidays and festivals. Although he practiced every Friday in a mosque, he was
not completely successful in mastering the sacred texts.[7] His
failure to absorb the teachings of Islam would ultimately impe-
ril the credibility of his cover.

As Eli's departure drew nearer, a briefing was dedicated to
the cover story he would have to commit to memory. The
Mosad, Yitzhak began, had "borrowed" the identity of one
Kamal Amin Taabet, a deceased Lebanese Moslem of Syrian
descent, who had been raised in Egypt and later emigrated to
South America. Kamal was born in Beirut in 1930 to Saada
Ibrahim and a Damascene textile merchant, Amin Taabet, who
had left Syria to find a better life in neighboring Lebanon. His
elder sister, Aina, had died when he was three, a year after the
family had moved again, this time to Alexandria. In 1946 a
wealthy uncle emigrated to Argentina and, once established,
urged the family to follow him. Kamal's father who had been
sorely affected by the postwar recession, readily accepted the
offer. He sold his textile shop and, in 1947, left for Buenos
Aires. After the Taabets' arrival, the two brothers joined a third
partner in opening a store on Legazi Street; but the venture
failed, and they were forced to declare bankruptcy. Amin
Taabet died in 1956; Kamal lost his mother a half year later. He
lived for a while with his uncle, while continuing to work for
the Maradi Agency, a travel concern in the capital. The Mosad,
Yitzhak explained, had built the new cover around this authentic personage. Eli would be able to expound pro-Syrian sentiments by explaining that his father had never relinquished his
citizenship and had passed down a love of the old country.
Amin Taabet often insisted that Kamal return to Syria as soon
as he had accumulated a small fortune. To strengthen his story,
Eli could also claim that although he had no memories of
Damascus or Beirut, he knew Alexandria well.[8] "After you
have established your descendancy," Yitzhak concluded, "you
won't encounter any difficulty in convincing the Arab community that you are eventually planning to return to the United
Arab Republic."

Not long after this meeting, on an afternoon near the end of 1960, Yitzhak gave Eli forty-eight hours to prepare for the voyage to South America. Nadia received the news that he would leave for a six-month trip to Europe with mixed emotions. Although she had expected his departure, it still came as something of a shock. In a matter of hours, though, she summoned the entire family for a hasty farewell party. Eli's brothers were astounded to find him sporting a bushy mustache. Maurice, who knew that he had always strongly objected to wearing one, asked him why he had suddenly changed his mind. "You look like an Arab," he added jokingly. Eli replied evasively that he had grown one so that he could shave it in thanks if he had a son.[9]

Eli returned to the apartment on Allenby Street only to learn that his flight had been postponed indefinitely. In the coming days he grew increasingly restless. Yitzhak was just as anxious to see him go but said he would have to wait until the necessary arrangements had been made to help him establish a cover.

The order to leave came forty-eight hours later. Gideon, a young Mosad operative who would become Eli's case officer under Yitzhak's supervision, drove him to Lydda Airport. In Zurich, Eli was told, he would be awaited by Israel Salinger, the Mosad station chief for Europe, who would from then on oversee all transit arrangements. Eli's "security passport" would be exchanged for that of an Israeli resident in Chile; a legitimate Argentinian visa had already been granted for three months. Sometime during that period, Abraham, the Mosad's station chief in Buenos Aires, would provide him with Argentinian papers issued to Kamal Amin Taabet.

Book Three
The Mission

7
Kamal Amin Taabet

Swissair flight 200 from Zurich to Buenos Aires was uneventful. The clouds which had obscured the coastline when the plane circled to land in Montevideo began to break early Friday afternoon during the short run from Uruguay to Argentina. The Convair 990 Coronado remained in the air for more than ten minutes awaiting tower clearance before beginning its descent over the mouth of Río de la Plata.

The landing at Ezeiza International was negotiated smoothly at 1:05 P.M. as scheduled. Engulfed by the usual hubbub of airport activity, Eli made his way through the tedious process of arrival. He located his luggage, and after what seemed an endless wait, he cleared customs and headed toward the first sight of the city.

The pleas to prospective fares from Argentine taxi drivers were as aggressive and persistent as those Eli was accustomed to in the Mediterranean. He managed to explain to one driver, in a combination of English and his limited Spanish, that he wanted to be taken downtown near the center of the city. By midafternoon he had checked into a small hotel the Información Turistica had recommended in the San Martín district, not far from the Stock Exchange.

On Saturday morning, Eli walked to the Café La Paz on Calle Corrientes y Montevideo, a celebrated gathering place for writers, artists and politicians. His contact was due to arrive at eleven. According to instructions, there would be no signs or passwords; the Mosad operative would identify him from a photograph.

Minutes before the hour, a short, stout man, well in his sixties, strode over to the table, greeted him with a hearty *bonjour, mon ami*, then introduced himself as Abraham. His heavy shock of white hair, Eli later remarked, gave him an almost Biblical cast. After a brief chat in Hebrew about the flight to Argentina, Abraham lowered his voice slightly and moved to the matter at hand. He disapproved of the choice of hotel and suggested that Eli find a furnished room in a less central neighborhood. "You must remain as inconspicuous as possible," he cautioned, "until your documents are ready."

The conversation, meanwhile, had shifted, at Abraham's suggestion, from Hebrew back to French. Eli was to master Spanish, learn Argentinean customs and the country's political structure; he would also explore the capital fully—its transportation system, restaurants and cultural facilities. "Above all," Abraham warned, "keep away from the Jewish quarter, and, for the time being, avoid the Arabs and their meeting places."[1] Before leaving, he gave Eli the name of a Spanish teacher and told him to leave the hotel on Sunday morning and take the streetcar to the Cabildo on Plaza de Mayo, where he would be waiting.

On Sunday, at 10 A.M., Abraham was standing in the shadow of the Cabildo. He had already looked through the Clarin's classified pages and found a small *pension* in Barrio San Marin. Using an assumed name, he had phoned the landlady, who promised to hold the room. When Eli arrived, Abraham gave him the details and the two agreed to see each other again on the following afternoon at 2 P.M. in the library of the School of Law and Social Sciences at the Universidad Nacional. Eli would have to complete a large number of questionnaires in order to obtain Argentinean papers. Abraham had the temporary use of a cubicle at the library "for research," where they could work undisturbed without arousing suspicion.

When Eli arrived at the *pension* within a half hour of leaving the Cabildo, he found that the vacancy was in a three-story white stucco house, built almost to the cobblestones of a narrow side street. The owner, Señora Trinidad Rodríguez, was a plump, dark matron in her fifties, beneath whose weight that age had added remained the fading outlines of a once-attractive woman. Eli was led up a flight of stairs to Apartment 5, a small but clean and cheerful room. There was no telephone. The windows, extending from floor to ceiling, looked out onto the street. "He checked the shutters," the landlady later recalled, "and seemed satisfied that they would assure complete privacy."[2] Eli paid two weeks' rent and moved in the same day.

As soon as the stores opened on Monday, he set out to purchase new clothes. "The style of your suit," Abraham had remarked, at their first meeting, "is unmistakably Middle Eastern." He had then given Eli the address of a well-known shop on Calle Florida. Eli spent almost the entire morning submitting to the owner's fidgeting and fussing, leaving the store completely outfitted in clothes of South American weight and cut. On the way to the university for another meeting with Abraham, he stopped at a street photographer's stand for six passport photos. Before two, he climbed the steps leading to the Law and Social Science departments to begin completing the official forms.

On Tuesday, Eli made an appointment to see the Spanish teacher Abraham had recommended at her home in the old but still-fashionable northern suburb. Mari Cruz Echevarría was a tall, reserved woman approaching sixty, with penetrating blue eyes and white-streaked blond hair. From the appearance of her apartment, it was apparent that the Echevarría family had once known greater wealth. Rich Persian rugs were faded and worn; draperies, mottled by dampness and sunlight, kept the rooms in semidarkness. Señora Echevarría greeted him in French and, without further discussion, began the lesson. Eli, who had undergone an intensive three-week course in Spanish before leaving Tel Aviv, displayed an unusual feeling for the language. "He was a natural linguist," the señora later commented. "I never before had a pupil who learned so quickly and easily."[3]

During the next three months, for four hours a day, five days a week, Eli devoted himself to his studies. As soon as his Spanish was reasonably fluent, he decided to spend several days at Mar del Plata, the Argentinean Riviera. Limited by a strict budget, he traveled the 250 miles to the resort by train, third class and stayed at the Playa Perla, whose hotels, though less luxurious than those on other beaches, were more than comfortable. He took care never to appear near the Playa Grande, the variegated semicircle on the Atlantic with its thousands of sun-worshipers, or the sprawling Bristol Beach Casino, where he could have been seen by wealthy, vacationing Arabs who might later recognize him. When he met Abraham shortly afterward, Eli noted that he had gone so far as to strike up a brief friendship with a young couple who had come from Santiago del Estero, Argentina's oldest city, to work near Mar del Plata. Their only comment about his accent had been that they enjoyed meeting foreigners.

Back in Buenos Aires, Eli felt confident enough to unbend somewhat toward his landlady, Doña Trini, and her daughter, Juanita. The friendship with Juanita not only gave him an opportunity to practice his Spanish, but also provided him with a companion to visit some of the city's points of interest.[4] He was expected to be well acquainted with the capital by the time he had to face the hyper-clannish, suspicious Syrians. Awaiting the order to enter the Arab community, he roamed through Buenos Aires in the company of Juanita. It was a rare moment of relaxation, and he knew the importance of using the time as preparation for the pressures to come.

Eli toured the city, photographing museums, palaces and monuments. He window-shopped with Juanita at the expensive stores on Calle Florida, and spent evenings on the banks of the Riachuelo, the gay and noisy nightclub district. On Sundays they traveled in green-yellow buses or privately owned *micros* and *colectivos*, through the *barrios*, from the older Italian quarter of La Boca in the south to the modern districts north of Avenida de Mayo, where baroque mansions made way for high-rise apartments with penthouses and swimming pools. Juanita took him to the Fine Arts Gallery and the tomb of Jose de San Martín at the seventeenth-century cathedral, browsed with him for a *Série Noire* or a Simenon at the Ateneo bookstore, and, on weekends, accompanied him to a *programa triple* in a cheap theater on La Valle. Eli became a frequent customer at the sidewalk Café Petit on Avenida Santa Fe, where he would sit afternoons drinking Quilmes beer or the more expensive Río Tercero, and occasionally, a dry Cinzano with Fernet, a local gin.

In mid-January, Abraham phoned and arranged for a meeting at the Rosedale garden in Palermo Park. When Eli finished his report, Abraham handed him a booklet which listed the attractions of the park. Inserted was a pink, plastic-laminated *cédula de identidad* (No. 6150148) and a blue passport with gold inscription and Argentine seal in the name of Kamal Amin Taabet.[5] Eli did not have to wait the two years necessary to acquire naturalization papers, nor did he have to make a personal appearance at the Federal Police Station. It had taken the Mosad station chief ninety days to create Kamal Amin Taabet.

Many of the half million Argentinean Arabs, 10 percent of whom lived in the southwestern sector of Buenos Aires, considered themselves *tan Argentinos como cualquiera* (as Argentinean as anyone) and proudly asserted that they had assimilated easily and did not constitute—as they claimed Jews did—an isolated ethnic group. The Syrians, however, who resided in the capital's old southwestern area, maintained, for the most part, an inbred existence. Although many worked in banking and commerce, which brought them into contact with the mainstream of Argentinean affairs, strong Arab nationalist sentiments, a language barrier and the desire to preserve traditions limited their social activities to association with compatriots. It was in this chauvinistic community, wary of outsiders, that Kamal Amin Taabet attempted to gain acceptance.

With the confidence bred by familiarity with the capital, Eli began searching for an apartment near the Syrian section. He finally chose an airy, pleasantly furnished room on the second floor of Calle Tacuari 1485 which rented for forty pesos a day.

His new landlady, Carmen Arena de Eizmendi, was a good-natured elderly woman of Italian descent who had come from the south with her daughter and operated several rooming houses in the neighborhood. Taabet's cover proved effective with Doña Carmen. When later interviewed about her tenant, she was at first nonplussed: "Cohen? Never heard of him." But at the mention of the name "Taabet," she exclaimed with mingled disbelief and astonishment: "Amin? The Turk?" (The señora's knowledge of the Mediterranean had obviously been abraded by time and distance.) "Of course I knew him."

Señor Taabet, she recalled, usually left the house early in the morning and returned late at night. He was a quiet and charming man, and, as far as she knew, engaged in business. Doña Carmen was not certain of his occupation, but she did remember that when he remained at home, he never seemed to leave the bathroom. She added half-jokingly and half-querulously that "on those days no one else could wash. I never saw another man who took six baths a day." (The bathroom had served as a darkroom to develop photographs of Syrian officials in Argentina.) Learning that Taabet had been employed as an undercover agent for an unnamed government, Doña Carmen remarked, "That one a spy? " And throwing her hands up, she added, incredulously, "He couldn't harm a fly."[6]

Taabet's work, about which Señora de Eizmendi had been so vague, was for Transportes Donato Alvarez, a trucking firm in the Flores district. It was important, Abraham had advised, that he have some sort of occupation, in case inquiries were made about his source of income. Through a furniture dealer known as Kugler, Taabet was introduced to Señor García, one of the owners of Transportes. "I told him I was a merchant," Eli recounted, "and that I was interested in learning about business administration." García recalled "Taabet said he had an adequate monthly income, and was expecting to inherit a large amount of money. We took him on without salary, and he turned out to be very clever. As a matter of fact, we found him to be quite useful." Upon learning of Eli's activities for Israeli intelligence, Garcia was dumbfounded: "I was with the police

for twenty-five years, but I had no hint that Taabet was anything more than he made himself out to be."[7]

While Eli evolved the identity of Kamal Amin Taabet, Mosad
operatives in Argentina watched for any developments which
might have caused his cover to be challenged. The silent war
between Arab and Israeli intelligence services in South America
was raging with much the same intensity as in the Middle East.
The previous May, Adolf Eichmann had been captured in
Buenos Aires and flown to Israel. The Mosad recognized that
one could not infiltrate Arab circles on the heels of the Eichmann episode without facing the possibility of an extensive
investigation but was nevertheless certain that the Amin Taabet
story would hold.

As a Lebanese of Syrian descent awaiting a sizable inheritance, Taabet was able to move freely wherever Syrians met. The
ebb and flow of expatriate life in Buenos Aires centered on
hotels, private clubs, restaurants, bars and theaters. It was in
this milieu that Taabet first began meeting influential Syrians.
The handsome eligible bachelor became a favorite of the ladies,
while his modesty and ironic sense of humor helped him win
friends among the men. Most important, the acquaintances he
made were convinced he was an ardent nationalist, deeply
concerned with developments in the Arab world and fully
committed to helping his people.

While making inroads socially, Eli strengthened the foundation of his cover by opening an account and establishing credit
in the local branch of the Syrian-Lebanese Bank. Mosad agents
in Buenos Aires arranged through a Sephardic businessman for
an introduction from the bank's president, Moïse Azzize, who
personally vouched for Amin Taabet. Relations between individual Arabs and Jews in Argentinean business circles had always been amiable. In the past, Sephardic Jews had played
prominent roles in the development of nonpolitical Arab organizations; several had even been members of their executive
committees. The efforts of Arab diplomats and emissaries of the
Arab League to Promote anti-Zionism and destroy the power

presented by Jewish solidarity with Israel had inhibited social intermingling. But some old friendships remained intact, and unknown to Eli, a favor had been granted on the basis of these ties.

Under the pretext of taking out a subscription, Amin Taabet visited the offices of *Alam al-Arabi (The Arab World)*, a weekly newspaper supported mainly by Syrians but also read by other Arabs. He paid 450 pesos for twelve months and stayed to talk with the sixty-year-old editor and owner, Abdul Latif al-Hashan, a correspondent for various Syrian newspapers and one of the elder statesmen in the Arab community. "Amin told me he was single and had come from Alexandria," al-Hashan said of their first meeting. "I don't know how he was able to get hold of one, but he produced an old Egyptian passport to prove it." Kamal even had photos of himself with his parents—perfect montages made on a Buenos Aires background.

Taabet struck up a cordial relationship with al-Hashan on the basis of a mutual interest in Arab problems. The young man forcefully expounded his views on Arab nationalism, so impressing the editor that he was urged "to visit us soon. We want to see more of you here."[8] Taabet left his telephone number and thereafter frequently received calls from al-Hashan at the office.

The friendship with the owner of *Alam al-Arabi* led to membership in the Asociación Islámica. At the Islamic Club, on Calle Bogotá 3449, Taabet met Suleiman Ahmad, a local businessman. Although he had spent most of his adult life in Argentina, Ahmad's Spanish was halting and uncertain. "One night he came in and sat down at my table," Suleiman remembered. "From then on, he came every night, drank coffee and played cards." Taabet was able to cultivate Ahmad's acceptance and goodwill with little difficulty. Admitted Suleiman: "I liked him from the moment we first met."[9]

Like al-Hashan, the range of Ahmad's acquaintances was extensive. Taabet was introduced to Kabalam Khalil, the association's vice-president, a wealthy and prominent merchant with many business operations in the capital. Despite the interest Khalil took in him (or perhaps because of it) the merchant's later replies to questions about Taabet reflected great bitterness. Khalil had been deeply hurt by the deception. "Amin did not impress me very much. He spoke little and traded mostly on his expected inheritance."

Taabet was known as an elegant dresser, Khalil admitted, "and never missed a dance." He also spent some of his leisure time outside the community, often socializing with his employers.[10] "We used to be like a little family," recalled the partner of Señor García, a Paraguayan who preferred to remain anonymous. "We lunched together every Saturday. Taabet loved *asado* [barbecue], and he was some eater! *Dios mio,* what hunger! He ate like a horse." Amin liked fiestas, loved mature women and was crazy about *futbol* (soccer), recounted Ricardo, a clerk with the firm who often went out with Taabet.[11]

Many in the Arab community viewed Eli as a potential leader, if and when he returned to Syria. He had publicly espoused anti-Zionist views and had demonstrated his concern for the cause of progressive Arab nationalism by becoming an active member of the Argentinean Arab Youth Movement and joining the Syrian Cultural Movement and the Arab League Society.

At the prompting of al-Hashan, the name Kamal Amin Taabet was added to the invitation list for most of the receptions at Arab diplomatic missions. He became a familiar figure at UAR cocktail parties and dinners, and was a welcome guest at the Lebanese consulate general on Calle Martín. On more than one occasion, Taabet was seen in the company of UAR Ambassador Ahmed Abdallah Tehema. Another diplomat he met at these gatherings was the UAR military attaché, Amin al-Hafez, a Syrian colonel and a close friend of al-Hashan. Taabet often visited Hafez in his second-floor office on Avenida Viamonte before the colonel was recalled to Cairo, but the two had talked on enough occasions for Taabet to ascertain that Hafez was leaning toward the then illegal Socialist Baath Party.

Regular reports of Eli's success in contacting UAR officials were sent to his superior at Mosad Headquarters. After seven months, satisfied with his progress, Tel Aviv ordered Abraham to instruct Eli to terminate his preliminary mission. In the first week of May, Eli told Doña Carmen and Señor García that he planned to visit his uncle, who was ill, and informed his Syrian friends that he was leaving to assume the inheritance and tour the Arab states before resettling in Syria. On the thirteenth he went to see al-Hashan at his office on Calle Campaña 621, paid for another year's subscription, and received letters of introduction to al-Hashan's son, Kamal, a cousin in Alexandria, a banker in Beirut, and a close friend in Damascus, the attorney Habib Khareb.[12] Khalil supplied more recommendations to relatives who held high positions in Lebanon and Syria; other letters were practically forced on Taabet by friendly Syrians. These references from "persons beyond reproach" provided the additional proof that Kamal Amin Taabet existed and was known by at least one influential segment of the Arab community in Argentina.

UAR officials were more than pleased to supply a transit visa for Egypt, and the Lebanese consul promptly issued a tourist visa for six months. The travel arrangements completed, Taabet arrived at the airport on May 16, 1961, accompanied by a number of close friends. The Syrians bade him farewell with Arab embraces and kisses, a final salaam and *vaya con dios*. Fifteen minutes later he boarded a flight to London en route to Tel Aviv.

8
Journey to Damascus

Following stopovers in London and Zurich, a connecting Lufthansa night flight took Eli to Munich and a conference with the station chief. The Mosad representative who called himself Salinger was unusually inquisitive and turned the meeting into an exhaustive interrogation. Although he had seen Eli's periodic reports and was thoroughly familiar with his mission in Buenos Aires, Salinger insisted on additional information. Eli had to spend most of the first day and night in a cramped hotel room answering questions; even a hasty dinner at a nearby restaurant did not provide a respite.

Near dawn, Salinger ended the questioning as abruptly as it had begun, instructing Eli to compile a detailed account of his efforts to establish a cover. An exchange was then made: Eli handed Salinger the credentials of Kamal Amin Taabet, his Argentinean documents and clothes, and, in turn, was given two pieces of luggage, two suits, shirts, underwear and a toothbrush. On top of the neatly packed garments lay a French "security passport" under an assumed name. "It was a great release to be myself again," Eli later told a friend in the Mosad. "The tension of assuming a second identity was beginning to become unbearable."

The Air France flight from Paris landed at Lydda Airport on Friday morning in the last week of August, 1961. Gideon, who had seen Eli off eight months earlier, now waited outside customs. Unlike Salinger, he wore no official mask and offered only praise for the agent's performance in Argentina. Yet apart from the amiable conversation en route to Tel Aviv, little was said about the future. Gideon promised there would be no immediate debriefings and drove directly to Bat Yam.

The welcome Eli received from Nadia held none of the expressions of relief and the tears of later visits, when she would come to suspect the true reason for his absence. Nadia was still secure in the belief that he had been working in Europe for Mishlachat Hakniot. Any apprehension she might have felt during his absence was dispelled when letters and postcards had arrived from Germany, Switzerland, Belgium and France. (They had been written before Eli's departure for Buenos Aires and were mailed by Salinger and his agents on the dates noted in the correspondence.) Paychecks had also reached Nadia regularly, and the presents Eli now brought further convinced the family that he had been away on ordinary government business.

Nor was Nadia suspicious when Gideon came to see her husband at the beginning of the week on the pretext of a friendly visit. Before leaving, he took Eli aside and passed on the order to report to the Operations Department for advanced training. The initial courses were to be conducted in the same private apartment off Allenby Street, where he was to live for the duration of his stay in Tel Aviv. As far as Nadia was concerned, he would have to depart once more.

The first phase in a refresher class for techniques previously learned was conducted this time by a former Army communications instructor known as Yehuda. Under his supervision, Eli practiced the Morse code for long hours each day until he acquired a "fair fist" and increased his transmission rate until he was capable of sending and receiving 80 to 100 words a minute—an impressive speed for an agent without much field experience. The meticulous Yehuda also taught him to dismantle and repair new types of miniature shortwave transmitters blindfolded. Outside class, Eli studied communication plans and memorized frequencies and time schedules which would eventually be utilized. He then recorded exercises for the technicians who had to familiarize themselves with the nuances of his transmission so that they would immediately identify his grip when receiving him. Successive courses in concealed writing, coding and decoding followed.

The experience Eli had acquired as an amateur proved invaluable in the advanced photography class which opened the course in new intelligence methods. Using facilities of the Mosad laboratory, he reduced hundreds of documents to the size of a typewriter period, mastering the sophisticated microdot process invented by the German Abwehr (military intelligence). At the same time he was drilled in the identification of Syrian units and Soviet weaponry until he was capable of distinguishing at a glance between the various insignias and different types of Russian arms, armor and aircraft. Modiin further briefed him on the organization of the UAR Army and its commanders; the Shin Beth created more complex exercises in trailing and detection, and ex-paratroop instructors supervised target practice and demolition.

Throughout the fall, Eli worked diligently in the Mosad's Syrian Department, assimilating reports and analyses of the intelligence community on the Northern Region of the UAR. The dossiers examined every facet of Syrian life—political, military, social and economic. Reviewing the exhaustive material, Eli thought he could never retain all the facts, but comprehensive tests revealed that he had absorbed the information and nearly memorized the Syrian *Who's Who*, along with more intimate details about political and military figures.

The intensive training program had been planned on the assumption that Eli would enter the Northern Region as the ardent unionist and Nasserite Kamal Amin Taabet. Yet no sooner did he familiarize himself with this political guise than an unforeseen event occurred. Minutes after five o'clock on Thursday morning, September 28, Eli was abruptly awakened by a call from the head of the Syrian Department who had just been notified by the officer of the day at Mosad Headquarters that instead of opening its regular morning broadcast with a reading from the Koran, Radio Damascus had come on the air at 4 A.M. with a communiqué from a self-styled Supreme Arab Revolutionary Command of the Armed Forces announcing that Syria had seceded from the United Arab Republic. Eli promised to come to the office at once.

At six thirty, before leaving the house, he tuned in the early news on Kol Israel, but both its Hebrew and Arabic programs only mentioned the coup in cautiously worded terms. Eli was somewhat startled by the development. Although the Mosad and Modiin were aware of the increasingly hostile attitude toward Egypt in the Northern Region and the intrigues fostered by anti-Nasserites, no takeover by elements opposing the union had been foreseen. The prestige of President Nasser was still immense, and the Mosad considered even his fiercest adversaries too frightened to come out into the open. Israeli intelligence had expected agitation from right-wing nationalists and conservative forces, but its analysts had deduced that an anti-union putsch had few chances of succeeding.

Eli arrived at Mosad Headquarters within the hour, and from there followed the coup closely. The apparent break between the two countries entirely altered Eli's orientation toward his mission. From a Nasserite émigré, he would now have to become an ardent Syrian nationalist. To achieve such a political identity, every new detail had to be analyzed. Since the battle between Syria and Egypt was being waged with equal intensity over the air waves, the revolt was not difficult to follow from Tel Aviv. Eli monitored Radio Damascus and Cairo's Voice of the Arabs, received hourly reports of broadcasts from other stations—particularly the well-informed Radio Beirut—and watched Arab television news programs on the control room panels. In addition to the foreign press, he read Mosad analyses and flashes from operatives in Syria, Egypt and Lebanon. By the time the day had ended, a clear picture of the situation in Damascus emerged.

The putsch, like the last three Syrian coups, had been hatched by Brigadier Abd al-Ghani Dahman, commander of the

Damascus garrison, and Major General Muwafak Asassah, deputy commander of the Air Force, with the aid of the 72d Armored Brigade and four colonels whose infantry, commando, Air Force and General Staff units were stationed in and around the capital. The rebels' strategy was simple: Following the tested method for seizing power employed since 1949, they planned to occupy key buildings in Damascus and arrest the present leadership. If successful, other garrisons were bound to join the rebellion. And with the Army in full control, the politicians would doubtless follow suit.

The conspirators had to be extremely cautious. The First Army of the UAR (what had once been the Syrian armed forces) was commanded by Lieutenant General Gamal Faisal, a staunch supporter of President Nasser and a close friend of his personal representative in the Northern Region, the vice-president, Field Marshal Abd al-Hakim Amer. Faisal, like his Egyptian deputy, Major General Anwar al-Kadi, was a fervent unionist. He had carried out the integration of the Syrian and Egyptian armed forces, had accepted Egyptian officers on his General Staff, and was zealously trying to preserve the new creation and make it work. It was this military hierarchy and the civil government supporting it that the conspirators were planning to topple.

The 300-strong force committed to the junta had been ordered into Damascus not earlier than thirty minutes before H hour. At 1 A.M. tank units rolled out of the Katana barracks, the largest military base in Syria, some 17 kilometers southeast of the capital. Half an hour later, armored cars and trucks carrying infantry began streaking north from a camp near al-Mazza. At exactly the same time, the meharistes (Bedouins of the Desert Guard) left their garrison at Dumeir, 39 kilometers to the east. At Harasta Air Force Base, a squadron of Mig-17's stood ready to strafe military installations that might put up resistance.

At 1:50, all units began moving into position: Infantry detachments secured the airport and al-Mazza Prison; roadblocks were erected near the ministries of Health and Education, the

Syrian University on Palestine Street and the square in front of the Hidjaz railway terminal; armored units surrounded the Parliament, the Syrian Bank and the Officer's Club on Afif al-Salihiya Street, while military police occupied the Palace of Justice, the Gendarmeri and the Muhafazet (City Hall) of Damascus.

The first skirmish took place at exactly 2 A.M. The meharistes broke into the telephone and telegraph exchange, fired a few rounds at the sentinels and occupied the building. A handful of soldiers who guarded the Damascus radio station surrendered after a brief struggle. In the meantime, two Soviet-made T-54 tanks lumbered into the gardens of the Serail which housed the central government offices, their cannons aimed menacingly at the entrance. The guards, seeing that the odds were against them, laid down their arms without combat. Another tank and a number of armored vehicles blocked the road on al-Jamhuriyeh Street, covering the Central Police Station, which offered no opposition. The same tactics were employed at the Defense Ministry and the General Staff Headquarters, where intense sniping came from the floor housing the Second Bureau; only after promises to respect the lives of the unionists were made over loudspeakers did the attackers take possession of the building.

Meanwhile, Lieutenant Colonel Abd al-Krim an-Nahlawi, adjutant to Field Marshal Amer, and a fellow conspirator, Lieutenant Colonel Haidar al-Kuzbari, burst into the presidential Muhajerin Palace at the head of a half dozen meharistes. They rushed up the stairs, shooting at the sentinels and killing two bodyguards. Marshal Amer's Albanian *garde du corps* tried to resist but was virtually annihilated after a short and bloody battle in which reinforcements overran the palace.

Wielding their pistols, the colonels burst into the field marshal's bedroom and arrested him in the name of the Supreme Arab Revolutionary Command, "the representative of a free and independent Syria." Amer roared in outrage to get out. Nahlawi pointed a gun at his head, thundering, "Don't make me use violence. Understand that we shall stop at nothing to achieve freedom."

Still in his pajamas, Amer was then bundled into a car, driven to the General Staff complex and confined to an office of the First Army Command, where Faisal and al-Kadi, who had also been taken into custody, were waiting.

With the three highest-ranking officers in the Northern Region secure as hostages, the six-man junta felt an initial surge of confidence. They immediately contacted local commanders considered sympathetic to their cause and asked for help in subduing the 5,000 Egyptian troops stationed around Damascus. Almost all readily offered their support. By three o'clock the insurgents were masters of all the key installations. Special detachments were then sent out to arrest politicians loyal to the UAR. There were few cases of resistance; only scattered machine-gun fire from rabid unionists awakened some drowsy Damascenes.

By 4 A.M. the entire Damascus region was in the hands of the rebels. The junta now felt secure enough to call military commanders around the country, inform them of the coup and request their adherence. The majority promptly responded, by issuing fiery statements of allegiance.

Most of the populace heard news of the coup at breakfast when they tuned in to Radio Damascus. The announcer read the first of the Revolutionary Command's nineteen communiqués, informing the Syrians that they had been liberated from Egyptian oppression. It was this broadcast that had prompted the officer of the day at Mosad Headquarters to notify the head of the Syrian Department, who, in turn, had alerted Eli.

Within the hour, the Army issued three more communiqués promising stern action against saboteurs and intriguers and urging the population to "treat your brothers the Egyptians with generosity, care and sincerity."   All airports and harbors were then closed by Communiqué No. 4.

The news of the secession sent Syrians dancing through the streets of cities and villages to the shouts of *Kanet Auja wa-Adalnaha* (She was curved and we have straightened her); from the Druze tribesmen of the south to the Yazidi devil-worshipers in the north, the entire citizenry seemed to have embraced the revolution. Everywhere the UAR's red, white and black banner with two green stars was torn down, and the old green, white and black tricolor with three red stars was hoisted in its place. In Tel Aviv, Eli read eyewitness reports from the border describing how Syrian officers had virtually uprooted the flagpole and triumphantly raised the old flag. Within a few hours, all UAR emblems in Syria had disappeared, as if the forty-one-month-old alliance had never existed.

At 8:45 A.M. in Cairo, President Nasser strode into Studio No. 1 of the Voice of the Arabs to present the Egyptian version of the crisis. "What occurred in Syria today," he began, "is much more serious and dangerous than anything that has happened until now. . . . The rebels in Damascus have betrayed Arab ideals. They are nothing but a group of reactionaries and separatists." As for the junta's demand to dissolve the union, he threatened: "I will never proclaim this . . . no matter what hardships I may face. . . . Our banners, the banners of Arab nationalism, will not be pulled down. . . . I have given orders to the soldiers of the First Army to move on Damascus and crush the rebellion."

As soon as he ended his speech, Radio Damascus countered with telegrams of support from field commanders, and Communiqué No. 5 claimed complete victory for the movement. Units in northern coastal areas, however, still resisted take-over. The commanders considered themselves the representatives of the central government in Cairo, and the soldiers remained loyal to their officers despite the new junta's promises of "pay increases, free sweets and movies each night."

At General Staff Headquarters, negotiations with the detained vice-president continued throughout the early afternoon. Outlining the Army's grievances, the rebel officers claimed that they had never intended to carry out a coup but had believed that their commands were in danger and merely wanted to rid themselves of Cairo's control and turn the union into a federation with Egypt. If these requests were granted, the Revolutionary Command would dissolve itself and the UAR could continue to stand.

Amer conveyed the officers' demands to Nasser and recommended that the president accept a reorganization of the chain of command, the withdrawal of the 15,000 Egyptian troops from the Northern Region and the return of Syrian officers attached to the Egyptian Army. The rais decided to bid for time and told Amer to continue negotiating while he consulted his Cabinet.

As Eli listened to the recriminations between Damascus and Cairo, he deduced that the negotiations with Amer were not going well. "Arab brothers," Cairo wailed, "your union is in danger from the imperialists and Israel. . . . You are the ones to defend it." Damascus responded with accounts of Egyptian tyranny and dictatorship.

Almost on the heels of these last denunciations, Communiqué No. 9 was completely to unnerve those who had thought the coup had succeeded:

> The Supreme Arab Revolutionary Command does not want to disrupt Arab national achievements. It has submitted the problems and aims of the Army to the vice-president and commander in chief, who understood the real affairs of the Army and took appropriate measures to solve them in the best interest of the unity and strength of the armed forces and the UAR. Military matters have returned to their normal course. . . . You are listening to the broadcast of the United Arab Republic from Damascus.

Cairo, now totally confused, rebroadcast the president's morning speech, while Damascus furiously repeated its previous announcements and statements until 2:05 P.M. when the junta's Communiqué No. 10 was read on the air. Amer, the Revolutionary Command now told the confused Syrians, who "had pledged to do away with the opportunists and saboteurs . . . went back on his promise." Communiqué No. 9 was revoked. A curfew was imposed, and all Syrian military personnel on leave were ordered to rejoin their units.

The rebels, in fact, had pleaded with Amer "to return the sabers to their sheaths, so that the water can continue to flow along its course." But the marshal, while stalling the negotiations as instructed, managed, in veiled terms, to ask Nasser for reinforcements. Technicians who were listening in promptly notified the junta. Realizing they had been duped, the rebels broke off the talks and notified the field marshal that he would have to leave Syria that afternoon. Amer was allowed a final call, during which he told the president bluntly: "The union is lost. The Syrians are opting out."

At 5 P.M., junta representatives escorted Amer, Faisal and the ministers of the UAR to Syria to the airport and, after an incongruously cordial ceremony, cleared a military transport for takeoff to Cairo. Minutes after the plane left, Radio Damascus proclaimed: "The regime of tyranny is over."

Turning to the Voice of the Arabs, Eli thought it was curious that instead of an expected announcement confirming the news from Syria, all that could be heard were the brassy sounds of marching bands. The explanation for the silence was given by Nasser in a broadcast at 5:30 P.M. After defending the aims of the union at length, the president excitedly told his listeners that a popular movement was now under way to save the UAR. The people of Syria, he claimed, were battling in the streets to restore unity. "I am unable to dissolve the UAR," Nasser cried out with pathos. "This is beyond my authority. . . . I am responsible before every Syrian, every Egyptian and every Arab for the protection of the UAR. . . . I call on every mutineer to face himself, his soul, his heart and his conscience. I say that every rebel must bear the responsibility of the mutiny in which he became involved and which affected the security of this republic, its future and the struggle of its brave and valiant people for freedom and for justice."

A special decree was issued forthwith, relieving the six rebellious officers of their commands. The Syrians answered with Communiqué No. 13, ridiculing the order.

Nasser reacted swiftly. Two thousand troops were rushed to Alexandria and embarked on merchant marine vessels. In the early hours of the evening, an emergency naval task force raised anchor for Latakieh. With the coastal zone still in the hands of unionists, Nasser planned to launch a counterattack and conquer the rebel-held territories. The moment Damascus learned it would be attacked, it issued a communiqué imposing an after-dark curfew; all borders, ports and airfields were to be sealed by 9:35 P.M. Secure under the rebels, secessionist Syria retired for the night.

While the Egyptian Navy was taking up positions along the Syrian coast and paratroop units prepared to join with unionist troops in Aleppo and Latakieh, pro-rebel units stormed the building of Radio Aleppo. The program was silenced in the middle of a paean, "Beloved Nasser, lover of Egypt and Syria," and returned with a tirade against "Nasser the tyrant, who wished evil for the Arab people." After hard street fighting in the city, the local garrison finally went over to the rebel side. Latakieh Radio was forced off the air at midnight, and the UAR's last stronghold in the Northern Region fell to the insurgents.

Egyptian operatives in the area transmitted news of the loss to military intelligence in Cairo. President Nasser was immediately notified and withdrew the order for disembarkation. (Two airborne commando companies which had received the order too late and had already jumped north of Latakieh were forced to surrender.) "Arabs will not kill Arabs," Nasser said later, explaining his tactical retreat." The real reason behind his decision, however, was a problem of logistics. The Egyptian forces were not equipped for major landing operations; they had no amphibious capabilities to invade, nor enough men to hold a hostile country 150 maritime miles away.   On Saturday,

On Saturday, October 2, the Supreme Arab Revolutionary Command proclaimed independence from the UAR and created the Syrian Arab Republic. Branding Nasser everything from "dictator" to "criminal," it emphasized that, if attacked, Syria was ready to fight again to maintain its freedom. Later in the day, the military turned over the reins of government to the civilians, headed by forty-year-old Sorbonne-educated professor of law, Dr. Maamun "The Trusted One" al-Kuzbari. A former minister of justice, Kuzbari proceeded to appoint an eleven-member transition government and promised his countrymen "a true and democratic way of life," a constitutional government and elections in four months.

As the Kuzbari Cabinet was being eased into office, Nasser went before the microphones once more, seeming much calmer, yet infinitely sad. "I feel it is not imperative that Syria should remain part of the United Arab Republic," he began. "I ask of all who insist upon the preservation of the UAR to realize that what is important now is the Syrian people." The break between the Egyptians and the Syrians was complete, Nasser added. Therefore, he would not oppose Syria's request to reenter the United Nations and the Arab League as a separate entity. Nasser's voice was breaking near the end, as he called upon Allah to keep Syria and bless its people. But Egypt would not accept the new regime, he cautioned, until he was certain that it spoke for the will of the Syrian people.

The developments in the Syrian Arab Republic were of great concern to Eli, who was approaching the end of his advanced training. The weeks after the coup gave him no definite indication of what course the country would take. Although the Revolutionary Command had abandoned the stage to the politicians, the Mosad anticipated that the Army would remain the final arbiter of power. "We have all returned to our barracks and our duties," the chief of staff, Major General Abd al-Krim Zaher ad-Din, had stated. "After rescuing the ship, we handed it over to the people for them to pilot it. Politics is not our profession or our ambition." Nevertheless, he warned, the Army would stand ready to defend "our homeland against the aggressors, plotters and subversive saboteurs."

During the next three months, a curious air of unreality pervaded Syrian life. The government was busy removing the 27,000 Egyptians who had worked in the Northern Region, as Premier Kuzbari continued to reiterate his dedication to panArabism and proposed a new federation with Egypt. On the domestic front, few but the wealthy were satisfied with the revolution. While the premier publicly vowed that Nasser's land reform would be carried out and the workers' share of profits would increase, he denationalized industry and returned thousands of hectares to the landowners.[1] It was during this unstable climate of renewed independence that Eli prepared to leave for Damascus.

Having successfully completed the five-month program, Eli was permitted a weekend with his family. It was at home, far removed from the isolated world of espionage training, that Eli became fully aware his mission would be not merely an intellectual exercise, but a game of death. He knew little of the alien world he would encounter while playing the part of another man, and as he later confided, he was human enough to feel fear at the prospect.

Nadia had always been sensitive to his changing moods, and throughout the weekend, Eli was careful to conceal his apprehension. He tried to keep his emotions under tight control, calling upon habits developed over a lifetime of similar experience to focus on the day at hand and somehow enjoy it. But the effort was not entirely successful. "He was a little sad," Nadia remarked, "when he left for the second time."[2]

Upon his return to Tel Aviv, Eli discussed the mission with Gideon over espresso at the Café Tchelet off Rothschild Boulevard. His objective, Gideon told him, would be to infiltrate the upper echelons of the Syrian government and gather intelligence on every level. The transmitter and other necessary equipment were to be supplied by Salinger in Europe. He would meet his anchor man, Majid al-Ard, a wealthy Syrian sheik in Genoa. There would also be a contact in Damascus: Georges Seif, the son of a Christian Syrian emigrant who had returned from Argentina and was now employed by the Ministry of Information. Like Sheik al-Ard, Seif would be unaware of Eli's identity. "He is convinced that you are a militant Syrian nationalist who represents ultraconservative interests," Gideon explained. A basic rule of the silent war in the region was that the traitor-operative must always believe that his employer is not the worst enemy of his country. "Lead the left-winger to think that he is working for a Communist network, and the right-winger for a conservative organization," Gideon added. If Arab contacts knew Eli's true identity, they might betray him, for, in their eyes, Israel was the devil incarnate. Gideon instructed Eli not to attempt to locate or approach Seif if they should meet by chance. The Syrian would have to make the first move.[3]

There were more last-minute briefings before Gideon ushered Eli into the office of Iser Harel. The diminutive, balding *memune* greeted him warmly in Hebrew marked by a strong Russian accent. Dressed in an elegant suit and open white shirt, Little Iser looked somewhat miscast in the austere surroundings. The *memune* was gratified by the groundwork laid to date. The evaluation report had described Eli as close to a professional as training could produce, and Harel was said to have expressed admiration for the determination and detachment attributed to his agent. Harel gave the operation his unqualified approval. From that point on, the case officer, Gideon, would personally guide Eli's activities with the aid of a few select officials from the Special Operations Department.

On the afternoon of December 28, Eli was driven to the airport by his immediate superior for a trip to Munich via Brussels. Just before departure, Gideon gave him an envelope containing $500, wished him good luck, and parted with a fond but rather sorrowful shalom.[4] He had come to like the diffident agent and was sorry to see him leave.

In Munich, documents were again exchanged with Salinger; Eli turned over his "security passport" and received the papers of Amin Taabet. He was instructed to buy a ticket for the *Ausonia* luxury liner of the Italian Adriatica Line, set to sail from Genoa to Beirut via Alexandria on January 3. While on board, he would make the acquaintance of Majid al-Ard, "who will ease your entry into Lebanon and Syria."[5]

A few hours after his meeting with Salinger, Eli left for Zurich, where he took out an Italian transit visa and a Syrian "repatriation visa." On the same day he opened a checking

account in a local bank and gave the number to one of Salinger's subordinates who handled financial matters. Funds
would be deposited for his use and transferred through Beirut
to Damascus under the cover of business transactions with Swiss
import-export firms.

The Mosad operative in Zurich gave Eli a miniature radio
transmitter—"the most powerful and sophisticated at the
time"—which would enable him to send a signal directly to Tel
Aviv. The radio had been hidden in a secret compartment of a
converted American blender; a long-range antenna was wired
into a cord of an electric shaver. (As a much sought-after
appliance, the blender could be brought inconspicuously into
Syria as a gift.) Until a secure communications pattern was
arranged, Eli would transmit innocuous messages. Only after
establishing himself was he to use a ciphered code system and
operate on a prearranged schedule. The codes had been written
in invisible ink on sheets of white paper and placed between his
personal stationery. High explosives were inserted in hollow
bars of Yardley soap. A bottle of aspirin contained a number of
cyanide capsules.[6] As an extra precaution, Eli would carry one
with him at all times.*

Eli spent the final hours of 1961 alone in a Zurich hotel
room and boarded the night express for Genoa on January 2.
When he arrived in the Italian port, the liner was standing high
above dockside. Before he was settled, the ship pulled anchor
and was steaming toward Naples.

"On the following morning, while I was sitting on the
tourist-class deck chatting with a group of Egyptians," Eli later
said, "a man approached us and joined in the conversation."
The acquaintance of Sheik Majid al-Ard was made with formal
introductions, as if it were a first encounter. The talk soon
turned to the coup in Syria and the more recent rightist putsch
in Lebanon. Taabet's participation was minimal. Being a repatri-

---

*Mosad operatives sometimes receive cyanide tablets for sabotage purposes. They
are not instructed to use them in case of capture; suicide is always a decision of the
individual.

ate, he refrained from expressing opinions and mainly listened. Using a moment when the others weren't looking, al-Ard whispered, "Leave them and follow me." At a corner table in the ship's darkened lounge, the sheik mentioned that he had a new Peugeot on board and would drive Eli to Damascus. "A dear friend of mine, a security officer, works at the checkpoint with Lebanon," al-Ard said. "I will be able to ease you through customs."[7]

Majid al-Ard was a prosperous merchant in his early fifties, balding and slightly built. Favoring elegant, Italian-cut suits, he looked like an aging dandy rather than a staid Arab landowner. But there was a much more mysterious aspect to the sheik's character. Apart from his legitimate businesses, al-Ard had had a long and somewhat shadowy career as an adventurer. During World War II, when ultranationalism had been in vogue, he escaped to the Axis and settled in Germany. Lacking interest in political activities, he preferred not to collaborate with Arab exiles in aiding the Nazis. He realized that it would be more lucrative to become an intermediary in the sale of German military supplies to Arabs in Vichy territory than to spy for the anti-British underground of the Grand Mufti of Jerusalem, who headed the Arab Bureau in Berlin.

After the fall of the Reich, al-Ard worked as a sales representative for Lebanese firms. He later married an Egyptian Jewess who had emigrated to Syria and converted to Muhammadanism. Although converts were unequivocally accepted by Moslems, al-Ard complained that his marriage was being held against him by the Syrian authorities despite the fact that he was "far from liking the Jews." At the outbreak of the Korean War in 1950, the sheik turned up in Seoul as an accredited United Nations staff member. He then lived for several years in Argentina where, with the aid of wealthy and influential Arabs, he prospered before returning to Syria. In Damascus he went into business for himself and became a landowner.[8]

Majid al-Ard was considered a conservative in his political and economic outlook; he had no sympathies for the leftist Syrian leadership whose influence, he feared, was constantly growing.

It was most probably these center-right leanings that were behind his agreement "to spy for the West," in addition, of course, to the payments he received for his services.*

As soon as the *Ausonia* docked in the Alexandria harbor at 7 A.M., Eli went ashore with the first group of passengers. Though he feared that someone would recognize him, he decided to take a long walk through the familiar surroundings, in an attempt to rid himself of the anxiety he felt as an alien in enemy territory. He realized that even an encounter with a friend could be dangerous, for he later said, "I didn't dare glance at the faces of the people I passed and tried to appear as casual as I could."

Little had changed since he had left for Israel five years earlier. The sounds, the smells, he recounted, were still the same. But he could not help recognizing the irony of the situation: In his new role as Kamal Amin Taabet, the Arab, he was able to move about the city undisturbed—a freedom he had rarely enjoyed as Eli Cohen, the Jew. His first stop was Muhammad Ali Square, where he delivered a letter of recommendation to Al-Hashan's lawyer cousin. (In spite of the secession, proof of friends in Egypt could be of immesurable value.) The letter evoked a cordial conversation over a strong cup of Turkish coffee about the unstable conditions in Syria and a promise to remain in contact. Following the visit, Eli bought some mangoes at a street stall, then hailed a taxi and returned to his cabin, "after my passport had been stamped by the Egyptian police."9

Why did the Mosad direct Eli to travel by ship to Alexandria when he could have flown to Beirut for his meeting with Sheik al-Ard? Moreover, why didn't he remain on board when he could have easily feigned an illness? It was important that a credible foundation be established for his activities, Eli later

*The military court which later tried Eli and his accomplices established that the sheik was well aware Taabet worked for a foreign intelligence agency, yet believed it was that of a Western country or the North Atlantic Treaty Organization. (The Mosad was known to have recruited operatives under the guise of NATO among those who normally would have never agreed to ally themselves with the Israelis.)

explained. Better to take risks at the beginning and strengthen his cover. The sea voyage had been planned so that he could meet al-Ard under the most natural circumstances, within sight of other Arabs. Eli also had to deliver the letters of recommendation and make the acquaintance of influential Arabs who might later vouch for him if necessary. Most important, the route had been selected so that Taabet's passport could be stamped in Arab countries other than Syria, in order to eliminate possible doubts of officials in Damascus.

The *Ausonia* docked in Beirut at the end of her five-day voyage on the morning of January 8. The port teemed with armed soldiers and police; Eli sensed the tension among customs officials. Passport control was strict. All passengers, especially those bound for Syria, were closely scrutinized, but the Argentinean documents spared Taabet intense questioning. Inquiring about the tight security, he was told that four days earlier, a special decree imposing heavy restrictions on visiting foreigners had been issued in the wake of a rightist coup which had collapsed on New Year's Eve.

The local police were not eager to allow Syrians to remain in the country for extended periods. Both Eli and the sheik were given only forty-eight-hour transit permits.

The two registered in the luxurious Hôtel Plage and took adjoining rooms which overlooked the palm-fringed Corniche along the Bay of St. George. As soon as they had unpacked, Eli left to see the banker for whom he carried a letter of introduction from al-Hashan.

Al-Ard, meanwhile, attended to his own affairs. Beirut's center of banking and commerce was a financial haven for the sheik. Money changed hands with few restrictions and even less government interference. Bartering in the traditional Arab mode, local financiers dealt with international transactions as complex as Byzantine conspiracies, concerning themselves solely with a quick profit. Al-Ard's familiarity with the exotic world of Lebanese commerce would later serve Eli well when he sought to establish his import-export firm in Damascus.

Beirut was also the sheik's favorite playground. A retreat for oil-rich rulers and wealthy Arabs escaping Socialistic austerity, the half-Moslem, half-Christian capital seemed almost uninhibited compared to life in Damascus. Taabet and al-Ard did not overlook the pleasures the city afforded. For the next two days they toured bazaars, visited suqs and window-shopped at antique stores that sold the usual array of genuine and fake. Their nights were spent between gambling at the Casino du Liban and drinking in *boîtes* and bistros crowded with Arab dignitaries savoring the spirits forbidden by the Koran.

But the excursion was soon over. At 11:15 A.M., on Tuesday, January 10, Amin Taabet and al-Ard checked out of the Plage. With their luggage roped to the rack atop the sheik's beige Peugeot, they drove onto the Beirut-Damascus highway, beginning the 105-kilometer drive to the Syrian capital.[10] The road, at first crowded with donkey carts carrying crops into town, became deserted when they reached the eastern slopes of the snowcapped Anti-Lebanon Mountains. An hour later, they arrived in Chtoura, the last settlement before the international frontier, where the usually indifferent Lebanese customs officers made a cursory inspection of their baggage before Eli and the sheik were allowed into no-man's-land. The desolation of the terrain was now broken only by a stone cross atop a hill erected on the grave of a French pilot who had crashed there during the Second World War. In the distance, Eli could see the Syrian trenches and gun emplacements. Billboards advertising East European products, a schedule of Aeroflot flights to Moscow and an enormous map of the Arab world from northwest Africa to the Arabian Peninsula stood high above the road. No boundary lines marked the Arab nations. It was Syria's only meaningful contribution to pan-Arabism.

The crossing proved easier than Eli had anticipated. The sheik was warmly greeted by a young lieutenant in charge of customs and passport inspection. The two embraced and kissed. Al-Ard introduced Taabet as "a brave old friend who is returning home" and took the officer aside for a private talk. (The sheik

had told Eli in Beirut that the lieutenant, whom he affectionate-
ly called Abu Haldon, was, in fact, the counterespionage officer
Nasser ad-Din Waladi, who often "made an additional pound
here and there by helping friends smuggle goods from Lebanon
into Syria.") Feigning reluctance, Waladi eventually accepted
700 Syrian pounds ($125) as "a loan," chalked off their luggage
without inspection and allowed al-Ard's car to pass with a curt
shukran (thank you).[11]

An hour's drive later, the two arrived at the sheik's farm on
the outskirts of Damascus, where Eli concealed his radio and
equipment. After a restless night's sleep he insisted, over al-
Ard's protestations, that they depart as soon as possible. The
sheik could well understand Eli's wish to reach the capital, but
his sense of hospitality was nonetheless offended; he suggested
that his guest at least spend the next several nights in a hotel
owned by a friend.

9
Mosad Operative

By the time al-Ard left the farm to drive Eli over the last miles of his journey to the Syrian capital, ominous granite clouds had swirled in from the west, darkening the skies of Damascus.. Despite the threat of a thunderstorm, the thoroughfare was thronged with military and civilian vehicles, forcing the sheik to cruise slowly and follow the traffic. Al-Ard spoke restlessly without interruption, jumping from one subject to another. He detailed his voyage to Paris and Rome, boasted about commercial successes in South America and even recounted amusing anecdotes about his experiences in Nazi Germany. Eli listened intently, nodding with interest at all the sheik had to say, but asked only few questions.

Al-Ard soon switched to politics, analyzing the anti-unionist coup and the reestablishment of the republic. He spoke glowingly of the Kuzbari administration and praised its economic achievements. Eli realized that the sheik's enthusiasm was genuine. Only once did he interrupt to ask about the contacts al-Ard had at the Ministry of the Interior. The sheik resolutely avoided a direct answer, and Eli led the conversation to another path.

Upon reaching the city's limits, al-Ard pointed at an Army base they were passing on the left. Eli immediately recognized the rows of one-story wooden and concrete barracks built by the French during the Mandate. He knew from briefings that the garrison served as unofficial headquarters for many politi-

149

cally active Syrian officers. On the opposite side of the road, the Damascus International Fair, a permanent trade exposition emblematic of the UAR's drive leftward and its attempt to revitalize the region's anemic economy, was practically deserted in the wake of the right-wing, anti-unionist coup. But the Russians, Chinese and East Europeans who had erected impressive pavilions—only a few Western nations were represented— still continued to display the achievements of their brands of Communism.

The sheik entered the city through Faruk al-Awal Boulevard alongside the Barada River. He crossed a medieval bridge, passed a series of gardens and turned into Rue de la République, where he stopped to secure lodgings at the orange-hulled New Semiramis Hotel. While Eli was waiting in the lobby for al-Ard to locate the proprietor, he could not help noticing the state of decline into which the Semiramis had fallen. Musty, ornate furniture and faded limestone columns streaked with blue gave evidence that the hotel was no longer attracting the prosperous American and European clientele who had swarmed through Damascus before the UAR government grew increasingly hostile toward the West. In an effort to bolster the sagging trade, an official notice, tacked behind the front desk, stated that children under sixteen and "servants of tourists" were entitled to reduced rates. A second bulletin, entitled "Paragraph 25, Decree of the Ministry for National Economy," made a curious bureaucratic attempt to reassure travelers that they were welcome. The directive ordered all hotels to receive tourists with "respect and politeness" and instructed the police to protect visitors "free of charge and without gratuity."[1]

The sheik introduced Eli to the proprietor as an old friend "who has just returned from Argentina to settle in the fatherland." He implored him to treat his guest "as you would treat me" and departed, promising to call the following day.[2] Eli had meanwhile given the clerk his Argentinean passport needed to complete the *fiche de police*—a questionnaire required of all foreigners. A black Sudanese carried his luggage to the third floor, where Eli found that the accommodations were drably

Spartan. As he unpacked, Eli resolved not to prolong the search for an apartment.

During the next ten days he toured Damascus with al-Ard, acclimating himself to the new surroundings while making discreet inquiries about available apartments. The capital was not entirely alien to him. He had been briefed about life in the city by Damascus-born Mosad instructors; he had studied maps, films and aerial photographs of the main quarters and had often "walked" through its streets by means of a scale model. Yet despite the Mosad's efforts to foster a sense of security, nothing could quite prepare him for the multiplicity and clamor of the Syrian capital.

Damascus, the oldest existing city in the world, lies at the edge of the fertile Ghuta plain in southwestern Syria. A metropolis of 526,000 which its inhabitants call al-Shaam, the capital is an oasis built on both banks of the Barada River ringed by desert and arid hills. For centuries Damascus had maintained contact with the outside world only by means of camel-driven caravans which lumbered across the sands. Such geographical isolation was not the least of causes for its fierce parochialism. Yet despite modern communications, an intolerance of outsiders bordering on xenophobia continued to exist and had been aggravated even further, Eli sensed, by the stormy dissolution of the United Arab Republic.

The city he explored during the first week contained some of the most striking contradictions in the Middle East. Its modern sections on the south bank of the Barada, with broad, treelined avenues, reminded him of Tel Aviv and Alexandria. But in the Syrian capital the clash of cultures was far more dramatic. Businessmen in styleless European suits and *keffiyehs* held by golden or black ropes, workers in blue coveralls and teen-age boys in open-collared sport shirts stood out strikingly next to the tarbooshed sheiks, turbaned officials in striped silk robes, brown-cloaked Iraqis and Saudi Arabians in long *kumbazi*. The contrasts among the female Damascenes were even more glaring. Black-veiled Moslem women dressed in traditional dark robes were outnumbered by the coiffured society ladies, semi-veiled and short-skirted teen-agers and schoolchildren in regulation blue and white frocks.

Juxtaposed and overlapping twentieth-century Damascus lay the rectangularly shaped ancient city with its contorted narrow streets, mosques, mausoleums, public baths, fountains and palaces still unbowed after eight centuries and a Mongol invasion. Eli wandered through the dust and grime and smell of ages surprisingly gratified. He lost himself in alleyways curling in unexpected directions, walked the twisted lanes with hands stretched out touching the walls, strolled under arches and passageways, staring into courtyards of windowless houses which looked grimly uninviting from the outside but were the quintessence of luxury within. Rejecting the services of an old and bearded dragoman guide, he toured the sites of the honey-colored Citadel alone. There he found a fanciful world of shimmering arabesque, dotty as a desert mirage: the sanctuary of Suleiman the Magnificent, the Palace of Azam Pasha, the pencil-shaped Tekiyeh and green-tiled Sinaniyeh, the monuments of the Saliniyeh suburb, the domed and vaulted Azem Khan, the tomb of Saladin and the mausoleum where the head of John the Baptist was said to be entombed.

In the center of this labyrinth of time-eroded alleys, horn-blowing Fiats, Renaults, Czech Skodas and early vintage Ford taxicabs were almost brought to a standstill by villagers riding mules or leading donkeys and elderly men on bicycles with water pipes strapped to their backs. Oblivious to this pandemonium, a medieval-looking conglomerate of Circassians, Armenians, Turks, Kurds, Ismailis and Yazidis in loose-fitting trousers and bright brocade sashes went about their business. Peasant women in full-length *festan*, their foreheads circled with gold coins, Alawi girls with tightly drawn embroidered bodices and deep-violet head scarves, Druze women in dresses girdled at the waist and circular caps covered by white veils and Bedouins with chins tattooed in blue stars followed their men in impassive silence.

Eli could barely find his way through the tangle of suqs

where Damascenes bargained with Teutonic bluntness. Markets by the dozens crisscrossed the old city: a bazaar for narghiles, a suq of antique shops, a street where carpet merchants laid out their wares, an alley of jewelers who sat in tiny glassfronted stores, a chain of shops which catered to the more practical needs of the Bedouins, and markets for silk, shoes, spices, coffee and sweetmeats, fruits and vegetables and secondhand clothes. The scenes Eli encountered were reminiscent of the *1001 Nights*. Sherbet sellers skirted in red and white, brass ewers strapped to their chests, approached him with bowls clicking and the cry *Berid ala kalback* (Refresh your heart). Juice vendors crushing lemons and carrots under a vise entreated him to "drink the juices of Damascus and make love five times a day."

Eli was unable to escape the turmoil enveloping the renewed Syrian republic even at the coffee shops and restaurants he frequented. The cafés by the Barada, a continual forum of political intrigue, were filled with students attracted to Socialism, workers flirting with Communism, disgruntled Army officers discontented with the government, amateur politicians who spoke knowledgeably on affairs of state and some government officials possessing reliable information. Pan-Arabism and the union with Egypt were still the most popular topics, but Eli overheard as many interpretations on the way to accomplish them as there were patrons.

Since Ottoman rule, the *kahwa* (café) had been an accepted meeting place for conspiring merchants, Army officers and government officials. Some establishments were closely identified with the political leanings of their customers. In fact, the police and Internal Security Services, who found truth in the Arab proverb that "the head of an idle man is the workshop of Satan," had mapped and classified the city's coffee shops and rarely failed to ask a suspect which one he patronized.

The furtive atmosphere marking the Damascene café seemed a most appropriate setting for the hatching of plots and counterplots. Patrons sat on low stools around small wooden or straw tables, playing trictrac and dominos, drinking Turkish coffee from small porcelain cups or smoking narghiles. The radio, turned to the highest volume, played Arabic songs, interrupted only by hourly news broadcasts. Against this background, governments were toppled and created. It was, of course, no easy matter to discover which way the winds of change were blowing, for one largely overheard rumors and false information. But the conversations were nevertheless monitored by a host of police informers, military intelligence and counterespionage agents, pro-Nasser and anti-Nasser spies and part-time operatives working for every party on the right and left. "The number of secret agents," the sheik had warned Eli half-jokingly, "is even larger than the number of soldiers in the country."[3]

While closely watching the subversive elements, the civilian government attempted to prevent the population from reacting in favor of another union with Egypt by continuously urging support for the armed forces "which had secured the country's independence from the UAR" and by creating a climate of siege in the large cities, particularly Damascus. Patriotic feelings were aroused by exhibits of new weapons at the Museum of the Syrian Army and displays of artillery pieces and tanks captured from the Jews in the jihad (the holy war) of 1948. There were also blunt reminders that the state was largely buttressed by the presence of the military. Helmeted soldiers patrolled the streets in Russian-made jeeps and half-tracks, military policemen stood guard at the bridges and in public buildings, martial music dominated the airwaves, and posters everywhere shrilly warned citizens: "Beware! The enemy is listening."

With the sheik's aid, Eli narrowed his search for an apartment to the Abu Rummaneh district, a predominantly residential neighborhood holding the General Staff Headquarters, the offices of the United Nations Mixed Armistice Committee and ten embassies, legations and consulates general. Eli told prospective landlords that he had decided to reside in Damascus permanently and required a large apartment or villa which could serve both as a home and office for a commercial enterprise he was planning to form. There were, however, two requirements he was unable to mention: The building could not be too isolated so that his movements would come under needless scrutiny, and there would have to be a large number of aerials already installed on the roof to provide an inconspicuous site for his own antenna. The absence of these prerequisites later caused him to reject, on one pretext or another, many otherwise suitable apartments.

Less than two weeks after Eli had checked into the Semiramis, he was shown the apartment he was looking for. Located on the fourth floor of a building across from the General Staff Headquarters, it consisted of five rooms, including a comfortable salon with a balcony overlooking the Second Bureau, a modern kitchen and pleasant bath. Persian carpets, Damascene tapestries and a telephone—a luxury for nongovernment employees—were additional inducements. The landlord demanded a monthly rent of 325 Syrian pounds. Eli found the sum reasonable, but only after the customary procedure of bargaining did he agree to make a full year's payment of 3,900 Syrian pounds ($1,000) in advance.[4] He then asked al-Ard to bring the compromising equipment from the farm and help him move his belongings to the new home. (Only later did Eli realize that the apartment lacked an alternative escape route. The main staircase led to a flat asphalt-covered roof, cluttered with laundry lines and antennas, which offered no hiding place. The neighboring buildings were too far apart to facilitate a flight over the rooftops. The only other means of exit was a thick water pipe that extended from Eli's kitchen balcony to the ground.)

One night, as soon as he was reasonably settled, Eli dismantled the antique copper lamp suspended from his bedroom ceiling and placed the miniature transmitter in the opening for the wires. He ran the antenna in his razor cord from the fourth-floor window to the roof—a relatively short distance which would ensure fewer disturbances—and attached it to a master aerial he had previously installed to face Tel Aviv. There was not a more ideal location in the area to establish a radio post. No mobile direction finder could pinpoint a specific set in such a forest of transmitters, much less distinguish between an illegal wireless and those used by the diplomatic corps, the UN or the military.

Using his Abu Rummaneh residence as a base of operations, Eli began to lay the groundwork for his business cover. The sheik introduced him to prominent wholesalers dealing in local crafts with whom he discussed plans to export Syrian art objects and furniture to Europe and South America. Swiss and Argentinean companies, he told them, had expressed interest in buying decorated coffee tables, polygonal stools, trictrac boards, boxes made of camel bone and chests carved from rosewood. To the retailers of foreign goods who appeared more than politely interested in his import scheme, he mentioned a list of luxury items which could be added to the firm's catalog. To prove that his resources were abundant, he presented the Argentinean references and alluded to a substantial inheritance on deposit in Belgian and Swiss banks. Most merchants greeted his project with enthusiasm; even those who did not suggested the names of others who might be willing to transact business. "I was shocked at the credulousness and naïveté of many important Syrian citizens," Colonel Suidani later commented, "who were taken in by Cohen's stories, believed that he had vast foreign bank accounts and accepted gifts from him while giving him classified information."[5]

Many Damascenes with whom Eli negotiated were members of the more speculative and ambitious Christian minority who exercised an influence on the business community out of proportion to their numbers. Three of his main suppliers were shopkeepers in the Bab Tuma district at the east end of the Street Called Straight. His major customers were Moslems in the Old City, yet he also had contacts with Kurds from Akrad, east of Salihiye, and Armenians whose industriousness and acumen even al-Ard regarded with a mixture of jealousy and admiration.

The acquaintanceship with some of the more important businessmen soon developed into close friendships. Eli often lunched with them at al-Aga, Ghazal and Morocco, gave dinner parties at the Oasis and Assari Club or entertained at the luxurious Scheherazade nightclub in Rabueh on the route to Beirut.[6] In the course of conversations, inevitably never far from the subject of politics, he sought to create the impression that he was a staunch nationalist, while eschewing a preference for one of the established political parties. He lauded the break with Egypt but qualified his view by expressing belief in a pan-Arabic union, with Syria leading the alliance. The opinions he advanced were never at odds with those of his companions—a carefully modulated stance which soon established him as a "reliable" émigré.

Eli's new friends recommended him to officials in the ministries of Finance, Commerce and the Interior, where he applied for permanent residency and an import-export license. In a country with an unstable economy, the investment of foreign capital in locally made products was considered a pledge of confidence in the new government; his application was given unreserved approval. The Amin Taabet Import-Export Company began operating as soon as all legal matters had been cleared. Eli rented warehouse space and bought a small stock of local goods, from which he made regular shipments to Switzerland, West Germany and Argentina.[7] The legitimate importers he dealt with insisted on wares of high quality, a demand not easily satisfied. The unexcelled craftsmanship which had once been the pride of Damascus had dwindled into mediocrity: The jewelry, leather and glass lacked both delicacy and durability; the rich inlay work had lost its elegance and sense of design. At best the work of the old masters was now slavishly reproduced. Yet Eli managed to obtain some merchandise wrought with the old excellence.

One of the companies he supplied in Buenos Aires had been set up by Abraham while two others were formed by Salinger in Munich and Zurich for the sole purpose of doing business with Taabet. The correspondence with the Mosad fronts served to transmit veiled messages. Merchandise ordered by the Israelis contained secret compartments into which Eli inserted microfilms of documents and lengthy reports. The business transactions of the firm proved a most reliable conduit; the Mosad was able to send all the hard currency—dollars, pounds sterling and Swiss francs—Eli needed for his clandestine operation without arousing the slightest suspicion.[8]

Eli allowed some of his friends and business associates to transfer private funds to Lebanon and Switzerland through the firm. He used the same method whenever he had to win over a government official, offering him a business deal instead of a direct bribe.[9] The major beneficiary from such manipulations was the sheik, but many others also profited from Taabet's wealth. In spite of his openhandedness, the company showed handsome profits. Eli kept the books meticulously and presented his superiors with yearly balances. The money he did not spend was transferred back to European banks and later returned to the Mosad treasury.[10]

At the beginning of February, his business affairs in order, Eli phoned Kamal al-Hashan at his office. The young attorney, who had been informed earlier by his father about Taabet's arrival, was eager to hear firsthand about his family and happily agreed to see him the following day. The two Kamals met in the Old City at a sidewalk café on the Street Called Straight. After reminiscing about life in Argentina, they discussed the import-export venture. Al-Hashan offered to advise Taabet on any legal problems concerning the firm and, with a traditional "My house is your house," invited him to his apartment for dinner. That evening, Eli was introduced to one of the attorney's friends, a dark, melancholy-faced Army lieutenant, Maazi Zaher ad-Din, the nephew of the newly appointed chief of staff.[11] Eli sat quietly as the lieutenant and al-Hashan discussed personal matters, but the moment Maazi began criticizing the manner in which the country's affairs had been managed under the UAR, he readily joined in the talk. He nodded with approval when the lieutenant charged that the Egyptians were not very fond of fighting, although they enjoyed talking about it, and smiled knowingly when the subject was switched to "Eezraeel," replete with the waving of spoons and arms extended in dramatic denouncements. Maazi's passion displaced his reason, turning the monologue into a burlesque. If the uninhibited performance was characteristic, Eli judged, the acquaintanceship with the lieutenant promised to be rewarding.

Al-Ard came to Abu Rummaneh several nights later and was told about the encounter with Maazi. The sheik, who happened to know the lieutenant, was delighted. "Maazi is the man you may need most," he told Eli. "He works at the General Staff and is very close to his uncle." The young officer was known as a *bon vivant*, al-Ard added, and had no difficulty living up to his reputation. Eli immediately urged that they all meet, and the sheik made a note to call Maazi and arrange a reunion.

On the weekend, during the midafternoon rest period, a taxi left Eli on a street corner in the Old City where the Christian Quarter meets the Moslem. He walked down Straight Street under the vaulted roof of rusty, corrugated tin, then turned abruptly right by the second Roman arch and entered the Café Shaam. He sat at a corner table, ordered a pot of tea, a narghile and a *shesh-besh* (backgammon) board, which he then prepared for a game with the sheik. The café was almost deserted; only a few patrons were smoking their afternoon water pipes while discussing the latest political developments. From time to time, some stopped talking and listened to the sad refrains of Oum Kalthum and Fairuz blaring from a transistor radio behind the counter.

Al-Ard arrived on time. He ordered Turkish coffee and, waiting for his narghile to be lighted, started the game by throwing the dice. The sheik told Eli that he expected Maazi to join them shortly, but before he could say more, they heard a cheerful *Mas 'salam* (May peace be with you). The lieutenant embraced al-Ard and seized Taabet's hand between his own. As soon as the amenities were dispensed with, the three engaged in a heated discussion about the present regime. Taabet responded to Maazi's discontent with apparent openness. The young officer was at his most tribal when talking about inter-Arab politics and domestic affairs. He criticized the civilians for fumbling with politics "like bears spinning wool" and asserted that the power should be given back to the colonels and the generals. Taabet could not agree more, and the sense of Maazi's last words set the tone of his own remarks. Before the lieutenant finally departed, Eli invited him to his home. "I'm giving a party for my new friends," he explained, "and I would like to consider you one of them."

It was well past eight in the evening, a few days after he had met Maazi when Eli finished developing a roll of film in his improvised darkroom. He held the microfilm up to the light, then, satisfied, rolled it onto a spool that he tied with a rubber band. He took a small Damascene backgammon board with ivory ornaments, into which he had built a cache, and, sliding a panel, removed one leg and opened a hidden compartment. He placed the microfilm in the cavity, sealed it hermetically and, after wrapping the game in a large carton, wrote a Swiss address on his firm's label and set the package aside.

Eli was putting away the darkroom equipment when the phone rang in his bedroom. An unfamiliar voice inquired about Kamal. Hesitating, Eli identified himself. The man on the other end responded, "This is Georges." There was a short silence before Eli inquired when and where he could see the caller. Georges suggested a theater in the neighborhood. An old Egyptian film was playing, and there were bound to be fewer people at the second performance, which started at nine fifteen. Eli was about to ask how they would recognize each other when Georges replied, "Don't worry, I will find you. Sit in the left aisle and save an empty place for me."

Eli entered the austerely modern Alhambra Theater shortly after the newsreel had ended. A tall, lanky man, wearing dark glasses and a light-brown suit, took the seat next to him as soon as the feature began. Continuing to look at the screen, he said simply, "I am Georges." There were no code words or signs. Seif went on in low voice, explaining that in order to make their relationship less vulnerable they would have to be introduced socially sometime in the near future. Since al-Ard was a friend, he would see him soon, try to lead the conversation to Taabet and, without the sheik's suspecting, have an introduction arranged. Eli suggested the possibility of meeting at his upcoming party. "I will try to be there," Seif reassured him. "After that," he added, "it would not be difficult to develop a friendship."

Throughout the movie, Seif elaborated on his role. As a high official of the Ministry of Information, he could supply valuable political and military intelligence. Among his responsibilities were the Radio Damascus programs for Syrians abroad—a position which might allow him to have Eli work on a volunteer basis as programming director for South America. This would offer the possibility of gaining entry into official circles. "I may even be able to present you to the ministry's director general," he said as he prepared to leave.[12] When Eli turned to his right, Seif was gone.

For the first days of February, between 8 A.M. and 6 P.M., Eli kept a watch on the General Staff Headquarters and the Palace of Guests. He had been able to locate the Communications Room and Second Bureau offices without difficulty and, choosing a spot from which he had a relatively unobstructed view of the building, photographed its security and the arriving and departing personnel with a telescopic camera installed by a window in the corridor leading to his bedroom. The castlelike complex was ringed with barbed wire and patrolled by special units; military police guarded the gates and corners of the main structure and were posted at annexes. As darkness fell, floodlights mounted on the rooftops and watchtowers blanketed the entire area. The lights in the Second Bureau, Eli discovered, were a highly accurate barometer of the political situation in Syria. If they were turned off at the end of the day, the evening would probably be uneventful; if they remained on late into the night, conditions in the city promised to be critical.

The frantic activity Eli had observed at the General Staff throughout the second week of February seemed to indicate that the Army was again agitating. When Maazi ad-Din alluded to a state of uneasiness among the military leaders of the coup, Eli considered the information vital enough to be transmitted without delay. In the early morning of the twelfth, he removed the copper lamp in his bedroom and extracted the wireless from the cavity in the ceiling originally intended to house the wiring for a hanging lamp. He then attached the antenna to the radio and connected it to the Phillips receiver purchased in Beirut. After encoding a short message, he waited until the clock struck seven, the hour at which nearly all transmitters in the embassy district would be functioning. He sent the prearranged signal to Tel Aviv, gave his exact bearing, repeated the number 88 several times and waited for a reply. Seconds later, Eli heard a coded number which indicated that the Mosad center was ready to receive him. His message was brief: He reported the apparent restiveness of the Army and followed with "Found apartment. Starting work." He then added the words *Mul hamate* (Across the street from headquarters) and signed off.[13]

10
Eichmann's Negotiator

In the final weeks of preparation for the establishment of his business, Eli noted that the major topic of conversation among Damascenes after the subject of Syria's return to statehood was the trial of Adolf Eichmann, a prime figure in the extermination of European Jewry. The café habitués directed a storm of indignation at Israeli intelligence, which had apprehended the former SS *Obersturmbahnführer* in Argentina almost a year earlier; the uniformly hostile Syrian press fanned the flames by glorifying Eichmann and describing David Ben-Gurion as a Jewish prototype of the SS man. As the proceedings opened in Jerusalem on April 11, 1961, the daily *an-Nasr* editorialized: "Having skillfully set the stage, the Zionist authorities in the occupied land will today begin the play of revenge for the alleged Jewish victims of the Second World War in Germany.... Israel cannot try Eichmann," the paper asserted, "because it is itself an unlawful authority, claiming the right to represent world Jewry, when it has committed all the crimes of which it now accuses Eichmann. How can it try him when it should be tried itself?"

Leading Arab newspapers Eli bought each day printed everything in the way of anti-Jewish diatribes. From Cairo to Amman and from Beirut to Baghdad, the media mocked the trial as a comedy, contending that the deeds of the accused called for the very opposite treatment he was receiving: Eichmann was in line for a commendation. "Why should he, who participated in cleansing Germany of the disease known as Jewry, be tried?" asked the Jordanian Jerusalem *Times*. A cartoon which appeared in the Lebanese daily *Al Nahar* showed Eichmann standing on a heap of skulls. The caption read: "He is being tried for his mistakes. He didn't kill them all."

Arab commentators in the region argued that if the Israelis could capture and judge Eichmann, "the Arabs have the right to try Ben-Gurion and his gang." Some even claimed that no great numbers of Jews had actually been killed by the Germans. Indeed, stated Radio Amman, "the Nazis only caused the death of several hundred." Other propagandists portrayed Eichmann as a hero and asserted that the Israelis actually owed their existence to him. "He is worthy of having his statue placed in every village, city and street in Israel," commented Cairo's *Voice of Palestine*. "Whether Eichmann likes it or not, he is the prophet of the Jewish State and its real founder. . . . After all, in the name of Eichmann, in the name of the gas chambers, in the name of the death camps, in the name of Hitler and in the name of the millions the Zionists claim were destroyed by Eichmann—in the name of all these, imperialism carried out its crime in Palestine."[1]

Compared with such logorrhea, the actual coverage of the trial by the Damascus press was scanty. As the proceedings entered their second week, the Syrians were becoming visibly concerned by its revelations. Many influential Arabs feared the testimony before the court would create world sympathy for Israel and reveal that Arab leaders had openly supported the Nazis, thus seriously compromising their self-righteous charge of Israeli genocide of Arabs living in Palestine. But, above all, there was anxiety that Eichmann would disclose the activities of Germans in the Middle East now working closely with the Arabs. Publicity surrounding the case had also raised the specter of an additional threat: If the Israelis could kidnap a German national in a Latin American country, what would stop them from attempting a similar coup in neighboring Arab territory? Some in Damascus feared such a commando operation was not unlikely.

* * *

One of the first assignments Eli undertook during his proscribed assimilation period was the investigation of former Nazi
officials living in Syria. His major source of information was the
sheik. Having lived in Berlin during the war, al-Ard had been
close to the Germans who had overseen the activities of Arab
collaborators in the Reich. Eli was uncertain of how far the
sheik's present loyalties extended but assumed that he might
have kept in contact with émigrés who had fled to Syria to
escape war crimes charges.

One evening, during a discussion of the Eichmann trial, Eli
asked the sheik whether he was familiar with any of the Germans residing in Damascus or, for that matter, elsewhere in the
Middle East. The response he received was encouraging. The
sheik had a good friend named Rosello who "had dealt in
Jewish affairs during the war" and now worked as an adviser for
the Second Bureau. Eli wanted to meet Rosello, but when the
sheik wavered, suggesting that an introduction would have to
wait for the proper opportunity, he did not persist. Al-Ard
promised to bring up the matter with the German.

The following morning, Eli radioed Mosad Headquarters that
he had located a German involved in "the Reich's Final Solution of the Jewish Problem." He passed on the name Rosello
and requested instructions.[2] The message was forwarded at
once to the department whose responsibilities included the
investigation of Nazi war criminals. A Mosad liaison with Atam,
the Special Investigations Branch of the Israel police, asked that
Eichmann be questioned about a German who called himself
Rosello and presently lived in Damascus. Atam sent on the
request to Bureau 06, which had prepared the Eichmann case
for trial. The bureau's chief in turn ordered *Pakad* Avner Less,
who had been interrogating Eichmann since his internment in
Israel, to pose the question. Within days, the Mosad was notified that the prisoner had identified Rosello as the former Reich
official Franz Rademacher.

An immediate inquiry regarding Rademacher's whereabouts
was sent by the bureau to the Zentrale Stelle der Landesjustiz-

verwaltung, the Central Office for the Prosecution of War Criminals in Ludwigsburg, West Germany. (The center compiled data on Nazi war criminals, attempted to locate those responsible and prepared the cases for trial.) The Zentrale's director was well acquainted with the case. He immediately cabled Tel Aviv that Rademacher had escaped from Germany in 1952, while on bail awaiting prosecution for war crimes. The federal authorities knew he had fled to Syria, but his current residence was unknown.

The files of Yad Vashem, the Jerusalem Martyrs' and Heroes' Memorial Authority, were found to contain an extensive dossier on Rademacher. Documentation centers in Paris, London, Berlin, Munich and New York also supplied additional material. From all these sources, Bureau 06 drew up a summary of the criminal allegations against Rademacher and forwarded it to the Mosad's liaison.[3] The facts provided a chilling picture of an ambitious Reich bureaucrat whose flatly worded memorandums had led to the slaughter of thousands.

Franz Karl Rademacher was born on February 20, 1906, in Neustrelitz, Mecklenburg, into a lower-middle-class family with a long tradition of government service. The son of a poor railway clerk, he had to pay his own way through school and began working at the age of sixteen. He attended the Volkschule and Gymnasium in Rostock and earned the *Abitur* which qualified him for college in 1924. He enrolled in the law school of Munich University and, after successfully passing the examinations in 1928, was granted a license to practice law.

While still an undergraduate, Rademacher had enlisted in the elite Ehrhardt Brigade of the paramilitary Freikorps, which had been created by unemployed and disaffected soldiers after the Reichswehr disintegrated. Its members were hostile to the Weimar Republic and sought an outlet for their violent energies. But Rademacher had joined too late to participate in any of the Free Corps' military campaigns. The movement, however, fostered his racist ideas and spawned a savage nihilism which would have a profound effect on his career.

Only weeks before graduation, the Freikorps was ordered disbanded, and Rademacher turned his interest to the Nazi Brown Shirts. As a dedicated member of the SA, he was asked to report to its leadership on his superiors at the Foreign Ministry. But Rademacher was reluctant to become an informer and demanded out. His *Standartenführer*, who was also a good friend, helped him get an honorable discharge, and Rademacher left the organization at the beginning of 1934. The young lawyer's diligence and dedication were not forgotten, however. Two months after Adolf Hitler captured the Chancellery in March, 1935, he was rewarded with a membership in the NSDAP, the German National Socialist Workers Party.

During the next three years Rademacher worked for a meager salary as a junior secretary in the Mecklenburg State Justice Ministry while dedicating every free moment he had to the party. But the ambitious young lawyer was disatisfied with his post. He underwent additional tests and was promoted to juridical assessor. After four years with the state legislature Rademacher decided to leave and, as soon as he became a state adviser, in June, 1937, began looking for a more promising appointment.[4] Aided by the reputation he had gained as a Nazi in good standing, he secured the position of legation secretary in the Cultural Department of the Auswärtige Amt, the Reich's Ministry for Foreign Affairs.

While in Berlin, Rademacher searched for permanent quarters. The housing situation in the capital was critical; large apartments were scarce and rents were high. As a government official, he was entitled to a requisitioned apartment, but claimants were numerous. The search for homes left behind by deported Jews had stimulated an inexhaustible cupidity in the Reich, and each ministry constantly prodded the SS to set aside apartments for its personnel. Rademacher used his personal connections and only weeks later was able to inform his superiors in the personnel bureau: "I have succeeded, privately, in obtaining a promise that a Jewish apartment will be liberated for me by a special measure, provided I repair it at the cost of 700 marks. . . . In view of the present crisis, I see no other way of finding a suitable apartment at a reasonable price. I do not have the 700 marks, and in this situation, I am requesting a special grant of 700 marks." The loan was approved, but before Rademacher could make use of it, early in 1938, Wilhelmstrasse transferred him to South America.

Rademacher's first assignment was Rio de Janeiro. Since the Reich had initially envisioned a Jewish national home in the Amazon, it was his responsibility to press the government for approval of German plans for Jewish emigration to Brazil. The project was dropped in its preliminary stages, but the flattering reports of Rademacher's efforts did not go unnoticed in Berlin. After Germany's march into Prague, in 1938, he was transferred to Montevideo, where he was involved in Germany's direct and largely successful effort to intervene in the domestic policies of Uruguay. But after a quarrel with an interned officer of the pocket battleship *Graf Spee*, he returned to Germany in April, 1940, at his own request.

The beginning of the war found Rademacher firmly established in the diplomatic ranks. Yet he preferred the active service and attempted to volunteer for the Kriegsmarine. Foreign Minister Joachim von Ribbentrop was so incensed by the near loss of one of his men to the Navy that he reassigned him, as punishment for his willfullness, to what seemed a relatively unexciting post in the Abteilung Deutschland, the Political Department, headed by Undersecretary Martin Luther. A former Dahlem furniture mover, Luther was an intimate and political ally of Von Ribbentrop, who capitalized on the friendship with his superior to accumulate power within the ministry. The Politische Abteilung chief immediately recognized his subordinate's potential and helped him move rapidly up the ladder. The thoroughness of Rademacher's work and the extreme care he took not to offend the wrong people assured his success. In June, he was appointed head of Referat DIII, the section handling Jewish affairs in Axis-occupied and satellite countries.

At the beginning of the war, Germany was still stumbling through the first phase of its "Solution of the Jewish Problem"—emigration from the Reich. The execution of this policy was overseen by the Reichssicherheitshauptamt (RSHA), the Main Security Office of the SS. Its Jewish Bureau IVB 4a, headed by Adolf Eichmann, together with Luther's department—particularly Referat DIII—decided upon the measures to be taken against the Jews outside Germany. Rademacher was entrusted with the administration of Jewish matters referred to the Foreign Ministry. The young diplomat immersed himself in his duties with such unusual enthusiasm that he soon became known as the omnipotent *Referent in Judensachen*, Chief of Jewish Affairs.

Among his first assignments was one of the most puzzling curiosities of the Nazi regime—the Madagascar Plan to resettle the Jews of Europe on the island of Madagascar, off the coast of Africa. Hitler, apparently still concerned about world opinion, had as yet rejected mass murder as a solution and was hoping to receive the wealth of the Jews in exchange for their lives. The Führer envisioned getting ransom payments for the émigrés from abroad in much desired foreign currency. After the fall of France, he took a personal interest in the proposal, causing the bureaucratic wheels to turn more quickly. A working plan prepared by the SS was eventually passed on to Von Ribbentrop to solve the political problems involved. The foreign minister instructed Luther to assign the project to Referat DIII. The eager Rademacher completed the task on July 3, 1940, submitting a memorandum "The Jewish Question for the Peace Treaty," which outlined the necessary diplomatic moves to be initiated as a preliminary step to institute the plan. In his *aide mémoire* he wrote:

> The imminent victory presents Germany with the possibility, and, according to my opinion, the obligation to solve the Jewish question. . . . The desirable solution [is to] remove all the Jews from Europe.
>
> * * *
>
> The peace treaty with France [shall contain] a clause whereby France is to put the isle of Madagascar at our disposal for the solution of the Jewish question . . . the approximately 25,000

Frenchmen domiciled there are to be evacuated and compensated. The island will be transferred to Germany as a mandate. . . . The part of the island that is not required for military reasons is to be put under the administration of a German Police Governor, who in turn shall be subordinated to the administration of the *Reichsführer* SS. Otherwise, the Jews will get autonomy in the territory: their own mayors, their own police, their own post and railway administration, etc. . . .

* * *

[The Jews] will remain under German domination as [hostages] for the future good behavior of their racial comrades in America.

* * *

This generosity shown to the Jews by Germany, in granting them cultural, economic, administrative and judicial autonomy, can be exploited from the point of view of propaganda.

With Luther's enthusiastic backing, Rademacher tenaciously set about promoting the idea which appeared to be on its way to success. Party officials jumped on the bandwagon, and the young bureaucrat's prestige rose along with the support for his proposals. Yet Rademacher was not caught short when the plan's death knell began to toll with victory in the East. On February 10, 1941, he wrote that the war with the Soviet Union had created new opportunities to end the Jewish problem. The Führer, he added, had decided in favor of the newly conquered Eastern territories as the future Jewish homeland. Late in the summer of that year, Luther echoed his *Referent* in a memo: "The Madagascar Plan," he noted, "in fact has been outdated as the result of political developments."

Rademacher's obvious talents for bureaucratic infighting were utilized by Luther to maintain his own standing in the Reich. The lives of the Jews would merely be the pawns in the deadly game of one-upmanship. On September 8, 1941, Edmund Vessenmayer, German roving ambassador in the Balkans, and Felix Benzler, minister plenipotentiary to the puppet government of Serbia, cabled the Foreign Ministry from Belgrade, accusing the Jews of sabotage and revolt and urging their deportation to Rumania. Luther was far from pleased with the diplomats' initiative and replied that the ministry deemed the suggestion inappropriate. The rejection did not inhibit Benzler and Vessenmayer. Within forty-eight hours, they wired another recommendation, insisting that a "quicker and draconian solution in Serbia is most urgent and a practical necessity. . . ." Deportation to the occupied territories in Russia or Poland was given as an alternative to the envoys' original proposal.

Luther, feeling pressured, turned the matter over to Rademacher for prompt action before the representatives in Belgrade could receive encouragement from a higher-up in the SS. Rademacher proposed they ask Eichmann's opinion and, with Luther's approval, called Bureau IVB 4a from his office. Eichmann listened quietly as the Vessenmayer-Benzler correspondence was read to him. Rademacher jotted down his remarks and handed the paper to his superior. The note read: "Eichmann says no possibility of reception in Russia and General Government [Poland]. Even German Jews cannot be disposed of there." He then scribbled on the margin of the telegram from Belgrade: *"Eichmann schlägt erschiessen vor* [Eichmann proposes shooting]."

In a memorandum to Luther written later that day, Rademacher concluded that deportation was unnecessary; the shooting of a large number of Jews would prove a satisfactory solution. On October 10, accompanied by two of Eichmann's key aides, Rademacher was dispatched to Belgrade, with instructions personally to "oversee the disposition of the problem." He spent four days in the Serbian capital. At a conference before returning to Berlin, he detailed the steps to be taken. "The males would be shot by the end of the week. . . . Women, children and old people, as well as 1,500 gypsies (except the men, who are to be shot) would be concentrated in a ghetto in the gypsy sector of Belgrade." They were to be given a minimum of food for the winter, and "as soon as the question of the Final Solution . . . was solved, and the technical means made available," they would be deported to the East. By May, 1942, Referat DIII could announce that "there was no longer a Jewish problem in Serbia."

Rademacher's list of accomplishments grew swiftly. When

asked whether it would be feasible to deport Rumanian, Slovak and Croation Jews living in Germany, he volunteered to take up the issue with the governments involved, "as a courtesy to Bureau IVB 4a." He swiftly completed the diplomatic arrangements and informed Eichmann that the three governments had consented to the expulsion of "their Jews living in Germany . . . to the ghettos of the East." This close collaboration with the SS would earn him the title of Eichmann's Negotiator.

At the beginning of 1942, Rademacher was preparing for a conference that would irrevocably resolve the "Jewish problem." The agenda he had received from the RSHA called for a discussion of the implementation of the Fuhrer's latest mandate—the physical annihilation of all Jews living under the control of the Third Reich.

The secret meeting opened promptly after a noon luncheon on January 20, in the offices of the RSHA, the former German Interpol headquarters, Am Grossen Wansee 50/58, a fashionable suburb of Berlin. Top police officials and fifteen directors general from various ministries listened as Reinhard Heydrich, the chief of the RSHA, emphasized the authority of the SS over Jewish matters. Heydrich, who had been appointed Commissioner for the Preparation of the Solution of the European Jewish Problem, noted that experiments with emigration in the West indicated the need for a more expedient method. The old policy had come to an end on the order of SS Reichsführer Heinrich Himmler. The Jews would now be deported to the East for eventual extermination. The new program was to be carried out in the countries under Nazi domination and, in addition, neutral Ireland, Spain, Sweden, Switzerland and Turkey. (According to Heydrich's figures, 11,000,000 Jews were scheduled for the Final Solution.) In the ensuing discussion over the political implications of the plan, Luther presented Rademacher's report, "Ideas and proposals of the Foreign Ministry for the Solution of the Jewish Problem in Europe." The Wansee Conference accepted all his recommendations.

When a second Final Solution Conference was called by

Adolf Eichmann on March 6, Rademacher was again invited to attend. This time the officials dealt with the problem of *Mischlinge*, products of mixed parentage and marriages. After brief deliberations, they concluded that the *Mischlinge* within the reproductive ages should be subject to sterilization, "which is to be considered a gracious favor." This decision raised the problem of dealing with more than 70,000 "tainted" persons. The conferees urged "divorce by compulsion" and the prohibition of marriage by children of mixed parentage. According to a later report Rademacher sent to Luther, the proposals became policy after a third Final Solution Conference, held in Berlin on October 27.

In the spring of 1943, Rademacher found his position jeopardized by an internecine struggle for power which would ultimately cause Luther's downfall. When a number of young *Referenten* who had been loyal to the head of the department came under investigation, he again requested permission to join the Kriegsmarine. This time he did not have to force his plea through channels; Von Ribbentrop arranged for the transfer without delay.[5] For the rest of the conflict, Rademacher served on a minesweeper; he saw action as a cadet and was eventually promoted to lieutenant.

On V-E Day, Rademacher's ship was lying in a Danish fjord. The British occupation forces commandeered its crew to clear the mines along the coast of Denmark. During one such mission, the vessel was slightly damaged and had to be docked for repairs. While the crew was interned at the Staumühle Center No. 5, Rademacher organized an underground information service for his fellow prisoners of war. But the camp authorities never discovered his real identity and finally released him with the rest of the naval personnel.

Rademacher settled under an assumed name in Hamburg, where he worked for a while at odd jobs. On September 2, 1947, the CIC of the American Seventh Army identified him as the former Foreign Ministry *Legationsrat* and sent a team of agents to arrest him at his home. But Army Secretary Kenneth

Royall's reluctance to allow the occupation forces to continue prosecuting those involved in the Final Solution spared Rademacher a summary trial. "He escaped prosecution," an observer remarked, "because he was needed as a witness in the Nuremberg Trials, and he avoided giving evidence because he was awaiting trial himself." A little less than a year after his arrest, however, the Department of the Army turned the Rademacher dossier over to the West German authorities.[6] Bonn decided to prosecute and transferred him from an Allied detention camp to the Nuremberg Prison. While completing the indictment, the Germans freed Rademacher on bail and on May 20, 1949, he was back in Hamburg looking for work. Within days, the former *Referent* was hired by the Hamburg cigarette magnate Phillip Reemstsma as his private secretary. Rademacher also resumed his political activities and began to write for the anti-Semitic tract *Die Anklage*. The Germans meanwhile had ended their investigation but scheduled no trial. Yet when pressure from Jewish organizations in the United States mounted, the Office of the High Commissioner complained, and a warrant for Rademacher's arrest was issued once again on March 18, 1951. There were more delays, but five months later he was behind bars.[7] It took still another two years before the case was aired.

On Monday, February 2, 1952, Rademacher finally came before a Nuremberg court. The three-judge tribunal and a jury of six were presided over by Landesgerichtsdirektor Wilhelm Schramm. In his opening brief, State Attorney Heinne contended that the defendant was responsible for the murder of more than 15,000 Serbian Jews and the deportation of 80,000 from Rumania and 108,000 from France, Belgium and Holland. Nearly all had been sent to the Auschwitz death camp, where more than 80 percent were gassed or shot. The accused denied the charges on all counts, placing the onus of guilt on his superiors—many dead or missing. And when incriminating documents he had signed were presented to the court, Rademacher blandly asserted, "It was my duty to write such letters."

The six-week trial did not cause much of a stir in Germany.

Thirty prosecution witnesses, among them a handful of former high officials in the Foreign Ministry, testified before an almost empty courtroom. On some days the only spectators were members of the press. They heard Rademacher claim that he had not been aware Auschwitz was a death camp; he had always understood the deported Jews "were building roads and working in factories." Rademacher remained unmoved even when a defense witness, Dr. Paul Schmidt, former press attaché in the Auswärtige Amt, told the court that all German diplomats had been informed about the SS plans for the mass execution of the Jews of Europe long before the program was carried out and that the Wansee Protocol had been circulated at the time throughout the ministry.

Prosecutor Hans Güttler listened to the repeated denials, then presented a final piece of evidence—an expense account, headed "Liquidation of Jews," prepared by Rademacher upon his return from Belgrade. At this point, the defendant broke down. He admitted to knowledge of extermination plans and conceded giving false testimony. The defense counsel, Dr. Hans Tipp-Fürth, an experienced war crimes attorney, attempted to change the direction of the trial. He asserted his client was merely following orders and carrying out national policy. The judges, however, were unyielding in their refusal to widen the issue. Güttler, in turn, contended Rademacher had based his defense on "a notorious series of lies," and demanded a sentence of life imprisonment. On March 17 the jury brought in a verdict of guilty. "It is difficult to believe that Rademacher, in his pose as *Judenreferent*, did not know what was really happening," stated Judge Schramm in issuing sentence. "His expense account showed that he knew very well the fate of the Jewish victims. . . . He seems to have been fully aware of the fact that the Jews whom he was deporting were being taken to extermination camps." The court sentenced Rademacher to three years and five months' imprisonment—three years for the killing of the Serbian Jews and five months for the deportation of the Belgian Jews. The Rumanian charges had been previously dismissed for lack of evidence. With the twenty-nine months

Rademacher had already spent in jail taken into account, he was due to be released in a half year.

The outcome of the trial aroused the emotions of both Jews and Germans and was seen in certain quarters as an indication of things to come. "It is a bad omen for what sentences on war criminals will look like after the whole affair is handed over to the Germans," predicted the World Jewish Congress. The German press criticized the court's justification for the brief prison term ("there had been no base motives behind Rademacher's actions") and advocated the state seek a stiffer punishment. The prosecution decided to appeal, while Dr. Tipp-Fürth, encouraged by the leniency of the sentence, felt he could do even better. He filed a counterappeal, hoping to secure his client's immediate release. In July, however, the Bundes- gerichtshof (Supreme Court) ordered a new trial, scoring the judge's permissiveness and referring the case to a different court.[8] Rademacher was again freed on bail.

Because of a growing outcry against the rise of neo-Nazism in Germany, Rademacher believed he might not fare as well in a second trial and decided to leave the country. He had no one to care for; his wife and two of their five children who survived the war had left him and were living in East Germany. A close friend, Robert Kramer, publisher of *Die Anklage*, undertook to arrange the escape. The ODESSA underground, engaged in spiriting out ex-Nazis facing federal charges, helped Rademacher flee to Monaco in the first week of August. After a short stopover in Monte Carlo, he moved on to Marseilles. A local agent in the French port took him to the Spanish consulate, where he was issued a passport in the name of Thom Rosello. He then obtained a Lebanese visa under that alias and sailed for Cairo via Beirut.[9]

Sporting a bushy mustache which made him look ten years younger, Rademacher arrived in the Egyptian capital to find that his trial had caused an uproar in the German community. (The neo-Nazi periodical *Deutsche Ehre* had jubilantly called his escape "an extraordinary feat of rescue from the clutches of the

Jewish jackals.") Many of the Nazis who had found refuge in Egypt rushed to greet him with offers of sanctuary and a variety of positions in the government. None of these posts, however, attracted his interest. He was neither a soldier nor a propagandist, he asserted, and would not be comfortable in either of the two careers open to Germans. Rademacher eventually decided Egypt was not a suitable place to establish roots and left for Syria.

Safely ensconced in Damascus, he attempted to make a place for himself in Syrian society. Once again, there were difficulties. He established an import-export firm in the capital; but conditions were not favorable, and the venture failed. Deeply discouraged, he wrote in June, 1955, to the West German government, declaring his willingness to surrender, "if I am granted safe conduct to Germany." The letter was posted in Cairo and addressed to the German ambassador in Egypt. No return address was included. Speculation had it that Rademacher was fearful for his life in Syria; another theory held that he merely intended to sidetrack German investigators by planting the notion he was still living in Egypt.

Whatever plans Rademacher had of returning to Germany were disrupted by the 1956 Sinai campaign. The Suez clash worked to his benefit. The diplomats of the Von Ribbentrop school were now following the Wehrmacht advisers into Syrian government service. With his specialized background in Jewish affairs, Rademacher found his star shining brightly. The Second Bureau offered to employ him as special adviser to the Palestine Department.

His rise in stature, though easing whatever fears he may have had, did break his cloak of anonymity. News of his current role began to filter back to Bonn. Near the end of 1957, Arabs studying in West Germany publicly admitted Rademacher was holding "a high position with the Syrian government." The Bamberg District Court at once issued a warrant for his arrest, while the federal police renewed the investigation and asked Interpol to locate the fugitive. The Bavarian Ministry of Justice even considered making a request for extradition, and in 1958 the federal government started planning the move. But a realistic appraisal of the Syrian political situation clearly showed that any efforts to obtain such action would meet only with failure. At the moment Rademacher was too important to the UAR government. Since he was considered a Spanish citizen, the Syrians could use his cover as a ground for refusing extradition. Bonn subsequently decided to allow matters to continue as they were, but instructed the legation in Damascus to keep a close eye on him.

In the early 1960's Rademacher again dropped out of sight. He moved to a different section of the city, broke off all ties with the German colony and lived in seclusion with a mistress. He remained in the pay of the Second Bureau, but German agents ostensibly were unable to locate him, although he was still using the name Rosello. Two possibilities were broached, both leading to the conclusion that the Germans were not really interested in bringing him to justice. A diplomatic source in Bonn told the authors: "We had more important things to do than find Rademacher." Another theory never explicitly denied by German officials was that Rademacher had been working as an agent of the "Gehlen Organization," the West German foreign intelligence agency. He had been allegedly recruited with the promise that extradition efforts would be discontinued and the Bavarian authorities would drop plans for his prosecution.

It was during this period of isolation that the name Rosello was first mentioned to Eli by Sheik al-Ard.

After amassing the report on Rademacher, the Center radioed Eli to investigate Rosello as thoroughly as possible but warned him to be cautious with the sheik and, above all, not to endanger his ultimate mission. Upon receiving the order, Eli called al-Ard to ask his advice on a business matter and near the end of the conversation remarked that he was looking forward to meeting the sheik's German friend, "who had fought the Jews during the Great War." Al-Ard said he would try to contact Rosello as soon as possible. On the following morning, the sheik phoned that arrangements had been made for Friday afternoon.

Al-Ard arrived in Abu Rummaneh at 3:30 P.M. Eli kept the talk casual as they drove the short distance over the Nabek Bridge into the fashionable Jisr district. The Peugeot stopped in front of a modern three-story white-stone building at 18 Abdul Rahman al-Chabander Street between the Syrian Bank and the Girls' Teachers College. A carefully landscaped garden surrounded the apartment house. In the lobby the sheik rang the bell under "T. Rosello." With the answering buzz, they began to climb the three flights.

A thin, balding and well-dressed man received them at the door. Behind him stood an attractive woman, obviously not Arab, of about the same age. The man momentarily eyed Eli, then invited them inside with a traditional *marchaba t'fadalu* spoken with an unmistakable German accent. The sheik introduced Kamal Amin Taabet. Accepting his outstretched hand, the host answered, "Rosello." Al-Ard, who had stood by smiling, benignly placed an arm around Eli's shoulder and remarked that Taabet was a faithful friend who could be trusted. "You may tell him your true name without fear," the sheik added. Apparently reassured, Rosello bowed with Prussian correctness and responded, "Rademacher, Franz Rademacher."[10]

The formal barriers removed, Rademacher's companion served Turkish coffee. Between the sips of thick, sweet brew, the conversation flowed easily to personal matters. Rademacher described at length the life he led as an émigré in the Damascus Nazi colony. His list of acquaintances was impressive—the German diplomat Otto von Hentig, Wehrmacht Colonel Rainer Kriebel, adviser to the Syrian Army, Eichmann's aide Alois Brunner and Hadj Amin al-Husseini, the Grand Mufti of Jerusalem. Eli sensed that Rademacher was relieved to talk with people he could trust, and al-Ard's assurance was seemingly enough excuse to pour out his bitterness and self-pity before a stranger. "The Jews and West Germans look for me everywhere," he blurted at one point. "They accuse me of having killed Jews during the war. But here in Damascus," he added for the benefit of the two Arabs, "I am relatively safe and permitted to hold an honorable post."[11] Rademacher avoided mentioning, however, the precise nature of his work. Eli, careful lest he show excessive interest, asked no questions. Before they left, Rademacher expressed the hope of a future meeting. Eli was delighted to accept. The sheik appeared pleased that his friends had been able to get along so well. It added to his standing with both.

In the early morning of the next day Eli transmitted the coded details of his encounter with Rademacher. Tel Aviv replied: "R. was one of Eichmann's aides. Continue surveillance. Send supplementary information." In a second report from Eli regarding Rademacher, the final sentence read: "Offer myself to liquidate R." The Mosad's ambiguous reply was: "Avoid any action on R. which could jeopardize principal mission."[12]

In a later message, Eli suggested that Rademacher be disposed of by means of an "explosive letter" (a deadly incendiary device developed by Israeli intelligence). One evening, following an affirmative answer from Mosad headquarters, he sat at his dining room table mixing chemicals. After liquefying a fine powder by heat, he thoroughly coated the inside of an envelope with the substance, inserted a tiny detonator and sealed it by a special process. That same night, he dropped the letter-bomb addressed to Thom Rosello into the "Damascus Only" slot at the main post office near the Serail. On the following afternoon the phone awakened Eli from his midday nap. It was the sheik, who blurted out that "the Jews have finally gotten Rademacher." Taabet expressed shock and asked for more details. The German, al-Ard related, had received a bomb in the mail which when opened, exploded in his face; he was rushed to the Municipal Hospital, but the sheik knew nothing about his present condition. As soon as al-Ard hung up, Eli consulted the phone book and dialed the hospital's number. Asking for patient information, he inquired about the condition of a T.

Rosello. A friend, he added, wished to know. After a pause, the clerk informed him that *Said* Rosello had been "slightly injured but was out of danger.*

*Rademacher soon recovered from his wounds, but the disclosures at the Cohen trial had again brought him into the limelight. On March 19, he was arrested by the Second Bureau, charged with espionage for Israel (Syrian counterespionage built up a case of guilt by association) and publicly denounced as a threat to national security. While awaiting trial in al-Mazza, Rademacher asked the West German consul for aid. But when told that Bonn would help only if he returned home and stood trial for war crimes, he decided to take his chances with Syrian justice. Rademacher would not regret this decision. The evidence of his innocence overwhelmed whatever case the government could present; he was acquitted but not reinstated to his post. On September 30, Rademacher left Damascus for Munich. His plane, however, was mysteriously diverted to Nuremberg. As it landed, the Federal police welcomed Rademacher with a warrant for his arrest. When finally brought to trial on March 21, 1968, he pleaded not guilty to all charges, testifying that he had tried to help the Jews whenever he could, even to the point of disputing Eichmann. After three-month-long proceedings, a Bamberg court sentenced him to five years' imprisonment, asserting that he had not played a major role in the extermination of European Jewry. The forty-nine months he had been in custody since the end of World War II were to be taken into account, and Rademacher was released to join his mistress in Bad Godesberg.

11
The Corporal

The 7 P.M. news broadcast on Sunday, March 8, 1962, had been over but a short time when Eli was alerted by a special bulletin: "Today our valiant soldiers have inflicted a poignant defeat to the armies of the Zionist enemy. [Our units] have damaged the Zionist vessels of war on the Tiberias Lake. The enemy has suffered heavy losses and has retreated before the Syrian Army." Eli was by now reaccustomed to the florid language of Arab news commentators, but the announcement aroused his interest. He had heard a markedly different version on the morning program of Kol Israel.[1] Jerusalem reported that the Syrians opened fire without provocation on fishermen laying their nets in the northeastern sector of the Sea of Galilee, which the Moslems call Tiberias Lake and the Hebrews Yam Kinneret.

Since the Israeli-Syrian Armistice Agreement was signed on July 9, 1949, exchanges of fire between Syrian military positions and Israeli patrol boats had been commonplace in this most coveted fishing ground where the border line runs parallel, 10 meters from the water's edge. (The entire Sea of Galilee is in Israeli territory.) The Syrian National Guard, posted at fortifications which stretch along 5 kilometers of hills overlooking the water, kept Israeli fishermen under constant surveillance, occasionally harassing them by firing on their armed escorts. Syrian fishermen periodically took to the lake under military cover in an effort to establish fishing rights by their presence. Damascus had always argued that villagers living along the eastern shore had the right to draw water and fish by virtue of a Franco-British agreement signed in 1923. Israel rejected this convention, yet offered to issue individual permits to Syrians through the United Nations Mixed Armistice Commission. Fearing such requests would imply recognition of Israeli authority in the area, Damascus categorically refused, and Syrian fishermen continued to cast their nets in the Kinneret in search of the Galilean haddock, famous since Biblical times as St. Peter's fish.

At the beginning of the fishing season (which lasts from November through April) an Israeli patrol had spotted fifteen boats ready to be launched. Modiin reconnaissance units of the Northern Command were sent to investigate and brought back information that the Syrian Army had guaranteed protection to Arab fishermen. The Israeli police dispatched a number of patrol boats into the sector, forcing the Syrian Southern Command to reconsider and order the fishermen to stay out. The Israelis then relaxed their vigilance, and fishing was resumed under the watch of a single police vessel. But Wednesday night, March 4, a launch had been caught in the flare of a probing searchlight and was strafed by machine guns; only a sudden storm ended the incident.[2]

A little before five o'clock on Sunday morning, as the mists were beginning to fade, a small fleet of Israeli fishing boats from Kibbutz Ein Gev started spreading heavy nets along the northeastern shore. An armed launch that had been scurrying swiftly back and forth moved closer into position offshore to protect them. The commander, Shariv Nadav, stood on the bridge as usual, scanning the hills with his binoculars. "The area seemed quiet, almost peaceful," he later recalled, "but I sensed something strange in the air." Syrian soldiers in the entrenchments of Nukeib were observing them go about their duties. Suddenly there was a whirring sound, followed by an explosion. Nadav speeding perilously toward shore. For a grim moment he considered the alternatives, then spun the wheel a full turn, bringing the launch around sharply, its bow canting upward in the water, averting the crash that seemed imminent.

Nadav had seen the shell strike. "It was much more powerful than the mortar projectiles we were used to," he explained. Two of his men, somehow uninjured, struggled to their feet as the piercing blasts of the boat's alarm began to sound. The trigger-tense Syrians now began spraying the deck with machine-gun fire. One of the crew, Benjamin Zered, ran to the engine room, but before he could reach the safety of the stern's armed protection, a second shell landed directly in his path, severing one of his legs. A shocked second passed before Nadav calmly replied to Zered's painful cry for help: "We will take care of you as soon as we get out of range." A moment later the commander was wounded in both knees. Using his elbows, he dragged himself to the wheel and steered the craft out of the bay. Crew members who rushed to his side were ordered to aid Zered first. Nadav finally turned over the wheel to Hanan Nol and gave himself an injection of morphine.

When the pain eased, the launch commander instructed his radio operator, Hilel Minster, to summon assistance. In its flight out of the range of the Syrian guns, the boat had been pushed beyond its capacity, burning out one of the two motors. Slowed almost to a stop, it floated haphazardly while the crew tried to put out the fire on deck. The fishermen, who had sought refuge deeper at sea, were looking on helplessly. In the opposite direction, two United Nations observers stationed at Post Fox tried in vain to establish the exact location of the incident. They could not see Nukeib but had heard six explosions and identified the sound of heavy machine guns. Unable to investigate further (as regulations prohibited them from moving more than 50 meters from the wooden watchtower without a Syrian liaison officer), they radioed UN Headquarters in Jerusalem that an exchange of fire was taking place somewhere in the vicinity

were still waiting for help. A half hour later they finally spotted
another launch cutting a path toward them. The vessel took the
stricken craft in tow, pulled it clear of the danger zone and led
the fishing boats to safety.[3]

The clash, Eli learned, had evoked intense and heated debates
at the weekly meeting of the Israeli Cabinet that Sunday afternoon, but the statement later issued in Jerusalem by the
Council of Ministers was vague. The Cabinet merely agreed to
"take the necessary measures to assure that such incidents
would not be repeated." Eli, nevertheless, decided to investigate the political and military aspects of the crisis, and, if
successful, radio his findings. On Monday morning, he called
Kamal al-Hashan and arranged to meet him in the afternoon.
During their conversation Eli mentioned "the incident in the
news," offered a layman's analysis of the military situation on
the border and asked al-Hashan's opinion on the previous day's
events. When the attorney appeared to avoid the subject, Eli
immediately let the matter drop.[4]

Throughout the week he monitored café conversation and
spent the rest of the time at the window of his apartment,
observing activities at the General Staff Headquarters. He stayed
at this post intermittently for three days and nights. On Thursday, there was an abrupt change in the normal pattern of
arrivals and departures. Chauffeured limousines, both military
and civilian, began arriving in increasing numbers; staff officers
and high-ranking government officials remained in their rooms
throughout the night. Rumors, as usual, were rife in the capital.
One of Eli's friends assured him that a military coup was in the
making. The officers involved, the informant said, planned to
take advantage of the border tension to gain public support for
the Army and utilize the movement of troops to carry out the
actual plot. Eli learned from another source that Colonel Abd
al-Krim an-Nahlawi, who had backed the civilian government
since he helped initiate the break with Nasser, was growing
impatient with the parliamentary system of President Nazem
al-Kudsi and what he described as the "incompetent ministers"

of Premier Maaruf al-Dawalibi. Nahlawi, a moderate rightist, was heading a power struggle against both the Socialist officers in the Southern Command and the pro-Nasserites at the Homs and Aleppo posts. In addition, his strongest ally, Colonel Abd al-Ghani Dahman, commander of the Damascus Garrison, controlled the key armor division. Eli also discovered through Maazi that his uncle, the commander in chief, Lieutenant General Abd al-Krim Zaher ad-Din, was still indecisive. The Syrian press added to the confusion. Its impassioned editorials on the "Zionist danger"—the first warlike appeal to public opinion since Eli's arrival in the capital—appeared to be preparing the people for renewed hostilities with Israel.[5] But as long as Zaher ad-Din withheld his support or backed the opponents of Nahlawi, Eli decided a takeover was highly improbable.

The activity he had been able to observe and the information he gathered supported Eli's deduction that the Syrians were not preparing for a full-scale war. He had verified the fact that the Damascus Garrison had been put on alert and the Southern Command was ordered to take precautions against an Israeli retaliatory operation. In other areas, though, only a partial mobilization had been taking place. On the morning of March 13 Eli finally coded a message to his superiors, then retrieved the tiny transmitter from its hiding place in the ceiling, connected it to the Phillips and the antenna, and clicked out his code number. Within seconds the prearranged signal returned from Tel Aviv. Eli tapped out a situation report, stressing the unusual movement of troops in the capital. He informed Tel Aviv about the emergency alert of the Damascus Garrison and pointing to the virulent anti-Israeli attacks in the press, summed up with "border attack most probable," and signed off.[6] Tel Aviv acknowledged and requested more data on the general climate.

The information that the premier and defense minister, David Ben-Gurion, received from intelligence sources was enough to cause mounting concern and spur the prime minister to call a special session of the Cabinet to discuss what action, if any, Israel should take in case Syrian attacks were intensified. Ben-Gurion phoned his ministers and set a meeting for the morning of March 11. "Conditions on the Syrian border" was the only item listed on the council's agenda. The ministers considered two major questions: Was the Kinneret incident just another manifestation of the continuing tension that had existed in the area for the last thirteen years, or was it a new development of much greater significance? Had the attack been planned in Damascus as part of a propaganda campaign to show the Arab world that Syria, not Egypt, was most active in the anti-Israel struggle and therefore the country to look to for leadership? Political analyses and intelligence data were evaluated, but after a heated debate the Cabinet referred the matter to the Knesset Committee for National Defense, which had full powers to determine the approach to be followed. The official statement was laconic: "The government considers the situation on the northern border as extremely grave."

The four-man parliamentary committee headed by Ben-Gurion met the same night to examine the problem. The prime minister wanted Zahal to retaliate at once, but his three colleagues recommended patience. Ben-Gurion argued in vain that the Syrians were planning a series of skirmishes that could lead to a more decisive confrontation. With three votes against the premier's proposal, the committee decided to let Damascus take the next step.[7] Should the Kinneret incident be followed by a similar one, Israel would respond with force.

In the meantime, the intelligence community intensified its surveillance of Syrian affairs. The day after the Center near Tel Aviv decoded Eli's message, Modiin informed the Operations Division of the Matkal (General Staff) of "heavy concentrations of troops and armor behind the Syrian lines and a steady movement of equipment on the Damascus-Kuneitra highway in the direction of the Golan Heights." Pikud Zafon (the Northern Command) was ordered to dispatch a scouting party to infiltrate the Syrian lines and confirm the intelligence. The patrol commander reported that a large number of tanks and armored vehicles had been brought up to the fortifications overlooking the Kinneret while elements of the Third Battalion of the Second Brigade had been spread along the line as reinforcements for the National Guard.

The General Staff viewed the buildup with alarm and, on March 14, reinforced all units along the Syrian border from Tel Dan to Tawfik.[8] Israeli intelligence had concluded that the Syrians were, in fact, preparing for a confrontation with Zahal in the area. Damascus was thought to have envisioned more attacks on fishermen so it could again raise the question of Israel's sovereignty over the lake before the United Nations. The Israeli government was now convinced that Syria sought a full-scale encounter to bring about new UN arbitration of the disputed border territories.

Late in the afternoon, conflicting complaints reached the Tiberias office of the Israel-Syrian Mixed Armistice Commission (MAC). When the chief of staff of the UN Forces, Major General Carl Carlson von Horn, was told about the attack, he immediately called the Swedish MAC chairman, Commander O. W. Melin, and asked that observers visit the site of the conflict on both sides of the border. The investigation of his blue-bereted observers was inconclusive. "There was no evidence of brewing trouble," Von Horn later wrote. "Whatever my own 'sixth sense,' I did not see this new incident as anything more than sudden thunder on the Sea of Galilee."

The Israelis, however, were apprehensive that the situation might easily deteriorate. On the morning of the ninth, Foreign Minister Golda Meir summoned Von Horn to her office in the Jerusalem Kiria. Chain-smoking in her oversized chair, she advised the general that Israel regarded the attack as extremely critical. "Tell them," the foreign minister warned in her booming voice, "that they are playing with fire." Von Horn, infuriated by her less-than-diplomatic orders, almost lost his Swedish placidity. He remarked that she could hardly expect the UNTSO chief of staff to act as "a post boy for messages that might be construed as open or implied threats." He had been assigned to the trouble spot, he told her, to keep the peace, not provoke hostilities. Recognizing that her warning was likely to produce a strong reaction, Golda Meir reassured the general that she had no other intention but to make her views clear. As the Israelis had no direct line of communication with the Syrians, Von Horn unbent somewhat and promised to inform Damascus.

Since Commander Melin was headquartered in the Syrian capital, the Israeli delegation could meet with him only on his occasional visits to Tiberias. Therefore, Foreign Minister Meir's message had to be radioed to Melin, who in turn saw the chief of staff, General Namek Kamal, on March 10. The Syrian reply came in the morning. Two police boats escorting fishermen were machine-gunned from entrenchments in Mussadiyeh, between al-Kursi and the mouth of the Jordan. Von Horn's Blue Berets were again unable to establish which side shot first; during the twenty-five minute exchange, they merely heard the sound of gunfire. The Syrians told the MAC that Israeli launches had fired upon their positions with Bren guns and 20 mm cannons. The Israelis reported fire from automatic and antitank weapons. The only evidence of a skirmish was an injured Syrian girl, who later died from her wounds.

While Damascus lodged a formal complaint, Jerusalem decided to go a step beyond by appealing to the UN Secretary-General. Golda Meir asked U Thant to intervene, emphasizing with deliberate understatement that unless he did, "the matter could become more serious." Characteristically, the Secretary-General first requested more information about the dispute from Von Horn. But before U Thant could act, a second duel took place on the Sea of Galilee. During the early hours of March 16 an Israeli launch was shot at from Kafr Akeb, near al-Kursi. In Jerusalem, Foreign Minister Meir had fired another message to U Thant demanding to know whether the latest attack was Syria's answer to the authority of the United Nations. The direct appeal came after Moshe Erell, her director of Armistice Affairs, and his counterpart from the General Staff, Colonel Yaakov Monbaz, senior delegate and chief liaison officer to the UN, had been unable to reach General Von Horn. But UNTSO's staff was deliberately keeping the general in the dark about the latest developments in the mounting crisis; Von Horn, who had lost his wife a day earlier, was attending her funeral in Bethlehem, Jordan. The two Israeli officials were given no choice but to discuss that morning's events with UN subordinates, and on such a level, a consultation proved fruitless. It was this local indecisiveness which prompted Golda Meir to wire New York.

Reports of troop movements on both sides now flooded the MAC. It became obvious that a buildup was in progress. On the Israeli side, the Blue Berets were barred from strategic positions. Commander Melin also reported a distinct hardening of the Syrian attitude; despite pleas from liaison officers, local commanders had refused the United Nations access to potential danger zones. "It was quite obvious to all our observers in Tiberias, Kuneitra, Damascus and Jerusalem," Von Horn later wrote, "that both sides were moving toward a head-on clash."[9]

David Ben-Gurion had just finished his morning yoga exercises when the first sounds of the Syrian guns swept across the lake. The prime minister slowly put on his robe, walked over to the window and, looking out onto the lake, growled: "We must put an end to this!" His wife, Pola, who had been watching, reproached him for even thinking about government duties during his vacation. It had taken much prodding to convince the stubborn septuagenarian to take a respite from his heavy schedule. The prime minister was not an easy man to look after. The only thing planned on his workday was breakfast; his other meal hours were as uncertain as his bedtime. But no retinue of aides could have protected the Old Man's health as well as his dark-haired, animated Pola. She had to impose her will on occasion, but when she argued, he usually obeyed. As February gave way to March, Pola realized her husband was on the verge of collapse. This time she insisted that he take a weekend off, but the situation on the border would not allow the prime minister to be absent from his Jerusalem office. He protested, and Pola practically had to whisk him away to their favorite retreat, the Galei Kinneret Hotel in Tiberias—the only place where he could relax completely.

That March 16 the Ben-Gurions took breakfast in their room. The prime minister repeatedly asked Pola to call his military adjutant, but she promised to comply only after he had finished eating. At eight thirty, Colonel Haim Ben David was finally permitted to see the premier, who instructed him to contact the Northern Command and request details about the skirmish. *Aluf* (Brigadier General) Meir Zorea was quick to call back with a full report. A morning message about another skirmish had roused him from bed and after hasty investigation had sent him rushing to his headquarters. Ben-Gurion listened carefully, asked a few questions, thanked Zorea and hung up.

Meanwhile, Colonel Ben David was trying to reach the *ramatkal* (chief of staff), Lieutenant General Zvi Zur. Ben-Gurion himself phoned Golda Meir to inquire about UN activities in the area. At 10 A.M. Modiin chief Meir Amit and the *memune*, Iser Harel, were ordered to Tiberias for an urgent meeting. By 2 P.M. the minister of defense and his two intelligence chiefs were huddled in conference with the chief of staff and General Zorea. As always when planning an important move, Ben-Gurion thought best on his feet. He paced back and forth across the room while talking, occasionally relaxing in a chair. "The Old Man looked somewhat drawn and nervous," one of the officers recalled, "although he was in excellent physical condition for a man of seventy-five." The youthful walk and alert eyes contrasted strongly with his harsh, wrinkled face, sheathed by the famous crop of white hair. Ben-Gurion listened carefully to intelligence reports, then analyzed the political situation: He had made up his mind—in compliance, of course, with the decision of the Knesset Foreign Affairs and Security Committee—to retaliate forcefully against the Syrian emplacements on the eastern shore. When he asked Zur whether Zahal could successfully perform such a mission, the chief of staff replied the operation. The general answered with a clipped *muchan!* (Ready!). Zur then suggested Nukeib as the target. Ben-Gurion quickly agreed. One of the generals hesitated, and others voiced objections. But the Old Man was impatient with vacillation and did not tolerate intimations of dissent. He said, "It will be Nukeib," and closed the session.[10]

An hour after he had left the Galei Kinneret Hotel, Major General Zorea called his staff together to plan the operation. With Chief of Staff Zvi Zur at his side, Zorea led the conversation through the maze of diverging views until, gradually, a definite plan took shape. "Nukeib was a difficult objective," Zorea later admitted. Situated on the summit of a hill, the outpost's forbidding terrain alone could have held off an attacker. In addition, the Southern Command had organized its defenses according to the Russian system of three concentric rings spread over an area of 300 square meters. The outer circle consisted of six bunkers with emplacements for Gorianov machine guns and a B-10 recoilless cannon, connected by trenches dug deep into the rock and protected by a semicircle of minefields only open in the rear. Its destruction demanded unorthodox tactics and a quick bold strike.

General Zorea's plan to capture Nukeib was marked by the audacity which characterized his previous campaigns. The attacking force was divided into four groups: Force A was to destroy the entrenchments near the village of Nukeib South; Force B would secure the village itself; Force C, which had been split into two sections, was to block the road to Bir as-Shkum, north of Nukeib, and cut off the eastern route to Kuneitra; Force D would be kept in reserve ready to support the other detachments. After reviewing the plan once more, the general gave his officers the go-ahead.

Zorea's staff set out to reconnoiter the objective. A boat took them to a point 300 meters off the coast from where they examined Nukeib. They studied the roads leading to the village

Command sent out a patrol on a final reconnaissance mission. A last-minute check of Syrian forces completed, Zorea was notified that conditions on the northeastern front had not changed. He only then allowed the colonel in charge of the retaliatory forces to alert the officers of the Sayeret, the commando battalion of the Golani Brigade, and support units. "When I received the order to prepare for an operation in enemy territory," Sayeret commander Major Zvi Ofer later recalled, "I alerted my men . . . even before I was given full details. It was a race against time. [The men] were already on the trucks that would take them to Kibbutz Ein Gev when their officers issued final orders." It was nearly 9 P.M. when the blacked-out convoy of jeeps, ambulances and half-tracks mounted on platforms led by a command car with lights on, entered the kibbutz's courtyard.

At 10:15 the colonel ordered the Sayeret into a corner of the vast Ein Gev amphitheater. The briefing was short: They were to "attack the village of Nukeib South and destroy the positions around it"; radio silence would be imposed until H hour, which had been set for 11 P.M. The colonel concluded with a warning not to fire upon women and children. A quarter of an hour later the lights were turned off in all Israeli settlements on the eastern shore.[11] Since blackouts were always in effect during artillery bombardments, the Syrians were not expected to be aroused by the sudden darkness.

Force A was still getting ready to leave when the colonel's courier arrived with the message to move out. Major Ofer gave the order and took the lead, sending ahead two guides the kibbutz had supplied. It was only a distance of 3½ kilometers in a straight line from Ein Gev's eastern gate to the target, but rather than follow the shorter coastal route, Ofer took a long detour, turning to the hills. The company filed rapidly along the dirt road which crossed a huge banana grove and soon passed the marker of the international border line. As he reached the slopes, Ofer decided intuitively to choose a more strenuous climb. "For some odd reason," he later explained, "I felt it much safer for tactical purposes." At the top, he diverted one platoon to the original course. A short time afterward a burst of fire was heard from the direction the unit had taken. Ofer's major force had narrowly escaped an ambush.

Force B, led by the thirty-two-year-old Major Benyamin Anbar, had left Ein Gev only minutes after Ofer, making its way north along the asphalt road. While still in Israel, some ten minutes from the village of Nukeib South, a scout halted the column. As he advanced to reconnoiter the field, a flare burst directly above their heads, followed by a volley of bullets. The men scurried for cover. Anbar judged that three light machine guns and seven or eight rifles fired upon them from a range of 150 meters. Since the surprise factor had already been lost, he decided to break radio silence and requested permission to liquidate the ambush; the colonel consented and set back H hour by twenty minutes. Shelled by mortars and fired upon from two sides, the enemy retreated.

To regain some advantage, Anbar led his troops into Nukeib from the north, instead of the east, as originally planned. He found that the inhabitants, some eighty families, had begun fleeing soon after stray shells had landed on several houses. Their flight made the capture of the village a simple matter; it would, however, complicate the mission of Major Ofer and his men.

Force C had just moved into its assigned position to cut off the retreat north when a mounted patrol of seven national guardsmen rode straight into its roadblock, only to be routed by superior firepower. Force D, the motorized reserve unit which had left the kibbutz last, heard the exchange as it drove with lights off along the lake road. After passing Ein Gev's marked minefields, the column turned toward a prebattle position where it would await the strike order. As soon as the half-tracks veered into the fields, explosions echoed from under six vehicles. they had entered a recently planted minefield of which intelligence had known nothing. In keeping with radio silence, a command car was dispatched to Ein Gev to borrow a tractor and a bulldozer from the kibbutz to clear a path through the slope and extricate the half-tracks, but both machines were immobilized by a mine. In a desperate effort to rescue the column, combat engineers resorted to digging out mines by hand but soon realized they were hopelessly mired. The minefield had been laid too intricately to allow for quick evacuation. The engineers managed to tow only two half-tracks back to Ein Gev; the tractor and four others were blown up and left behind. The colonel could only hope that there would be no need for reserves to aid the attacking forces.

By now Ofer had also heard the battle starting prematurely on both his flanks and decided to attack. He was about to shout the order to fire when he spotted the villagers, fleeing Anbar's forces, entering the narrow path between his men and the Syrian fortifications. For an electric moment, Ofer pondered whether to open fire. He could not order an attack, he later said, "without killing them all," and passed on the word to wait. The Syrians, however, had by now become aware of Ofer's exact position, and they began shooting wildly. Although he was outside the range of fire, a stray bullet felled one of the lieutenants, but Ofer stubbornly waited until the last villager had walked by his left flank before starting the assault with the order *Kadima aharai* (Forward, after me).

The Syrian commander called for a withering mortar barrage, momentarily halting Ofer's advance, yet a few rounds of Uzi submachine guns enabled the company to reach the barbed wire fence. The men tried to blast an opening with a bungalor, which failed to go off. They finally had to use the old infantry expedient of two men throwing themselves across the wire, to allow the others to break through.

The Syrians had come out of their initial impasse relatively fast. "In the command bunker," Private Ahmad Yechia Hussein later recounted, "the corporal ran to the phone and shouted, 'The Jews are coming, the Jews are coming!' . . . then everybody fired and the whole thing started. . . . Suddenly somebody passed me running and shouting that they had overtaken us." The lieutenant in command, a corporal, and Hussein hovered in the bunker. The battle was raging for some time when the phone rang. Hussein heard the officer argue with the party on the other end before he was disconnected. There was a second ring; the lieutenant tried to answer but was killed while reaching for the receiver. Seeing him fall, the corporal fled. Hussein picked up the phone. It was his colonel. "I told him that we had been taken," Hussein explained, "but he insisted that we stay and fight. 'Don't leave your post until death!' the colonel shouted and hung up."

The national guardsmen were putting up a determined stand in the outer ring. One squad had been battling fiercely to hold open the perimeter of their escape route, but Ofer easily destroyed their southern flank. He fought his way in hand-to-hand combat from trench to trench. When another of his lieutenants was shot, Ofer took charge of his platoon and broke into the second ring. He was greeted by a cluster of hand grenades. A number of Syrians defended their foxholes with bayonets and daggers. Said Ofer later, "We took every inch and held it with our teeth."

The platoon fighting from the south was advancing slowly, while the one coming from the north was being held up by heavy fire. Unable to complete the pincers movement, Ofer radioed Anbar for help. The commander of Force B had just given the order to dynamite the buildings used by the Syrian Army when Ofer requested assistance. He had encountered virtually no resistance in the village. A machine gun blazing from one of the houses had been quickly silenced, strongholds on the western edge had been eradicated, and the men had swept through to the other end. Anbar arrived within minutes and attacked the outpost from the east. At one point, he was so close to Ofer that the two exchanged shouts to prevent their men from firing on each other.

The Israelis now closed in from all sides. By the time the last bunkers were being cleared their ammunition was running low. They picked up Russian weapons from the dead, using them to fight the last hundred yards. The white bunker overlooking the valley, which had served as headquarters, was still holding out. Its defenders were rolling hand grenades down the hill. Two direct bazooka hits halted their fire and Ofer, covered by his men, dropped in a hand grenade, silencing the last enemy.

It was almost 1 A.M. when the shooting ceased. But the moment Nukeib had fallen to the Israelis, Syrian long-range mortars and artillery zeroed in on the summit, forcing the Sayeret to carry out mop-up operations under heavy shelling. Anbar's demolition teams finished dynamiting the houses in the village and the bunkers on the hill, while Ofer's men inventoried the confiscated weapons. Czech and Russian guns and ammunition were carried back to Ein Gev. The lightly wounded returned on their own, while the serious cases were driven to a provisional hospital. Syrian parachute flares now illuminated the area to a midday brightness, and snipers swarmed the hills, making the retreat increasingly difficult. The Syrians had also begun shelling Kibbutz Haon and Ein Gev forcing the population into shelters. Israeli artillery from across the lake attempted to shield the retreat, but when it failed to quell the Syrian batteries, an air strike was ordered.

Seated on a heap of Russian munitions, Ofer called the command post in Ein Gev. His report was terse: *Haesek beiadi* (It is in my hands). He then gave the colonel their casualty figures: five men killed, ten badly injured (80 percent officers and NCO's) and two missing. His men had also counted thirty-seven Syrian bodies, none of them with rank. No Syrian wounded had been left behind, and one straggler, Private Ahmad Yechia Hussein, had been taken prisoner.[12]

Ofer next organized details to comb the occupied territory for the two missing, his sergeant major and Corporal Yosef Devir. He personally led a squad which searched the nearby fields. Each soldier repeatedly called the names of the two men, stopping to peer at the faces of scattered corpses by the light of Syrian artillery. The major's concern for the missing was much more than that of a commander for his men. He had asked his sergeant major to stay behind and supervise the logistics involved in the unit's transportation from the battlefield, "but he was so offended and kept begging me to take him along," Ofer recalled, "that I finally gave in and used him as my liaison with the other units."

The search continued even as the bombardment intensified. "We remained there for two hours," General Zorea later said, "more than was needed to dynamite the bunkers. . . . We could have finished much earlier . . . but we didn't want to return before finding the missing men." Commenting on the sergeant major, the general added, "I believe that he was injured and might have run in the wrong direction. . . . It sometimes happens when a man is wounded. If he would have stayed within the area, we would have found him." As for Devir, Zorea remarked that his disappearance was a mystery. His friends claimed that "they saw him until a late stage of the operation. He was gone only after the shelling began."

By 3 A.M. the search parties had remained behind alone. An hour later the first wave of Mirages III swooped down on Ein Gev, fanning out over the Syrian positions in a long plummeting dive. The threat of expanding the clash into a major encounter apparently convinced the Syrians to stop the bombardment. As the skies above the Golan Heights began to redden, their artillery ceased firing, leaving the sector enveloped in a welcome stillness. "With the coming of dawn," concluded General Zorea, "we had to discontinue the search and complete the withdrawal."[13]

On the Saturday following the battle, UN observers in Damascus were told that the body of an Israeli sergeant major had been found near Nukeib. Zahal's representative to the MAC at once demanded an inquiry into the whereabouts of the missing corporal. The Syrians replied that Devir was not in their hands, "either dead or alive."[14] Despite the admission about the sergeant major, the Israelis did not believe the assertion regarding Devir. It was commonly known that Israeli citizens who had fled across the border or had been kidnapped by National Guard patrols were held in Syrian jails. Jerusalem assumed that Devir had been secretly confined either to the military prison of al-Mazza near Damascus or the remote desert penitentiary in Tadmor. When the Syrians denied having captured Devir a

second time, Zorea dispatched a search party into enemy territory; the patrol found no trace of the corporal's body. A
special board of inquiry later ruled out the possibility of dis-
memberment by an artillery shell, reinforcing the theory that
Devir was still alive.[15] Since the Northern Command had been
unsuccessful in solving the mystery and all contacts with the
Syrians through the MAC had failed, the Modiin chief, General
Meir Amit, asked Iser Harel to investigate.

In the last week of May, Eli received a coded message
requesting him to locate Devir. There was no need for elabora-
tion; Eli had been following the daily accounts of the battle of
Nukeib reported daily on Israel's Arabic program. Ironically,
Nukeib was also the topic in Damascus, where the media had
heralded the battle as a resounding victory. The four half-tracks
which Zahal had left lying in the minefields were being displayed
as proof of the triumph before jeering crowds and wide-eyed
schoolchildren in the capital's Marjeh Square. Eli first mentioned
the incident to Maazi in the course of a conversation, inquiring
if any Israeli had been captured as a result of the battle. "I was
not there," the lieutenant replied, "but as far as I know, we did
not take a single prisoner."[16]

Sometime after his talk with Maazi, Eli made the acquaintance of the military police commander of the al-Mazza district
and attempted to find out through him if Devir was being held
in the dungeons of the Damascus military prison. The commandant assured him that no Israeli taken at Nukeib had ever
been imprisoned there. Toward the end of the year, Eli tried to
determine whether Devir was among the twelve Israelis confined
in the Tadmor military prison. Posing as a tourist interested in
the archaeological findings of what had once been the ancient
Greek trading center of Palmyra, he traveled 500 kilometers
north into the Syrian desert to the crumbling village of Tadmor.
The detention camp and the old French fortress where the
Israelis were being kept was but a short distance away. Eli went
to see the elderly camp commander, Captain Omar, and his
prison warden, Sergeant Awad, for whom he had brought a

warm letter of recommendation from Maazi. But the two officials were reluctant to show him the compound. Eli never got past the commandant's office and could find no evidence of Devir's presence there. Back in Damascus, he still continued probing for leads. Only after Modiin officially closed the dossier did he discontinue the search.*

*The Devir mystery was finally solved in 1964, when eight of the Tadmor inmates were exchanged—some after twelve years of imprisonment—for a number of Syrian prisoners. They recounted that Devir, who had been wounded in the battle, was captured by the National Guard after the Israeli withdrawal. In Kuneitra and Damascus he was submitted to ceaseless questioning under severe torture but refused to give his interrogators details about Zahal. He was finally transferred to Tadmor, where he succeeded in committing suicide before the end of 1963. The Syrians were said to have buried his body in an unmarked desert grave.

12
The Coup

It was still dark, early in the morning of the last Wednesday in March, when a series of insistent telephone rings awakened Eli. Switching on a light, he glanced sleepily at the alarm clock which showed only seconds past five forty-five. As he reached for the receiver, his thoughts stumbled through the possible reasons for a call at such an hour. Then he heard Maazi's deep voice, filled with quiet excitement, say, "It finally happened, *ya ahi*. The Army has taken over." Eli sat up listening attentively as the lieutenant went on explaining how, during the night, the High Command had herded together assemblymen and senior government officials at the General Staff compound before dispatching them to the al-Mazza Prison. The president, the prime minister and nearly the entire Cabinet had been placed under house arrest. His uncle, Maazi added proudly, who had emerged victorious from a recent inner struggle for power, headed the ruling junta; he was expected to assume both the political and military leadership and become the country's next strong man.

Maazi felt his own chances for promotion were excellent. The Bureau for Officers Affairs would no doubt now award him the long-overdue rank of captain coupled with an important command. But Maazi was looking forward not so much to the change of status and the monetary remuneration as to the political recognition and influence the captaincy assured. Once elevated to the conspiratorial class of officers, he would have to be taken into account by politically ambitious higher-ups making coup calculations. The lieutenant interrupted his monologue to point out that an emergency broadcast had been scheduled for the opening of the morning radio program and concluded: "I thought you would be interested in following the events from the very start." Eli thanked him for his trust and invited him over for a game of backgammon.

As soon as Maazi had hung up, Eli peered through the curtains. Tanks and armored cars guarded the entrance to the General Staff, and reinforced squads patrolled the fully lit grounds. The activity in and around the complex resembled the clamor prior to the Nukeib retaliatory operation. Military limousines, staff cars and Land Rovers hurriedly entered and left the premises. Eli could hear no gunfire, though, and deduced that the roundup of politicians—many of whom lived in the Abu Rummaneh Quarter—had procceeded without incident. Minutes after six, he turned on the radio and listened to the medley of John Philip Sousa marches which followed the daily reading from the Koran. He could picture the Army deploying its forces in the classic coup maneuver they had practiced only six months ago to the day: columns of T-54's and Russian-made armored cars advancing through the streets; troops moving into strategic positions around key government buildings; commando units occupying the radio and television stations; military policemen sealing the International Airport and waving away incoming planes. The leaders were different, but the pattern was always the same.

The sunrise broke like a fireball over Mount Kassiun, setting the city ablaze with a thousand hues. Just as Maazi had predicted, at precisely 6:50 A.M. an excited newscaster read an announcement of the High Command. The proclamation, titled Communiqué No. 19, informed the public that the Army had assumed power that morning "to preserve the achievements, security, stability and freedom won by the revolution of September 28, 1961." The officers' concern with public opinion was obvious from their calling the first communiqué "Number 19." By continuing the sequence released by the Supreme Revolutionary Command during the secessionist coup, they could pass themselves off as the same cadre, claim that they were only trying to revive the orientation of the September '61 Movement and show they had never been hostile to the union.

Preventive security measures followed in rapid succession. At 7 A.M. borders were closed. Ten minutes later the junta announced the dissolution of the National Assembly. At 7:20 came the expected resignation of President al-Kudsi "for reasons of health" and less than a half hour later that of the Dawalibi government.

While the broadcast continued, Eli ciphered two messages he had prepared a day earlier, relaying what he had learned about the recent power struggle in the Army and the Syrian-Iraqi military collaboration, adding another with Maazi's early information on the coup. He included his own comments on its significance, promised to assemble more facts and sought new instructions. Tel Aviv acknowledged receipt and, according to a prearranged emergency plan, scheduled a second transmission for later that night.[1] By then Eli was expected to have more data on the day's events and the center would be ready with detailed instructions concerning the new situation.

Within a little more than an hour after the initial take-over announcement, the High Command was prepared to make further explanations. In an elaborate statement read on the air, the officers tried to justify their actions against the legitimately . elected government by blaming treacherous deputies for having influenced the legislative and executive branches to abolish laws that protected the workers and peasants. "We had to intervene in order to stop such illegal practices," an Army spokesman explained. The junta's role, though, he promised, would be provisory; the Army was determined to stay out of politics and return to the barracks as soon as the internal situation permitted it. Giving the people an inkling of its future intentions, the High Command pledged to safeguard civil liberties, protect the rights of the fellaheen, encourage private enterprise, promote constructive Socialism and build a society based on love and brotherhood. While following a policy of "positive neutrality" in foreign affairs, it would pursue a stronger initiative in inter-Arab affairs, take positive steps to achieve unity on a concrete basis "with liberated Arab countries, especially beloved Egypt and sister Iraq," back the struggle for freedom and independence of Arabs everywhere, and employ every means at its disposal to liberate Palestine.

But despite such early explanations, confusion was rife among the commanders of military installations in the remote north, south and southeast—particularly those along the borders with Lebanon, Turkey, Jordan and Iraq—who had not even suspected that a cabal of thirty senior officers from the Central Command and the General Staff were conspiring. Like a great many of their field commanders who had also been kept in the dark, they were unable to react reflexively. The uncertainty gripping much of the officers' corps in the early hours of the morning was so complete that an outpost near Azaz on the northern border was seen by Turkish soldiers in Kilis alternately hoisting and lowering the UAR and Syrian flag five times between 8 A.M. and 2 P.M., before finally deciding on the current green-white-black banner with three red stars. But the peripheral commands soon overcame their indecisiveness, hastily reaffirmed their loyalty to the commander in chief and gave their approval to the junta's act.

In the early afternoon, Damascenes at last began venturing into the streets and many businesses reopened. Eli went to see al-Hashan at his office and later met Sheik al-Ard for coffee. He also had a fruitful exchange with Seif about the coup's political implications, then set out for home. Shortly before the curfew began, while walking along Abu Rummaneh Boulevard, Eli noticed a disturbance near the residence of Nazem al-Kudsi. The presidential mansion and the nearby Turkish embassy were surrounded by red-capped military policemen and commando troops in camouflaged coveralls and battle gear. As he was watching, Eli saw the soldiers bundle al-Kudsi into a military limousine and drive off. The president, he later learned, was taken to the relatively comfortable al-Mazza Hospital, outside the prison walls, where he was later joined by Premier Dawalibi and fifteen of his ministers. Some ninety deputies and senior administration officials arrested earlier on charges of "corruption and sabotage" were squeezed into a neighboring ward.[2] By the time darkness enveloped the capital the situation seemed calm. Radio Damascus canceled its program of marches, but kept on broadcasting warnings against "treacherous rumor spreading." The curfew was still rigidly enforced; but on Sunday, after an uneventful night, the borders were reopened, and life returned to normal.

Thursday evening, over dinner, Eli learned from Maazi about the behind-the-scenes events that had prompted the coup. The lieutenant, through his connection with the *atabek al-assakir* (commander in chief), knew the most minute details of the revolt, and Eli could easily reconstruct the mosaic of events, analyze the junta's moves and predict its future intentions. Two weeks earlier, Zaher ad-Din had summoned all brigade commanders to Damascus to discuss a proposed *entente cordiale* between Syria and Iraq. The brigadiers weighed the economic and tactical gains that such a pact might bring and, in spite of strong opposition from Nasserites who considered the pact a counterbalance to union with Egypt, decided to favor the Iraqi policy.

After this agreement had been reached, a heated discussion ensued on internal policies. The divergencies of opinion aired at the conference were irreconcilable: the leftist Nasserites led by Brigadier Abd al-Ghani Dahman, commander of the Damascus area, and Colonel Abd al-Krim an-Nahlawi, director of Officers' Affairs at the General Staff, sought the initiation of talks for an immediate return to the UAR fold; a scattered group of rightists, whom the Army had allowed to remain in active service after the purge which followed the secessionist coup, wanted to maintain the status quo of conservative independent rule; and

and peasants' demands. The debate remained inconclusive, and Zaher ad-Din had no choice but to adjourn the meeting.

The chief of staff nevertheless considered himself responsible for finding a way out of the impasse and, taking the initiative, went to see al-Kudsi. During a tête-à-tête at the Muhajerin Palace, Maazi recounted, his uncle harshly criticized the government's policies; he argued that in order to resist the blandishments of Nasserism, some sort of Socialistic measures had to be adopted to satisfy militant leftists. The president agreed but would not add his voice to the discontented. He was helpless, he claimed. Dawalibi held unrestricted power over the conservative majority and Zaher ad-Din would have to talk to him.

The commander in chief went to see Dawalibi the following day. When the premier heard his complaint and learned about the ill feeling at the brigadiers' conference, he was incensed. Protesting vehemently against military interference, he reminded Zaher ad-Din of his pledge to keep to the barracks. The general gloomily warned Dawalibi of the Nasserite officers' wrath, which he could not contain for long, and threatened to join them if the situation was not remedied. The next day when Dawalibi publicly denounced the Army's interference in political affairs, Zaher ad-Din's official reply was to demand his resignation.[3]

The Nasserites of Dahman and Nahlawi had followed Zaher ad-Din's interventions with rising interest and backed him as long as it suited their purposes. But when the rift between the moderate officers and the conservative politicians was widened, they realized that Zaher ad-Din and his followers would not tolerate insubordination much longer, and decided to take the initiative themselves. Yet before they could act, the Second Bureau informed Zaher ad-Din, who at once assembled his entourage of middle-of-the-roaders and gave them to understand that they could no longer remain aloof from active politics if they wanted to retain their posts; then, in a skillful political maneuver, he announced his full support of the coup the meeting with Dahman and his colonels at Central Command Headquarters. Clarifying his views, he had argued that the time was most propitious to assume power: Al-Kudsi and Dawalibi had fallen into disfavor while the prestige of the Army had soared after its performance a fortnight earlier at Nukeib. Zaher ad-Din offered the unionists his official support and the cooperation of the intelligence services, the military police, the Air Force and the Navy. The issue of union with Egypt, though a matter of principle, would have to be discussed later. A temporary formula acceptable to both sides, such as the immediate resumption of talks with Nasser, could be worked out. If agreed, Zaher ad-Din proposed that the leadership of the junta should fall to the highest-ranking officer involved—himself. The unionists were somewhat skeptical about his intentions but finally opted for collaboration.[4]

During the weekend two lieutenants from the Ministry of Defense with whom Eli was acquainted confirmed most of the facts revealed by Maazi, and Eli transmitted the verified information to Tel Aviv.

Early Friday morning the sheik called Eli to tell him that more than a dozen of the city's wealthiest businessmen had been arrested by the military police, among them the heads of the *Khumasiyeh*, "The Company of Five." (The fourteen-year-old trust, which derived its name from the five constituent family firms which exercised a considerable influence on the Syrian economy, had been nationalized in 1960 by the UAR but was returned to its owners in gratitude for the encouragement and financial aid they had given the secessionists.) Other deputies who had been members of economic and financial parliamentary committees were also imprisoned at al-Mazza.[5] But the information on Zaher ad-Din's failure to create a civilian front for his junta was the achievement of Georges Seif.

In an effort to assemble a cabinet of technocrats, Seif learned, the commander in chief attempted to negotiate the formation of a transitional government with three untainted deputies. The politicians, fearing their ultimate fate would be

similar to that of Dawalibi's team, promptly refused to cooperate and were sent straight to al-Mazza. Zaher ad-Din had to
swallow his pride and grant the directors general of all ministries
temporary administrative powers to act as ministers in order to
keep the bureaucratic machine functioning.[6]

The general's failure to win civilian backing caused friction
among his Nasserite collaborators, who began suspecting that he
was deliberately avoiding a democratic solution and planned to
pronounce himself Syria's sole leader. Their fears were further
strengthened when Zaher ad-Din issued orders forbidding the
disclosure of the names of officers who had initiated the coup,
allegedly to present an image of total unity within the armed
forces. The well-informed Egyptians, however, were not about
to permit him to hide the differences among the members of his
junta behind a façade of military camaraderie. In a highly
accurate account, the Cairo press described the rift and published a Who's Who of the March coup, listing the seven Nasserites of the Dahman-Nahlawi faction and some of their twelve
adversaries in the Zaher ad-Din group.

To counter Cairo's claim of dissension within the High Command, Zaher ad-Din called a press conference for Friday afternoon. Using both Seif's and Maazi's influence, Eli was able to
obtain an invitation.[7] The commander in chief appeared at the
Officers' Club in the company of his ally Brigadier Dahman,
who looked on doubtfully as his superior explained to a group
of selected newspapermen that the coup had been engineered
by socially concerned officers and was aimed solely at "the
destruction of the corrupt reactionary politicians." He denounced capitalists, speculators and separatists and proclaimed
that the armed forces would not tolerate corruption, isola-
tionism or government indifference to socioeconomic problems.
The officers were determined to enforce social changes, restore
"constructive and just Socialism," promote unity and bring
about an improvement in relations with Egypt.

The press was not overly impressed; some dispatches even
expressed the opinion held by the majority of Syrians that the
officers' real intentions had been to reinstate the union. Fearing

the hostility of the public, Zaher ad-Din issued immediate orders to the Radio and Television Directorate to avoid all references to "sister Iraq" and "beloved Egypt" and to reassure their listeners that "Syria will not fall again into the arms of any Arab nation."

The broadcast of such vague policy statements caused mounting concern among both conservatives and Nasserites in the north, the rightists' and unionists' traditional center of power. After only three days of military rule, the opponents of the Damascus junta in the Homs, Hama and Aleppo provinces were beginning to become restless. The conservatives were the first to react. Halaf at-Tilawi, one of Eli's business contacts in Homs who witnessed the disturbances, later described them to him: On Saturday morning, March 31, groups of Moslem Brethren and rightist activists marched on the provincial government and the local military headquarters, voicing support for the ousted premier. The police asked the Army for help, and the commander of the Homs Garrison, upon orders from Damascus, sent out his troops to quell the demonstration. But no sooner had the Army been ordered back to barracks than a pro-UAR mob took to the streets. Before the police could check it, the demonstration turned into a mammoth pro-Nasser rally which lasted well into the evening.[8]

Meanwhile, in Hama, Socialists and conservatives joined in a demonstration against the abolition of the legitimate government, while Nasserites, who had no love for either the left or the right, organized a rally in favor of reunion with Egypt. After violent clashes with the police and casualties on both sides, the three factions were dispersed.   Before the day had ended, an uneasy truce settled over the city.

As the demonstrators of Hama and Homs were being driven from the streets by combined Army and police forces, Aleppo conservatives set out to voice their disenchantment with the junta. Angered rightist militants, strengthened by a ragtag army of unemployed factory workers, cotton pickers and unskilled laborers furiously battled steel-helmeted riot squads but were driven back and away. Those who remained behind were rounded up and trucked off to jail. Sheik al-Ard, who had gone to Aleppo on business after the situation in the capital had improved, was caught in the middle of the violent demonstrations. Forced to remain in the city throughout the weekend, he witnessed the events at first hand; his account later allowed Eli to make a detailed report about the circumstances that led to the Aleppo putsch.

At noon a few hundred Moslem Brethren stormed into the streets, smashing a statue of Nasser, turning over buses and setting fire to streetcars. Ordered to stop the mob, the police simply fired into the multitude. The result was pandemonium. Angry roars were pierced by shrill cries of pain as rifles mowed rioters down. Twenty men were killed and more than a hundred wounded; the rest fled in panic.

The manifestations of protest did not end with the dispersal of the Brethren. The Nasserites, impatient with the junta's stand on unity and infuriated by the tour de force achieved by the conservatives and the extreme right, also decided to voice their demands in public. Students, workers, fellaheen and Palestinian refugees from a nearby camp marched into the center of Aleppo with signs reading FIDAKI DAMI, YA NASSER (Yours is my blood, Nasser) and NO LEADER BUT GAMAL. Army and police cordons opened as they passed. Intoxicated by this victory over the forces of order, the mob's reason for the day's demonstrations was soon forgotten. They attacked shops, wrecked, burned and looted unopposed. The Army and the police at first made no effort to stop them, but when the riot threatened to consume the entire city, they finally intervened and dispersed the demonstrators.[9] As riots petered out, a curfew was imposed. Yet Aleppo continued to seethe with threatened violence.

Late Saturday night an agreement to rise against the Damascus junta was reached between Nasserite leaders and officers of the Homs Garrison. Sunday at dawn, the infantry brigade stationed in and around the city, reinforced by the staff of the Homs Military Academy, took over the barracks, the municipality and the radio station, jailed pro-junta opponents and began broadcasting unionist propaganda, urging Damascus to under-take immediate unity talks with Egypt.

When Brigadier Jasim Alwan, commander of the Northern Command headquartered in Aleppo, was notified that pro-UAR officers in Homs were defying Damascus, he did not send an armored detail to punish them but expressed sympathy for their cause and, after a series of consultations with his staff, contacted the rebellious officers and their civilian supporters—the provincial governor, the chief of police and city officials—and offered to join them in waging an aggressive radio campaign against the junta.

At a meeting Alwan demanded that his subordinates commit themselves to the cause of unity. His adjutant, the Druze Lieutenant Colonel Hamad Ubayd, and seventeen officers readily swore him allegiance. Alwan then confined Baathites and neutral officers to the barracks and arrested both followers of the Damascus junta and anti-Egyptian conservatives. A small force was dispatched to secure the regional military installations, occupy public buildings, seize the radio station and raise the flag of the UAR over the fortress of Aleppo.[10]

Eli learned about the creation of a rebellious Aleppo junta from a broadcast of an intercepted cable Alwan had sent the Egyptian ambassador in Beirut requesting aid, arms and paratroopers. Zaher ad-Din, in an attempt to sway public opinion to his side and neutralize the rebels, countered with an appeal to patriotism. Pointing to the Nukeib incident, he claimed that the Israelis were preparing a new offensive; he entreated the nation to close its ranks and "volunteer for action against the Jews." Eli viewed Zaher ad-Din's appeasement move with great concern. He informed Tel Aviv of the creation of special emergency recruiting and training centers and reported the opening of military camps to civilians; it was, he thought, a step which suggested that the junta was favoring the creation of a national militia to channel the hostilities of its opponents against the Israelis.[11]

Zaher ad-Din's strategy proved successful. On Sunday night a struggle developed between his and Alwan's supporters in

Aleppo. In the exchange of fire between the factions, two officers and five soldiers were killed. The pro-Damascus troops were rapidly reinforced from Palmyra, and the rebels soon crumbled. To resolve the differences which still existed, the officers in the Northern Region suggested that Zaher ad-Din bring the representatives of the five regional commands of all units to the conference table. Zaher ad-Din was capable of quelling the Aleppo revolt with the loyal forces at his disposal in Katana and Kabun, but he knew that such an act performed without the backing of the officers' corps might shatter the delicate balance he had achieved among the three rival factions during the weekend. He feared that the uneasy peace which had reigned after their struggle for supremacy would not last long if the officers at unit level were not given the opportunity to express their opinions and work out their differences. Zaher ad-Din, who hoped to achieve unity in the Army, understood that the proposed conference was an ideal way to break the deadlock. He expressed his approval and a meeting was set for the following morning at the Officers' Club in Homs.

When the commander in chief and his entourage arrived, a fleet of staff cars and limousines was already parked at the entrance. Eli later learned that all faction leaders and their close collaborators, except for the Aleppan rebels, were present. Zaher ad-Din spoke bitterly about dissension in the ranks and the mutiny of the Aleppo Garrison. He analyzed inter-Arab problems and warned against a hasty union with Egypt or Iraq. His emotional patriotic speech against extremist unionists was warmly received; the majority of the officers shared his moderate views, though opinions varied widely on individual issues such as union with Egypt. After a night-long acrimonious debate, all unit commanders pledged their support to the commander in chief, denounced Dahman, Nahlawi and Alwan for seeking personal power and agreed that extremist officers, both unionist and anti-Egyptian, should be discharged.

The Homs Officers Convention also supported the reinstatement of a civilian government of moderate leftist persuasion but rejected the reconvening of the National Assembly. Zaher ad-

Din's suggestion that al-Kudsi be reappointed president of the republic received the officers' approval, and the commander in chief was given a free hand in choosing a prime minister and installing a Cabinet of technocrats which would answer to the military alone. The officers also agreed in principle that a popular plebiscite be held to determine if, when and how union with Egypt could be consummated. A Command Council of some forty officers was then created to supervise military and civilian affairs and prepare a referendum on union with Egypt to be held after a return to normality had been achieved. The new arrangement, Eli realized, was no more than a civilian façade for Army rule; the High Command planned to maintain its supervisory position for a long time to come.

Monday morning Zaher ad-Din ordered President al-Kudsi transferred from al-Mazza back to house arrest. He then again assembled local and foreign newsmen to announce that the new Command Council of the armed forces would guarantee moderate Socialistic reforms, an eventual return to "a clean democracy" and a national plebiscite on the question of reunion with Egypt.[12] But while he was talking, pro-UAR riots erupted in the capital. Zaher ad-Din reacted swiftly. The troops he sent into the streets dispersed the demonstration by firing on the crowds. The junta immediately sealed the borders, closed the airports, imposed strict military rule on the capital and the surrounding countryside, arrested dissidents and reimposed the curfew. The disturbances, however, prompted a clarification of the position of the Damascus junta on the issue of Arab unity. Zaher ad-Din insisted that the High Command "favors unity with the liberated Arab countries headed by Egypt, providing that this unity be established on proper foundations, that the country's honor and existence be safeguarded by preventing the recurrence of past mistakes and that these foundations be subject to a free plebiscite."

The seven unionists who were about to be deactivated in

they decided to join Alwan, who was already entrenched in Aleppo, and form a unionist junta that would proclaim the territories under the jurisdiction of the Northern Command as a part of the Northern Region of the UAR. As soon as the seven had arrived in Aleppo, the local radio station intensified its propaganda war against Damascus. "We belong heart and soul to Nasser," an announcer shouted. "We are his lion cubs. Long live Arab unity." The unionist junta now braced for the worst. In case their rule was theatened, they hoped to defend the city and later, if outside help could be found, even move on the capital.

During the night the General Staff prepared to launch a military operation against the rebels. A tank battalion and several batteries of recoilless guns were dispatched to Aleppo, while the Air Force was instructed to prepare a sortie over rebel-held territory. At dawn Eli heard Radio Damascus issue an ultimatum to the insurrectionists, ordering all officers and soldiers confined to barracks, but only a while later denounce them as "traitors who were taking orders from their masters in Cairo." After the ultimatum, the streets of Aleppo filled with confused unionists who boosted their own morale with chants of "Allah is with Abdul Nasser." Alwan, though, began to plan the region's defense. He distributed weapons to his civilian supporters and deployed units in a circular defense line on the roads to Damascus, Homs, Deir ez-Zor, Antioch and Latakia.

As troops of the Aleppo junta were moving into position, Zaher ad-Din dispatched two Mig-19's from Harasta to silence the abuse-showering radio station of the rebels. Minutes later, at nine fifteen, wailing sirens warned the Aleppo population of an air attack. The jets dropped two bombs on the station's transmitter some 20 miles to the south, missing the target. Then, in a show of force, flew over the city before returning to their base. An Aleppo newscaster excitedly announced the attack and bitterly protested the bombings. Describing the situation as desperate, he begged Nasser to send paratroopers to save the city and help maintain a beachhead for the UAR. Damascus

At the headquarters of the Aleppo junta, some officers were beginning to doubt Alwan's ability to maintain a political bridgehead for the UAR in Syria. They recognized the uselessness of a military confrontation with the Damascus junta, on whose side fought many of the ground forces, the Air Force, Navy and armored brigades. When advanced rebel outposts on the road to Damascus informed Alwan that a tank column of fifty-six T-54's was driving northward, a number of aides in Alwan's entourage expressed disbelief in final victory. But the brigadier still ordered his units to fight holding actions outside the city. Some of the field commanders were not prepared to back Alwan that far. Afraid of the consequences an unconditional surrender might bring, they urged him to negotiate.

Alwan was helpless. Cairo, instead of sending troops had offered to mediate. Without aid and with tanks at the city gates and troops from Deir ez-Zor closing in, Dahman and Nahlawi now also favored negotiations. Alwan decided to submit. He ordered Radio Aleppo shut down and sent a message to Zaher ad-Din humbly informing the commander in chief that the troops in Aleppo would obey confinement orders while talks were held. Damascus agreed and offered a truce.

In the early afternoon a compromise was reached. The High Command promised to abide by the Homs Convention, but the eight-officer junta would have to go into exile. Each would be consoled with a $3,000 stipend from the national treasury and receive a diplomatic post. Low-ranking officers, though, would be relieved of their duties and court-martialed.   Alwan had no choice but to agree. While his seven fellow plotters were speeding toward Beirut, the brigadier prepared to relinquish command. Like one of his ancestors who had surrendered the citadel of Aleppo 500 years earlier to a lame Ottoman soldier armed with only a club, he handed over the northern area to Luay al-Atassi, commander of the eastern area, who had arrived from Deir ez-Zor alone. Alwan, however, scorned fleeing into exile; he donned a civilian suit, left headquarters by the back door and went underground.

216 The Shattered Silence

The Aleppans dispersed heavyhearted, leaving behind littered streets and buses plastered with photographs of Nasser. Eli, who had been alerted earlier that "an important and happy announcement" was forthcoming, heard on the six o'clock broadcast that the rebellion was over and the situation had returned to normal. Barely thirty-six hours after the uprising began, the Aleppo putsch, Syria's second in a week and eighth in thirteen years, had ended in a fiasco.

With the Army hovering in the background—Zaher ad-Din had named himself minister of defense in addition to retaining supreme command of the armed forces. Maazi now had easy access to invaluable political data; on the basis of his confidential information, Eli was able to satisfy the demands of the Center for concrete intelligence on Syria's return to civilian rule.

In a move to restore the reins of government to the politicians, Zaher ad-Din released the president but kept most Parliament members under house arrest and deprived them of their political rights. On the thirteenth, al-Kudsi was officially returned to the Muhajerin Palace, where he accepted the resignation of the National Assembly, Premier Dawalibi and his entire Cabinet. In a broadcast to the nation, the president dismissed the coup as "merely the result of differences of opinion about the ways to realize the aspirations of every Syrian Arab for unity, democratic life and Socialism" and promised "to formulate and promulgate legislation that would lay down the democratic basis of our future lives." With Zaher ad-Din's blessings, he then entrusted Dr. Bashir Azmeh with the creation of a transitional government. The new premier refused to form a cabinet of old-guard politicians and looked for his ministers among the professors "of pronounced leftist tendencies" in the Faculty of Medicine of Damascus University. Sworn in on the seventeenth, he presented a fourteen-point program, promising a referendum on union with Egypt, renationalization of the Company of Five and cancellation of the amendments to the 1958 Agrarian Reform Law; he then set out to reorganize political life by returning public freedoms and lifting the ban on political parties.

Before Eli could make good use of the information Maazi now supplied, he received a stunning message from the Center asking him to return home for a debriefing. "Inform if can get away," the message read. "Submit departure scheme." Eli radioed a plan which would enable him to leave in June. Tel Aviv acknowledged and offered additional guidance. The case officer finally authorized his departure and instructed him to proceed with the arrangements. By mid-May Eli had advised his friends and business contacts that he intended to go abroad to "close some import-export deals." Less than a month later, still managing to cover ministerial resignations and a cabinet reshuffling, he left for Beirut and, after a short stay in Europe, proceeded to Tel Aviv.

13
The Keeper of the Secret

Eli felt somewhat elated when the gray-clad policeman at Lydda Airport greeted him with a warm shalom, cleared his papers and returned them with a curt thank-you. The sudden surge of confidence was a rare experience for a man who lived constantly in the shadow of destruction. He crossed into customs and, after a brief check, gave his baggage to a porter and strode into the main hall. With arms full of presents, he walked rapidly, his eyes searching for Nadia; he knew that she had been told of his arrival and would come to meet him. He finally caught sight of her, as she stood at the barrier near Gideon, who held little Sofie, her face lit by a happy smile. Eli seized them both in his arms and laughed heartily as they covered him with kisses.

Gideon was overjoyed to see him. "It's good to have you back," he said warmly as they shook hands; Eli noticed that he was sincerely moved. As they walked to a waiting car, he showered Nadia with questions, but when they drove off, he suddenly became silent. Nadia rested her head on his shoulder and watched him as his eyes toured the countryside. Less than six months had gone by since his last visit, and there were so many changes. The country had been busy building itself.

Hatchia Street still held its familiar Friday afternoon mood: old men hurrying to the synagogue; mothers rushing home from the beach; children on bicycles; girls chatting in front of houses; men sipping a cold drink on the terrace. He was home, and

218

home meant safety and happiness. The house was full of flowers and gifts of chocolate and fruit brought by his parents, relatives and neighbors who had come to greet him. Gideon, who had by now become one of the family, stayed until all the well-wishers had left, but when Eli drew him into a corner and attempted to give him a short account of his experiences in Damascus, the case officer cut him short. There would be no debriefing on this day. The only object of his visit was to make Eli feel safe and welcome.

As soon as the weekend was over, the long exhausting debriefings began. Eli met his superiors in a conference room at Mosad Headquarters, where a tape recorder and a slide and movie projector had been installed. As he started to make his first report on the setup in Damascus, Eli was aware of his superiors' burning interest. He told them of his strategically located residence, drew layouts of the apartment ("If they catch me," he observed dryly, "I can always jump from the fourth floor and end it all"), and sketched the caches he had built. He detailed his daily routine, explained his business cover and the contacts he had made, and reported on the efficiency of his anchormen.[1] Gideon made some suggestions for improvements but approved the overall arrangements. He then asked Eli to write a detailed report on his achievements, account for his finances and make suggestions for a widening of his assignment.

For the next few days, Eli explained and amplified the messages and documents he had sent during the last six months and others he had brought with him. "His memory was vast, accurate and highly disciplined," one of his superiors would remark, "and he had a thousand stories to tell about the situation in Syria." He had acquired data of the highest importance, and there was much more to come. It was an impressive achievement. Any doubts Eli's case officer may have had about his performance and his value were now laid to rest.

Mosad officials held a number of additional conferences in which the handling of his anchormen, Sheik al-Ard and Georges

Seif, was discussed. Eli suggested that the Information Ministry official remain his major source for political information on Syrian and inter-Arab affairs, while the sheik continued to cover the economic field. Gideon took notes, nodded occasionally and asked only few questions.

Eli began to speak about his prospective sources. He described at length his relation with Maazi Zaher ad-Din, stressing the lieutenant's potential as a source of information. His superiors regarded his contact with Maazi as a considerable accomplishment. Their friendship would have to be cultivated to permit a flow of political and military intelligence.

Gideon and his superiors accepted many of Eli's suggestions, but since he seemed overeager to engage in a wide variety of assignments, they had to calm him down by setting a number of immediate objectives, leaving the decision on the others for the future. He was instructed first to concentrate on political and economic reports, leaving for a later date the acquisition of more technical military data on the armed forces, particularly the Southern Command. Yet general military information was a field he could undertake. The Mosad was interested in Syrian preparations for mobilization, the character and destination of arms shipments and troop and vessel movements. Eli was urged to report any unusual military event regardless of how trivial it looked to him.

These, however, were all long-range goals. He would first have to strengthen his cover. More money, it was determined, would be pumped into the import-export firm to increase his standing in the community. He would nevertheless have to act slowly and with patience. "Always remember that wise Arab proverb," Gideon stressed, " 'Hurry is written on the hoof of a donkey.' "

Eli's systems of communication were also reviewed. Mosad requests for information, it was agreed, would continue to flow through "open" correspondence, while microfilmed documents he acquired would be sent to fronts in Europe and South America, where the respective station chiefs would transfer them to headquarters by diplomatic pouch. Finally, more complicated transmission arrangements were imposed, and Eli was given a new set of codes and ciphers. He was at last told to repeat the instructions and complied flawlessly.

A last meeting was dedicated to the possibility of his entering political life. Mosad analysts had concluded that the parties of the *ancien régime* whose leadership now participated in the al-Azam government were outmoded and ineffective. The moderate and conservative parties, outlawed for so long, were disorganized and powerless; the Nasserites were strong but fractioned; and within the Socialist camp, the Communists presented no potential. The probability of any of them rising to the fore was minimal. The political force Eli should join would have to have a strong following in the Army because more military coups were predicted in the near future.

The only party that had proved extremely effective in spite of its inner difficulties was the Baath Arab Renaissance Party. After the secessionist coup in 1961 the Baath had experienced two major splits and was under constant attack from its dissident wings; it was also constantly harassed by the Nasserites and by the present government, which had closed its organ and sentenced the editor to jail. Yet the Baath's propaganda campaign and organizational effort had been extremely successful, and the party's active opposition to the government had proved the efficacy of its militants. But more important, the Baath had the strongest following in the Army. Between members and sympathizers, Baathite officers formed a force with which the Nasserites would have to reckon. Mosad officers suggested that Eli's acquaintance with a number of Baathites in Damascus could prove invaluable if he ever chose to gain entrance into the party. He would have, though, to await further developments and report to the Center before making a move.[2]

After the debriefings followed a short period of training. There was still much for Eli to learn—new radio techniques, coding procedures and the use of micro cameras. "He proved an apt pupil," an instructor later remarked. Encouraged by his successes and driven by an obsession for greater accomplishments, Eli displayed demonic energy in absorbing the new material.

While at home, Nadia often asked Eli about his travels a-broad. He described the countries he had visited, related some minor anecdotes but carefully avoided discussing his work. In reality, he excelled in his effort to keep Nadia ignorant of his true mission, yet often wondered whether she really believed him. He could not of course discern precisely how much she guessed, although it sometimes appeared obvious that she sensed he was leading a clandestine life. Whatever her thoughts, Eli knew that he would have to keep his secret throughout the long, lonely years to come. This dishonesty had already begun to cloud his married life. The strain of being one person to his wife while he was two others to himself made it almost impossible to live.

On the rare occasions when they were alone together, the subject of his departure was raised. Nadia wanted to know why he could not take her and Sofie to Europe at least occasionally, and Eli had to employ every possible argument to persuade her of the impossibility of such a trip. He had to move from one place to another at a moment's notice and could never subject her and the child to such a strenuous life. He spoke of the future and promised her solemnly that within a few years all would end for the better. In the meantime, she would have to trust him and accept the bleak situation.

After an eight-week stay, Eli prepared to leave. When he finally flew out of Lydda toward the end of September, he carried concealed in his luggage a second powerful radio, a new set of codes and a micro camera with thousands of feet of high sensitivity film.

Eli landed in Damascus only days after his meeting with Salinger in Zurich. He found the grimy, depressed city of sullen men, noisy policemen and reckless drivers unchanged. The streets were thronged as always, yet there was an oppressive ambiance in the air. The students still agitated, and the police were constantly on the lookout for potential plotters. The talk in the cafés was politics as usual, though taxes and women were still favorite subjects. Although everyone was interested in which general would be next to seize power and how unity with Egypt should be accomplished, what really concerned the average Syrian was how to stay alive and make ends meet. Most Damascenes had lost confidence in their politicians, who paid lip service to Arab unity but never honored their pledge to hold a plebiscite. The same officials had restored the Agrarian Reform Law with amendments benefiting the landowners and went on making promises to nationalize the monopolies.

During Eli's absence, relations with the Soviet Union had been strengthened and the rift with Egypt had grown deeper. Labor strikes, demonstrations of Nasserites, Brethren and Communists, ministerial resignations and dismissals, arrests and releases of politicians had become commonplace. The unstable situation was further complicated by the mutiny of Parliament members, most of whom had been deprived of their political rights and kept under house arrest ever since the coup.

Through Seif's office, Eli acquired details of the event. To dramatize their plight and put an end to the state of emergency and the transitional form of government under army tutelage, a number of deputies met in the Damascene residence of Khaled al-Azam, to draft a demand for the restoration of constitutional life. A week afterward the six-foot bespectacled al-Azam defiantly called a full session of the banned Parliament against the will of the High Command. Barred by troops from entering the chamber, the 157 deputies again assembled in al-Azam's mansion and, in a plenary session, reaffirmed the validity of the preunion constitution. President al-Kudsi, hearing of their mutiny, asked al-Azam to form a new government; a vote of confidence by cheering deputies eased Azam into office.

Zaher ad-Din was furious, yet could do nothing but withdraw opposition from a return to parliamentary rule and assent to the change. On September 17, after Dr. Rashir Azmeh submitted his resignation, the wealthy industrial landowner, nicknamed the Red Millionaire for negotiating the 1957 Soviet-Czech arms deal, formed a twenty-one-man cabinet of national unity with no Nasserites or Communists and promised general elections within a year.[3]

Eli found the situation in the Army no less confused than in the government. Maazi spoke gloomily about his uncle's supporters, who had no real goals and talked in vague terms about saving the country, restoring order, repressing reaction and affecting reforms. On the basic problem of Arab unity and particularly union with Egypt, they were both eloquent and contradictory. They claimed that unity was needed but would not elaborate on how it could be achieved.

This ambivalent attitude of the High Command had angered the officers' corps, causing dissidence even among the supporters of Zaher ad-Din. Junior officers in field units were holding discussions and openly voicing discontent. Fearing another revolt, the commander in chief and President al-Kudsi toured the bases reassuring the officers of the sincerity of their intentions and urging "national unity to face imperialist designs." Yet, to prevent open rebellion, the High Command ordered a second wave of large-scale dismissals coupled with appointments of senior police and security officers.

After Zaher ad-Din had sent the Army back to barracks, scores of Nasser supporters had been arrested, and seventeen officers who had taken part in the Aleppo revolt brought to trial. The commander in chief then promoted himself to lieutenant general, reshuffled the High Command to include "officers who enjoyed the confidence of all units" and carved several appointments for his own supporters, among them Major General Namak Kamal, a protégé whom he had recalled from a training tour in the Soviet Union and named chief of staff.

Although Eli's observations indicated that the Army still had the final word in internal policy, the civilian government felt strong enough to curtail its powers. The politicians first repealed a decree giving military commanders full control of their area—a measure which had been in force since the coup—and, on December 23, lifted the state of emergency and appointed al-Azam military governor. The Army was outraged. Some offi-

cers decided to strike an audacious blow against the High
Command, which would not call the civilians to order.

When Zaher ad-Din received word that Nasserite sympathizers were once more agitating, he again used his favorite method
of promotions, transfers and dismissals to stop them. The cashiered officers included Abd al-Krim an-Nahlawi and his friends,
who had been waiting since April in Swiss exile for orders to
assume the diplomatic posts they had been promised. When
Nahlawi learned of Zaher ad-Din's treachery, he contacted two
dozen young officers who served in the armored brigades stationed in Katana and near Damascus and urged them to rebel,
promising to return with three of his friends to assume the
leadership of the revolt. The plan, set for January 9, called for
the tank officers to alert their troops and move on Damascus,
where they would present demands asking the High Command
to reinstate Nasserites to active service and dismiss Zaher ad-
Din. Nahlawi would be there by the time the tanks were ready
to enter the city. But before the plotters were able to start out,
Second Bureau informers alerted the commander in chief, who
deployed loyal troops of the Damascus Garrison throughout the
city. Nahlawi arrived on time, but his junior partners were
immobilized.

Unionist university and high school students who heard of
the revolt swarmed into the streets of Damascus and Deraa and
rioted in Sananayn. Scores were injured in the clashes, and
Zaher ad-Din sealed the borders for fear of outside intervention.
He dared not, however, arrest the rebels, who used his hesitancy
to call on President al-Kudsi for arbitration. A triumvirate
headed by the president sat with representatives of both sides
but after an all-night session ruled that Nahlawi and his friends
return to Europe to assume their diplomatic posts in Bonn,
Prague, London and Bern. The following morning, as soon as
they had left, twenty-four of their supporters were arrested, and
before noon, tension had eased.[4]

This time Eli had been privy to the attempted coup almost
from the very beginning. Through Lieutenant Suleiman al-Rajula,
a new friend who worked for the Second Bureau, he found out

about the tank officers' intentions; Maazi filled him in on the rest. Shortly before dawn, the lieutenant had called and in an excited voice recounted the happenings at the Presidential Palace. Eli was still able to transmit in the morning that the middle-of-the-roaders had won another victory over Nahlawi's rebellious Nasserites. Astounded by the rapidity with which Eli had acquired the information, the Center decided to score a propagandistic victory over the Arabs and released the news. A bulletin on the attempted coup and the all-night session was broadcast by the Voice of Israel on its late-morning program—a practice that the Mosad's Psychological Warfare Department later used with much of Eli's information.

During the fast of Ramadan, on Friday, February 8, a popular and auspicious day for revolution in the Middle East, a cabal of Baathite and independent officers deposed Iraq's dictator, Abd al-Karim Kassem, and hastened to declare "unity of aim" with Cairo. With the establishment of the pro-Baath regime in Baghdad, Mosad analysts foresaw an imminent collapse of the fragile parliamentary regime in Syria. In his last report, Eli had held the failure of the politicians to be an absolute certainty. Stressing their disorganization, their submission to the military and their vague position on unity with Egypt, he predicted the fall of the al-Azam regime and the rise of the Baath. Now that the policy of moderation, compromise and parliamentarianism had been shattered, the prestige of the Baath had soared. Although the party was still the smallest and weakest of the Socialist forces in Syrian politics, its success in Iraq, Eli believed, proved that it had an immediate future in Syria. The Syrian Baathites hailed the new Iraqi regime and urged unification with both Egypt and Iraq. But before al-Azam could take the first step, the party set out to undermine his efforts. Upon the request of the Syrian Regional Command the Iraqis invited its representatives to confer on the suggested union in Baghdad. The undiplomatic move of discussing unity with the opposition was a political slap in the face to al-Azam. The Cabinet crisis which followed the departure of the Baath delegation on February 17, would ultimately cause the middle-of-the-road government to come tumbling down.

In this transitional period, Maazi continued to supply tidbits of information on the rampant intrigues within the High Command while Sheik al-Ard concentrated on economic matters. Yet political events were covered mostly with the aid of Georges Seif. During Eli's absence from Damascus, Seif had added to his duties as head of the press and radio section in the Ministry of Information those of supervisor of foreign programming at Radio Damascus. In both his capacities, he attended government functions, public meetings, official ceremonies, ministerial briefings and off-the-record press conferences. His access to such sources had made him a gold mine of political information from which Eli sifted many of the messages he then radioed to the Center.

Within weeks after his return, Eli became a frequent visitor at the Information Ministry and was introduced to Seif's colleagues. The guards came to know him so well that they no longer asked for the special permit mandatory for visitors; Eli would later utilize this laxity to enter Seif's office at night and photograph documents that could not be taken out. His habit of going through Seif's dossiers would prove almost disastrous. As he was once reading classified material, Seif's immediate superior entered unannounced. The astounded official reprimanded Seif for his negligence and threatened him with an investigation. But Seif managed to convince him that Taabet had no particular interest in political matters and was reading the documents out of sheer curiosity.[5]

As the collaboration between the two intensified, their personal friendship also strengthened. Seif came to Eli's apartment with increasing frequency and would stay long hours to discuss the latest political developments or gossip about his higher-ups. He never failed to appear at the parties Eli gave and often brought his colleagues or friends with him. On one occasion, Seif arrived with an uninvited guest, a young and husky major, Salim Hatoum, who commanded the guard at the General Staff complex across the street and the nearby radio and television station. Hatoum turned out to be a heavy drinker and connoisseur of good food, whose illicit escapades were openly discussed that evening. Although somewhat reserved at first about his work, the major took an immediate liking to Eli and soon became a steady participant at the bachelor evenings in his apartment.

A native of the Druze Mountain, Hatoum was the son of a wealthy family with a military tradition. At an early age the family determined that Salim and his brother Jaris would follow a military career and in preparation for the Homs Military Academy, sent them to a private *lycée* in Beirut. While Salim kept to himself, Jaris befriended a Lebanese who first introduced him to Jewish culture. After his friend's family emigrated to Palestine, Jaris returned home strongly impressed by the determination of his young friend to help in the Yishuv's resistance to the British. Jaris himself later crossed into the Galilee, contacted the Haganah and volunteered for active service in Zahal. During the 1948 war he served in a Druze unit and rose to the rank of captain. He would finally convert to Judaism, take a Hebrew name, marry a young Israeli and become an adviser on minority questions to the mayor of Haifa.[6] Eli, who knew of Hatoum's sensitivity to "the treachery of Jaris," never mentioned his name in their conversations although the incident was a topic of murmurs among the major's political enemies.

When Eli therefore expressed the wish to become a member of the Baath, Hatoum eagerly promised to sponsor him. (With the rise of the Baath to the fore, Eli had requested and received the Center's permission to join the party.) Taabet fulfilled all basic requirements for becoming a Baathite: He was an Arab emigrant, pronounced nationalist, over eighteen years of age and member of no other political group. Thus only days after his request, Eli was invited to a meeting of a Friends' Cell, the training ground for new members. Unlike other Baath sympathizers who had to be active for at least one year before being sworn in, Eli was approved within weeks by the higher echelons. One cold evening in February, he was summoned to the home of a district leader, who solemnly administered the oath. In Hatoum's presence, Eli swore "upon his honor and belief" to be "faithful to the principles of the Arab Baath Socialist Party, keep its trust, follow its rules and execute its plans." After promising to become "a true example of the struggling Arab," fulfill his duty to the Baath, pay his monthly dues and abide by the party's constitution, he was assigned an area cell. The three isolated members of his cell would meet for discussions once a week at his home or that of another comrade; occasionally they would receive orders to carry out diverse clandestine propaganda missions. Within a short time, Eli learned the ways of the Baath and became acquainted with its pyramidical structure and organization.*

As the Baath had a poor following in merchant circles, the enrollment of an importer-exporter was therefore considered an important breakthrough, and Eli's way to the top was rapidly negotiated. Hatoum discussed Taabet's leadership qualities with Michel Aflak, the secretary-general of the Regional Command, and Eli was singled out for quick advancement. In a meeting of cell members who formed the company in charge of the Abu Rummaneh Quarter, he was elected to its command, which in turn nominated him secretary of his area cell. It was not long before the leadership of the division composed of friends he had made in the lower echelons proposed him for the post of *Amin Sir* (keeper of the secret), or company secretary. As such Eli

*The Baath membership is organized in secret area and work cells of three to seven people. The next level in the organizational ladder is the *firkah* (company), which comprises three to seven cells; two or more companies constitute a *shubah* (division); the county or department *fir* (branch) is made up of two or more divisions. The political and ideological direction of the party is assumed by a regional command. (The Baath which operates in Iraq, Syria, Jordan, Lebanon and Arab countries from the Atlantic Ocean to the Persian Gulf has a regional forum in each state.) The highest policymaking and directive organization is the National (inter-Arab) Command in which all regions are represented. Some of the command posts are elected by the membership, but most are appointed from above. The suggestions of subordinates, however, is usually respected by local leaders. The membership is mainly drawn from among intellectuals, officers and students and in smaller numbers from among workers, employees and businessmen.

first came in contact with the division secretariat, which, impressed by Taabet's enthusiasm and dedication, would support his election to the command of the Damascus Branch. When the branch secretary also made a favorable report to the regional level, Eli's name was finally brought to the attention of the secretary-general, who expressed the wish to meet him.[7]

In time, Eli was taken to see Michel Aflak. The founder and ideologist of the Arab Socialist Baath Party lived in a modestly furnished four-room apartment not far from the city's center. Aflak, whose mild manner had earned him the nickname of the Professor, was a pale, slight man of painful shyness, deep sincerity and frugal habits; he appeared more like the Gandhi of Arab Nationalism, as some of his disciples called him, than as the man who defied the Arab world's most powerful political figure, Gamal Abdul Nasser. During the amenities, his two small children played underfoot while his wife, Anid Bashir, a young and successful physician, served coffee and sweets. "The party," Aflak began as soon as she had left, "had many intellectuals but not enough executive and technical talent." It needed a cadre of young people like Taabet. "We need more funds, more men, more time, more of everything," he reiterated his favorite saying. The party wanted determined and efficient young revolutionists who could assume positions of leadership should it emerge from the opposition. "Only a few, an elite," he preached, "are aware of the nation's maladies and can struggle to correct them." He now talked about the need for such an elite, mixing his flowery Arabic with French.

Eli, who had been entrusted with the task of widening the party's support among merchants and businessmen, understood Aflak's anxiety for effective leadership. In his contacts with the lower echelons, he had found them high-spirited idealists, drunk on Aflak's rhetoric but with a great deal more heart than head. They had no broad understanding of organization and were utterly lacking in initiative. As Aflak went on to talk of party politics, his reputation as a middle-of-the-roader came to light. "I stay away from power," he said mildly. "I'm incapable of governing." He deplored the weakness around him and despised the political leaders who vied for prominence and control. He was confident, though, of accomplishing his visionary goals of leading the party to power and Syria toward "unity, freedom and Socialism."

Eli would meet Salah al-Bitar, the party's number two man, at Aflak's home only a short while later. A co-founder of the Baath and inseparable friend of Aflak from the time they had studied together in Paris, Bitar had been imprisoned four times during his career as a member of Parliament and holder of various portfolios in the old regime. Where the secretary-general talked of Socialism, Bitar, now editor of the party's organ, *al-Baath*, was occupied with the nationalist aspects of Baathism. He was considered the party's tactician and would in fact engineer its rise to power. Bitar was taken in by Eli's convincing enthusiasm, and their meeting gave rise to a fast friendship which would later prove invaluable to the Mosad.[8]

The virtually complete polarization of political forces after Nahlawi's attempt had meanwhile resulted in a wave of savage violence in the major cities. By mid-February street brawls, gang wars, looting and lynchings in Homs and Kamishlieh had left many dead and large numbers of wounded. Dismayed by the rising tide of violence, some Army officers began to consider resorting to force. The majority of the officers' corps, however, remained indecisive and reacted only gradually to the rampant civil disorders. Maazi had told Eli of various plots being fermented, yet Eli's own investigations revealed that the cabals were confined to local garrisons and had no broad support.

The strongest nucleus of conspiracy, Eli learned, had developed in the Kuneitra Garrison when the commander of the Southern Command, Muhammad Ziyad al-Hariri, a stubby, mustachioed brigadier of strong unionist convictions, heard from his friend, the director of Officers Affairs at the General Staff, that Zaher ad-Din and his coalition of anti-Nasserites in the High Command were planning to eliminate the unionist elements in the Army by pensioning, dismissing and transferring a large number of them. Hariri discussed the matter with his subordinates, who placed themselves unconditionally under his orders. He also received pledges of support from Colonel Rashid Kutaini, a former military attaché in Jordan whom Zaher ad-Din had recently appointed head of the Second Bureau, and Brigadier Muhammad al-Sufi, commander of the Homs Garrison. The imprisoned Colonel Luay al-Atassi, whom Hariri contacted through a loyal emissary, also acknowledged the general's nominal leadership of the plot and was made honorary leader of the conspiracy.

Unable to whip up solid support, and despite his reservations about political conspirators, Hariri began to consider civilian aid. Although he was not a member of the Baath, Hariri sympathized with its Socialist and pan-Arab aims. He felt close enough to the moderate faction of Aflak, which preached union with Egypt and Iraq, to take the secretary-general into his confidence and invite him to join the cabal.

Eli, who gathered information on the coup from Baath sources, learned of the executives' debates from Aflak. The secretary-general was by no means convinced of Hariri's political capacity, yet he knew that the party's only hope of attaining power was to collaborate with the military and later to try to outsmart them. He apparently hoped that in the aftermath of the coup the general would unwittingly provide an opportunity for his elite of revolutionaries. He did not expect to achieve Baath rule in a matter of weeks or even months but was convinced that a swift and successful coup would considerably enhance Baathism. He had therefore advised the executive to support the rebels.

As soon as the leadership voted for collaboration, preliminary orders regarding the manner in which the Baath would take part in the rebellion were sent to militant cells by the Damascus Branch Command. Students and workers were armed and organized n paramilitary units as a clandestine militia to sustain the Army. A fierce spirit of *fedai* (a sense of sacrifice) soon developed among the young during the conspiratorial period. "They had a much stronger sense of loyalty to the party," Eli would later report, "than the soldiers had to their country." Eli would not take part in actual street duty during the night of the coup. His orders were to wait in his apartment until he received word from Hatoum that the radio station was secure in rebel hands before proceeding there to help supervise the rebels' information and propaganda effort.

On the morning of March 7, as a messenger hurried to Aflak with final instructions, the General Staff notified Hariri that he had been relieved of his command and appointed military attaché in Baghdad. The general did not acknowledge the order and some hours later received a radio message instructing him to consider himself under arrest. Hariri at once summoned his co-conspirators and quickly arranged for a banquet to be given at the Kuneitra Officers' Club in honor of his departure. Early that evening, the Harirists overpowered all the officers loyal to Zaher ad-Din as they arrived to attend the farewell party, disarmed and jailed them in the command's stockade. With the Southern Command secure in rebel hands, a small force of paratroopers, ten armored cars and twenty jeeps set out for Damascus. The bulk of Hariri's force, some 1,800 men, would cautiously follow.

At 4 A.M., almost eleven hours after leaving Kuneitra, Hariri's main force finally entered Damascus from three directions. At the General Staff complex, Major Salim Hatoum awaited the rebels with open gates. But as he and his guards were about to join them, they were suddenly attacked from within. A fierce fight developed for the control of the vital compound as Zaher ad-Din and his entourage tried to repel the assault. Hariri's avant-garde caravan entered the compound without effort, inflicting heavy losses on the staff officers who finally laid down their arms.

As the take-over was slowly being completed, the commander of the Damascus Garrison and the chief of the military police placed themselves at the disposition of the rebels; one detachment of MP's was ordered to secure the immediate release of Colonel Luay al-Atassi and a number of Baathite and unionist officers from al-Mazza Prison while other units were dispatched to arrest deposed officers, ministers and high government officials.

By five o'clock most government centers and military installations in and around Damascus had surrendered. Minutes later,
Eli received the expected phone call. The radio and television
studios had been liberated, Hatoum tersely informed him and
hung up. Eli quickly headed for the station, passing a cordon of
troops and checkpoints of armed civilians before hurrying up-
stairs to assume the task with which the party had entrusted
him. While supervising preparation for the early broadcast, Eli
kept in constant touch with the General Staff complex. Radio
Damascus would not begin transmission until the junta had released its first official statement.

The Baathite NRC in Baghdad who was privy to the coup
began getting impatient when Radio Damascus failed to open its
broadcasts as usual and attempted to contact the Syrian leadership. But with all international lines of communications shut
down, it broadcast a direct message requesting the operators of
the Damascus station to switch their radiotelephone to the
Baghdad wavelength. While Syrian technicians fulfilled the request, Eli hastily summoned Aflak, then talked to the Iraqis and
informed them briefly of the situation.[9]

At 6:30 A.M. Harari and his officers finally issued their first
proclamation and settled down to the task of building a military
and government machine capable of subduing the nation. To
handle immediate problems, they created a twenty-one member
National Council of the Revolutionary Command under the
nominal chairmanship of Luay al-Atassi.* The NRC then formed a
twenty-man Cabinet headed by Salah al-Bitar. Eleven ministries
went to members of the Baath and nine to supporters of Nasser.
All posts were held by civilians except those of Defense and
Interior. (As his minister of the interior Bitar chose Amin
al-Hafez, a little-known colonel but veteran Baath militant, who
was recalled from a study tour in the Soviet Union to assume the
post with the rank of brigadier. Within less than four months,

*The Council of the NRC was composed of eleven military with subordinate
civilian assistants. Nasserite and independent unionist officers held the majority. The
Baath contingent of eight, led by Secretary-General Aflak, was later joined by representatives of the Nasserite Arab Nationalist Movement, Socialist Unionist Front and
Arab Union Front.

Hafez, whom Eli had met while he served as UAR military attaché in Buenos Aires, would emerge as the leading figure of the Syrian Baath.)

At 7 A.M. a curt radio announcement imposed a general curfew. Thirteen minutes later Eli released the NRC's Proclamation No. 1 which stressed "in the name of God the Merciful and the Compassionate" the desire for unity with Egypt. At 9 o'clock Proclamation No. 2 returned thirty-three officers to active service and rewarded the coup leaders with swift promotions. Atassi became commander in chief, Hariri chief of staff and Kutaini his deputy. By 3 P.M. calm had finally settled over Damascus; the insurgents were obviously in firm control.

In the monitoring room, Eli closely followed the broadcasts from Egypt. Cairo made no comment on the coup. Nasser would not radio his greetings to the new regime until Saturday at eight. Significantly, his guardedly cautious salutations were addressed to the predominantly Nasserite NRC rather than to the Baath-dominated government. "The Syrian-Egyptian attempt at union," he said with restraint, "had been a pioneering and practical experiment from which we benefited a great deal. . . .The experience gained will be ammunition for the Arab future and for Arab unity." What steps might be taken for a new union were pointedly left unspoken. The NRC's reply cable came within hours: "Syria had taken revenge for the secession and had washed away its disgrace." It was now "returning to its rightful course—the unionist and Socialist course." The NRC was willing to proceed with a new entente and even concede to Nasser the role of *primus inter pares*.[10]

The March coup was a landmark in Eli's career both as a Baathite and as an agent. As he had become securely established in his relations with the party leadership, his cover, the basis for his clandestine work, was greatly strengthened. At the same time, his analysis of the insurrection and the series of political reports he sent to the Center signaled the beginning of his real mission.

For weeks after the coup, Eli amassed material for the preparation of a comprehensive study the Mosad had requested. He discussed with Aflak the social and ideological implications of the revolution, prompted Hatoum into clarifying for him the relations between the military factions in the NRC and asked Seif to investigate the precise consequences of the revolt. The result was a painstakingly researched report. It offered, in addition to his own observations, what he had heard from friends and chance acquaintances and the material he had sifted from *al-Nidal*, the confidential publication distributed to branch leaders, views and reactions of Baath higher-ups, addenda of microfilmed documents and a set of Baath directives Seif had secured from the Ministry of Information. Indefatigable in obtaining intelligence on the revolt, Seif had more than made up for the loss of Maazi's invaluable aid. (With the fall of Zaher ad-Din, Eli had lost Maazi as a source of information. After the arrest of his uncle the lieutenant had to relinquish the post of district commander of Adlib, near Aleppo, and was dismissed from the Army. He would later assume a minor position in the Ministry of Municipal Affairs.)[11]

Eli's accurate and full assessment of the revolt established his reputation. His study turned out to be of far greater value than records of troop strengths and secret documents and would carry considerable weight in Tel Aviv. When Premier Ben-Gurion summoned Cabinet members and Army chiefs for consultation on the implication of the Baath coup, his Mosad advisers on Arab affairs were able to present him with invaluable material. They were convinced that the coup would effectively enhance the reputation of the Baath which could act as a counterbalance to Nasser's influence in the Arab world.

Eli spent the rest of the hectic week after the coup shuttling between Seif's office and Hatoum's quarters. The information he acquired from the workings of the National Council of the Revolutionary Command was invaluable. It was at that time that he also began frequenting the office of the prime minister, where Aflak and the Regional Command has installed their temporary headquarters.

After the visit of an Iraqi delegation to Damascus, Nasser began fearing that the Syrian and Iraqi NRC were trying to

establish a common front before proceeding to Cairo for unity
talks and instructed the media to denounce violently the hesitation of the Syrian leaders. The NRC was quick to react. Early
Thursday morning Seif called to inform Eli that the Council,
worried by Cairo's pressure, had decided to take the first halting
steps toward the formation of a three-state federation. To placate Nasser, a seven-man delegation headed by Vice-Premier
Nihad al-Kassem had been appointed to initiate the unity talks
and ordered to proceed to Cairo at once. Eli had not expected
such swift reaction to the campaign of hate and subversion
which had marked Cairo's efforts to force Syria back into the
UAR fold. The Baath's reluctance to negotiate an immediate
union with Egypt was notorious, and he had thought that the
party's predominance over the Nasserite groups was an assurance against such action.

In an effort to find out more about the move, Eli rushed to
see Hatoum, who helped him gain entrance to the compound of
the General Staff only to find the Council adjourning. As the
participants were leaving the premises, Eli was told that the
delegation to the Cairo unity talks was already on its way to the
airport. He wanted to know if al-Kassem had been given specific
instructions; Hatoum reassured him that nothing but a general
agreement to start talking had been reached in the Council. The
Nasserites, he explained, expected Kassem to come back with a
pact, but the Baath had secretly urged its chief delegate, Economics Minister Abd al-Krim Zuhur, to stall for time and get
Nasser's reaction to a federal union on the basis agreed upon
with the Iraqi command. The outcome of the talks, however,
would prove that the Council had gravely miscalculated
the willingness of the rais to return to a Baath-influenced
union.

As soon as the delegates had left, Eli installed himself at the
temporary party headquarters to await details of the Cairo conference. From that moment and until the secret talks ended
fifteen days later, he would leave his post only for a few hours
before dawn, officially to rest but in reality to transmit the
most important items of information he had gathered during
the past twenty-four hours.

Late Thursday night, Kassem and his colleagues briefed Damascus by phone on their first conversation with Nasser. They had arrived in Cairo at 4 P.M. and were joined a few hours later by an Iraqi delegation headed by Saadi. Shortly before 7 that evening, they were already closeted with Nasser at his home in Manshieh al-Bakr, where they conferred until midnight. Their host, Zuhur informed, had shown reservations from the very start and would not consider the real issues unless he received a satisfactory answer to the question "Who was now ruling in Damascus? " But none of the Syrians was absolutely certain who really sat in the NRC. "Then with whom should we talk? " Nasser had inquired, annoyed. "Must I deal with ghosts?" As he insisted on names, Hariri explained that they were trying "to keep the Council's membership a secret to ensure its collective character." Nasser, however, was not satisfied. "It would be wrong," he warned, "to begin these proceedings by having secrets from each other."

Shortly before dawn, Eli transmitted the essence of this first conference to the Center and made notes for a report he would later send on microfilm through Europe.

On Saturday at 2 P.M. when the talks were resumed in Cairo's ornate Kubbeh Palace, Eli and Seif sat by the phone in the company of Information Minister Sami al-Jundi, awaiting Zuhur's reports. It was 10 P.M. Damascus time before the economics minister finally called. After six hours of mutual accusations, Nasser had suggested that each delegation meet on its own to clarify positions. He would have to wait two hours before the Syrians would finish consulting with Damascus. Eli was present at the Baath conclave which discussed the new position to be adopted by the Syrian delegation. Aflak had remained unperturbed upon hearing that Nasser would not deal with the Baath; he had expected the talks to collapse even earlier. Yet the regional leadership was worried about the reactions of their partners in the NRC and instructed Zuhur to stall the negotiations until a common stand could be reached with the independents, the military and the Nasserites.

At a briefing Bitar gave al-Jundi, Seif and other senior Information Ministry officials late Saturday night, Eli learned that the talks had been conducted without a set agenda or order of business. They had drifted from topic to topic, always returning to the same central issue—the creation of a federal union. Nasser had seemingly had no illusions about his partners in the talks. He was ready to unite with Syria and Iraq, but "if unity is to be with the Baath party," he had explained, "I am absolutely not prepared to hold any discussions." (He later withdrew his reproach of the Iraqis but maintained his stand toward the Syrians.) The Baath's control of Syria, he had argued, would provide a grave impediment to any unity scheme. "I am certain," he had concluded, "that we shall differ before four months are over." Nasser had therefore been reluctant to press ahead. "By Allah," he had exclaimed, "I am the one who is most afraid of unity among us."

Zuhur rejected the proposal: "There could be no unity without Egypt." The Nasserites in his delegation made it plain that the union with Egypt was "a matter of life and death" for Syria. "If we return with empty hands," one delegate had remarked, "it will be a shock not only to our people but for the entire Arab world." Nasser's response to this clamorous demand was then spelled unequivocally: "Unity of states is not enough," he had stated icily. "It is the unity of the political leadership that is important." Steadfastly, he held out for one Socialist party, a strong central government under his leadership and a unified military command—a setup similar to the UAR he had earlier formed with Syria. The Syrians differed with him on the issue of the presidency and of political parties; they insisted on a collective leadership, the maintenance of local autonomy and the freedom to organize political parties—a loose federation with common defense and foreign policies. The Baathites doggedly stuck to their conception of unity. No honeyed words would seduce them into returning to the 1961 arrangements that first muzzled, then banned their party.

After fifteen hours of secret talks, disillusionment had set in as Nasser realized that the Baath would not accept a union under Cairo's centralized control. A last conference on March

17 had produced no solution. Eli notified Tel Aviv that the Syrians had left the first round of talks embittered, without clarification of the issues they had come to discuss. They had no plans for the resumption of the talks or, for that matter, their own further intentions.

After the delegation had been debriefed, Eli's reports indicated that the Iraqis were closer to Nasser's concept of unity than to that of their own party. The common front with their Syrian brothers was in danger of collapsing. Fearing isolation, the NRC reacted swiftly. On March 19, four leading Syrian Baathites—Aflak, Bitar, Atassi and Colonel Fahed al-Shaer—flew to Cairo unannounced. From the airport, they made an appointment with Nasser for an initial courtesy call and rushed to the Republican Palace. The Egyptians were puzzled and unprepared. The formalities were brief, and before ten minutes had passed, the two delegations were involved in a long argument which grew increasingly bitter.

But the talks soon became as repetitive as before. Nasser continuously accused the Baath of treason. Atassi repeatedly asked him to speak about the future and forget the past, but the rais remained unforgiving. Yet despite the unbreachable chasm that separated Nasser and the Baathites, a six-point basic plan for the creation of a loosely organized tripartite federation was reached before the Syrians returned to Cairo. The agreement, mainly Atassi's achievement, called for a tristate plebiscite on the issue of the presidency and allowed for a twenty-five-month transitional period before the formal amalgamation.

Damascus gave Atassi a victor's welcome. After listening to his report, a cheering council unanimously elected him president, an act to which Eli gave his loud approval. A third round of talks conducted by a seventeen-man Syrian delegation finally yielded the April Seventeenth Agreement. Egypt, Syria and Iraq united their 38,000,000 citizens in a tripartite federation almost the size of India with one president (Nasser), one capital (Cairo) and one flag, that of the UAR with three stars.

As the Damascus NRC ratified the charter, the Israelis remained unperturbed. Eli had radioed: "Paper federation approved. Baath no intention carrying out pact." Like many other skeptics, its analysts would believe in Arab unity when it happened.[12] The Cabinet, which had been briefed on the talks, refused to be threatened into action by Atassi's boast that "the Jews will have no value when we stretch from the Atlantic Ocean to the Persian Gulf. They will be only a drop in the sea and will disappear completely *Insh'Allah* [with God's will]." Ben-Gurion refused to cut short his Tiberias vacation.

The tripartite agreement was quickly compromised. Only three days after the unity manifesto had been signed, Egyptian intelligence intercepted a letter from the Iraqi military attaché in Damascus to Deputy Premier Saadi informing him that the Syrian NRC had no intention of honoring the pact and had in fact decided to eliminate the remaining Nasserites in the Army. Learning of the Baath's real intentions, Cairo intensified the hate propaganda and stepped up subversive activities in an all-out effort to regain enough influence to force the Baath to stay in the union. The Syrian Nasserites were ordered to strike and stage demonstrations in the big cities; students gleefully cooperated and poured into the streets chanting the name of their hero. As violence mushroomed, Atassi appointed Interior Minister Amin al-Hafez deputy military governor. Aflak and Bitar, who coordinated the work of the NRC and the Cabinet, knew that their support in the Army was not sufficient to face the combined forces of the Nasserites. Yet they hoped to ride the storm to come with the help of Hafez and the two armored brigades now under the firm control of Baathite officers. The tanks Hafez sent into the streets quickly dispersed the rampaging students. The toughness with which he quelled the disturbances would firmly enhance his credentials with the party leadership.

The rift between Nasserites and Baathites seemed irreconcilable. It appeared inconceivable, Eli would report, that the two movements ever again could work together, but the Baath realized that its position was not attainable. The Nasser forces had by no means been defeated and were still extremely powerful.

To prevent further deterioration of their relationship, Bitar resigned the premiership on May 11. The natural choice to succeed him was the moderate pro-Nasser Information Minister Sami al-Jundi, who had taken no sides in the Nasser-Baath struggle; Bitar thus hoped that al-Jundi would be acceptable to both Cairo and his rivals.

Eli had met Seif's superior shortly after he had been nominated minister of information. During the last turbulent months, al-Jundi had come to consider Taabet a close friend and often consulted him on the issue of reunification. He felt such confidence in their relationship that he freely discussed party problems with Taabet, who often sided with him in internal matters and factional disputes. A native of Salamiyah and former dentist with political ambitions, the forty-three-year-old blond, blue-eyed al-Jundi was a member of the Nasserite Socialist Unionist Front in which he had risen to a position of leadership. Opportunistic but shrewd and well aware of the need for caution, he had mastered the devisiveness of Arab politics. He refused to identify too closely with his own party and would not show his hand by participating in minor conspiracies against the Baath. His ambiguous stand, however, would ultimately force him into the open. While still loyal to the Nasserites, he began to express sympathy for the moderate politicos of the Baath and became a frequent visitor at Aflak's Damascus apartment, where he occasionally saw Eli.

As premier, al-Jundi hoped to placate the Nasserites and gain a breathing space to consolidate his position. He attempted to form a cabinet with six Baathites, six Union Socialists (his own former party) and two Arab Unionists, but his efforts proved futile. Cairo's Voice of the Arabs had made it plain that Nasser considered him a front man for the Baath, and the Syrian Nasserites took their cue from Cairo and refused to participate in his Cabinet. Al-Jundi unsuccessfully negotiated for two days, before conceding defeat. Tired and disappointed, he appeared before the cameras of Damascus television to tell the nation that all the Nasserites were politicos with a bourgeois mentality who cared only for posts and portfolios.

Bitar was forced to take over again and form a new sixteen-man Cabinet, overwhelmingly dominated by the Baath. Al-Jundi's pro-Baath record stood him in good stead; in recognition of his services as interim troubleshooter, he was offered the double portfolio of information and national guidance minister. Eli had remained al-Jundi's ally until he realized that the party was becoming increasingly apprehensive over the growth of his power. And Taabet was more interested in party alliances than in the friendship of al-Jundi. In the ensuing power struggle, he would take an active part in the intrigue against al-Jundi and throw his influence on the side of his enemies. The minister would ultimately be cashiered and banished to an ambassadorial post in France.[13]

In June, alarmed by the intensification of Nasserite subversion, the Baath decided to curtail the powers of the defense minister and chief of staff, Ziyad al-Hariri, who was showing unusual compassion for his Nasserite subalterns and had once too often come out against the party's policies. Secure in his power, al-Hariri left Damascus on June 28 at the head of a goodwill delegation to Algiers.

As soon as he had gone, the Baath tried to draw support away from him by intrigue and called upon Hafez, the real power behind its military faction, to carry out the ouster. The minister of the interior, who saw the opportunity of removing a last obstacle to his personal power, was more than willing to oblige. He initiated a purge of Harirists, reassigned Hariri himself to the post of military attaché in the United States and sent him instructions to proceed directly to Washington via Paris. The general disobeyed, returned to Damascus on the twenty-sixth and angrily summoned the NRC, which met at the General Staff Headquarters in a somber atmosphere. The Council wrangled over the dismissals for two days and nights.

As tension mounted, the Iraqis threatened intervention on the side of Hafez. With the armored brigades in and around the capital under the control of Baathite officers, Hariri understood that to attempt a coup would be sheer suicide. On July 7, he finally yielded and was placed under house arrest before being banished to Vienna, from which he was later sent to a diplomatic post in Paris.

After Hariri's ouster, Hafez assumed all his posts. Atassi had no choice but to promote him to major general and appoint him chief of staff. His loyalty and cold efficiency also earned him a second post in Bitar's Cabinet—that of minister of defense. [14]

Eli could have made no better choice when he befriended Amin al-Hafez in Argentina. The tall, broad-shouldered general with thick silvery hair, prominent nose and dimpled chin was only forty-nine when he attained the summit of politics in Syria. Born in 1914 to a poor Aleppo family of Suuni orthodox Moslems, Hafez had moved to Damascus when his father became the representative of the Westinghouse Corporation in Syria. While teaching in one of the capital's elementary schools, he met Aflak and Bitar. As a young man with strong Socialist convictions, Hafez joined the Baath Party soon after its creation. But four years later, for unknown reasons, he joined the Army and enrolled at the Homs Military Academy. Still a cadet when the first Arab-Israeli war broke out, he was nevertheless sent to the front,where he earned the rank of lieutenant. Hafez was one of the few Syrian officers to emerge from the war with an enhanced reputation and quickly rose to the rank of major. With the advent of the UAR, the Bureau of Officers Affairs sent him to pursue his studies at the Cairo Staff College. Yet no sooner had the Baath withdrawn its support of Nasser than Hafez was promoted to colonel and banned to the post of military attaché first in Madrid and later in Buenos Aires. At the time of the secessionist coup, partly because of his Baath connections, Zaher ad-Din assigned him to head the Army's training branch; Hafez repaid the commander in chief by siding with him against the Aleppo insurrectionists. But differences soon arose between them, and the High Command again sent Hafez on a study tour, this time to the Soviet Union, from which the party would recall him to take charge of the Ministry of Interior.

As soon as Hafez had assumed his ministerial post, Eli had

sent him a congratulatory note and, at the Center's suggestion, began following his career closely. The general had immediately shown his iron hand in dealing with the enemies of the revolution. He established the rule of the party by reshuffling the security forces, crushing the Communist underground, checking the students and containing the Nasserites. His forces of order dispersed demonstrators, enforced curfews, conducted unrelenting arrests and operated security courts full time. His loyalty to the party would earn him the post of deputy premier.

The general's quick advancement prompted Eli to ask Seif to arrange a meeting with him. Only days later, the two were cordially received by Hafez at his home in the Abu Rummaneh district. Eli told the general about his business venture, discussed party affairs and placed himself entirely at his disposition. Taabet's patriotic enthusiasm and sincere and modest manner favorably impressed Hafez, who expressed the wish to see him more often, both in private and at Baath functions. As Eli's star began to shine in the party, he became a frequent guest at the house of the Hafezes and, before long, enjoyed the confidence of Madame Hafez and the friendship of the general, who readily permitted Taabet to call him by the intimate name of Abu Abdu, the Father of Abdu, his eldest son. After knowing Hafez better, Eli was puzzled by his political success. The general lacked charisma and was not a moving speaker. Although he projected self-confidence, he did not possess the volatile temperament that was a hallmark among his compatriots. He never lost his temper, even when provoked, and would utter harsh words in a quiet, cold way. Even in private, Eli noted, the general lived up to his reputation for being an extremely circumspect and distant man. He was impenetrable, somewhat stiff, gave answers reluctantly and would not readily be drawn into specifics. "You could talk to him for an hour," a friend once told Eli, "and suddenly realize that he hadn't said ten words."[15]

Early in July, the branch leadership proposed Eli for the regional command. Aflak presented the nomination, and Hafez,

Hatoum, Bitar and al-Jundi seconded his appointment. Within days, Eli was seated in the NRC as an observer without a vote and only a while afterward was accepted as a full Council member. Shortly after his appointment, a rift developed between the civilian moderates of Bitar and the military radicals of Hafez. The clash had placed Eli in a difficult position. Aflak, hoping to appease the Army, had sided with Hafez; because of his friendship with the general and Hatoum, who backed Hafez, Eli was forced to do the same. In a secret vote to elect a new executive, the old guard, including Bitar, was defeated and every rightist Baathite swept out of office.[16]

Nasserite officers who had survived the purges that followed Hariri's dismissal now doubled their efforts to wrench the power from the Baath in order to redirect the actions of the government and reintegrate Syria into the UAR. Eli was privy to their scheme from the very beginning. Earlier in July, he had heard from his friend in the Second Bureau that Jasim Alwan, who had fled the country after the abortive Aleppo revolt, was back in Damascus plotting rebellion. Cairo had approved his coup plan and had promised paratroopers and air support. As Nasser planned to denounce the federation agreement on the anniversary of the Egyptian revolution, H hour was finally set for two days before, the morning of July 18.

At 10:15 A.M., as planned, only a half hour after Atassi and al-Jundi had flown to Cairo, Alwan's infantry, signal corps and military police units, supported by Air Force personnel and civilian co-conspirators, converged on Damascus. Four rebel Mig's swooped over the Abu Rummaneh district, bombed the radio station but missed the transmitter which had to be dynamited by a sabotage team. Heavy fighting broke out in the heart of the city as the insurgents attempted to seize the Defense Ministry and General Staff complex. The astounded rebels were soon driven back from all strategic centers by troops loyal to Hafez. But the general was himself taken by surprise when a major in charge of the guard at the General Staff compound ordered his troops to withdraw before the rebels. Toting subma-

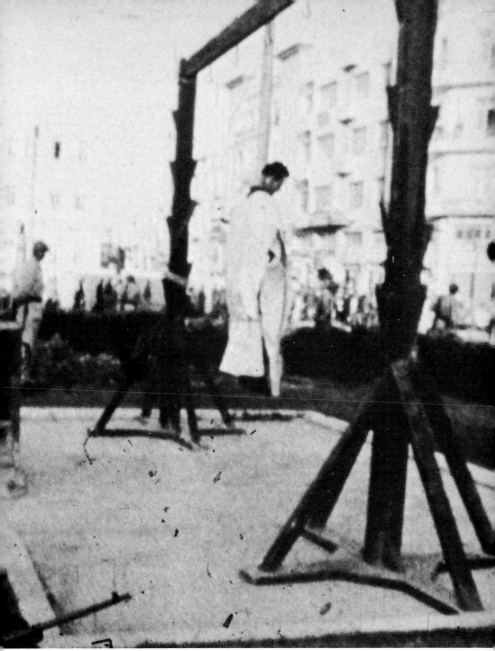

The body of Eli Cohen hanging in Damascus' Marjeh
Square.

Bamahane

The Cohen family in Egypt.
Eli, at four, is at extreme left.

Cohen-Sidon

Samuel Bakhur Azar, a self-portrait. "Sami," Eli's best friend, was later convicted of espionage and hanged in Cairo in 1954.

Eli's Bar Mitzvah. Portrait of the Cohen children.

Bamahane

A page from Eli's Egyptian *laisser-passez* used to emigrate to Israel.

Eli's Israeli identity card.

The wedding of Eli and Nadia Cohen.

Haolam Haze

Sofi's first birthday party. Eli entered the Mosad, Israel's supreme intelligence and security agency, shortly afterward.

Bamahane

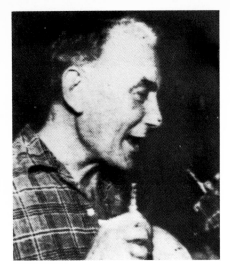

Benyamin Gibli, chief of Israel's military intelligence corps.

author's archives

Iser Harel, known as Little Iser, first chief of the Mosad.

author's archives

Meir Amit, Harel's successor.

author's archives

Café La Paz in Buenos Aires, where Eli used to contact Abraham, the Mosad station chief in Argentina.

The house on Abu Rummaneh Street where Eli lived in Damascus (left), and the Muhajerin-Abu Rummaneh Quarter, the center of Damascus' diplomatic and military communities.

One of Eli's transmitters, hidden in a Damascene backgammon table.

Haolam Haze

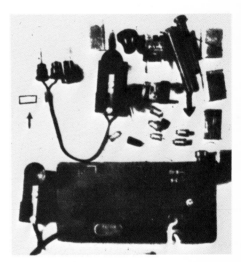

A dismantled miniature transmitter and Morse key alternately used by Eli to beam coded messages to Tel Aviv.

Haolam Haze

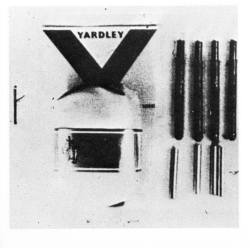

Dynamite sticks and detonators, hidden by Eli in bars of Yardley soap.

Haolam Haze

The mailbox of the Kamal Amin Taabet Import-Export firm in Damascus.

Haolam Haze

Canceled checks and business correspondence found in Eli's apartment after his capture and arrest.

Haolam Haze

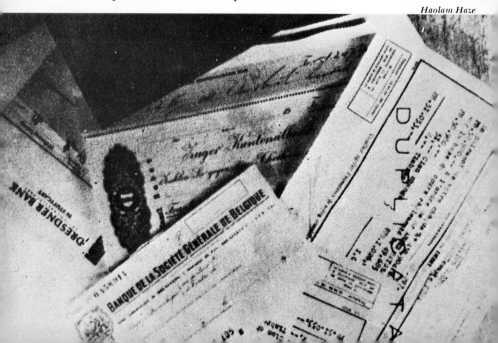

Portrait of Eli Cohen taken on a visit to Israel during
his mission in Damascus.

Keystone

Syria's president, Major
General Amin al-Hafez,
shown here with Egypt's
late president, Gamal
Abdel Nasser.

UPI

Salah al-Bitar, Syria's
prime minister.

author's archives

Michel Aflak, secretary-
general of the Arab So-
cialist Baath Party.

author's archives

Sami al-Jundi, Syria's
ambassador to Paris.

Haolam Haze

Eli and Saliha on the Beirut seashore.

Eli, with a group of Arab friends, at a masked ball in Damascus (Eli sitting with glasses and false nose, second from left).

Haolam Haze

Eli, posing during his personal tour of the Golan Heights fortifications.

The Golan Heights fortifications, across from the Sea of Galilee. The picture is taken from the Syrian side.

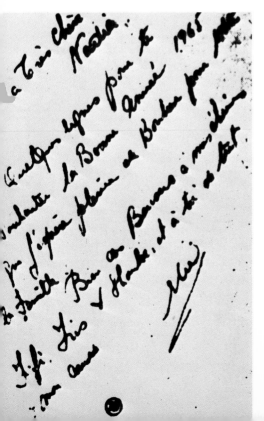

BAT-YAM
ISRAEL

A postcard Eli sent to Nadia from Belgium, shortly after he left on the trip to Damascus from which he never returned.

The last New Year's card Eli sent Nadia from Europe read: "A few lines to wish you a happy 1965. I hope you and the family will have a good year. Kisses to Fifi, Iris, Shul, and to you with all my heart."

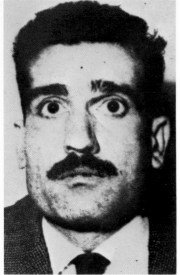

Eli' police portrait, taken after brutal interrogation and torture.

Typical of the pleas for clemency received from world leaders was this cable from Belgium's president, Camille Huysmans.

Colonel Ahmed Suidani (first on left), chief of Syria's Second Bureau, with Leonid Brezhnev during a trip to Moscow.

The military tribunal which judged Eli and thirty-six collaborators. Lieutenant Colonel Sallah Dalli, president of the court (center), and Colonel Salim Hatoum, Eli's friend and confidant (second from right).

The prisoners in the dock before the military tribunal. From left to right in the first row: Eli Cohen, Sheik Majid al-Ard, and Lieutenant Maazi Zaher ad-Din.

Parents

(handwritten letter in Arabic and French)

author's archives

The last letter Eli wrote his wife (in Arabic and French) urged her to remarry.

The unveiling of Israel's monument to the memory of Eli Cohen on top of a hill at the forest planted in his name.

Haaretz

chine guns, Hafez and a group of staff officers had to repel the attack themselves.

The paratroopers and air support which the UAR had promised never came and after a fierce four-hour battle, the capital was firmly secured by government forces. Loyalist pilots flew over the roofs in a show of force, and by 2:30 P.M. as Radio Damascus limped back on the air, it was again in Baath hands. Hafez rushed to inform the Syrians that the effort to "disturb the peace," engineered by "a small group of civilians backed by a few armed soldiers," had been crushed. The list of casualties was enormous. Reports of the number of dead alone ranged between 170 and 900.[17]

As Damascus was placed under curfew, the country remained buttoned up, its borders, airports and harbors sealed. Atassi returned undisturbed from a ten-hour unsuccessful conference with Nasser and rushed to the military hospital to kiss the soldiers wounded defending his regime. Later that evening, a summary military court passed death sentences on three leaders of the coup and the NRC convened in an emergency meeting to consider the verdict. Atassi expressed sympathy for the unionists and objected to the sentences. But the civilian faction, Eli included, despairing of reconciliation with Nasser and suspicious of Egyptian instigation of the coup, sided with Hafez in voting for execution. The next day at noon, the commander of the Signal Corps and five of his NCO's were shot in the courtyard of al-Mazza. Two hours later, two more noncommissioned officers and twelve civilians were brought before the firing squad. By July 22 hundreds of Nasserite suspects had been rounded up, and the number of executions reached twenty-seven. Warned Hafez: "Let them think twice before trying again. And if they do try, let them be ready to die."

Although executions were by no means foreign to Syrian tradition, the shooting of political opponents had been unknown for more than fifteen years. The cruelty with which Hafez quelled the rebellion therefore impressed both friend and foe and helped consolidate his power to what seemed an impregnable degree. The party elected him president of the NRC and supported his appointment as commander in chief to succeed the overriden Atassi, who had stepped down from both posts without comment. With these latest elevations, Hafez now held six top posts: three in the Cabinet (deputy premier, minister of defense, and minister of the interior); one in the party (president of the NRC); and two in the Army (commander in chief and military governor). Sometime later, with the resignation of Bitar, he would also assume the post of premier. There was thus little exaggeration when, in August, Hafez was introduced to a rally as "the man of steel."[18]

As the figure of the five-foot-six Aleppan general loomed gigantic against a background of blurred mediocrity, Eli received instructions to strengthen ties with the new strong man and immediately intensified his visits to the Hafezes. He now used every opportunity to see the president at the Muhajerin Palace, where a yard-long model of a Russian T-54 tank dominated his marble office. The general, anxious more than ever for support from a civilian in the NRC, never refused Taabet an audience and received him in a cordial mood at all hours. As Eli put himself at the disposal of Hafez, he soon came to enjoy the powers of an éminence grise. Their close collaboration in the NRC would continue until the end.[19]

14
Saliha

Since his rise to prominence in the Baath, Eli had not ventured to ask or even intimate that he be allowed to visit the southern frontier zone. The Syrians could sometimes be lax over security matters, but the outposts along the Israeli border had been made inaccessible to all civilians except those cleared by the General Staff to whom the Southern Command had issued special passes. Yet it was crucial that Eli gain access to the sites. The 47-mile armistice line which ran parallel to the old international frontier between Syria and Palestine—with several encroachments caused by three demilitarized zones in the northern, central and southern sectors—was the shortest border with any Arab state but also the most troublesome. Land claims by both sides, brought about by the ambiguous terms of the 1949 Armistice Agreement, had caused numerous clashes between the opposing forces. At nearly every point along the heights on the edge of the Golan Plateau the Syrians had a tactical and topographical advantage. From ridges and mountains towering some 1,800 feet above the northeastern fingertip of the Upper Galilee, infantry and artillery emplacements overlooking the demilitarized zones threatened a chain of kibbutzim spread out along the border, forcing the settlers to spend many of their days and nights in concrete shelters. These outposts served the Syrians not only as a defense line but also as a potential launching area for a ground assault against Israel. They were thus comparable to the drawbridge across a moat; if the Israelis were vulnerable here, the way would be open for total disaster.

Zahal observation posts kept the Syrian positions under constant watch. To track troop movements in the area, reconnaissance units of the Northern Command made deep penetrations into the Golan, and IAF planes scouted and photographed aboveground activities from the air; in addition, Modiin maintained a small army of Arab informers from among the villagers of the Bakaa. But the Syrians, by constructing a labyrinth of trenches and bunkers which crisscrossed the fortifications, had so effectively screened their armor and artillery from the prying cameras that the types and precise locations of the weapons could be determined only by an observer at close range. The Mosad therefore ordered Eli to give top priority to the gathering of information about the Syrian fortifications along Israel's northern frontier.

The influence wielded by Hatoum and, until the March coup, by Maazi eventually opened the door of the border area for Eli. Both his friends, who admired the rapidity with which he had ascended in the party ranks and respected the influence he now wielded, were eager to dissipate the skepticism he had often expressed concerning the readiness of the armed forces by proving the efficacy of troop deployments along the border with Israel. Eli thus managed to accompany one or the other of them three times during 1963 on inspection trips to the lines. On his first visit Maazi took him to Baal Zabdi and Bloudanehi. Late in the spring, he drove with Hatoum to Tal Azazziyat, the fortifications in the northern sector of the demilitarized zone—a 45-mile journey from the capital. As they twisted their way along the Damascus-Kuneitra highway through the dreary Hauran plain, a vista of desolation spread before them. The panorama of this Biblical land of Bashan seemed scarcely changed since ancient times. Stony, barren wastes were followed by a chain of rocky yellow-brown hills, boulders and occasional patches of scrub. Eastward, though, the soil was black and rich. Weathered by underlying basalt rock and much rainfall brought by strong winds from the sea, the Bakaa, as the region was commonly known, had once been the granary of the Roman Empire in the eastern Mediterranean, but centuries of neglect had turned it into a bleak, sparsely cropped and thinly populated area where the poorest among Syria's poor fellaheen dwelled. Most of the peasants barely eked out a living by tilling the soil and raising sheep and goats for absentee landlords or by growing some wheat, barley or oats for themselves on an acre or two of rented land.

In place of the rich crops which this soil had yielded before it lost its fertility, the Syrians had created a 15-mile buffer zone of barren, mine-infested wasteland into which they built a series of military installations where a large portion of their armed forces was concentrated. The area, code-named the Elaal War Zone, came under the jurisdiction of the Southern Command headquartered in Kuneitra; it comprised—on a permanent basis subject to slight changes—two infantry and one armored brigade, several field and long-range artillery battalions, a few commando companies, a variety of support troops and a number of National Guard and mounted border patrol units. A peripheral line of Maginot-type fortifications—concrete observation posts, machine-gun emplacements, antitank bunkers and firing trenches—built atop the ridges bordering with Israel, were strengthened by tanks buried in the ground to provide stationery artillery and backed by long-range, rapid-firing 130 mm cannons and 122 mm mortars hidden behind the cliffs along a 20-mile line between Tal Kunheila in the north and Tawafik in the south.

After a torturous hour, choking from the dust, Eli and Hatoum arrived on the outskirts of Kuneitra, the southernmost urban center of trading and smuggling fame, where the narrow highway turned into a twisting main street. With its jumble of crooked alleys, squarish stone homes, mosques and minarets, odorous bazaars, veiled women and skirted men, Kuneitra was typical of most Syrian towns. In the poor quarter, narrow, shabby streets seemed more like a repository for filth and human waste. Housewives used them as a garbage dump, casting about panfuls of water and remains of food. Hoards of scab-covered, undersized children with uncombed hair, sick eyes and running noses, clad only in underwear or nightgowns, played among the refuse. Swarms of green-black flies festered over the dung. Dogs, cats, chickens, camels and horses strolled around unbridled and unmolested. Barefooted men stood knee-deep in mud washing their jackasses; one of the donkeys brayed plain-tively until a mare came running and rubbed his neck to quiet him. It was the only public display of affection between the sexes that Eli would witness during his stay.

Hatoum suggested that they stop for lunch at one of the restaurants where arak flavored with anisette was served with a plethora of hors d'oeuvres, followed by dishes of greasy roast lamb buried in mounds of pilaf. The nearby bazaar over which hung a familiar odor of oils and spices was teeming with idlers, coffee vendors and beggars hunting for baksheesh. Across the street, butcher shops with chunks of raw meat hanging from iron hooks and stands piled sky-high with fruits and vegetables swarmed with Druze clients from the surrounding villages. Even the merchants selling old clothes, the cobblers who repaired shoes with tire rubber and the tinsmiths who fashioned house-wares from discarded cans had their hands full. And only a stone's throw away, at the terminal, where trucks and buses arrived and left in a steady stream, taxi drivers hawked for customers with the traditional *Shaam, yallah as-Shaam!* (Damas-cus, going to Damascus!), constantly cutting prices to lure pas-sengers away from the buses.

Shortly after lunch, Eli and Hatoum drove to the western end of the town. They passed a residential quarter of modern concrete villas the Army had built for officers and, at the fork on the highway, turned right and north. A few miles ahead rose the headquarters of the Southern Command, a two-story saw-shaped building dwarfed by the snowcapped Jabel as-Sheikh, the Biblical Mount Hermon where Nimrod the hunter had made his home and near which the tribe of Dan had settled when fleeing the Philistines. Its gaudily painted portal was topped by a green, orange and purple shield embossed with a nationalist slogan and the Baath dream map of an Arab empire—stretching all the way from the Atlantic Ocean to the Persian Gulf. A guard armed with rifle, cartridge belt and steel helmet asked Hatoum for his credentials. He glanced at the papers, saluted smartly and let them pass.

As Eli ran the gauntlet of checkpoints to the main entrance, he gained an inkling of the respect in which senior officers were held when a lieutenant dared question Hatoum's intentions. The major gave the subordinate a no-holds-barred bawling out. He was on friendly terms with the commanding general, Abd al-Ghani Dahman, and had come to pay him his respects. The lieutenant stuttered an apology and quickly cleared the way. Hatoum led Eli up a red-carpeted spiral staircase to the second floor; after a short wait in an anteroom they were ushered by an adjutant into a small office, where General Dahman received them with a cordial embrace. A thick Persian carpet, an elegant desk, a stiff-backed chair and a battery of telephones filled the room. Dahman, a broad-shouldered, muscular man of over forty, had a slightly lined face, a prominent nose and groomed mustache. His eyes, two burning coals, were topped by shaggy brows and contrasted sharply with his quiet temperament. After much coffee and even more party politics, they talked about the virile qualities of the Arab soldier and his manliness in battle. The general spoke slowly in a deep, rich voice used to command, ripping out words in explosive Arabic. With Allah at their side, Dahman believed the Syrians could fight until all Palestine was liberated from the Zionists. In the meantime, he promised, their shells would batter the Jews until they surrendered. But that was the extent of his remarks about border problems. If Eli had any illusions that Dahman would produce a map of the front and give him a full briefing, he swiftly lost them. Though charming and soft-spoken, the general avoided any references to frontier matters and refused to go beyond a simplified explanation of his role in the area.[1] There was nothing for Eli to do but forget his frustration. He did not hesitate, though, to be lavish with his compliments. This was no time or place for subtleties, and he decided to leave on this pleasant note lest he overplay his hand. The general kissed Hatoum and embraced Eli, who pledged to visit him soon at home. Minutes later, the two were retracing their circuitous way back through the corridors and checkpoints until they eventually emerged from the grounds.

After supper, a group of Hatoum's friends, members of the general's staff, invited them to see an Egyptian movie showing at a theater near the Officers' Club. It was a nightly diversion which Kuneitrans rarely missed. The audience was almost all male. Many were holding hands or mildly necking. After two hours of melodrama justice triumphed over feminine unchasteness and they all proceeded to the adjacent club for a drinking bout which lasted until morning. The club was the only place in Kuneitra where officers could spend the evening. The town, though unconcerned about homosexuality, took pride in its purity. There were no nightclubs or brothels, except private soliciting. The lack of any type of cultural life forced the military to spend their evenings sitting at sidewalk cafés playing backgammon, discussing politics or listening to the blaring radio while toying with their strings of amber beads. They went to bed early and awoke before dawn.

Eli hosted the party where generous quantities of liquor—usually beyond the means of many officers—were supplied. The talk was uninhibited, and he impressed his guests with a knowledge of military affairs uncommon in a civilian. Throughout the evening, a local Druze photographer he had commissioned took pictures of the assembled captains, majors and colonels, who seemed flattered that Taabet wished to have a permanent record of the occasion.[2] Shortly before dawn, Eli and Hatoum were shown to one of the more comfortable billets at the club.

Eli's generosity earned him the undaunted admiration of the young officers. His fame spread to such an extent that the following morning he was allowed to use his camera and speak freely to anyone he wished at the Southern Command—a privilege reserved only for high-ranking visitors. He even managed to get a briefing in front of an aerial map, a guided tour of the radar station the Army had built on a ridge of the steep hill across the road from headquarters, trips to bases in the vicinity and permission to inspect the fortifications of the northern sector.

A day later an officer was assigned to accompany Hatoum and Eli on their tour of the lines. They whizzed past Masada, catching a bare glimpse of Mughr Shaar and on the far left passed Ain Fit. A hairpin curve, a plunge down a steep incline, and the staff car began the climb toward Baniyas, the lush, green village blessed by pools and cascades of water which flowed from the river after which it was named. From there, the road led westward, straight to the side of Tal Azazziyat. They followed a wadi for several hundred yards and began crawling along the ledge dug into the living rock, spiraling upward steeply through rugged and serpentine terrain. Eli soon found himself on the leveled ground of a high plateau surrounded by three layers of mines and barbed wire. In the concrete command bunker, they were greeted by a heavyset, dark-haired captain, a militant leftist Baathite, who had recently returned from a training exercise in Cuba and was to leave soon for an artillery course in Czechoslovakia. Eli obligingly brought the officer up to date on party affairs and was in turn briefed on the defense plan of the position.

Tal Azazziyat, a central strongpoint of the Syrian heights, was perched atop a three-pronged ridge of volcanic rock. Its hedgehog of concrete pillboxes, firing trenches, antitank and artillery bunkers and underground sleeping quarters were built to withstand air bombardments. The *tal* was held by a force totaling some 200 men, constituting two infantry companies armed with rocket launchers, bazookas and heavy and light machine guns and supported by tank crews in static emplacements and a small field artillery unit manning Czech recoilless cannons and heavy mortars. To the west, facing the Israelis, a belt of mines and barbed wire fence stretched in a 600-foot perimeter around the main compound. Together with similar positions manned by 100 men each on the nearby Baniyas Plateau, Tal Kunheila on the northern flank, Tal Iaher 700 feet higher to the south and rearguard headquarters in Baniyas and Masada, Tal Azazziyat formed a defense barrier of the northern demilitarized zone. Its fortifications were backed by a second line of national guardsmen from the surrounding villages and heavy artillery batteries with a range of 15 miles emplaced in the ridges of Mughr Shaar, Tal Hamra and Ain Fit which regularly raked the kibbutzim of the Upper Galilee and the Huleh Valley below. Facing the Syrians along the land that stretched between the Sea of Galilee and the hills of Canaan, thirty-eight agricultural settlements organized in the Upper Galilee Council formed a border defense belt under the jurisdiction of Israel's Northern Command. Fronting, flanking and backing the kibbutzim were defensive positions manned by rugged commando-trained units of the Golani Brigade, most of whose men had been born and reared in the shadow of the Syrian guns.

From the summit, the whole of Israel seemed spread below. The white cubic houses of Dan and Shear Yeshuv lay at Eli's feet. Farther westward, beyond flocks of grazing sheep and tractors creeping along newly plowed fields, he could clearly see the roofs and water tower of Dafna. To the south, within rifle range, the settlements of the Huleh Valley stood naked and vulnerable.

Beyond Dan's wheat fields, the wadi, a narrow stream bed, was dried up. The grove through which the Dan River flowed, a favorite retreat for hikers, was now totally deserted. A triple line of willow, oak and poplar trees led to a labyrinth of slit trenches dug waist-high and carelessly camouflaged with eucalyptus branches. The kibbutz itself looked unchanged—the dining room, the hen houses, the school and even the museum of natural history where he and Nadia had admired the rare specimens of Israeli wild life. Men and women in rubber boots were working in the fields, harvesting wheat, cutting sugarcane and picking cotton. He could distinctly see the young girls in the apple orchards clinging to their long ladders and the weather-beaten fishermen standing knee-deep in the breeding ponds with rifles slung over their shoulders.

The sylvan scene, Eli knew, was deceptively peaceful. With the Syrians towering above them to the east and the Lebanese to the north, kibbutz members lived in a constant state of siege, protected only by the assurance that an attack would bring a massive retaliation by Israeli troops dug in nearby and reinforcements stationed only hours away. They spent most nights on guard, slept with their rifles near their beds and provided military escorts for their herdsmen, tractors and combines.

The Syrians kept a twenty-four-hour lookout on the settlers, monitoring their every move. They knew when the *kibbutzniks* went to work, ate or returned to their rooms. They followed them with their binoculars into the orchards, watched the shepherds leave with their herds and kept tabs on the tractors which plowed the fields adjoining the border. From time to time, they raked the settlement with heavy machine guns or shelled it with bazookas, mortars and field artillery. Shellings sometimes came with such regularity that the settlers named them "Syrian rainfall." The *kibbutzniks* became such experts in anticipating the bombardments that the moment their lookouts saw the Arab shepherds across the border disappear, they gathered their children and went underground. (Eli clearly remembered the Dan children. They were a healthy breed, though somewhat mature and melancholic. They seemed to have lost the joys of childhood from having spent most of their lives in bunkers.) At night, a blackout usually signaled the coming of an incident. As soon as the lights failed to go on or were turned off on the Syrian hedges and in the villages across the border, the settlers knew that a shelling was imminent and prepared to spend the night in deep concrete shelters. Their fears almost invariably materialized; overnight the Syrian shells flattened houses, smashed chicken runs and destroyed cow barns. But after each attack the settlers would emerge and with a fatalistic sense of mission start anew, clearing the destruction and rebuilding their kibbutz.

From Tal Azazziyat, Hatoum and Eli drove east along the Baniyas-Masada asphalt road. Near Ain Fit, a group of Russian advisers inspected long-range artillery emplacements, which Eli

photographed without interference—an activity apparently expected of visiting politicians. By the late afternoon the two
were back in Kuneitra. But before returning to the capital,
Hatoum stopped at the base stockade, a small military police
station on the road to Damascus, where an officer they both
knew was being held for political deviation before transfer to
the capital. Hatoum promised to use his influence to win the
officer's release and they left for home.[3]

Eli made one other trip to the border in the company of
Hatoum. The last time he traveled farther south, photographing
installations near the villages of Bir ash-Shkum, an-Nukeib and
al-Kursi. Below the Nukeib emplacements near the northeastern
shore of the Kinneret, he noticed a small fleet of fishing
boats spreading their nets. More to the south the Plain of
Jezreel stretched its flat, green floor across the breadth of Israel.
"Looking across," he later wrote, "I was struck by the tragic
folly of this unceasing war between Syria and Israel." The
farmers of al-Kursi and the fishermen of Ein Gev seemed so
much alike. They were enemies now but only because for
fifteen years Damascus had been spreading venomous propaganda which had stifled their best instincts. A sense of despair
overcame Eli at that moment and caused him to wish that he
could "seize a boat, cross the water and come home." The
Kinneret had suddenly become "a vast and terrible ocean"
separating him from his friends and family. The very fact that
his way would be barred, even if he were an ordinary citizen,
made him recognize that his isolation was "a necessary evil. I
felt like a lighthouse desperately passing its warning signals
through the night . . . to save the ship called Israel from the
dangers that were threatening it."[4]

Apart from supplying Tel Aviv with a *curriculum vitae* of
many officers of the Southern Command, Eli relayed photographs and sketch plans of the fortified bunkers and concrete
casements and supplied the precise coordinates of artillery emplacements near Mughr Shaar, Tal Hamra and Tal Azazziyat.[5]
From his own observations and the conversations he had been

privy to, he also reported on the strength and identity of the
units manning the lines—data that would prove of inestimable
value a few years later during the Six-Day War.

Hatoum, like Maazi, had once again become an unwilling ally
of enormous value, for without the major's friendship, it would
have been impossible for Eli to have obtained much of the
information that he had gathered about the border fortifications. He was almost naïvely confident that despite Hatoum's
inbred suspiciousness and penchant for seeing the darker motives behind every man's actions, the young officer remained
completely guileless about Eli's real intentions. As their friendship deepened, Eli eventually allowed Hatoum, who was married, to use his apartment as a trysting place, both for short
periods or for several months whenever he went abroad. His
certainty that the major harbored no doubts about his identity
was apparently complete, for while he carefully concealed the
transmitter and darkroom equipment in caches before leaving
for Europe, a meticulous search of the apartment would have
proved fatal.

Hatoum often spent the afternoons with one of his amours in
Eli's apartment, only a stone's throw away from his office. He
alternated between an attractive employee of the Turkish embassy and a curvaceous popular singer named Ludi Shamieh.
The major had first met Ludi while he was still in command of
the unit that guarded the General Staff complex and the nearby
radio and television stations. As commander of the most sensitive installations in Syria, he was wooed by his fellow officers
and wielded an enormous influence in the party. He thus had no
difficulty in convincing the television programming director to
feature Ludi.

At Hatoum's urging, Eli also helped boost Ludi's popularity.
He approached the director of Radio Damascus with a request
to give the young singer more exposure and went out of his way
to praise her charm and artistic potential to his newly cultivated
friend, Yussuf Khatib, director general of broadcasting and
television. He also spoke of her to Information Minister Sami

al-Jundi, thus earning the major's eternal gratitude. With Hatoum's influence in the party soaring, Eli did not have to insist. The government-owned station, unaffected by ratings of public criticism, allowed Ludi more and more time on the air, and she soon became a familiar face on variety programs.

The arrangement worked perfectly for all sides, except perhaps the Damascene viewers, many of whom found Ludi's singing so unbearable that they bought higher aerials in order to receive Cairo programs. The romance between Ludi and Hatoum provided ample gossip for the capital's *haut monde*, and their conduct drew sharp criticism from both the party and religious quarters. Hafez and fellow officers held the view that Hatoum was abusing his prerogatives and called him to task; only the major's position of strength saved him from expulsion.

Oiled by Hatoum's influence, Ludi had meanwhile become the undisputed star of Damascus television. Her affair with the powerful Baathite major also earned her the nickname of the Hatoum Barometer. Powerful Damascenes knew that as long as the radio blared Ludi's records and her cherubic face appeared on the screen for hours at a time, Hatoum's standing in the party remained undisputed; but as soon as her programs were curtailed, it was a sign that either an internecine struggle for power had been rekindled or the major had temporarily fallen into disgrace.[6]

Besides Hatoum, Seif and Maazi were also permitted to make private use of Eli's quarters, and eventually another officer would be brought into their confidence. Colonel Sallah Dalli, a Hafez protégé and member of the party's military committee, became a frequent guest. During Eli's second winter in Damascus, the phone would often ring early in the morning with either of his friends inquiring whether they could bring a companion over at midday or between five and seven in the evening. Eli usually laughed indulgently, promising to oblige. He would place the key under the doormat and leave the apartment shortly before the caller arrived with his steady girlfriend or casual companion. Seif and his secretary, Reita al-Huli, a plump brunette of peasant stock, were regular visitors and Dalli steadily entertained an Italian stewardess of Syrian Arab Airways whom he had met at a party Eli had given after his return from Europe.[7]

Eli's expansiveness did not go unappreciated, since even the Marxist-oriented Baathites still found it necessary to heed in public the Moslem prohibitions against sexual freedom which were still stringently adhered to by the older generation. Polygamy and concubines had once flourished in Damascus—although not for the last fifty years—but the culture had never tolerated unseemly public behavior. No hotel could have been used for an assignation, and there were scarcely any brothels left in the city. Only several generations before, an unveiled woman on the streets was automatically assumed to be a prostitute and could have been slain without fear of retribution by any male passerby. Since then the status of women had not changed greatly. Most could not talk freely with a man even in an accidental encounter, much less see him socially, for this could easily taint their reputations. A woman who had been touched by another man was often not considered suitable to become a bride. Only when a couple was betrothed could they venture out in public, and those who did were always the younger and more independent, usually college graduates and girls who had discarded the veil and old-fashioned views and had chosen to live in the modern suburbs of al-Mazza on the road to the International Airport.

The conception of romantic love was not prevalent in Syrian society; marriages were arranged between the girl's father and her suitor. The price of the dowry would increase in proportion to the girl's beauty, and young men often complained bitterly that fathers asked as much for their daughters as they had spent on them since birth. After marriage, most women were still relegated to a lowly status. They could not leave their homes at will and rarely spoke with their husbands' friends or indeed conversed with their own husbands in public. The men never talked about their wives and considered it an insult to be asked about them by a friend.

Yet the distinctly second-class status of Syrian wives, which

Hatoum, Seif and the others considered a circumstance that justified their indulgence in affairs, did not give them complete leeway—even with the students and career girls they dated. Syria was a country where informers still reported clandestine meetings of "free" youngsters to their parents and where innocent kissing in public could bring a jail term. Baath leaders in particular had to maintain at least an outward appearance of asceticism befitting a revolutionary party; gossip of open sexual dalliances was not the best publicity for a regime which proclaimed its belief in austerity and attacked the indulgences of the privileged classes.

Apart from the indebtedness accrued to him, Eli had another reason for allowing his friends to use the apartment. It often served as a meeting place for Hatoum, his fellow Druze officers and the rightist Baathites of the major's faction, all of whom were brought together by a common disdain for the overbearing Russian advisers, instructors and technicians of the Soviet military mission. The officers would gather in Eli's "Green Room," an opulently appointed salon decorated in a monochromatic color scheme, where they could talk undisturbed. Little did they know that behind the walls, Eli had installed a tape recorder and camera operated by an automatic timing device. elsewhere. But above all, Eli recognized that the irrefutable evidence of potential conspiracy could be used, in an extreme situation, for the purpose of blackmail.

In a country where a man's financial resources largely determined his suitability as a husband, Eli was considered among the most eligible of bachelors and more than one of his friends tried to marry him off—especially with young and attractive émigrées from Argentina. His charm, handsomeness and political position gave him an almost irresistible appeal. He traded on these advantages for his own purposes. Several secretaries in the Ministry of Defense and a young woman who worked in the Radio and Television Directorate at the Information Ministry had made known their interest in him. Without overtly encour-

aging them, he treated them warmly enough to win their affection and obtain useful bits of information to which they had
access. Some of the girls were more than willing to help in the
advancement of his political career and saw it as their duty to
make for him an extra copy of the letters their superiors wrote.[8]

Eli was also involved though in a much deeper way with a
young Damascene named Saliha, a relationship which would
finally cause him a great deal of anguish because of the obvious
conflicts with his other life. The girl's father, Abu Mahmud, had
been a large landholder before the Baath came to power and
still owned a number of shops near the Suq al-Bzaniye. Abu
Mahmud, a close friend of al-Ard's, had been introduced to Eli
by the sheik; he was suitably impressed by the young man. Eli
and the old merchant struck up a genuine friendship and often
spent their afternoons or evenings together. Abu Mahmud used
to accompany the sheik and Eli to the Hammam al-Jose, one of
the oldest bathhouses in Damascus, and frequently aided Taabet
in buying the best bargains from Damascene antique dealers. He
somewhat resented Eli's reluctance to join him when he prayed
at the Shian Pasha Mosque, but the two met almost daily at a
café where Abu Mahmud would chew salted nuts or smoke a
narghile while playing backgammon and relentlessly discussing
politics. He usually railed against the Baath, which had stripped
him of most of his estates, proclaiming somewhat unconvincing-
ly that he would soon leave Syria. At one point Mahmud tried
to use Eli's influence in the party and offered $10,000 if he
would intervene with the Ministry of Agrarian Reform on his
behalf. As "a loyal member of the Baath Party and the Arab
revolution," Eli tactfully refused.

Abu Mahmud nonetheless saw Eli as a most promising husband for his daughter and introduced him to Saliha, a rather
plain-looking, though shapely, girl in her mid-twenties with
dark-brown hair and brown eyes. What Eli truly felt about
Saliha is not known, but while it was not essential that he
appear to be seriously interested in a woman, such a relationship gave him an added dimension of stability, almost as tangi-

ble an asset as his business interests. He regularly visited Saliha and her family at their luxurious Ottoman-style house in the new section of Damascus, north Chuhada Street, and was always greeted formally, shown into the *iwan* and served coffee by Saliha or her mother, a heavyset woman who rarely spoke. The woman would then light the narghiles (waterpipes), and the ritual of smoking and political talk would begin. After their betrothal, Eli and Saliha were often seen together. They picnicked on the shores of the Barada, occasionally saw an Egyptian or Indian movie, or nightclubbed at the Orient Palace on al-Hidjaz Street. On some weekends they would drive out to a summer resort in Bludan in the Anti-Lebanon Mountains, to Beirut or to the Meadow Lakes east of Damascus, almost always chaperoned by either Saliha's father or brother.

The girl apparently became deeply attached to Eli, and when she later began to suspect that he was gathering intelligence for some purpose, she led herself to believe that it was to further his own political career; through her friends who worked for the government, she eventually supplied him with information.[9] Their relationship though, could not remain casual for long. Both the sheik and Saliha's father soon became less than subtle in their entreaties that they marry. But after consulting with Tel Aviv, Eli decided to stall as much as possible before taking the final step.

In the spring of 1963, Eli was startled to read in the French press that Iser Harel had suddenly resigned as head of the Mosad and *memune* of all security services following a bitter feud with Prime Minister Ben-Gurion over the Mosad's activities involving German scientists employed by Egypt. Eli was well aware of the Mosad's efforts to investigate the scientists and technicians working to develop Egypt's aeronautics and missile industries since Faruk's reign. Both Naguib and Nasser had extended their contracts, but largely because of the country's shaky economy, a lack of skilled Arab personnel and Russian reluctance to help, nothing of much substance had been achieved. Yet after the launching of the Sputnik, Nasser had decided to undertake a massive effort to construct long-range missiles and placed the project in the hands of a trusted intimate, Colonel Mahmud ad-Din Khalil, the head of Air Force intelligence, promising that this time no shortage of funds would impede the work.

Khalil calculated that without the support of the Russians, Egypt had no choice but again to seek out the technologically sophisticated Germans, and military attachés in Europe were ordered to comb the Continent for experts who wished to cooperate. In the spring of 1960 a number of prominent rocketry experts who had been guaranteed lucrative salaries arrived in Cairo aboard a Lufthansa Comet IV. Among the visitors were Dr. Paul Görke, a former Luftwaffe engineer renowned for his work in radar and infrared rays; Dr. Wolfgang Piltz, a white-maned rocket designer and propulsion expert; Professor Eugen Sänger, director of the Institute of Jet Propulsion in Stuttgart; and his portly administrator, Dr. Heinz Krug. Not long after, a site was chosen ten miles east of the capital where the new weapons would be developed. Khalil wasted no time. Five thousand fellaheen were trucked daily into the area and in one month, working round-the-clock shifts, managed to erect a vast complex of hangarlike buildings (innocuously code-named Factory 333) and constructed a new highway link between the center and the International Airport. While the missile assembly plant was rising on the desert sands, a launching area, complete with pads, blockhouses and gantries, was being readied 40 miles west of Cairo. By the time the facilities were completed, planeloads of German technicians, some with their families, had begun arriving in Egypt and were settled in a new village near Factory 333.

In less than one year, two types of ground-to-ground missiles carrying conventional warheads had risen from the desert launching pads. Al-Zafer (The Victor), patterned after the French Véronique, was designed to carry 400 pounds of explosives, had a range of 230 miles and could be launched from mobile platforms; al-Kaher (The Conqueror), based on designs of the German V-2 rocket, had a maximum payload of 1 ton of explosives and a range of 370 miles, but could be fired only from fixed emplacements.[10] What particularly concerned the Israelis was that the enormous expense and effort expanded on the project could not have been for the sole purpose of developing weapons for conventional warfare. They knew that the missiles' guidance systems were not sufficiently refined for use against military targets; the weapons could thus be fired only against urban centers. Yet if this were Egypt's aim, they could have more easily employed the Ilyushin bombers received from the Soviet Union which carried a larger tonnage of explosives. It seemed clear that Nasser ultimately intended to arm the missiles with atomic warheads.

What the Mosad later learned about the type of warhead that the Egyptians wanted to use was indeed chilling. Dr. Otto Franz Jocklick, a former Wehrmacht captain and later secretary of a clandestine neo-Nazi organization in the Tyrol, who had just returned from Cairo, unexpectedly contacted Israeli agents in Europe. According to Jocklick, a prominent Austrian radio therapist and X-ray specialist, an agent of Egypt's director of Special Projects, Colonel Mahmud Khalil, who claimed to represent a new cancer research laboratory at Cairo's Central Hospital, had approached him with a request to purchase large quantities of radioactive cobalt 60 "for medical experiments." The Egyptian had assured him that he would be well paid for his services. After a few more meetings the two agreed on a delivery system, and within months, lead cylinders containing the cobalt 60 began arriving in the Egyptian capital. Jocklick was then invited to Cairo, briefed about the true nature of the project and asked to supply increased shipments. The master plan, code-named Project Ibis, called for equipping Egypt's Air Force with 900 missiles of both types, to be later supplemented by a long-range (590 km) missile named al-Ared (The Vanguard), all with radioactive warheads. Jocklick refused to collaborate and, upon his return to Europe, contacted the Mosad. He offered as proof of Egypt's plans invoices and bills of lading covering the shipment of quantities of cobalt 60 far too large to be used simply for medical purposes.[11]

Israeli agents in Egypt, who had been on the alert for moves to develop more devastating warheads, confirmed Jocklick's story. Jerusalem now had a difficult decision to make. The situation called for an anguished appeal to world opinion, even a request for United Nations' intervention to halt Cairo's aeronautical buildup, atomic research, missile programs and chemical and bacteriological warfare projects. But accusations involving atomic warfare could not be made without adequate proof, and disclosing the evidence available would inevitably reveal the sources from which it had been obtained, endangering the Mosad's Egyptian networks. The price was simply too high. Jocklick, on the other hand, was not a creditable enough witness to be used in a propaganda assault. Besides, there was the danger that such a fantastic story would not be believed. A solution based on open propaganda and appeals for help was therefore discarded.

Mosad officers finally decided on a plan of action. As most of the German technicians at Factory 333 were unaware of the true nature of Egypt's Project Ibis, they decided to try two parallel approaches: appeal to the non-Nazis to desist from participating in a new act of genocide, and wage a campaign to frighten the Nazi diehards and neo-Nazis of the younger generation with threats of violence. The messages were to be conveyed in both cases through relatives in West Germany. The families of employees in Factory 333 were soon visited by Israeli agents who told them of Egypt's plans to annihilate the Jewish state. They were urged to relay the Mosad's veiled and sometimes direct threats to Cairo in order "to avert any untoward accidents."[12]

But neither threats nor appeals to conscience had any immediate effect, and no Germans left Factory 333. The Egyptians successfully launched their missiles and exultantly displayed them before cheering throngs at the parade marking the tenth anniversary of the revolution. "Our missiles," Nasser boasted rather undiplomatically, "can reach any point south of Beirut." The target could only have been one nation.

The Mosad ordered the initiation of a campaign of terror. A private plane carrying the wife of Hassan Kamil, Nasser's purchasing agent in Europe, crashed in Westphalia, killing her and the pilot. Dr. Krug left his office one morning at the Jet Propulsion Institute and was never seen again; his abandoned car was found several kilometers from his home in Munich. Hans Klingwachter, head of a laboratory in Lörrach which supplied parts to Factory 333, was on his way home when a sedan blocked his way, a man got out and thrust a pistol into the car, firing point-blank; the police found the abandoned sedan in Vienna. A "letter-bomb" intended for Dr. Plitz was opened by his secretary, seriously maiming her. A number of scientists were killed by parcel bombs received from Germany.[13] The Germans in Cairo were terrified. When they began receiving threatening letters mailed from Cairo, many hurriedly left Egypt.

As part of the campaign of intimidation, Jocklick and a Mosad agent who called himself Josef Ben Gal met Dr. Görke's daughter in Basel and attempted to convince her to persuade her father to leave Egypt. The Swiss police, whom the girl notified about the meeting, arrested the Austrian and the Israeli and charged them with coercion and illegally acting as agents of a foreign country. Their trial exposed some of the intelligence operations Harel had been conducting against the scientists. Jocklick's testimony, however, would ultimately arouse world opinion and bring undreamed-of results. He had managed to purchase more than $4,000,000 worth of cobalt 60, three times the amount of radioactive material needed to destroy the population of Israel and render the country inhabitable for at least five years.

The disclosures at the trial brought into the open the feud between Ben-Gurion and Harel over the handling of the missile affair. Until the early sixties the premier had held Little Iser in high esteem and had considered him one of his most trusted advisers. Harel had successfully carried out special missions for Ben-Gurion in Europe and the Arab countries and had personally led Mosad agents in the abduction of Adolf Eichmann. Their relationship, however, had been strained when an investigation by the Shin Beth, Israel's counterespionage service, revealed that Israel Baer, Zahal's official historian and Ben-Gurion's military adviser and close friend, had been a Russian spy for the last twenty years. The gulf between them had widened farther when the *memune* joined a cabal of the Mapai Party which attempted to depose Ben-Gurion. But the premier, who felt that Harel's performance had always been beyond reproach, kept him in his post and continued to rely upon his advice in intelligence matters—until that day when Harel put the German scientists' dossier on Ben-Gurion's desk. The *memune* claimed that he held incontrovertible proof that nothing less than the existence of Israel was at stake.

Ben-Gurion at first went along with Harel's plans to intimidate and, if necessary, liquidate, the scientists who were working toward Israel's destruction. But after the Basel incident, when the premier found that the Mosad's actions and Harel's statements over the issue were causing anger in Bonn, he began to fear that relations with West Germany were being undermined. When the *memune* suggested that he approach President Konrad Adenauer and request that his government either recall or take other action against the scientists, Ben-Gurion categorically refused.

The premier believed strongly that he could not risk a showdown with Adenauer over the issue. Germany, perhaps somewhat ironically, was Israel's major supplier of arms, and Ben-Gurion advocated a policy of appeasement with Bonn. Further, he could not agree with Harel that Israel faced any great danger; but even if the scientists did in fact present a potential threat to Israel, he would have to call a halt to the operations. Yet Harel continued to assert that the Germans in Cairo presented a genuine menace. However, when recalled from a trip to Europe and ordered to substantiate his allegations, the *memune* angrily replied, "It will be my successor who will provide this proof." The following morning, Ben-Gurion received Little Iser's formal resignation.

Harel was quick to enter political life in order to publicize his grievances against the premier. He charged Ben-Gurion with appeasing the Germans—an unpardonable policy and an "affront to the Jews of the Auschwitz generation." Harel felt the

Old Man's rejection of his assessments only proved that the government was ungrateful to the men who had risked their lives to halt the Egyptian missile project.[14] But whatever the premier's own deductions from the data he was supplied, it would seem that at the least he had taken a calculated risk. Ultimately, the scientists left Factory 333 for moral reasons or out of fear, and the Egyptian missiles were never armed with cobalt 60.

But the short-term effect of the affair, the last of a series of *cause célèbres,* proved devastating to the prime minister. With public opinion very much on the side of Harel, Ben-Gurion's position had been hopelessly undermined; several months after Harel's resignation, he relinquished the posts of premier and minister of defense to Levi Eshkol and retired to his home in the desert settlement of Sde Boker. For Little Iser, the missile affair had ended seventeen years of intelligence work—a career marked by Machiavellian ploys which nevertheless enriched the Mosad's espionage record.

Eli's curiosity was piqued by the question who would be named to succeed Harel; yet until he returned to Israel, he had no way of knowing who was now directing his mission. At the weekly Cabinet meeting after Harel's resignation, Ben-Gurion informed his ministers that the man he had chosen to replace Harel was Major General Meir Amit. The appointment of Amit came as no surprise to the intelligence community; as head of Modiin he was the second-ranking officer in the services.

The tall, solidly built forty-nine-year-old Amit had been a soldier for more than half his life. A sabra, born in Tiberias to immigrants of Russian descent, he had studied agriculture in Givat Hashelosha and graduated from the Balfour Gymnasium in Tel Aviv, where he first joined the Haganah underground. Upon receiving his diploma, Amit joined Kibbutz Alonim, where he met his wife, Yona, and settled for the next eleven years. Like his predecessor he served in the Jewish Auxiliary Police before devoting his full time to clandestine operations. During the 1948 war Amit commanded a battalion and won an early reputation for bravery. He would later lead his motor-ized commando unit against the Syrians, battle the Iraqis and, after recovering from a wound he received on the Jordanian front, pursue the Egyptians to the tip of Eliat. At the war's end he led the famed Golani Brigade until the General Staff decided that he could fight better from behind a desk. Impressed by his tactical abilities, Chief of Staff Moshe Dayan offered him the Operations Division.

While running the gauntlet of regional commands, Amit's career threatened to come to an abrupt end when he was gravely injured during paratroop maneuvers in the Negev. The long period of recovery which followed finally caused his re-lease from active duty and he decided to pursue a new career. He enrolled in New York's Columbia University and two years later received a master's degree in business administration. But when the new chief of staff, Yitzhak Rabin, heard that he was searching for a position in industry, Amit was offered the command of military intelligence.[15] From there, the road to the Mosad was quickly traveled.

Amit admitted that the transition from a field command to intelligence work had not been without difficulties. Less flam-boyant and autocratic than his predecessor, he was a diffident man who could not be roused to anger, mild-mannered, yet somewhat cynical. Unlike Harel, who shunned keeping official records of either his decisions or the activities of the service, Amit ordered that a stenographer be present at every confer-ence and Mosad operations be carefully documented. A firm believer in scientific methods who did not share Harel's taste for espionage fiction, Amit instituted the recruitment of university graduates and refused to employ Israelis or others with criminal records, a practice common in the past. He preferred to train men of solid qualities rather than mold reliable agents out of sharp characters. His ideal operative was a good linguist, skillful detective, accomplished psychologist and social extrovert—all in one. Amit therefore ended the practice of disciplining employ-ees for negligence or incompetence. "If an agent, no matter how highly placed, does not observe the discipline, he has to resign."[16]

Amit inherited from Little Iser a vast variety of operations already in progress. The most fruitful of all, though, was the mission carried out by Operative 88.

Crescent and Swastika

The magnitude of the threat to Israel's existence created by the German scientists in Egypt had made it strikingly clear to the Mosad that the contributions ex-Nazis were capable of making to Arab states could not be underestimated. At the time Eli had completed his report on Franz Rademacher an estimated 100 former Reich officials lived in Damascus. Their influence was thought to be less powerful than in Egypt, but the reverberations of the missile affair had caused enough concern for the Mosad to request that Eli resume his investigation.

Whatever the assistance these ex-Nazis were giving the government in the early 1960's, Eli had ample evidence to indicate that, in the past, Damascus had been much more anxious than the Egyptians to enlist their aid. Even before the Arab-Israeli conflict, in an effort to diminish the French influence in its armed forces, Syria was recruiting military instructors from among the German officers and NCO's who had served under Field Marshal Rommel. (The Syrian Army had been under French tutelage ever since its creation during the Mandate as an auxiliary force to the metropolitan Troupes du Levant; its recruitment, training and equipment were supervised by a special military mission directly responsible to the governor-general. But neither the Third Republic nor the pro-Nazi Vichy administration and later General de Gaulle's Free French Forces attempted to modernize the auxiliaries.)

After the French withdrawal, an unofficial Brotherhood of

Friends of the Axis had come into being in Syria when Vichy supporters, veterans of the 1941 pro-Nazi putsch in Iraq and repatriates from the defeated Reich, who held high civil posts in the government, convinced the generals that German advisers could bring about improvements which the French had been unable or unwilling to institute. The General Staff at once realized the potential, and asked former SS Lieutenant Colonel Akhram Tabassa to organize the repatriation of followers of the Grand Mufti's Arabian Freedom Movement who had fought with the German Arab Legion during the war. A first contingent of Arab SS men was later joined by scores of low-ranking German officers and NCO's who had managed to escape from British POW camps in Cyprus and Egypt. Hundreds of jobless Wehrmacht officers were also hired as soon as the remnants of the Afrika Korps emerged from captivity.[1]

The General Staff's enthusiasm for the Germans was due in part to ideological rapport and past allegiance to the Reich, but the major reason was grounded in simple necessity; as a young nation with little military know-how, Syria was willing to pay handsomely for the martial skills possessed by German officers. After the region had been scoured for foreign military experts, Damascus launched a recruiting program abroad. A number of former Nazis armed with Syrian passports were sent to Germany and Austria in search of old comrades-in-arms still willing to fight the Jews. As they offered salaries of up to $535 a month plus special hardship bonuses, the response was overwhelming. The Germans underwent a crash course in Arabic and were then sent to Rome and Geneva, where clandestine processing stations patterned on the French Foreign Legion had been opened in the Syrian legations.

The hiring of military advisers was also done through intermediaries. Officers of the French and Spanish Foreign Legions contracted fugitive SS men to fight in Indochina and sold them to the Syrians for $350 to $500 per capita. The Germans were smuggled through the French Zone in Germany and Austria under the guise of legionnaires and were delivered, for embarkation in an Italian or Turkish port.[2] The American and British high commissioners could do little to stop this illegal traffic and, as a result, dozens of German officers were routed to Damascus.

One of the first major tasks undertaken by the Nazis was the training of a ragtag volunteer army composed of Yugoslav and Albanian Muhammadans who had fought for the Reich, British deserters from the Eighth Army and an assortment of Axis collaborators. The responsibility for molding this undisciplined force was given in large part to a thirty-man contingent under the command of Major General Graf von Strachwitz, who had led an infantry division in Europe.[3] The performance of the volunteers turned out to be almost as bleak as that of the Syrians themselves; repeated setbacks in the early months of the Palestine war forced the General Staff to make a plea for more German advisers.

A second team, consisting of SS officers, Luftwaffe pilots and panzer specialists, was entrusted with the reorganization of the Syrian Army along the lines of the Waffen SS. But whatever the military acumen the Germans could offer, it was hardly enough to compensate for the shortcomings of the Syrians and their volunteers under fire. The Army's failures subsequently opened the way for other Wehrmacht and SS veterans who came to Damascus in growing numbers to undertake the task of revitalizing the armed forces. The effort was now directed by a one-time Wehrmacht general, Hermann von Stutterheim, and his adjutants, Colonel Rainer Kriebel, a former instructor in military tactics at the Berlin War Academy, and the cavalry expert, Colonel Heinz Heigl. The reshaping of the armor brigade and special units was placed in the hands of Colonel Hans von Zempelhof, Major Herbert von Fürst (alias Abdullah Harb) and Captain Keil (alias Mahmud Zanubitch), who had fought under General Hans Guderian on the Russian front. Finally, the overhaul of the Second Bureau became the responsibility of former Gestapo Colonel Rapp.

By the early 1950's the presence of as many as fifty German advisers in such high-level commands had begun to cause Syria some embarrassment. Anxious to dispel any misconceptions arising over the true role of the German officers, President al-Shishakli was at pains to stress that they were merely filling Syria's need for military specialists. If any of the émigrés had shown an inclination to interfere in the country's politics, he told a West German newsman, "I would not have permitted him to remain in his post for more than one hour."

After the USSR entered the Middle East as an arms purveyor, German technicians and Russian advisers had to collaborate for nearly two years. In February, 1957, President al-Kuwatli officially terminated an era by dismissing the German military advisers to make way for the Russian and Czech military mission. Kriebel and Heigl left last after they were decorated for "outstanding services to the Syrian nation."[4] With the advent of the union, more and more Soviet personnel reached Syria. But with the Egyptianization of the Army and the security services (the 1,100 officers dismissed and 500 transferred to Egypt were replaced by 2,300 Egyptians) a second wave of former Nazis arrived to advise the Second Bureau and the Special Bureau, Syria's political police.

The German technicians and specialists remained and, for a while, Germans and Russians meshed their activities fairly well. But differences soon arose, and the Russians attempted to take over and oust the Nazis. Colonel Abd al-Hamid Sarraj, the chief of the Second Bureau during the union, sidestepped the internal conflict. The German technicians, Sarraj argued, held key positions in the Army and communications and were necessary to prevent a breakdown; he insisted on cooperation with them. After days of heated and frantic discussion at the General Staff, Sarraj warned the Russians that they would have to continue to work together in the best interest of Syria, and for a while, Germans and Russians continued training troops, administering logistics and instructing security forces.[5]

With the intensification of the struggle against Israel, the Syrian security services, Eli learned, like their Egyptian counterparts, were also on the lookout for German advisers with experience in the "Final Solution of the Jewish Problem," to be employed as propaganda and information officers. That such specialists might also happen to be war criminals was very much incidental. The Mufti, in fact, argued at the time that the presence of Lieutenant Colonel Adolf Eichmann in Syria would create panic among the Israelis and sent an emissary, Hussein Khurani, to search for him in Germany.

By that time, thousands of German war criminals had successfully evaded detention, assumed false identities and were living in hiding. As soon as security measures had been relaxed, they formed the first clandestine group which helped comrades who were still lingering in internment centers awaiting prosecution. Under cover of aiding POW's, the group was given Allied blessing. Before long ODESSA (Organization of Former SS Members) was using an escape route code-named B-B to smuggle escapees from Bremen to Bari and later Rome, Venice and Genoa, from which they were shipped to South America or the Middle East. Haddad Said, the former SS Captain Rostal who was in charge of ODESSA's European branch, ran transports of up to forty men from Frankfurt and Munich to a distribution center in Augsburg, where they were given passports and false papers. Those slated for Cairo and Damascus were sent on to Memmingen, a medieval town in the heart of a secluded wooded region in southern Bavaria. They were then driven across the Austrian border in newspaper delivery trucks of the *Stars and Stripes* to Lindau on the Lake of Constance, where an ODESSA center operated under the cover of an import-export firm with branches in the Arab capitals. Those transferred to Bregenz applied, after they were joined by Austrian women and children who had been hired to pose as their relatives for passes to St. Gall in Switzerland. The crossings took place with the collaboration of the Austrian border police and the lenient French occupation authorities. ODESSA emissaries finally sent the fugitives by train to Geneva, from which they were flown to Beirut. A reception committee headed by Major Count Günther Elmar von Hardenberg screened them in the Lebanese capital, where

278 The Shattered Silence

an association for Christian German War Refugees—a cover for the secret German Aid Committee in the Near East—assigned them to their units in the Syrian Army and helped them on their last lap to Damascus.[6]

Syrian embassies in Bern and Rome had also served as stations for neo-Nazi underground movements, Eli was told. The Rome legation at one point served as headquarters for ODESSA. It was thus at the embassy's initiative that SS Colonel Walter Rauff, who was responsible for many of the early gassings of Jews, had arrived in Syria. Rauff had been taken prisoner by the American Army and spent more than twenty months in the Rimini POW camp in northern Italy before escaping in December, 1946. With the aid of a priest, he made his way to Naples, then to Rome, where for eighteen months he was given sanctuary in various monasteries. He was teaching French and arithmetic at an orphanage in the Via Pia when the Syrian embassy offered him a contract as technical adviser to the Special Bureau and arranged for his family to leave the Russian zone in occupied Germany and join him in Damascus. Rauff would later be chosen to head the personal guard of President al-Shishakli.[7]

The Syrians also aided another notorious Nazi, Franz Stangel, former commandant of the Treblinka extermination camp, where only forty out of 700,000 inmates had survived. At the war's end, Stangel, who had returned to his wife and children in Austria, was arrested by the CIC and underwent a routine investigation at Camp Marcus W. Orr in Glassenbach near Salzburg. Two years later he was transferred to the prison in Linz for having attended, as a former police officer, the Training School for Extermination at Castle Hartheim. In May, 1948, Stangel escaped while on his way to work at the Voest steel combine; ODESSA whisked him to Damascus, where he worked as a mechanic before the Second Bureau employed him as a specialist in Jewish affairs. A wealthy Indian socialite who lived in the Syrian capital hired Frau Stangel as governess for her children, and the Syrian consul in Bern issued the necessary visas. But after the announcement of Eichmann's capture, Eli learned that Stangel, his wife and three children, had disappeared from the Syrian capital.[8]

In addition to the investigations into the status and whereabouts of Nazis in Syria, the Mosad had an even more timely reason for a new inquiry: It wanted Eli to check reports that converted Germans had rather recently become active in arms acquisitions—an area of vital importance to the Syrians, who had little capacity to produce their own armaments. Tel Aviv had learned that sophisticated war matériel Damascus had been unable to obtain from Communist nations was being supplied by Germans trafficking in contraband weapons.

Through Rademacher and al-Ard, Eli had known that former Nazis were presently dealing in black arms; he was only vaguely aware, however, of their past or current activities. One of the arms merchants, Georg Fisher, an alias used by SS Hauptsturm-führer Alois Brunner, had been mentioned by Rademacher, but at the time, Eli had heard that "Fisher had left for Cairo." From the sheik, he now discovered that Brunner continued to operate his Damascus office with the aid of two partners— a German and a pro-Nazi Syrian. Brunner's past had been far from uneventful. As a member of Eichmann's staff in Bureau IVB 4a, he had been responsible for the deportation of Jews from Greece, France, Slovakia and Austria to extermination camps in Poland. In December, 1944, on special orders from the chief of the Gestapo, Heinrich Müller, all of Eichmann's subordinates were summoned to Prague and issued false papers; they were told to make appearances at different military installations under their newly assumed identities before going underground in Germany or Austria. Brunner arrived in Upper Austria before V-E Day, passed through Budweis and Römersdorf in the Lemback district, where he left his wife and returned to Vienna. He was arrested donning a Wehrmacht uniform and interned in the Wegscheid POW camp near Linz. Before he could be interrogated by the American CIC, he managed to escape and went into hiding in northern Germany. While his brother Anton Brunner was tried and executed in the capital, the federal authorities renewed the search for Alois. (Warrants for his arrest had also been issued by Austria, Hungary and Czechoslovakia.) Brunner contacted the ODESSA underground, which provided his new identity.

After a brief stop in Cairo, he moved to Damascus, where he worked for a local company bottling Coca-Cola. He then established a motion-picture distribution company which handled German-produced anti-Semitic films, such as the notorious *Jud Süss*. Brunner, who was later employed by the Grand Mufti and the Syrian Moslem Brotherhood, later became active in a much more lucrative enterprise. While working for Hadj Amin al-Husseini, he had grown friendly with a former Reich paratroop captain, Karl Heinrich Speath, who had acted as a middleman in the sale of Czech arms to the Algerian rebels. Speath employed Brunner in the Arab Medical Company, THAMECO, a drug firm headquartered in Lichtenstein which he used as a cover for the trade of black-market weapons. Brunner eventually established a similar firm in Damascus—an import-export firm he called the CATAR office. His partners were Karl Heinz Brinkman and Dr. Fuad Nahdif, a Fascist leader who had fled to Germany during the war after the French had outlawed his youth organization.

During the union with Egypt, Brunner was employed by the Special Bureau. Shortly before the 1961 coup, on September 13, he was notified that a package from Germany was being held for him at the central post office. Brunner picked up the package at the parcel post window and brought it home. As soon as he started opening it, there was an explosion. Brunner lost the use of both eyes, his left hand was badly damaged, and he received several chest injuries. Although private sources attributed the bomb parcel to the Red Hand,* it was obviously an

*The Red Hand was a rightist terrorist organization formed by French Army officers and settlers in Tunisia to counter Bourguiba's Neo-Destour Movement. It spread to other French-speaking nations of North Africa plagued by nationalist movements. Its agents on the Continent and in North Africa worked in intelligence, supplied contraband guns and liquidated opponents. Much evidence has come forward in latter years to suggest that the French SDEC gave it unofficial support. The Red Hand later merged with the OAS, the Secret Army Organization, a right-wing terrorist group founded after the revolt of the French Army in Algiers in April, 1961.

Israeli intelligence operation. Brunner recovered, and shortly after Eli had arrived in Damascus, he left for Cairo, where the Interior Ministry had promised him a pension.[9]

Brunner's CATAR office had often done business with Ernst Wilhelm Springer, one of the more exotic figures in the shadowy world of arms smuggling and a man who had aroused Eli's intense interest because of his reported dealings with the Acquisitions Department of the Defense Ministry. Eli knew that Springer, known in Damascus as Schtringer, had been Rademacher's friend and business partner. Al-Ard, who knew him for more than ten years, had been introduced to Springer by Rademacher one evening in the late fifties while he was dining at the al-Shark nightclub. As an SS officer, Eli learned, Springer had trained the volunteers of the German Arab Legion during the war. When he did not travel, Springer lived with his family in the small Schleswig-Holstein city of Bad Segeberg. In the postwar years, he had joined forces with General Otto Remmer, one of the founders of the Socialist Reichs Party and was considered one of the far right's best orators; he had also been elected as the party's representative to the Schleswig-Holstein State Assembly. Springer's political career, though, had ended after the party was declared illegal, and he became involved in the black market arms trade, gaining a reputation as the leading Omnipol salesman in the Middle East.*

Springer was rarely in Damascus for long periods of time, but al-Ard managed to arrange a brief meeting with Eli in the lobby of the New Omayad Hotel. A tall, broad-shouldered man in his early forties, Springer appeared cordial enough but revealed little of importance about himself.[10] He did not lead the kind of sheltered and oppressive life led by Rademacher that would cause him to talk impulsively with strangers. Yet Eli was eventually able to discover a number of interesting facts about the man. Springer had sold large quantities of arms to the FLN and

* Omnipol, the Czech-owned company, manufactured small arms and sold them as genuine Third Reich war surplus. The weapons were prefired, dated from World War II and given the insignia of the Third Reich. In this way they could be sold to non-Communist nations or rightist forces without any embarrassment to the Soviet bloc.

had dealt just as willingly with their implacable foes, the right-wing terrorists of the OAS. He was extremely inventive and in one instance had smuggled automatic pistols into Algiers by concealing them in airtight cookie tins. Besides the Syrians, his wide range of clients included the Tunisian freedom fighters, Katanga separatists, Moroccan rebels and the princes of the Persian Gulf. His readiness to sell anyone arms for a price, though, was inevitably risky; at least one attempt had already been made on his life by an assassin who planted a bomb under the seat of his car.[11] But Springer found compensation for some of the dangers involved. Despite the risks, one German arms dealer observed, selling to the Arabs at least ensured that the old cause would be furthered—"the continuation of the battle of the Western world against the common enemy, Judaism."

The status of the Jews who lived in Arab nations was of particular concern to the Mosad, which had helped organize illegal emigration and now helped the Research Department of the Foreign Ministry to collect and analyze intelligence on Jewish communities in the Arab world. While the situation of the Syrian Jewry was not a subject shrouded in secrecy, the government had not permitted any Jew to leave the country for the last eight years, and the few who had managed to reach Israel offered accounts about conditions in the *harets* that were often contradictory and always highly emotional. Intelligence analysts needed detailed information which could be supplied only by an objective observer, free from the strains imposed on the local community. Yet Eli's inquiry had to be discreet. There was no apparent reason why he should be at all interested in such a small and nearly invisible minority. Questions which might appear too pointed had to be avoided, and he could not chance making contact with Jews actually living in the *haret*.

What Eli learned through overheard conversations and un-obtrusive walks through the ghetto brought a profound shock of recognition from his own past. A once-flourishing communi-ty, existing since Biblical times, now lay wasted and largely ignored by all but the police. The sorry condition was all the more appalling because of the stark contrast with what had once existed. Less than two decades before, 30,000 Jews, many of them prominent merchants and professionals, had lived in Aleppo and Damascus. Throughout the Mandate, they had held important posts in the government and after the French departed, they were not excluded from positions in the new administration.

The emergence of the state of Israel altered the status quo with unusual swiftness. Virtually overnight, the Jews turned from respected citizens to despised aliens whose very existence was seen to pose a grave threat to Syrian security. After the United Nations voted to partition Palestine, eighteen synagogues in Aleppo alone were burned to the ground. As the reprisals worsened during the tense months before the war, the trickle of Jews who had been helped since 1930 to cross into Palestine became a tidal wave of humanity. By the time Israel declared itself a state nearly half the Jewish community had left Syria. In retaliation for the exodus, the government seized the émigrés' homes and property, in some cases turning over the abandoned dwellings to Palestinian refugees. Those who stayed behind did not dare venture away from the *harets* for long or risked returning to find their doors bolted and their possessions sacked by the security services.

By the mid-1950's intimidation and repression had reduced the Jewish population to 6,000. Eli learned that a small *haret* whose residents were of Turkish origin still existed in Kamishlieh, while a group of Jewish peasants remained in the Gezira near the Iraqi border. In the capital the survivors huddled together in the Haret al-Yahud, southeast of the Street Called Straight. They were permitted to leave the confines of the ghetto only for religious services and then under the watchful eyes of a police escort. Poverty was endemic. Jews were no longer considered employable by the government or private business, nor would public schools admit children from the *haret*. The only educational institutions remaining open were a Talmud Torah and the Alliance *lycée*; in both, Hebrew and the Bible were banned from the curriculum.[12]

The government did seek, however, to keep the Jewish Quarter inundated with anti-Zionist propaganda. A compulsory lecture was given each week to prominent members of the community by Eli's friend, the former director of foreign programming in the Ministry of Information, Louis (Heiden) al-Hadj, the translator of *Mein Kampf* into Arabic, who spoke on the evils of Zionism and the aggressive acts of Israel, which were "preventing them from obtaining their freedom." Under such pressures, symptoms of resignation and despair often surfaced. The Jewish Religious Council and several members of the community made a substantial contribution to the government during "Arms Week," and on one occasion an Israeli who had escaped from the al-Mazza Prison and sought refuge in the synagogue was betrayed by an informer and seized by the local police.[13]

The community struggled under a welter of restrictions and official decrees calculated to isolate its members from the rest of the world and eradicate any source of hope. Anyone found listening to the Arabic program of the Voice of Israel was subject to imprisonment; foreign visitors could not speak to Jews except to the septuagenarian Rabbi Shalel and his successor, Rabbi Nissim Andbo, the government-acknowledged spokesman. Zionist underground groups directed by Mosad operatives had been able to help Jews escape in the past by using false identity cards with the prominent red *Yahud* carefully deleted. But the penalties risked by those even suspected of making such an attempt were sufficient to persuade most Jews to remain in the *haret*. In one notable case, a military prosecutor asked the death sentence for eight Jews accused of trying to flee the country, despite the fact that there was no evidence that three of the defendants had ever considered such a plan.

Eli's report revealed that conditions in the *haret* had become even worse than the Mosad had imagined. Civil rights had long since disappeared, and all but the most basic forms of trade were prohibited. Since Arab craftsmen would not make repairs and there was no money for materials, the remaining buildings on the streets which had not been taken over by Moslems or

Christians had fallen into an irreversible state of delapidation. No Jew could travel at any time more than two and a half miles from his home; those who left their homes risked being set upon by Palestinians, whose acts of terror were dismissed by the police as justifiable revenge. Only the elderly and indigent seemed brave enough to venture out.

The police had also seen to it that the embodiments of Jewish faith were obliterated. A religious center in Djobar two miles east of Damascus was now taken over by Palestinian Arabs, and the synagogue where Elijah was said to have anointed Elisha had been converted into a school for displaced Arabs.[14] Almost every trace of the Jews' 2,000 years of existence in Syria, Eli wrote, had vanished.

Several weeks after the July coup that put Hafez in power, the Center again requested that Eli return to Israel. The new ensemble of the Cabinet and its hard-line policy toward Israel were not matters which could be dealt with in terse reports or coded messages. Military intelligence, apart from the political motives behind strategy, could be conveyed without explanation or analysis, but information about Syria's notably mercurial leaders and their policies often had little value without a knowledge of the nuances of their personalities and the possible motives behind their actions. Face-to-face consultations between the agent and his superiors, who had the perspective of viewing events from a distance, often produced fresh insights or raised valuable questions that would never have surfaced otherwise.

Another factor also influenced the Mosad to ask that Eli return. It had been more than a year since his last trip to Israel, and the longer he was removed from all that held value for him, the chances increased that he would commit a serious error as the chilling sense of isolation set in. Operatives occasionally needed to come in from the "cold," and Eli may have been more susceptible than most agents to the tensions involved in his work. The Mosad did try to inform him as quickly as possible about important family matters, which helped close the gap between life in Damascus and his real identity. That summer he had received a message notifying him that a new baby was on the way; his trip to Israel was to coincide with the birth of his second child.

Home was never far from Eli's thoughts. Messages sent to Europe often reminded his contacts there not to forget such things as birthday presents for Nadia or a gift for Sofie. One Saturday evening in July, after transmitting a report dealing with the Baath leadership, he added a postscript prompted by the news broadcast over Kol Israel, that the national soccer team had been defeated in an international match in Tel Aviv. "It is time we learned to win on the football field, too," the message read. "Pass on to the losing team my strong sense of national disgrace."[15]

Leaving Damascus for a short period was not a difficult matter. Eli needed only to explain, as he had the year before, that the exigencies of his import-export business made it necessary for him to fly once again to Europe. This time, however, he offered a second reason for his departure—a mission for the Baath in South America. Since he had become a militant party member, Eli had often discussed with the secretaries of his division and the Damascus Branch the possibility of forming an Argentinean branch of the Baath, similar to those already existing in Western Europe and the United States. Now that the party was in power, Eli argued, it would not be difficult to win new converts.

It was also an equally ideal moment, Baath officials recognized, to solicit contributions from émigrés who had prospered in Argentina, encourage them to import more Syrian goods and increase their investments in the private sector of the economy. Syrian merchants and landholders living in Buenos Aires had very little revolutionary fervor, but with the Baath in command they might be persuaded that any tangible signs of confidence in the new regime they could offer would be very much in their own interest. For this task it was agreed that Eli was ideally equipped, since he was not only an ardent Baathite familiar with the Syrian community in Argentina, but a successful entrepreneur with whom businessmen could readily identify. The proposal for a fund-raising and recruiting trip was received enthusiastically by the leadership of the Damascus Branch he consulted and was then passed on to the Regional Command, where the idea was given the same backing. With such unanimous support, Aflak was quick to give his approval.

The new status of the Baath as a national party supplied Eli with another reason for making the journey. Georges Seif, now the program director of Radio Damascus' broadcasts beamed to foreign nations, had proposed that Eli produce a regular five-minute program in Spanish and Arabic aimed at Syrians living in South America. It was hoped that the program, to be called *A Former Syrian Emigré Speaks*, would bolster the image of the Baath abroad. Not coincidentally the new program might serve to enhance Taabet's stature and open the doors for him within the Information Ministry. Eli had tentatively agreed to the idea, and Seif first channeled the proposal to his immediate superiors, the director of Radio Damascus, Ismail Habash, and then to Eli's friend the general director of broadcasting and television, Yusuf Kahtib. From there the plan was forwarded to al-Jundi's desk. The minister, who respected Eli immensely, found the idea an admirable way to help bridge the gap between the Baath and influential émigrés. After an elaborate meeting with Eli in his office, al-Jundi gave Seif the authority to proceed.[16] Eli, however, sought a delay before the program began. He told Seif he did not believe that it would be wise to begin airing the broadcast until he had conferred with Syrians in Buenos Aires and sought out their opinions about a viable approach to the program. The true reason was, of course, a matter he could not confide to Seif. Before finally agreeing to make the broadcasts, he would have to consult his superiors in Tel Aviv.

A few days before his departure, Eli gave an elaborate party to celebrate his return to South America on behalf of the Baath. He had planned a lavish affair and anticipated the evening with some pleasure; it would be a proper climax to his work in Damascus—a time for him to celebrate his success privately before returning to Israel. It was somewhat ironic then that in the course of the evening he would confront, for the first time since his arrival in Syria, the possibility of being exposed as a foreign agent because of a mistake which a schoolboy would have taken care to avoid.

Besides the habitués such as Saliha, Seif, Hatoum and Maazi, the guest list included an impressive sampling of Damascus *haut monde*—an array of Army officers, Baath officials on the rise and businessmen who were well connected with the new regime. It was an indication of the party's unfettered atmosphere that Hatoum had arrived with the popular and controversial Ludi. Seif was accompanied by his plump secretary, and some of the less orthodox businessmen had brought their wives. Eli had also invited an ample number of young secretaries from the ministries of Information, Defense and Agrarian Reform, along with several stewardesses from Syrian Arab Airways, to ensure that the affair would be a success.

The gatherings Eli held at his apartment were inevitably successful not only because the oppressive weight of having constantly to observe the proprieties was momentarily lifted but because of his unsparing efforts to ensure that his guests were present at a unique occasion. Gourmet foods to satisfy the most demanding appetites were served along with the finest Scotch whiskies and French liqueurs. Hashish heightened the mood, and before long the acrid smoke enveloped the rooms where the guests sampled the delicacies while lounging on sofas or relaxing Oriental style on cushions or carpets.

The party had long since passed the polite stage when Eli momentarily left Saliha's side to speak with Maazi, who had been standing by himself near the living-room library, thumbing, it appeared, disconsolately through a book he had taken from one of the shelves. As the two talked, a white code sheet covered with a grill-like design, which Eli had placed between the book's pages and forgotten, fell to the floor. Retrieving it, Maazi asked what the curious arrangement of Latin letters embossed on the design signified. Eli hardly had time to think of a reply and calmly said that it was a crossword puzzle. His answer apparently did not strike Maazi as peculiar, and they continued to talk about another subject.[17] Eli returned to Saliha, furious at his own carelessness, but certain that Maazi had suspected nothing. The lieutenant's behavior throughout the rest of the evening gave no clue that he was preoccupied with anything but enjoying himself. Indeed the young officer would not recall the moment for quite some time.

16
Red Star over Syria

During a stopover in Switzerland, Eli exchanged documents with Salinger, met the agent managing his business fronts and got in touch with the legitimate Swiss importers who supplied his firm and purchased from him the Damascene furniture and *objets d'art*. Several days later, he flew via Paris to Lydda, where Gideon was waiting as usual to drive him to Bat Yam. For the next week, at least, he would be completely free of any thought about his mission.

Nadia had not expected him to arrive for several more days and was both astounded and grateful to see him back. She had received postcards from Europe in which Eli wrote that he was uncertain whether he would be home in time for the birth of the baby. She had been understandably upset about his vagueness, but Eli had managed to arrive in time to take her to the hospital. Like all fathers, he paced the floor and skimmed aimlessly through old magazines until the doctor informed him that both Nadia and the child—another girl he was to name Iris—were doing well.

While his wife was resting at home, Eli escaped the intense summer heat by taking Sofie and his nieces and nephews to the beach. He spent the evenings with Nadia and the children and went out only to visit relatives and friends. The reunion was as joyous as the year before, yet for the first time members of the family became aware of a slight edginess in Eli. His brothers, above all, were puzzled, if only momentarily, by Eli's behavior. He would constantly follow the newscasts from Damascus and occasionally even speak Arabic with an easily discernible Syrian accent. When his mother once asked if he would like her to prepare "that favorite Aleppo dish you used to like so much," Eli replied that he had often had the same food abroad.[1] Maurice, who noticed that a box containing a doll Eli had brought for Sofie was marked Galeries Lafayette, anxiously inquired whether he had recently been in France. Eli inexplicably replied that he had not; he abruptly lost his temper when Maurice mentioned the package, nervously adding that he could not be expected to remember all the countries to which he had traveled. "Anyway," he snapped at his brother, "what is all this? Are you testing me?" and, without waiting for an answer, stalked angrily away.[2]

At Mosad Headquarters Eli was first introduced to Meir Amit, with whom he discussed at length his mission and the overall situation in Syria. Eli was subsequently debriefed by his superiors during a number of conferences in which he gave a full report of his part in the coup and his relationship with Baath leaders. The important contacts—Seif, al-Ard, Maazi and Hatoum—were analyzed thoroughly; Eli received advice about the manner in which they might be exploited further. A special session was devoted to the pressing question of whether he should heed Seif's offer and broadcast a daily program to South America. Mosad officials agreed that such a venture would unquestionably boost his prestige, yet by accepting a sensitive propaganda position and becoming a government employee, he would no doubt be subjected to a thorough security check, reaching beyond Damascus to South America and perhaps even deeper into his past. Whatever the adequacy of his cover, such an investigation was dangerous.

Eli argued strongly that the opportunity would allow him to widen his contacts both in and outside the government and should therefore not be lost. In Syria's present condition, lines of authority were often so vague that a check might well not be authorized, and even if it were, internal security was so haphazard that the investigation would no doubt be superficial. His superiors agreed that he undertake the broadcasts, which would be monitored in Tel Aviv. He would use a special code the communications department had developed to send messages he deemed too urgent to be delayed until the regular transmission time. In the months to come, Eli would relay information by means of passages from *Robinson Crusoe* he read daily on his radio program.

Eli returned to Paris at the beginning of September and, without delay, flew to Argentina, via Lisbon and Dakar. In Buenos Aires he was warmly greeted by his friends in the Asociación Islámica and especially by ak-Hashan, whose son had sent word that "Taabet would be returning on an important mission." Eli set out at once to make converts for the Baath cause. With the help of the Syrian embassy staff, his own contacts and the Arabs whose names had been supplied by the Regional Command, he organized a nucleus of recruiting officers and started a drive to form an Argentinean branch of the Baath.

Before Eli left for South America, the Mosad had deposited a large amount of money in the Syrian-Lebanese Bank from which he could draw if he failed to raise for the Baath what Damascus would consider a sufficient sum. As it turned out, there was no need to touch the contingency fund. Eli solicited $9,000 in contributions from a small group of Arab businessmen—an amount which was more than enough to impress Damascus. He humbly announced that he would add $1,000 of his own money to the total and assured the émigrés that, as soon as he got home, he would personally present the $10,000 check to President Hafez.[3] He finally urged all businessmen to import more Syrian products and increase their investments in the fatherland, suggesting that they use his name to ensure the full cooperation of the Ministry of Commerce.

Eli returned from Buenos Aires in time for the regional conferences that preceded the Sixth National Convention of the

Baath, which opened on October 5. Party headquarters, ringed by soldiers and guarded by tanks, was decked with banners proclaiming "One Arab Nation with an Eternal Mission" and "Unity, Liberty, Socialism." Although not a delegate, Eli was able to follow the Congress closely. As a member of the Syrian National Revolutionary Command and volunteer worker for Radio Damascus he had entry to most committees and with the aid of Seif and his friends in the party's Information and Propaganda Department was even able to follow debates held in closed session. He met many of the 120 Baath delegates from neighboring countries and student organizations abroad, whom he entertained at the New Omayad Hotel, a rendezvous of the international press, or at the nearby Café du Bresil.

The ideological evolution of the party (the congress attempted to clarify the vague policies of Socialization, austerity and collective farming) concerned him only as far as it meant a strengthening of leftist influence. He was much more interested in the confidential political reports of the delegates from other Arab countries and particularly those concerning their efforts to unify the party's organization in Iraq and Syria and to create a Palestinian force to resist the diversion of the Jordan River.

The messages Eli would send indicated an obvious shift to the left in the Baath, a development in which the Center was extremely interested. In spite of its acceptance of the principle of "positive neutrality" in foreign affairs, the party intended to strengthen ties with the Socialist camp. The reasons were not hard to find. The new inter-Arab leadership was younger and far more dogmatic. More than half the thirteen-member National (inter-Arab) Command was under thirty, and most belonged to the leftist factions in their respective countries and were known for their intransigence toward Israel.

One of the incidents which Eli witnessed and would report extensively was the downfall of his friend Salah al-Bitar. As the congress dealt with the reelection of the secretary-general, Aflak, who was under fire for his rightist line, agreed to sacrifice some of his moderate followers, among them Bitar, in order to maintain his grip on the party. But no sooner had Tel Aviv received the information than a split in the Baath leadership was followed by a *coup d'état* in Baghdad, which brought President Abd al-Salem Aref to power; his first actions were to purge the Iraqi Baathites, put an end to the Syrian-Iraqi unity scheme and allow a reconciliation with Nasser.

Bitar, who had always viewed with distaste the *sub rosa* struggle in the Iraqi party, now held no public office and felt free to denounce the Baathites whose internecine struggle had caused the debacle—Ali Salah al-Saadi, former deputy prime minister, and Taleb Hussein Shabib, his minister of foreign affairs. After profound differences and bitter personal quarrels had broken out among the party leaders in Iraq before the coup two factions within the party had crystallized: the extremists led by Saadi, who advocated swift Socialization and opposed reconciliation with Nasser, and the moderates of Shabib, who sided with the Egyptians in their efforts to create a federation. With the advent of the tripartite agreement, Saadi's position was undermined, but his followers, who constituted a majority in the Iraqi delegation to the Sixth Congress, restored his prestige and upon their return to Baghdad ousted his opponents. Shabib's adherents called a conference of the Regional Command in the Iraqi capital on November 10, overpowered the radicals, arrested Saadi and the next day sent him into Spanish exile. When the news reached Saadi's sympathizers, they poured into the streets of Baghdad and attacked the Presidential Palace and Ministry of Defense. Stunned Iraqi party leaders called Damascus urging the National (inter-Arab) Command to rush to their help and try to solve the crisis. Hafez and Aflak arrived within hours. For three days they arbitrated between the two factions and finally decided to exile Shabib and his colleagues to Lebanon. The Syrians declared the regional elections unconstitutional and took over the direction of affairs in Iraq until a new leadership could be appointed.

The elimination of their leaders and the Syrians' "intellectual trusteeship" of the party caused deep resentment among Iraqi Baathites. But the Syrians' take-over of the country's affairs also enraged the Army, which was already chagrined by the creation of an elite National Guard to "protect the revolution from within and without." Aided by anti-Baathites and Nasserites, Aref seized power. Hafez and Aflak were sent to jail and kept there until, ironically, a plea from their arch enemy Nasser set them free.[4]

The Saadi crisis further weakened the Syrian Baath now plagued by vigorous intrigues. But the rifts within the party were exploited by Eli to further his own position. He continued backing the rightist faction, diplomatically playing between Aflak and Bitar, yet always siding with Hafez's followers, and Hatoum in particular. However, when Bitar openly accused Saadi as being the cause of the debacle, Eli was among the few who did not turn against him

In the first week of January, 1964, without the party's authorization, Bitar held a press conference in which he viciously criticized the power-seeking Saadi and demanded his condemnation. The Regional Command was quick to retaliate: In an extraordinary meeting on the twenty-fourth it expelled Bitar from the party. Aflak's moderates were now frightened into action. Using his influence, the secretary-general called an emergency session of the Council and reinstated Bitar. Eli voted in favor.[5] His action would bring him Bitar's eternal gratitude.

The consolidation of power of General Hafez in the party, the Army and the government had created a development of major importance to the Israelis: As a sign of faith in the Baath, the Soviet Union relaxed restrictions on arms sales and lifted the partial embargo it had imposed before the party had seized control. *Pravda* considered the appointment of General Hafez as a victory of the "honest, energetic and patriotic elements" over the "treacherous, discredited clique of old-time politicians," and before long, Ambassador Anatoly Barkovsky presented his credentials to the general. It was therefore certain that the once-unabated flow of armor, heavy weapons and aircraft would soon again pour into the country. The Mosad had viewed these overtures with great concern since the capability of the Syrian Army to wage war depended almost entirely on the quantity and type of materiel that the Russians were willing to supply.

This symbiotic relation with the Soviet Union had not occurred overnight. Moscow had foreseen early that because of its pronounced anti-Western attitudes and restless political climate, Syria was a highly suitable target for infiltration. The USSR was not enamored, however, of the succession of governments which ruled Syria in the postwar years. The first cabinets were blamed for the persecution of Communists; Zaim was accused of catering to Western imperialism; Hinawi was labeled a British agent and Shishakli a Fascist dictator.

The Soviet Union's attitude softened noticeably in the mid-fifties, and Syria first received the Russian vote in the Security Council in its quarrel with Israel over the use of the Jordan waters. Cultural relations were soon established, and the Russians, who recognized the profound influence exerted by Islam on Arab culture, proudly showed Syrian visitors samples of the "absolute freedom enjoyed by Soviet Moslems." As Russian students, physicians and agricultural experts began to arrive in Damascus for prolonged stays, Soviet influence in the Middle East was sealed by an even more tangible sign of confidence. In September, 1955, Nasser announced the conclusion of an agreement with the USSR for the delivery of substantial quantities of armaments. In Damascus the rais was viewed as a great liberator who had eliminated whatever need the Arabs still had to rely on the Western powers. The Soviet Union thus emerged as the patron saint of Arab interests.

It was not long before Syria became the recipient of Soviet arms dispensations. After President al-Kuwatli visited Moscow on the eve of the Suez war, Russian cargo ships and planes laden with weapons began arriving in Latakieh and the military airfield at al-Hama. A news blackout over the shipments stirred suspicions in both Arab and Western capitals that Syria was becoming a major Soviet bastion in the Middle East.

The truth, however, was far more complex. The Syrians, for their part, had made an unprecedented and voluntary move toward collaboration with the Soviet Union; it had been agreed, nonetheless, that there would be no Sovietization of the Army and that the Soviet economic and social system would not be entirely emulated. The welcome Damascus offered suited Russia's needs, for Moscow had embarked upon a policy of aiding Third World nations and turning them into allies or client states, rather than satellites. Russian aid was not by any means dispensed to enable Syria to become self-sufficient; it was meant to bind it inexorably to the Soviet bloc. While the arms agreements would make Syria dependent on the Soviet arsenal and military know-how, economic aid was earmarked to bolster the state sector of the economy and create a Soviet-trained elite certain to play a considerable role in the country's future. A further advantage offered by Russia's growing involvement in Syria was not overlooked: Damascus had agreed to allow the USSR to use the country's ports and airfields as "forward facilities" where ships and planes could dock or land for repairs or refueling.

In the months following the Suez War, deliveries of Czech- and Soviet-made small arms, artillery, tanks and subsonic jet fighters were increased. Almost overnight, the Soviet bloc became Syria's prime source of imports. Russian and East European trade missions swelled in size; the Soviet Union alone had six economic missions in Damascus staffed with 250 technicians who surveyed the country's needs and planned development programs.

The strongly felt presence of the Communist countries had an immediate impact on Syrian politics. Conservative and pro-Western leaders were purged from the government, the press was prohibited from printing statements critical of the Soviet Union, and the moderate chief of staff was replaced by a Communist. By August, 1957, Syrian economic and military missions had traveled to Moscow, where they were assured of continued aid on all fronts. Syria's army would not suffer for lack of modern equipment; the armaments offered included Mig-17's, Ilyushin bombers, T-34 tanks and submarines.[6]

The unexpected union with Egypt was not looked upon with enthusiasm by Moscow, in part because Soviet leaders knew

298 The Shattered Silence

that Syria's Communist Party would be weakened with Nasser firmly in control. Yet when the SCP was banned along with all other political organizations in the Northern Region, Moscow was unwilling to rebuke Nasser. The USSR was not anxious to make any move that would threaten its growing influence in the area. After the dissolution of the UAR, arms deliveries to Syria were resumed, while economic aid, which had markedly declined during the union, was increased. But when the Baath achieved power, Russia placed heavy restrictions on arms acquisitions—a stinging rebuke to the party's leadership, whom the Soviets accused of behaving more like Fascists than Socialists.[7]

The Baath's temporary setback in its relations with Russia came at a time Syria was being increasingly wooed by Communist China, which was fast becoming the Soviet's potent rival in the Middle East. The Chinese CP had invited Arab Communists and Marxists to attend its Asian and Pacific Peace Conference in the early 1950's, and Chinese Moslems had made pilgrimages to Mecca with the party's approval. Inevitably, Egypt was the focal point for Chinese approaches, and following private talks between Nasser and Chou En-lai at the Bandung Conference in 1954, diplomatic relations had been concluded between the two nations. An exchange of diplomatic missions between Syria and China was not made until two years later, for Peking was aiming first to exert its influence on Egypt and Yemen.

After the arrival of the first Chinese diplomats in Damascus in July, 1956, Radio Peking bombarded Syria with propaganda to a degree only exceeded by Cairo and Moscow and, like the Soviets, denounced what it conceived to be Western imperialist designs on Syria. The Chinese mission was downgraded during the union, but when Damascus requested diplomatic recognition after the 1961 coup, the Chinese remained impassive, waiting until the United States and the Soviet Union had announced their intentions.

With the advent of the Baathites revolution, however, the Chinese were quicker to react. Only ten days after the 1963 coup, a note of diplomatic recognition was dispatched from

Peking. The embassy in Damascus quickly grew in size, becoming a major propaganda base and a conduit which channeled instructions from Peking's espionage apparatus. It also became one of Eli's primary objects of investigation. The Chinese envisioned Syria as another Albania, a base from which they could direct their campaign to dominate the underdeveloped nations of Africa and the Middle East. They therefore offered Damascus interest-free loans for arms purchases. But what Peking could deliver was often inferior in quality, if not obsolete.[8] The Russians, who in less than a decade had delivered over a third of a billion dollars in war matériel to Syria, now offered transport planes, surface-to-air missiles, submarines, destroyers and helicopters—equipment which was more modern than its own satellites possessed.

With the resumption of deliveries, the Mosad was particularly interested in reports that Moscow would soon ship a squadron of Mig-21 fighter planes to bolster the Syrian Air Force. Pilots who were training in the Soviet Union were on their way or had already arrived. It was still problematical whether they would become operational. A year earlier, after a squadron of four Mig-19's, had failed for several days to carry out their usual reconnaissance mission along the northern frontier, the Mosad had transmitted a Modiin request to Eli that he determine the reason for the canceled flights. Since the sorties originated from al-Mazza airport, Eli had an impeccable source of information; the commander of the base, Illeah al-Maaz, was a friend of Seif's. Without much difficulty, Eli was able to learn that of the squadron's four pilots, one had been grounded because of illness, another had suffered injuries in an automobile accident, while a third had been removed for "political deviation."[9] If they could not be replaced immediately, it was strikingly apparent that the training of Syrian pilots would be far behind schedule.

Despite this lag, it was essential for the Mosad to know whether the Syrian Air Force was, in fact, scheduled to obtain the faster and more dangerous Mig-21's, which could place them on a parity with the Israeli Air Force. Yet only a handful of Syrian officers had access to classified information about the shipments; although Eli was a member of the party's Defense Committee and had established a reputation of being more than nominally concerned with military matters, these officers were not accustomed to being questioned directly by civilians. A circumspect approach, similar to the one he had employed in gaining access to the frontier outposts, was decidedly the wisest course. Over a period of weeks Eli managed to make it clear to Hatoum that he would be interested in visiting the al-Hama munitions center, where all the war matériel which arrived in Syria were stored and classified before being transferred to other installations. The major presumably found nothing un- usual in Eli's request—his friend had left no doubt that he was satisfied by merely reading the reports prepared by the General Staff—and not long after Tel Aviv had forwarded its request, Hatoum arranged for a trip to the base.

A chauffeur-driven staff car took the two to al-Hama, where an adjutant showed them into the office of the base com- mander, Colonel Muhammad Tawil, a pudgy, aging officer who wore a Chaplinesque mustache. While an orderly served coffee, Tawil ordered an aide to ready a vehicle for a tour of the compound and launched into a near monologue covering the aggressiveness of the Jews, the latest border skirmishes and the Army's readiness to deal with the enemy. Throughout the obligatory excursion away from practical matters, Eli no doubt wondered if he would have the opportunity to use the minia- ture camera concealed in his pocket. All four walls of Tawil's office were covered with information of the most invaluable kind—boldly printed charts listing newly acquired weapons, drawn up according to country of origin, type of armament and date of acquisition and delivery. Other schedules showed yearly comparisons of shipments and the needs and requests of various Syrian units. As Tawil elaborated on the data, Eli most surely wondered if the information could be obtained elsewhere, for it seemed highly improbable that he could ever gain access to the colonel's office alone.

Near the end of the briefing, a junior officer who knew Hatoum requested permission to enter the room. Pleasantly surprised to see an old friend who had served under his command, Hatoum abruptly excused himself and left with his former subordinate. Seconds later, Colonel Tawil was summoned to another office to answer an urgent phone call. Since either officer could have returned at any moment to discover him in the process of photographing classified material, Eli did not risk wasting the few seconds it would have taken to aim the lens but merely snapped a series of shots in rapid succession. By the time the two returned several minutes later he was sitting in one of the leather armchairs gazing abstractedly out the window.

The visit to al-Hama produced a number of other important results. After Colonel Tawil had shown Eli and Hatoum a display of small arms recently acquired from the Soviet Union, China and "other allies in the East," he guided them through the enormous compound. Stacks of AK-47 assault rifles, lightweight mortars and bazookas were piled everywhere. In one area of the camp, Eli noticed that crates marked in Russian, apparently containing jet aircraft parts, still lay opened. When he inquired about the cause of the delay in assembling the new Migs, Colonel Tawil avoided a direct answer by estimating the amount of time needed to put the replacements for the Mig-19's into operation. Then, with a trace of embarrassment in his voice, he confided that even if the jets were made operational immediately, they could not be flown. "Thirty officers," the colonel added, "are still completing their training program in Moscow."

Reassured not only by Eli's credentials but by Hatoum's apparent trust in him, the base commander openly answered questions regarding weapons procurement and deployment. Yet at one point, when Eli sought some technical information, the colonel became noticeably reticent, offering the data only after Hatoum assured him that "Kamal's position in the party required that he have a thorough knowledge of weapons systems."

Apart from his momentary doubts, Colonel Tawil was obviously pleased with the outcome of the tour. As Eli prepared to return to the capital, he frankly told the colonel that after his inspection of the base he had much more confidence than before in the overall preparedness of the armed forces. He thanked Tawil for his hospitality and promised to make a detailed and complimentary report to "our illustrious Liwa al-Hafez."[10]

Following plans decided at a recent Arab summit meeting in Alexandria, the Syrians prepared to push ahead with the diversion of the headwaters of the Jordan that rise in Syria and Lebanon in order to cut off Israel's supply. Although Israel "could stop the Arabs from continuing its water project any time it wants," the Mosad wanted Eli to find out whether work had begun.

Before leaving for the border, Eli took Hatoum and one of his friends, Michel Saab, to dinner. Saab, a Lebanese engineer in charge of the channel excavations, gave Eli exact details of the area's topographical features and supplied him with a diagram of the channel and the large pumping station Syria was planning to construct. The following day, Eli and Hatoum headed south toward the encampment of the Saudi contractor by the Yarmouk headwaters. They reached the camp at the end of a dirt road just as the last artillery shells were falling into the clearing. A white jeep was parked near the barracks which housed the diversion project's office. Two UN observers and a Syrian captain were talking with al-Farah, while a group of Yugoslav engineers standing nearby heatedly discussed the incident. The shooting from the Israeli side had ceased and the Syrian positions above were quiet. Hatoum drove up to the Saudi and Eli walked over to greet him. But al-Farah was so fully engaged in conversation with the observers that he failed to notice him. When the contractor finally saw Taabet, he grinned expansively The UN officers, who were stationed seven kilometers away, had not witnessed the skirmish, but had heard explosions and identified the sound of heavy machine guns, Eli was told. They were unable to investigate further, as regulations prohibited moving more than 50 meters from their watchtower without a Syrian liaison officer. By the time a local commander arrived to escort them, the shooting had stopped.

As soon as the observers departed, al-Farah introduced Eli to the chief engineer, but the Yugoslav did not seem anxious to converse. Referring to the damage caused by the Israelis, he soon apologized for having to supervise the removal of the debris and left with a polite *"mas'salaam."* The Saudi began to sweat even more profusely as he tried to explain to his visitors what had happened, all the while leading them to his office. "They were unchallenged," he exclaimed. "No Mig's came out to fight them. Their planes zeroed in on the military positions in the mountains." The Israeli artillery had also shelled large portions of the canal dug close to the border and had partly destroyed the waterways. Once in the office, al-Farah proudly called Eli over to the map behind his desk and outlined the diversion plans at length. When the Saudi finished, Taabet casually remarked that he had considered buying land in the area. "I will have to get a map as soon as I return home so I can choose the best locations," Eli remarked casually. Hatoum quite innocently suggested that al-Farah lend Taabet one of his. The contractor agreed without hesitation. "Let me give you the one that has the markings of the water project on it," he volunteered, "so you will know which land is available and which is not." When Eli wished to know how he could reciprocate, al-Farah replied, "We will find something, don't worry. I am sure that you could help me in my dealings with the authorities."[11]

At Hatoum's suggestion, the Saudi took them on a tour of the desolation left in the wake of the attack. Eli photographed the scene rapidly. He wanted he said, to show the people at home what the Jews were doing. Al Farah encouraged him while a silent Hatoum walked docilely behind. A security officer who had been watching the three confronted Eli and angrily grabbed his camera. The area was considered a military installation, the officer informed him, and therefore classified as nonphotographable. Hatoum intervened, but they were still brought to a barracks which served as the local guardhouse. The excitable Saudi attempted to explain who his guests were, but Hatoum was visibly subdued and seemed almost to welcome the incident, as if it demonstrated the Army's alertness along the Israeli front.

The officer telephoned his superior but was unable to locate him. Meanwhile, he feigned apologies for "the inconvenience." Other officers began to arrive, yet no one was able to cope with the situation. The stars and insignias multiplied until a high-ranking officer strutted in. He studied the General Staff pass and presidential recommendation. He was desperately sorry, but the film would have to be sent to the military photo laboratory. He knew it might delay them, but it would only take a short time. Hatoum, who had only complained halfheartedly before, now protested strongly. After all, he pointed out, Amin Taabet was a member of the Regional Command and a personal friend of the president. He was surely beyond suspicion. The colonel could call General al-Shaer at the Southern Command who personally approved the trip.

The officer finally swayed and returned the camera untouched. After a vigorous round of handshaking and shoulder clapping, Eli and Hatoum drove off toward Kuneitra.

17
The Merchants' Mutiny

One of the duties Eli had never neglected in spite of his frequent trips to the border was regular contact with the business community. Although his political activism had forced him at times to disregard his import-export firm, he always found time for old acquaintances and continued strengthening the ties he had so carefully developed with al-Ard's aid. After the March coup he began to attend meetings of merchants and industrialists who sympathized with the Baath, never failing to stress that in the new Baathite society a vote for the party was a vote for their own well-being. If his recruitment of merchants was not overly successful, the party bureaucracy nevertheless held him in high esteem for his efforts.[1] The Baath had in fact found little support for its policies within the business community, mainly among owners of small independent enterprises who had always belonged to the conservative and Nasserite parties which were now banned. As a target of nationalization, they were the first victims of Socialization and suffered from great financial difficulty.

Eli found that the further deterioration of the economic situation had caused mounting concern and dissatisfaction among such merchants. In taking over, the Baath had found the country nearly bankrupt and tried to revive the economy with programs ranging from nationalization of industry to conversion of state land into collectives. But despite the planning, conditions had steadily worsened and by the end of 1963 had become critical. In a desperate attempt to modernize the economy, the Baath had driven the country into bankruptcy. An economic blockade and export embargo by Arab neighbors had brought the value of the pound tumbling down, and had caused unemployment to rise sharply.

The Damascene merchant had always been suspicious of the party's nebulous principles of social justice. On the one hand, it advocated that strict limits be placed on private possessions, while on the other it considered property a natural right guaranteed "within the national interest" and promised to protect that right, though "regulating its social functions by law."

But when businessmen withdrew their support, the party attempted to placate them by partially modifying its Socialist ideals—and agreed to a cooperation between the public and private sectors. "The government," Bitar promised, "would never be more than a partner in the private sector." Aflak echoed: "Baath Socialism recognizes the strength of the instinct for private property; it thus permits it while at the same time placing some restrictions on it."

As a Baath militant and successful merchant whose thriving import-export business brought the country much-needed foreign currency, Eli was regarded with high esteem in government circles. At a time when foreign investments had become almost nonexistent and local currency was deposited in foreign banks for fear of nationalization, the government was desperately seeking markets for its products and a successful exporter such as Eli was more than welcomed. Officials in the ministries of Finance and Commerce went out of their way to encourage him. His selfless dealings, always putting the good of the country first, soon reached the ears of government and party officials, further enhancing his reputation.

As the economic crisis worsened, friction increased between the Baath and Syria's merchants. The rift ultimately severed relations between the rightist and leftist factions in the party. Each had its own solution to the problem: The extremists demanded more nationalization while moderates urged encouragement of private initiative. By the end of March, 1964, the party was shocked into action by arms raids on police stations in Aleppo and Damascus staged by Moslem Brotherhood commandos; those were the first signs that the extreme right was plotting rebellion. The Army reinforced its garrisons in the big cities and prepared for the approaching storm.

On April 9, Hama's merchants, joined by anti-Baathites of all shades, struck in protest over the death of a Communist under investigation at the local jail. While the Minister of Interior hastened to deplore the incident, the Army dealt with the "destructive elements" trying to foment trouble by arresting nearly five hundred people. Realizing the true reason for the strike, a delegation of Homs businessmen was invited to Damascus to discuss the economy.

The merchants had begun to worry about the militantly Socialist program of the Baath when the government expropriated all landholdings over 25 acres and nationalized six of the country's largest corporations. Damascus would not go back on its policies but, in order to placate the business community, ordered the dismissal of the governor of Homs.

Despite these efforts, the Baath would face a major civilian rebellion when the merchants' strike spread to the midland city of Hama. On Thursday, the ninth, the town's population staged a mass demonstration to protest the sentencing to a year's hard labor of a fifteen-year-old student at the Uthman Hourani secondary school for erasing a Baath slogan and replacing it with "The Atheist Baath Is Against God." Although soldiers and police dispersed the angry mob by firing into the crowd, the boy's classmates went on strike. The sheiks and the mullahs of Hama's sixty-five mosques denounced Baathist oppression in their Friday morning sermons and within hours, incited by Moslem Brotherhood agitators, mobs filled the streets and routed the police. The Army opened fire, turning Hama into a charnel house. Reinforcements rushed from Damascus were sent straight into the core of the fighting and the numbers of victims on both sides mushroomed.

Alarmed, Hafez flew to Hama after ordering Hatoum to take charge of the operation. Eli, who had seen Hatoum a few days earlier before the party sent him to Homs and Aleppo to help placate the merchants, now met the major in Hama. Throughout the rest of the week Eli would stay near Hatoum and witness the fury with which Hafez crushed the civil rebellion; it was the ruthlessness the general displayed there that would earn him the nickname Butcher of Damascus.

Upon arrival on Sunday, Hafez tried to calm the population by ordering the release of the boy arrested the week before, and indemnities paid to the parents of a student killed a day earlier. His appeasement, however, was interpreted as weakness. Merchants again answered a call to strike and closed their stores. The curfew clamped on the city was effective only for one day. On Tuesday, the fourteenth, the Brethren went on the offensive and severe clashes broke out. As in the past, there was no prevarication from Hafez. When a detachment of soldiers was attacked from barricades, rooftops and minarets, all hell broke loose. Hatoum rushed to the scene in an armored car. Noticing that machine-gun fire came from atop the Sultan Mosque, he personally took command of the cannon and in a well-aimed shot decimated its 60-foot minaret. The shelling convinced the rebels that Hafez was ready to put down the revolt by any means; they notified him that they were ready to negotiate. But the general was in no mood to talk. He told them that unless they handed over their arms along with nineteen suspected leaders, the army would attack by dawn with overwhelming force.

During the night, Hafez moved up additional troops and T-54 tanks which smashed through rebel barricades. Armor and artillery hammered for hours at their strongholds driving them into last-ditch positions. The toll of the week-long battle: sixty civilians and twenty military dead and injured.[2]

Even as Hama was forced into submission, sympathy strikes broke out in other parts of Syria. A young man who attempted to defend the Baath at a mosque in Homs was beaten to death by the faithful. But the Hama incident had caused a stir which soon broke out into defiance.

Before returning to the capital, Eli witnessed another act of civil disobedience. The markets fell silent as the "suq bourgeoisie" rang down their iron screens in Aleppo and Homs, but the business community had underestimated Hafez's determination. He ordered the arrest of Aleppo's ten leading merchants and distribution of their goods to the poor and repeated the move in Homs. The Baathite National Guard aided by commandos under Hatoum's orders broke into closed shops and requisitioned the stock. The Damascenes at once reopened the shutters and business went back to normal.

When Hafez jauntily returned to Damascus, he promoted Hatoum to colonel and blandly approved a provisional constitution which technically lifted the martial law; yet he also signed a decree making the closing of a shop a crime punishable by twenty years' imprisonment. To an enthusiastic Baathite rally, he promised no appeasing measures. "In our good country," he told the crowds, "there are still feudalists, capitalists and exploiters. We consider them our sick brothers. We will try to cure them by simple medication, but if surgery is necessary, we shall not hesitate to amputate. . . . Our enemies," he added with a smile, "are playing games. We are not."[3] This policy was to be directed against the business community with increasing severity over the next few months.

As life in Damascus returned to normal, Eli learned through his contacts at the Ministry of Defense that the Second Bureau was planning to give active support to al-Fatah, a little-known organization of militant Palestinians who were seeking "to recapture the land stolen by the Jews" by means of guerrilla warfare. The Baath was now eagerly presenting itself as the true champion of the Palestinians. A Palestine program proudly announced that all restrictions on the movement of the refugees had been lifted and that the Army was seriously studying how to best help them in their struggle. Eli knew that the Army had long maintained elite commando units specifically assigned to infiltrate Israeli territory and carry out acts of terror and sabotage; he had also heard rumors two years before that former Palestinians who had held officer rank in the Syrian Army had been dismissed during the union because of their pro-Communist leanings, had organized a small number of refugees living in Damascus into cells which met regularly in private homes for theoretical discussions and small arms training. But upon investigation, he found that no more than 150 people were involved and radioed the Center that their relationship with the armed forces was nebulous at best.[4]

Al-Fatah, the abbreviated name for Harkat Tahir Falastin (Palestine National Liberation Movement), had been formed in Egypt ten years earlier; it never gained much of a reputation, though, even in the Arab countries. The group had adopted the Koranic word for victory and conquest—*fatah*—a name used by the legions of the first caliphs, the legendary armies that conquered in the name of Islam. The modern-day al-Fatah had started out as a paramilitary organization composed of young Palestinians living in the Gaza Strip. They were trained in demolition techniques by Egyptian officers but had to purchase the explosives with funds they collected among the refugees. In the mid-1950's the Gaza activists carried out a series of largely ineffective raids inside Israeli territory; after the Sinai campaign they regrouped and reorganized into fedayeen, calling themselves *al-Jabha* (the Front).

During the same period, young Palestinians enrolled in Syrian high schools and universities were beginning to find a common identity and banded together in a number of associations which not only engaged in ideological discussions but also offered its members military training. Most were supported by the Grand Mufti and received some help from the Syrian government. Egypt and Syria thus exploited the moral fervor of these youths whom they attempted to compare unfavorably with their more complacent Arab brothers.

Similar groups later sprung up at the universities of Cairo, Baghdad and Beirut, each spearheading local student movements. But not all the Palestinian organizations were looked upon benignly by the authorities, and some were forced to operate clandestinely. Jordan and Saudi Arabia jailed many of the activists, and the organizations in other Arab countries eventually became moribund.[5] Significantly, though, the movement was revived outside the Middle East, this time under the leadership of one man who was destined to play an important role in Arab affairs.

Palestinian students at the West German University of Stuttgart banded together around Aba a-Rahman (Yasir) Arafat, a charismatic young man in his late twenties, who had been president of the Palestinian Students Organization in Cairo University. Arafat was born in 1929 in Jerusalem, where, according to his own testimony, he had served during the 1948 war as secretary to Abd al-Kader Husseini, commander of the Jerusalem front. He later emigrated to Egypt and settled temporarily in Gaza, where he organized protests against the UN partition plan before enrolling in the Engineering Faculty of Cairo University. Arafat served as a second lieutenant in the Palestinian Brigade of the Egyptian Army which fought in the Sinai during the Suez War, but because of his membership in the Moslem Brotherhood was forced to flee Egypt. With the aid of a friend he was hired by a construction firm in Kuwait, and, while there, became the leader of the local al-Fatah chapter.[6]

Under Arafat, the al-Fatah unit at Stuttgart University eventually secured control of the large Egyptian-oriented Palestinian Students Organization and dispatched recruiters to campuses throughout Europe to raise funds and distribute propaganda among Arab émigrés. While al-Fatah emissaries established cells in Austria, Italy, Spain and Yugoslavia, Arafat and his adjutant, Halil al-Kazir, prepared for their ultimate goal—the readying of units for guerrilla warfare. In the early 1960's the two were invited to Peking, where they were given funds and an abbreviated course in guerrilla tactics. Upon his return to the Middle East, Kazir, who was a friend of the Algerian FLN leader Muhammad Haidar, received a promise of support from the government of Premier Ahmed Ben Bella, and subsequently, Fatah units were permitted to use Algerian military camps for training purposes. Arafat, who returned to Kuwait as a leader with a substantial following, won the backing of the wealthy Palestinian community there and the cooperation of the emir, who allowed al-Fatah to establish training sites around the capital. These programs, however, were doomed to failure; after weeks of harsh training, the former zeal of the majority of the students evaporated, and they chose to return to their books.

The setback convinced Arafat that if the movement was to achieve some success, it needed the strong backing and a base inside a country whose border fronted with Israel. Since the Egyptians were already sponsoring the Palestine Liberation Organization (PLO), Syria was an inevitable choice. Arafat came to Damascus from Algiers earlier that year with a letter from Boumedienne for General Hamad Ubaiyd. The Algerians had promised him money and arms; he wanted the Syrians to give him training facilities. He held a series of talks with the chief of operations at the General Staff and the head of the Second Bureau, who immediately saw the advantages of such a move. Al-Fatah could provide Syria with a guerrilla force to rival the Egyptians' PLO and fit in, however vaguely, with the Baath's enthusiasm for "wars of popular liberation." Unlike a classic guerrilla movement, al-Fatah was not expected to win the backing of the local population, but it could create the kind of excessive tension along the frontier that might spark an all-out war between Israel and the Arab states, for which the Baath longed. The party at first agreed to consider his request but only after Suidani intervened and convinced Hafez to back al-Fatah during a trial period was a secret pact closed.

Through Seif and Hatoum, Eli found out that the Second Bureau had agreed to aid Arafat by supplying his organization with equipment, money and propaganda outlets; the General Staff would help plan operations and arrange for its commando units to collaborate with the Palestinians whenever necessary. Eli also confirmed that al-Assifa, the military arm of al-Fatah, was preparing for publication the first number of its official organ *Saut al-Assifa (The Voice of the Storm)*.

But Arafat, who attempted to recruit Palestinians living in Syria, was unable to enlist enough students to fill the ranks of the proposed units. He had to rely on the Syrian Army, which ultimately established its own recruiting offices in refugee camps in northern Syria, Jordan and southern Lebanon. But even by using this approach, the plan to enlist only Palestinians had to be discarded. Membership, Eli learned, was offered to any Arab, including those with criminal records, with an inducement of a salary of 15 Syrian pounds per month and special pay for dangerous operations. Training, he discovered, was held in two large camps at Kabun and Kuneitra, with secondary facilities near Damascus.[7]

Toward the end of the year, *al-Baath*, the party's official organ, proclaimed that "Al-Fatah had embarked upon the only possible revolutionary path for liberation by transferring the battle to Israel." The Palestinians, the paper emphasized, "must put an end to routine delay, speeches and decisions." Simultaneously, al-Fatah printed huge ads in most Damascus newspapers, promising to start operations against Israel by the end of December.[8] Eli informed the Center and promised to forward a lengthy report on his findings.

Fall proved to be a period of hectic activity for Eli. As a member of the Defense Committee, he was invited to observe an armor exercise within the framework of the annual military maneuvers held on October 24 near the Israeli border. Only days later, he accompanied Lieutenant General Ali Ali Amer, commander in chief of the Arab Unified Military Command on an inspection tour of the southwestern front.[9] He hardly had time to radio the information gathered on this trip when Baath Headquarters informed him that the president, who was flying to Paris for treatment of a kidney ailment, had personally insisted that he be present at the official farewell to be held at the capital's International Airport. Although Eli had managed so far to avoid being photographed, he was unable to hide from the battery of hungry press photographers assaulting the delegation of party heirarchs, ministers and generals, who had come to witness the presidential departure.[10]

When Hafez returned on November 12, after a successful

operation performed by a Jewish surgeon at the American
Hospital in Neuilly, Eli was on hand to greet him at the airport.
Later that evening a palace aid called to inform him that Hafez
had expressed the desire to see him the following day. As soon
as he arrived at the Muhajerin Palace, Eli was ushered into the
president's chamber. Hafez received him cordially and answered
at length the inquiries about his state of health. The reason he
had been summoned, the president explained, was of great
importance to the party. He had followed Taabet's activism
with interest and knew of his closeness to Bitar. He therefore
wanted to entrust him with a sensitive mission: to carry a
missive of reconciliation to the former prime minister, who was
now in Jordan recovering from a "political illness." Hafez
elaborated with a long, flowery monologue which recapitulated
the events since "that shameful April mutiny."

The common action of the unionists, conservatives and
Brethren had proved that the secessionist-reactionary element
had not been entirely suppressed. Hafez, who had previously
opposed a rapprochement with Egypt, was now convinced that
the party's moderate civilians had been correct in their evaluations. The president finally realized that Bitar had never underestimated the power of Nasserite subversion and was therefore
right in seeking a coalitionary understanding.

Eli knew that Bitar's last resignation on October 3 had caused
Hafez little embarrassment, as the premier's withdrawals had
become almost a matter of course. Yet after the April rebellion
and September summit conference in Alexandria, he had come
to accept the necessity for reconciliation. Ruling with a predominantly military Council of the Presidency and a cabinet of
technocrats was no longer the answer. There was a need for
change which only Bitar could perform. His reinstatement was
imperative.

Eli was well aware that the iron rule of Hafez had immobilized the party, triggering intrigues and conspiracies that had
rocked the apparatus throughout the summer and most of the
fall. The rightist faction, which had held power in the Baath
since the coup, had been sidestepped by the Military Committee.

Bitar resigned and together with Aflak went into self-exile. With the rise of discontent in the business community, characterized by the April mutiny, Hafez now attempted to reconcile the merchants and capitalists who, though not satisfied with the party, favored a lesser evil—the rightist faction's practical approach to Socialization. Hafez had thus decided to soften his rule by forming a coalition with the moderate civilian Baathites headed by Bitar.

But the president had problems not only with the party. The rift between his partners in the Council of the Presidency had also reached dangerous proportions. Luay al-Atassi and Muhammad Umran had grown weary of carrying out Hafez's wishes and of aiding him to implement a dictatorial rule; they had even demanded the disbanding of the party's Military Committee and a return of the civilians to power. While Hafez was in Paris, they had started defying him by abolishing the national security courts. Hafez knew that Atassi was too weak and indecisive to have proposed such a move and that only Umran could have initiated it. He was particularly disappointed in Umran's actions as he had helped his swift rise through the ranks and had appointed him acting president whenever he went abroad.

The only one in the Council who now sided with Hafez was Salah al-Jadid. An Alawi like Umran, Jadid, who had risen from major to major general in only nine months, was a rabid anti-Nasserite and devoted party member. He had been retired from the Army for his political activism before the coup but was later returned by the Baath to active service. His militancy in the party had made him the nominal chief of the leftist faction. Yet Jadid's backing was a poor consolation to Hafez, whose differences with the Atassi-Umran duumvirate had snowballed. His isolation in the Council only convinced him further of the necessity for a more moderate position.

Privy to this situation, Eli left for Jordan at once and met Bitar in Jericho. This time the former premier was reluctant to return and haul Hafez out of the fire. But Eli used the pressing needs of the party as bait to lure the elder statesman back to Damascus. The civilian wing, he claimed, had backed Hafez ever

316 The Shattered Silence

since the July take-over the previous year and the president had always recognized the rightist faction as the ideological framework for his activities. He now also recognized the need for the political acumen of Bitar and thus would work closely with him. Bitar finally gave in and flew to Syria with Eli.[11] Shortly after he had resumed office, Aflak would return from a five-month self-exile in Europe.

It was with the detailed information he had gathered throughout the fall that Eli prepared to leave on his third trip to Israel.

This time Eli's trip was hardly as urgent as the year before, when the Baath had first seized power. But besides an annual review, the Mosad wanted Eli to be with Nadia in November, when their third child was to be born. Eli arrived in Bat Yam several days before Nadia gave birth to a boy—the son he had always wanted. He was so exhilarated by the event that he discussed with Gideon the possibility of inviting some of his Mosad colleagues to the circumcision ceremony. Gideon understood Eli's elation, yet had to reject the idea; even if his friends took the greatest care to disguise their professional relationship with Eli, the possibility still existed that someone outside the service might accidentally discover the truth.[12]

On this visit, nonetheless, members of the family were beginning to suspect that whatever the work Eli was doing, it involved more than an arms procurement assignment in Europe. Maurice later recalled that when trying on a pair of shoes Eli had given him as a gift, he noticed that the size was marked with a partially erased Arabic character. When Eli explained that he had purchased the shoes in Turkey, his brother jokingly reminded him that the Turks had not used Arabic script for almost half a century. This time Eli really lost his temper, accusing Maurice of needlessly prying into his affairs.[13] On another occasion, noticing that a package containing fragile Chinese miniatures Eli had brought with him was stuffed with propaganda tracts extolling the virtues of Chairman Mao Tse-tung, Maurice asked where they had come from. Eli coldly replied that he had been in Peking on a buying mission and, as if to offer proof, produced a photograph which showed him standing next to Premier Chou En-lai. It naturally struck Maurice as somewhat peculiar that Eli would find himself in the company of the Chinese Communist statesman, but the photograph appeared to be completely authentic.[14]

Maurice kept his doubts to himself; the rest of the family, however, also became aware that something was amiss. After the birth of his son Shaul, Eli had been in high spirits, but his mood had darkened with the passing weeks. Uncharacteristically, he rarely joked or expressed the wish to see old friends; to some of his relatives he appeared "nervous and bad-tempered." The cause of Eli's moodiness could have well been a matter that had always concerned him and grew even more painful now that he was again with his family: the decision whether to marry Saliha could not be delayed any longer. Ever since they had become engaged, he had—under one pretext or another—avoided setting a date for the wedding. But before Eli left Damascus Abu Mahmud had made it clear that he expected a definite answer upon his return.

The Mosad could offer no solution; his superiors suggested only that he attempt to fabricate another excuse. Yet if his story's credibility should be doubted, he would have to go through with the marriage.[15] Eli found little satisfaction in the Mosad's advice. He became increasingly restless and Nadia sensed his reluctance to leave. One evening, while spending the weekend with her at a luxury hotel in Caesarea, he admitted being weary of the separation from the children. Eli then assured her that there would be only one more trip abroad before he returned to remain in Israel permanently. "I will soon be able to build a villa and stop traveling . . . then it will all end and I'll be able to be with you and the children at all times, same as the other men in the neighborhood."[16]

In the early evening of November 13, Eli was at home in Bat Yam when Kol Israel broadcast its first bulletin describing a four-hour artillery and air battle with the Syrians which had broken out that afternoon near Kibbutz Dan. The clash was the most serious since the battle of Nukeib; scores of soldiers and civilians had been killed on both sides. When all the details were made known the next day, Eli realized that the information about the Syrian artillery emplacements he had supplied a year earlier had been a decisive factor in the outcome of the furious exchange.

Tension along the frontier had run high throughout the summer and fall, with twenty-nine separate incidents reported by UN observers in one four-week period alone. But at the beginning of November, the situation had become even more strained when an Israeli construction crew began repairing a portion of a patrol track which ran along the armistice demarcation line close to the DMZ. The track was used by the Mishmar Hagvul (Border Patrol) watching over the Dan River, the only tributary of the Jordan originating inside Israeli territory, whose dams and pumping stations had been prime objects for sabotage by Arab infiltrators. The Syrians complained to the MAC that the road encroached upon their territory and, to enforce the charge, laid mines on the path and fired upon Zahal patrols from positions on the heights less than two miles away. The Israelis were nevertheless determined to meet the challenge.

At 12:30 P.M. exactly on the afternoon of the thirteenth, an armored personnel carrier that lumbered defiantly along the track was showered by rifle and machine-gun fire from entrenchments southeast of Tal Nukheila. The patrol scattered under the covering fire from their own positions, but several minutes later—a time span which indicated that what was about to occur had been carefully planned—Syrian tanks, mortars and recoilless cannons at four different outposts simultaneously laid their own barrages on the settlements of Dan, Dafna and Shear Yeshuv. As the kibbutz members crowded into their underground shelters, the Syrian shells shattered the communal buildings, destroying garages, silos, a dining hall and two nurseries.

The Syrian delegate to the MAC finally agreed to a cease-fire proposed by the chairman who had raced to the site, but as the heavy artillery remained unsilenced after the set time period had passed, the Israeli commander of the northern front, Brigadier David "Dado" Elazar, decided to take drastic action. Since the Syrian emplacements could not be checked by short-range artillery he had available, Elazar recognized that an air strike would have to be ordered. It was not, however, a simple matter of contacting the closest air command and requesting planes. To launch an air attack against Syrian territory, whatever the provocation, required approval at the highest level. Elazar immediately contacted the chief of staff, Lieutenant General Yitzhak Rabin and explained the urgency of the situation. Rabin in turn sought permission from the prime minister; he managed to reach Levi Eshkol, who was on a tour in Rehovot and obtained his consent to the air strike. Elazar now called Air Force Headquarters in Tel Aviv. He was told that General Ezer Weizman was already on his way home but could be contacted over his car telephone.

Within three hours after the first fire exchange, Israeli jets struck across the border. Two low-flying Mystères opened the attack by napalming positions at Tal Azazziyat, Tal Hamra, Zawra Buqata and Tabata az-Zeit. A second wave of Super-Mystères, Votours and Mirages bombed and machine-gunned the artillery positions, setting them ablaze. An hour and fifteen minutes later, the shelling had stopped. The Syrians, astounded by the successful air raid—the Israeli jets had zeroed in on their positions with great precision—agreed to a general cease-fire.[17]

Following the study of reports filed by MAC observers, and weeks of turgid debate at the United Nations, the Security Council voted in favor of a resolution—predictably vetoed by the Soviet Union—condemning the Syrians for provoking the Tel Dan incident. At Mosad Headquarters, the successful retaliation of the IAF was considered the personal achievement of Operative 88.

Eli had barely returned from his last trip home when he received an invitation to tour the al-Mazza complex, which had been recently emptied of all prisoners. As he stood in the company of newsmen listening to the minister of information proclaim that "a new era free of coups" was dawning for Syria, he could not have imagined that he would be among the first to return to al-Mazza as a political prisoner.[18] While party intrigues were described as a thing of the past, Major General Salah Jadid and Michel Aflak, who had just arrived from a prolonged self-exile in Germany, were privately consorting to maintain the status quo. And as internal Baathite intrigue again became evident, Eli resumed his investigations of their source and nourishment.

Aside from new developments in the Baath, Eli informed the Center of imminent moves toward further nationalization. No sooner had Tel Aviv received the information than the feared decrees were issued. Shortly after the 11:30 P.M. news program on January 8, Radio Damascus had begun to broadcast martial music interspersed with slogans. "Nineteen sixty-five shall witness fundamental developments in strengthening the foundations of the regime," the commentator promised. Although such an occurrence usually signaled the start of another coup or government crackdown, Eli was not surprised; he had been anticipating an announcement of sweeping economic changes. Specific details came at 1:30 A.M., at the end of the traditional lamb and rice feast of Iftar that followed the day-long fasts of the month of Ramadan. The announcer read four decrees which virtually eliminated private ownership in the major industries. Eli had obtained detailed information on the reforms days before their disclosure, while they were still under consideration by the Economic Committee of the National Revolutionary Council. Tel Aviv had received first drafts of the decrees, followed by a lengthy report in which Eli discussed their probable impact on the Syrian economy, particularly the business community.

The theoreticians of the Baath had termed the program "autogestion," or self-management. It called for the take-over of almost all industries, but on a sliding scale that gave the government various degrees of ownership in different firms. Large enterprises were compensated in government bonds, while small operations remained intact. Of the 115 firms worth some $70,

000,000, which manufactured products ranging from beer to textiles, only 22 were taken over in their entirety; the rest were partially nationalized. Some companies changed management, while the executive structure of others was left standing, depending upon how large a percentage the government had taken. Under the provisions of the first two decrees, those businesses being run with the highest degree of efficiency were the least affected. The other directives guaranteed compensation to owners over a period of fifteen years at three percent—a rather dismal prospect in an unstable regime—and imposed sentences of death or life imprisonment to anyone attempting to obstruct the changes.

Overnight, the country was placed under a state of emergency. When industrialists rushed to their offices on the following morning, they found troops and tanks at the factory gates which had been locked and sealed with wax. At the government-owned banks, businessmen found their safe-deposit boxes opened and their foreign currency replaced with Syrian pounds. During the weekend, as discontent grew, President Hafez declared martial law, claiming that "Syrian reactionaries and imperialist allies abroad are trying to thwart the move." He dispatched troops to close the borders and ordered the Army to patrol the streets of major cities. Yet Syria's business community had not been caught completely unaware.

Many who had feared the worst had transferred the bulk of their holdings to Lebanon and Switzerland. Approximately one billion dollars had been smuggled out in less than two years, and many of the businessmen were now preparing to flee after their money. The ultimate result of the rumors and decrees proved even more devastating to the Baath. The flight of businessmen left few qualified personnel to operate many of the nationalized firms. Only one of the seventy new factory directors had any experience; the others proved that the regime was far from ready to tamper with the successes of capitalism. Hafez was quick to realize the dangers of lasting Socialization and allowed major industries to continue to function under the free enterprise system. But while the president was willing to compromise, he also made it clear that his new policies were not to be taken lightly. Special revolutionary tribunals, set up to counter opposition, summarily tried the first group of eight businessmen and unanimously sentenced them to death.

Eli, who did not follow their trial, would witness their march to the gallows as they passed the cell where he awaited his fate.

Book Four
The Ordeal

The Pirate Transmitter

The question of who deserved credit for the capture of Kamal Amin Taabet was a matter that did not go undisputed. The Egyptians, always anxious to belittle the Syrians, claimed that it had been their Mukhabarat (General Security Services), not Suidani's Second Bureau, which was instrumental in uncovering the operative. Taabet's trail, according to officials of the Interior Ministry in Cairo, had been picked up in 1964 during a visit of Lieutenant General Ali Ali Amer to the Syrian-Israeli front. One of the security officers had recognized a familiar face among the civilian representatives of the Baath who accompanied the general.

Upon further investigation, the party official known as Kamal Amin Taabet was discovered to have been an Alexandrian arrested three times as a subversive in the 1950's. Cairo forwarded the information to the Second Bureau, which then initiated its own inquiry.[1]

Suidani and Maaruf, for their part, were not outdone by the claims of a rival intelligence service. Both insisted that during the summer preceding Taabet's arrest, when Kol Israel broadcast a number of secret Cabinet decisions which had been previously discussed by the National Revolutionary Council, they had been alerted to the possibility that an operative had infiltrated the highest governmental echelons. The undetected pirate signal gave them more grounds to believe that many of the political and military disasters sustained by Syria in the 1960's could be attributed to a well-placed agent. Their suspicions grew even stronger in November, 1964, when Israeli guns zeroed in with astonishing precision on the long-range artillery emplacements on the southern border—a feat that would have been impossible without access to classified information.

Whatever the truth behind the Syrian claims, the Second Bureau had never won the reputation of being either reliable or effective. The major cause of its failure was a continual plague of purges, resulting from the internecine warfare between Baathite factions of rightist and leftist officers. Its counterespionage agency had always dealt more with internal politics rather than attempted to ferret out foreign agents. This failure to counter outside threats dated back to the bureau's formation shortly after the end of the French Mandate.

While Syria was still evolving into a modern republic, the new administration created a skeleton military intelligence organization, Makatib al-Tani, the Second Bureau of the General Staff, patterned on its French counterpart, the Deuxième Bureau de l'Etat Major which, like its predecessor, the fifteenth-century Espionage Civile of the Red Cardinal, Duc de Richelieu, was riddled by ineptitude and scandals. During the Second World War, the bureau had been a haven for collaborationists; it was therefore the Vichy element from which the Syrian officers had gained their expertise in political police methods.

With French and later German guidance of former Abwehr and Gestapo officials, a handful of Syrian officers in the auxiliary forces, of whom only a few had firsthand intelligence experience, attempted to create a proficient and subservient tool to gather political intelligence and military data on Zahal and even on their Arab allies, engage in counterespionage activities and maintain security in the armed forces. But the high-ranking officers who succeeded their French mentors began developing the intelligence and security apparatus in true Deuxième Bureau spirit, prostituting the services from the start in order to achieve personal political power. As a result, almost all the inspectors general of Police and Public Security, chiefs of the Second Bureau and heads of the Internal Security Services later became chiefs of staff, ministers of Defense or Interior and presidents of the republic. The most dismal aspect of their machinations surfaced after the creation of the UAR, during the union with Egypt.

Abd al-Hamid Sarraj, the soft-spoken chief of the Second Bureau since 1954, had accumulated so much power that he became a virtual ruler of the Northern Region. The thirty-six-year-old son of a wealthy Hama merchant, Sarraj was a graduate of the Gendarmerie, the Homs Military Academy and the French General Staff College. He controlled not only Syria's 15,000-man police force, Internal Security Services, and military intelligence, but also the Makatib al-Khassah (Special Bureau), a political police which spent more than 1,000,000 Syrian pounds a year on some 6,500 informers to sustain the union. "Sarraj wanted to know everything about everybody," Nasser's friend and confidant Muhammad Hassanein Heikal said of him. "He did not want to miss a movement or a whisper." Sarraj could hear an ant walking anywhere in Syria, one of his subordinates commented. So efficient were his spies that talkative Syrians learned to speak in whispers, developing an ailment known as the Syrian Twitch—a nervous compulsion to glance over their shoulders.

For more than three years, Sarraj handily disposed of officers and civilians who showed dissatisfaction with the regime. He fabricated espionage cases and prosecuted dissidents, bringing the most irresponsible charges against them. His arbitrary and ruthless policy finally brought the Northern Region to the verge of chaos. Toward the end of the union, Nasser attempted to break Sarraj's power by dividing the services into military intelligence and internal security and merging the Egyptian Mukhabarat with the Syrian Makatib to widen their scope and increase their efficiency. But the unrest felt in both organizations, stemming from a history of purges and political instability, combined with the traditional antagonism between the services, hindered the successful fusion of their operations.[2]

After the reestablishment of the Syrian Arab Republic in 1961, the Sarraj machinery was dissolved, and following a purge of Nasserite officers, the services were reorganized and placed under the command of right-wing officers, who, in turn, tried to use their power to liquidate Marxist elements and Nasserite Socialists in the Army.[3] With the advent of the Baath, the Second Bureau, in all its ramifications, was turned into a mere party tool. In a series of inner coups, officers loyal to one junta or another followed in rapid succession. Foreign espionage was almost totally neglected, military intelligence was employed mainly to maintain security within the Army, and counter-espionage was turned into a political arm and used to dispose of ideological opponents.

By the time Ahmad Suidani joined the bureau, its activities were still focused on both civilian and military foes and inter-Arab intrigue. The colonel adjusted quickly to an organization in which there was little efficiency and concentrated instead on exploring personal jealousies and winning the favor of his tough-minded and politically astute superiors. Unlike most officers of the Suuni (orthodox Moslem) sect, Suidani was of rural origin. Born to a peasant family from central Syria, he had enlisted in the Army before reaching the legal age and graduated from the Homs Military Academy while still in his twenties. Because the ranks of the intelligence services had been depleted by mass dismissals, he was transferred in the early 1960's to the Second Bureau, where his background, impeccable manners and knowledge of French and English gave him priority over many of his fellow officers. After three years of police work, the taciturn Suidani, nicknamed the Sphinx by his colleagues, was promoted to lieutenant colonel.

Following the 1963 pro-Baath coup, he worked closely with *Akid* Muhammad Shinawi and helped direct the Sovietization of the overall organization. As a fiery Marxist and sympathizer with the Vietcong and the Cuban revolution, Suidani was sent on an extended fact-finding tour of China and, upon his return, came to be recognized as a leader of the "ideological officers" in the Baath, enjoying substantial influence behind the scenes in the Army and party.[4]

Suidani, however, was much more concerned with his own future. A colonel at thirty-one, he hoped to become Syria's youngest general. As soon as he took charge of the intelligence machine in 1964, he insisted that his staff work exhausting hours and tolerated neither fumbling nor failures. He kept a half dozen officers drafting reports which dealt with political intrigues to the chief of staff, Salah Jadid; the minister of defense, Mamduh Jaber; and especially General Hafez. Suidani openly and aggressively courted the president's favor, a display of personal loyalty that many considered foolhardy in the insecure climate that characterized the Syrian political spectrum. Hafez, on his side, fully recognized Suidani's ability and loyalty but was made uneasy by the young colonel's obsessive ambition.

Suidani's reputation had preceded him to Moscow, where he flew on an official visit with a Syrian military delegation and was received with full honors. He found the chief of the KGB (State Security Service), Vladimir Y. Semichastny, and his first deputy chairman, Major General N. S. Zakharov, most willing to lend a sympathetic ear to the Second Bureau's needs. The tall, sandy-haired Semichastny, who also came from a working-class family, was said to have shown Suidani and his party some of the counterintelligence methods and tactical support sections in the massive stone structure on 2 Dzerzhinskovo Street which served as KGB headquarters. But most of the KGB's twelve directorates, particularly the divisions dealing in foreign espionage, were inaccessible.

Zakharov offered to supply the Internal Security Services and the Second Bureau with some of the more basic tools his scientific and technical branches had designed and manufactured, in addition to highly sophisticated audio and radio equipment, listening and detection devices, secret ink processors, weapons and other paraphernalia used by agents. The Soviets also agreed to accept a quota of Syrian intelligence officers to the Frunze Academy, the Russian West Point, and admit a select few to the

KGB's Judicial Institute for either a full four-year course or a special abbreviated program in internal security methods, gathering intelligence and counterespionage.

For good reasons, the Syrians were allowed only a glimpse at the other major instrument of Russia's secret power, KGB's rival, the Fourth Bureau of the Chief Intelligence Directorate of the Red Army's General Staff, or GRU. Suidani had met the small and wiry GRU chief, General Ivan Serov, during his visit to Damascus, when the sinister-looking officer was said to have showed no inclination to be cooperative. The Fourth Bureau had an extensive network of operatives working in Syria under the cover of diplomats, military advisers, technicians, Syrian Communist Party members, newsmen with the Tass telegraphic and Novotny press agencies and a number of "illegals" whose work could be jeopardized by collaboration with the local services. But Serov had changed its attitude and now offered Damascus the GRU's full cooperation.

Suidani returned with an oral pact for closer collaboration between the Syrian and Soviet services and the establishment of a permanent liaison in Moscow and Damascus. The Russians also promised to relay any information on Israel gathered by their agents. They pledged aid in the reorganization of the security and intelligence services, assistance in the creation of espionage schools, more advisers and new detection equipment. By bolstering the Second Bureau, they hoped to achieve another, equally important goal—to infiltrate the Syrian intelligence apparatus and, indirectly, other Arab services with whom Damascus maintained contact. The GRU nevertheless continued to deploy its operatives in seeking control of the Syrian Army and the Baath Party. For Damascus, however, the move toward Sovietization, in spite of the obvious hazards, ensured a tougher and more effective operation.

Syria, like other nations, possessed its own arsenal of sophisticated electronic eavesdroppers. The Second Bureau's monitoring equipment, of the type developed during World War

II by Section 3B of the Abwehr and later skillfully employed by the British and perfected by the Russians, had been in operation since August, 1958, when Soviet radar networks were installed throughout the country.[5] The monitoring stations, which probed the airwaves with their antennae, were located along the coast and around Damascus. But although the Syrian technicians who investigated the avalanche of whines and buzzes were supervised by Soviet advisers, attempts to pinpoint and track down enemy agents had, until that time, frequently met with failure. At the beginning of 1962 the central tracking station of the monitoring section near Damascus had detected a clear, but rather weak, unlicensed signal. In the months that followed, the trackers often isolated the alien beam from among the other signals; it was repeated on the same wavelength each day, generally between dawn and 8 A.M. But the transmission was too brief to give the old detection equipment sufficient time to locate the wireless. Recordings of the intercepted messages were sent to cipher units which failed repeatedly to break the code, yet from the short duration of the first transmissions, counterespionage deduced that the clandestine radio operator was not sending much information. It was only after the messages were lengthened that the existence of an operative was confirmed; it was further established that the transmitter was being operated somewhere in the northeastern section of Damascus. The trackers also learned to identify the pirate's fist on the Morse key and reported their findings to headquarters. Maaruf, who had been kept informed of developments, instructed that the transmissions be jammed, but before his order could be carried out, the clandestine post began changing frequencies and schedules, squeezing signals between other transmissions and often overlapping them.

By 1965 the tracking stations still had not determined the location of the controlling center to which the signal was beamed, nor were the direction finders able to pinpoint the pirate's precise location. Maaruf's only hope was that the more advanced Soviet instruments would provide the means necessary to solve the dangerous mystery.

*   *   *

At the beginning of the second week in January, only days after Eli had returned to Damascus, a meeting was scheduled by the chief of military intelligence and his head of internal security to discuss the employment of newly arrived Soviet equipment. Colonel Suidani arrived at the General Staff complex a little later than usual. He hurried into the building, climbed the wide staircase several steps at a time and walked along a corridor which led to his office in the wing reserved for the Second Bureau.

Suidani appeared drawn and tense as he listened without any apparent interest to the duty officer's report about the previous uneventful night. The colonel's eyes swept restlessly over the furniture. The room, whose windows overlooked the back courtyard, was soberly appointed, and a youthful portrait of the president of the republic looked down on a massive map of the Arab world. As soon as the major had ended his briefing and left, Suidani began searching through the stacks of papers neatly piled on his desk. He found the desired memorandum among documents marked "top secret," and before he could make some marginal comments on it, the intercom rang. An aide announced arrival of Lieutenant Colonel Azziz Maaruf and, seconds later, ushered the chief of the Internal Security Services into the office. The two shook hands, and Suidani told his subordinate to sit down.

For the next half hour the colonel paced back and forth, complaining heatedly about the shortcomings of the services. Apart from its proficiency as a political police force and several successful intelligence coups, he argued, the services' contribution to counterespionage operations had been practically nil. When Suidani paused long enough to indicate that he had finished, Maaruf protested. His drawn face became even more waxen as he attempted to explain that the bureau simply could not be operated efficiently; the staff was inadequate and the equipment antiquated. Maaruf's manner was respectful, but neither did he show fear or servility.

Suidani paused before replying. Maaruf had always supported

his political undertakings; as chief of counterintelligence, his influence was crucial in many areas. Suidani was therefore doubly careful in his reprimand. But the colonel made clear that he was not interested in technicalities. Pointing to the report he had been reading, which disclosed renewed agitation in the Army by the rightist Baathites, a faction led by the chief of the Special Forces, Colonel Salim Hatoum, Suidani confided to Maaruf that such machinations within the military were his prime concern. He also feared that subversive elements were making inroads into the security services. Suidani told Maaruf that he was even beginning to doubt the allegiance of some of his department chiefs and that he had no use for anyone within the bureau—from sergeant and up—who was personally disloyal to him. He insisted that tighter security measures be imposed on the personnel and that Maaruf work to increase the overall efficiency of his organization's surveillance procedures. The lieutenant colonel promised that the service would produce results and reassured his superior of his personal fidelity.

As Suidani listened, his deep-set brown eyes, quick to flash in anger or pleasure, became less fierce and more appraising. He walked around the table and placed his hand on Maaruf's shoulder. "I have known all along that I could count on your loyalty," he said in his low, resonant voice and, as if offering a gift to assuage the officer's feelings, revealed that new detection equipment ordered to replace the outdated devices now being used by the Monitoring Section had arrived from the Soviet Union on January 7. The equipment had been transported from the port of Latakieh to Al-Hama, where it had been installed in the section's detection vans. Suidani wanted it tested in Damascus without delay. The timing of this order, given so soon after the colonel had raised doubts about the loyalty of high government officials, could not have been more appropriate.

Lieutenant Colonel Maaruf transmitted Suidani's order for the test to Major Ali Maqdad, the departmental chief in charge of the Monitoring Section, as soon as he returned to his office. Maaruf also informed a senior official in the Ministry of the

Interior that the recently arrived Soviet equipment would be put into use and instructed him to issue a memorandum to all foreign missions, United Nations personnel, local organizations and individuals who operated transmitters with government approval, notifying them to maintain radio silence between midnight and noon the following Wednesday. A similar directive was sent to the General Staff, the Damascus Garrison radio centers and all the Signal Corps at Army bases around the capital.[6] Only the Air Force, Civil Aeronautics and the Air Defense Command frequencies would be left open. Maaruf stressed the need for strict adherence to the radio silence; the order could be rescinded only in the case of an emergency caused by an uprising in the capital or war on the southern border. The test period, Maaruf concluded, would also provide an excellent opportunity to "detect those pirate operators we have been monitoring but have been unsuccessful in pinpointing."

On the day of the test, Maaruf personally supervised operations at the central tracking station. All licensed and military transmitters were still at 7 A.M. An hour later the silence was suddenly shattered by a solitary, alien beam. The trackers monitored the same identification signal which had been discovered in the northern area of the city more than two years earlier. Realizing the time element was crucial, Maaruf ordered a radio detection finder crew into the streets. Within minutes two mobile tracing units were speeding toward the Abu Rummaneh Quarter. The laundry-type vans cruised the streets and avenues in the vicinity of Mount Kassiun, their looped antennae rotating on sensitive receivers, while technicians charted the probable direction of the signal via careful triangulations. The calculations of both tracers showed that the beam was coming from the new section of the Abu Rummaneh Quarter. As the vans advanced, the beep became stronger. The trackers entered the street off Abu Rummaneh Boulevard and stopped in the vicinity of the Indian embassy, where the sound became steady. Word of the location was immediately relayed to Maaruf, who remembered the embassy's complaints that its transmissions in the early hours of the morning were often disturbed. He quickly ordered Maqdad to disconnect the master fuses of all houses on the street in order to locate the one from which the signals came. Maqdad was successful at his third attempt. The pirate operator transmitted from a fourth-floor apartment right across from the General Staff Headquarters.[7] Maaruf at once notified Suidani. The colonel could not help expressing admiration for the operative's protective cover. His transmitter was surrounded by the powerful radios of ten foreign missions, the UN head-quarters of the Syrian-Israeli Mixed Armistice Commission and the communications center of the General Staff, each of which employed its own sets of codes. Even the few amateurs licensed by the government were located in this luxurious residential area. No better camouflage could have been devised for a pirate operator. If not for the introduction of the new equipment, he would never have been caught.

Twenty-four hours after the raid on Eli's apartment in Damascus, his opposite number arrived at the Mosad Communication Center, walked rapidly down the main corridor and entered one of the soundproof cubicles, closing the door behind him. Sitting heavily in a swivel chair, the radio operator turned on the high-powered transmitter-receiver, set it on a prearranged frequency and checked the Morse key. All seemed in order. He then proceeded to unlock a small safe and remove a number of cipher sheets and decoding books. The clock on the wall read 5:57 A.M. (7:57 Damascus time). He hastily put on his headset and began searching for the identification signal from Damascus.

The first clattering began at 6 A.M., as scheduled. The connection was excellent. Eli's signal came through without interference. The operator mechanically jotted the groups of numbers on a special form and was about to reply when he suddenly stiffened. He attempted to adjust the tuning dial, while at the same time clamping the headset harder against his left ear. Visibly baffled, he started checking his notes. There was no doubt that the man on the other end was Eli. He recognized the fist, speed and style he had become so familiar with during the past three years. That morning, however, the message contained an unscrambled last sentence—the prearranged danger signal. He understood that Eli was in trouble but could ask no questions.

336

The instructions for such cases were unconditional: Stall and await further details. Complying with the orders, he refrained from answering and rang for his superior. When the same message was repeated, again without error, he deduced that Eli was most likely being forced to feed the center misinformation.

By the time the second transmission ended the duty officer had arrived and was tersely briefed. He appeared dumbstruck as he read the incoming message over the operator's shoulder. When Eli's transmission that evening still remained unscrambled, the officer understood that he had been uncovered and issued the order to sign off and out.

The first evidence of Eli Cohen's arrest was logged at six thirty Tel Aviv time on Monday evening, January 25, exactly thirty-eight hours after the raid.

The duty officer rushed to notify the head of the Syrian Department, who, in turn, contacted Major General Meir Amit at his residence near Tel Aviv. Minutes later, the ground-floor telephone rang at Premier Eshkol's villa on Ben Maimon Avenue in Jerusalem. Although the prime minister's wife, Miriam, would usually not allow him to be disturbed until later in the morning, the sound of Amit's voice was enough to bring her to awaken her husband. The *memune* read the message to Eshkol, told him what facts he knew and commented that, indeed, Eli might have been compelled to transmit false data. He promised to keep the premier informed.

It took Amit only forty-five minutes to dress and drive to Mosad Headquarters. His top-level staff was already at work. In less than an hour after his arrival, an aide placed a summary of the Arab and world press on his desk. Amit found one fragment of information that confirmed his fears. The Lebanese daily *al Muharrer* had echoed a garbled report, originating in Syria, about the apprehension of "a dangerous Israeli espionage ring."[1] Friendly embassies had offered additional data, but the day's intelligence from operatives in Damascus and Beirut gave no clue to the veracity of Suidani's message. Later in the morning, the unit monitoring Arab stations supplied a transcript of a Radio Damascus communiqué confirming the arrest. When Kol Israel finally broadcast the item on its 1 P.M. news program, the Mosad had concluded that the Second Bureau's claim was based on fact.

Most international news services carried the story with few details. The Tel Aviv daily *Al Hamishmar* buried the bulletin on an inside page. Only two major Western newspapers would print it on the following day. *Le Monde* ran a brief account of the capture, while the New York *Times* commented that the accused "will be tried by a military tribunal and may face the death sentence."[2]

The *memune* understood that in order to prevent a summary trial the Mosad would have to ask the government to summon all its resources to help Eli. To ensure the success of such an operation, a news blackout would have to be imposed before Eli's exploits could be publicized. Amit realized that exposure of the case would only hinder the efforts to obtain a fair trial. Yet he knew that the authorities could not impose publishing restrictions, for under Israeli law, the government can act as censor only when the disclosure of information threatens national security. Eli's arrest voided any argument that secrecy would be breached if the facts about his mission became known. Amit, therefore, could not prevent the press from running the story, but he nevertheless decided to try to convince Israeli editors to cooperate.

With the approval of the minister of defense, he ordered his secretary to convene the editors' committee of the nation's press and gave the editors in chief a full account both of Eli's career and his assignment in Damascus. Amit explained the necessity of keeping the matter from the people, to avoid public clamor that would needlessly embarrass the Syrians and jeopardize the trial. The editors unanimously agreed to maintain a veil of secrecy for as long as the government deemed it necessary.[3]

At the first weekly Cabinet meeting on the Sunday following the disclosure of Eli's capture, Eshkol brought his ministers up to date on developments. Though the life of an Israeli agent was at stake, domestic political considerations, while unspoken, were not far from the surface. The prime minister was aware of the impact an internal crisis caused by an espionage blunder similar to the one that triggered the Lavon Affair might have on his career. Eshkol's popularity was at an ebb, as the nation prepared to elect its sixth Knesset. Even the premier's own Mapai Party had grown weary of his monotonous competence and regarded him more as a caretaker leader, a symbol of transition to a new, still-undetermined stage of political life. The prime minister also faced a Mapai convention in February and expected a showdown over his programs. Particularly nettlesome was former Premier David Ben-Gurion, who identified with the vociferous Young Turks of the party and had become exceedingly critical of Mapai's refusal to adopt his position on the Lavon Affair, by now Israel's major political *cause célèbre.*

Reviewing the Cohen dossier, Eshkol quoted from a Mosad report on Eli's four-year mission in Syria. The prime minister cautioned the Cabinet to refrain from discussing the incident with their advisers—not even in confidence; the only others who had any knowledge of the affair besides the intelligence community were the chief of staff, his closest aides and the Knesset Foreign Affairs and Security Committee. A blackout, Eshkol added, would be maintained by the nation's press.

The immediate problem at hand, the prime minister continued, was to force Damascus to consider the international consequences of any precipitous action against Eli. In view of the Syrians' reputation for justice, an execution without a trial was a real possibility. And if there were a trial, it could well be held summarily, *in camera,* and end with a death sentence. Even in the event the proceedings were public, there was scant justification for assuming that Eli would be allowed an adequate defense. Eshkol went on to propose a global rescue campaign to be launched under the aegis of the Foreign Affairs Ministry. Its objective would be to seek the intercession of world leaders in persuading the Syrians to hold a fair trial and, in the case Eli was given the death penalty, to marshal public opinion to save his life. Since Israel had never hanged a spy and the execution of a foreign national in peacetime was contrary to civilized practices, the Syrians could hardly justify such an action. Abstract appeals for equity, however, might not be sufficient, Eshkol emphasized. Contacts would therefore be sought to bargain with Syria for an exchange of prisoners.[4]

Despite the skepticism of some ministers, who claimed that Damascus was impervious to outside interference, the diplomatic effort was swiftly mounted by Golda Meir. Though the Foreign Ministry would first concentrate on pressing for a just trial, the ultimate purpose of the drive was made clear in coded telegrams to Israeli officials abroad. The messages contained three unqualified words: SAVE ELI COHEN.

At home, every foreign representative stationed in Israel was approached with the urgent request that his government intervene in the case. The foreign minister called her personal friend, U.S. Ambassador Walworth "Wally" Barbour, a Bostonian who acted as *doyen* of the diplomatic corps, and asked for his aid. The usually outspoken Barbour, though uncertain he could do anything, promised to cable Washington. Israeli politicians continued prodding him at his weekly Sunday open house and, whenever the opportunity arose, at public functions. When the French ambassador was approached, he promptly advised the Quai d'Orsay to use every means at its disposal to influence the Syrians. Yet West Germany's special envoy, Dr. Kurt Birrenbach, in Jerusalem to work out details for the establishment of formal diplomatic relations between the Bonn government and Israel, advised the foreign minister that since the two countries had announced mutual recognition, the once-cordial relations between his nation and Syria had deteriorated to the point where any overtures would be fruitless. Aside from the diplomats, visiting dignitaries (Lord Herbert Bowden and Supreme Court Justice Arthur Goldberg), businessmen and university lecturers were asked to contact their governments upon returning home.[5] The response was heartening.

The Ministry of Foreign Affairs recognized from the beginning that Moscow-oriented Damascus would most likely be roused by pressure from the Soviet Union. After Golda Meir had met with coldly diplomatic vagueness from Russian Ambassador Dimitri Chuvakhin and pleas to the Eastern bloc representatives went unheeded, the aid of a prominent Israeli Communist, plump, gray-haired Moshe Sneh, was enlisted. An ardent Zionist, Sneh requested the intervention of party hierarchs in Moscow, Bucharest, Budapest, Sofia and Prague, soliciting them to ask their governments to act in Eli's behalf.[6]

Emissaries of the secretary-general of the Histadrut, Israel's mammoth labor federation, meanwhile appealed to Socialist politicians and trade union leaders throughout Europe; their efforts resulted in a flood of cables to Damascus which urged clemency for Eli. The chairman of the Socialist International, Austrian Vice-Chancellor Dr. Bruno Pietermann, petitioned the Syrian ambassador to Vienna, while the moderate Socialist president of Italy, Giuseppe Saragat, and former Argentine Premier Arturo Frondizi entreated Hafez for an equitable trial and sentence. The mayor of Florence, Giorgio La Pira, who had been an intermediary for peace in the Middle East and held the distinction of bringing Israelis and Arabs together to a conference table, added his name to the list of those working to help Eli. Forty Swiss politicians and Dutch Labor Party leader Pieter Dankert petitioned Damascus. In Sweden, union chief Arne Geijer telegraphed the Muhajerin Palace, and leading intellectuals in Stockholm signed a petition addressed to Hafez, demanding justice for Cohen.[7]

In Belgium, Ambassador Amiel Najar briefed the aging, prestigious Camille Huysmans, ex-president of the Council of Ministers, who took up the cause as his own, writing, cabling and phoning Damascus. When his attempts proved fruitless, he offered to go to the Syrian capital and speak to Hafez directly.[8] The Queen Mother Elisabeth, known for her interest in humanitarian causes, granted an audience to Lieutenant General Moshe Dayan, then on an official visit to Brussels as minister of agriculture.[9] Afterward, the palace promptly wired Damascus.

On his European tour in mid-March, Eshkol privately discussed the Cohen case with Premier Harold Wilson and Foreign

Minister George Brown during a state dinner at 10 Downing Street. The Labour Party subsequently backed the Israeli chargé d'affaires in his solicitation of the Court of St. James's. Jerusalem could now count on Queen Elizabeth's support in their campaign to pressure Damascus. Lord Bertrand Russell, a name synonymous with international causes of every description, was an inevitable addition to the drive. Michael Foot and twenty-two of his colleagues in Parliament and Trades Union Congress chairman George Woodcock followed suit.[10]

The efforts to impress the Syrians reached beyond the palaces and ministries of the world's nations. Ehud Avriel, the Israeli ambassador to Italy, was dispatched to the Vatican, where His Eminence A. G. Cardinal Cicognani, the secretary of state, listened to him with evident concern. Following the meeting, Pope Paul VI requested the two Arabs recently elevated to the cardinalship to intercede. The Holy See also dispatched a special envoy to the Archbishop of Damascus, beseeching the prelate to enter an urgent plea with Hafez.[11]

Whenever political considerations outweighed moral issues, however, assistance was not offered as quickly. Ambassador Abraham Harman and Israeli attachés in Washington were given a cool reception by Philips Talbot, Assistant Secretary of State for Near Eastern Affairs, at a Foggy Bottom conference. Like Averell Harriman, President Lyndon Johnson's ambassador at large, who had been briefed about the Cohen case by Foreign Minister Meir and President Zalman Shazar during policy talks in Jerusalem shortly after Eli's arrest, Talbot was at pains to point out that United States opinion had little effect on the Syrians. The State Department was now in a particularly poor position to plead with Damascus after the recent exposure of a CIA espionage episode, which further strained relations between Hafez and Ambassador Ridgway B. Knight.

At the White House and on Capitol Hill, the response was little more encouraging. Walt Whitman Rostow, Johnson's special assistant for national security affairs, doubted the President could be helpful even on an unofficial level. Longtime

Congressional friends of Israel, who had been generous with aid in the past, showed understanding but could do no more than hope for a favorable outcome.

Despite the bleak official attitide, the usually influential American Zionist Council continued to lobby for the cause in Washington. While the Israelis stepped up recruiting of private support, Nobel Peace Prize winner Linus Pauling readily responded to the pleas for backing. Unexpectedly, Arab communities in Allentown, Toledo and Detroit also agreed to send messages to Damascus. They were joined by the Syrian Church and the Lebanese Bishop of New York, who appealed to Hafez's "noble Arab feelings."[12]

At United Nations Headquarters in Manhattan, members of the Israeli delegation, led by Cambridge-educated Michael S. Comay, persistently cornered everyone they thought might be of help. In the absence of Adlai Stevenson, Comay's aides spoke with Charles Yost, then third-ranking member of the U.S. Mission and former ambassador to Syria, who bluntly said that he was reluctant to intervene in an espionage case. Representatives of African nations receiving military and economic aid from Israel were more cordial but termed it "a waste of breath" to use the international forum to move the Syrians.

The pipe-smoking Russian ambassador, Nikolai Fedorenko, as usual charmingly polite, was no more sanguine than the Africans. Among the Western delegates, though, the Israelis found sympathetic listeners who were willing to cooperate. The British and French volunteered to serve as intermediaries and sounded out their Arab colleagues. They later reported that the Egyptian representative, Muhammad Awad al-Kuny, had merely shrugged at the request and the Syrian ambassador, George Thome, was gracious but as intransigent as ever toward Israel.

All along, the Israelis at the UN had sought to inform Secretary-General U Thant of the matter and enlist his support. When unofficial approaches were seen to have failed, a meeting was finally arranged. Thant received Comay's deputy, Yosef Tekoah, in his thirty-eighth floor office and listened impassively while puffing on a succession of black Burmese cigars. After

Tekoah had finished, the Secretary-General patiently explained that while he was personally sympathetic, his office had its limitations. When it came to espionage, there was nothing he could possibly do.

Israeli diplomats, nevertheless, doggedly persevered. Knowing that U Thant leaned heavily on advice about the Middle East from UN Undersecretary Ralph Bunche, a member of the delegation saw the latter privately at his Forest Hills home. Their conversation was amiable until Bunche learned the nature of his guest's visit. At that point, his voice hardened; there was no way, he said, that the Secretariat could intercede.[13]

As the international diplomatic community was probed, other, more unorthodox means of reaching the Syrians were being employed. In Buenos Aires, one Aaron Bagdadi, a fifty-seven-year-old Jewish textile merchant, wrote the Foreign Ministry, requesting that it act on behalf of his "nephew," Kamal Amin Taabet, a citizen of Argentina who was being held as a spy in Damascus. Bagdadi was summoned to the Cancillería on Calle Arenales and questioned at length.[14] A month before, the daily La Prensa had carried an Agence France Presse dispatch on the arrest of an Israeli agent in Syria, but it was not until several days afterward that the press discovered Taabet had claims to Argentinean citizenship. The story became front-page news throughout South America. Spurred by the publicity and Bagdadi's formal request, the Ministry of Foreign Affairs ordered its consul in Damascus to see Eli and attend to his immediate needs. Foreign Minister Angel Zabala Ortiz later officially asked the Syrian government to spare Eli Cohen for "humanitarian reasons."

Making use of Eli's status as an Argentinean, the Israelis retained a Buenos Aires attorney in the name of the Cohen family to seek assistance from any likely source. Vice-President Carlos Perrete consequently wired Hafez, and Alfredo Cardinal Palacios, lying on his death bed, implored the Syrian president, as a last wish before dying, to grant Eli clemency.[15]

* * *

Throughout the campaign, every quarter in France, the Western nation closest to Syria, had been besieged for aid. Walter Eytan, the balding, Bavarian-born Israeli ambassador to the Quai d'Orsay, had received the assurance of former premiers Edgar Faure and Antoine Pinay that they would entreat Damascus. At Eytan's request, Foreign Minister Maurice Couve de Murville had also asked the pro-Gaullist Tunisian envoy, Muhammad Masmudi, to urge his government to press the Syrians. Anticipating the official visit of Lebanese Premier Charles Helou, Eshkol meanwhile wrote President de Gaulle about Israel's Jordan waters policy and added that an expression of concern over the Cohen case from the president could have far-reaching consequences. De Gaulle brought up the matter with the Lebanese prime minister, who was said to have been startled when he later heard a similar plea from Cardinal Cicognani at the Vatican.

In nongovernment circles the Israelis won the support of French businessmen, educators, Catholic lay leaders (Jacques Medole) and jurists (Batonnier R. W. Thorp, president of the French Bar Association). Le Mouvement Français pour la Paix and both French labor unions, the Catholic CFTC and the Socialist Force Ouvrière, also pledged cooperation. No possibility, regardless of how remote it seemed, was overlooked in the desperate drive to help the captured agent. Israeli diplomats even contacted Dr. Maurice Kuss, the surgeon who had treated the Syrian president for a kidney ailment. Kuss wrote his former patient, asking him, "in the name of life," to save Eli.[16]

His letter, like all the others, went unanswered. The Muhajerin Palace had responded so far with total silence to pleas from throughout the world.

In his cell, Eli remained totally unaware of the efforts being made to save his life and could only guess whether the Mosad had informed Nadia of his fate.

After the initial interrogations at the Hamadieh base, Eli was transferred to the dungeons of Sigin al-Kala, the old prison in the heart of Damascus, from which he was periodically taken to a large room on the first floor of the General Staff Headquarters for more intensive questioning. Colonel Suidani, Major Tawara and occasionally President Hafez himself took part in the sessions. "I saw Eli Cohen a number of times afterward," Hafez later revealed. "I offered him cigarettes, but he refused. He did not drink either. He was in perfect control and conducted himself courageously and with dignity during those difficult hours." [1]

Although he held little back in discussing his personal life, Eli omitted certain incriminating information about his recruitment, training, acquisition of a cover in Argentina and accomplishments in Damascus. He had been thoroughly prepared for the eventuality of capture; he had practiced yielding slowly under intense questioning, creating the illusion that he was collaborating and that facts he had no desire to divulge were being successfully pried from him. Well aware that the knowledge shown by his interrogators was based on analyses of comparatively insignificant material detected by the police, Eli embroidered unimportant data, giving the impression that he was revealing much that was vital. His interrogators, at least in the beginning, did not recognize the maneuver, and Eli managed to avoid disclosing a great many compromising facts. But despite such stalling tactics, Colonel Suidani was able to uncover his Syrian accomplices and reconstruct some of his intelligence-gathering exploits. The Second Bureau, however, remained unaware of many of his actions.

During the time Eli was being questioned, a great many of his friends and business associates were seized. Their number eventually reached 500, including 17 women, among whom were employees of the Radio and Television Directorate, several secretaries at the ministries of Defense and Information, a number of socialites and airline hostesses and Saliha. Along with the others arrested were Eli's anchorman, Sheik Majid al-Ard; his collaborator, Georges Seif; and his close friend, Lieutenant Maazi Zaher ad-Din? None of Eli's contacts in the Army or the Baath was apprehended, as their status placed them beyond the reach of the investigation. Aside from President Hafez, these included former Premier Salah al-Bitar, Defense Minister Mamduh Jaber, the secretary-general of the Baath, Michel Aflak, Hafez's protégé, Colonel Salah Dalli, and Colonel Salim Hatoum. The Second Bureau was predictably quick in using the Taabet case to dispose of some political opponents, and Suidani rounded up several well-known anti-Baathites under the false charge of having helped Taabet in his espionage activities.

When Eli's interrogation appeared to have reached an impasse, Suidani instructed his men to begin more drastic questioning. Eli was to be transferred from the detention center to the dreaded Sigin al-Maaza al-Askari, the central military penitentiary where all political prisoners were ultimately imprisoned, and held there until his fate was determined. At twilight, after having spent only a few days in the capital's dungeons, Eli was escorted, handcuffed and manacled, from his cell at Sigin al-Kala to a closed Russian-built van. Preceded and followed by Land Rovers filled with heavily armed soldiers, the vehicle raced south through the suburbs. A few miles from the center of the city, the small convoy turned off the Damascus-Kuneitra highway onto a dirt road which led to the military prison. Minutes later, it passed through huge steel gates set in high stone walls and parked in the inner court—a paved yard surrounded by buildings all of whose windows were barred. As Eli emerged, he could not help noticing in the center by a round fountain a neatly stacked pile of birch lashes.

The massive, fortresslike penitentiary, erected by the French during the Mandate, jutted from a steep hill ringed by deep uncultivated valleys. The entire area was dotted with military installations which constituted the Mazza District. Although close .enough to the capital so that those confined behind its walls could hear the jets landing and taking off from Damascus' International Airport, the prison was practically isolated and impenetrable from within. Inmates who dared attempt to breach its high walls flanked by watchtowers were confronted by a barrier of barbed wire and mine fields laid over a wide radius. Escape from al-Mazza was tried only by those who had nothing to lose.

The guards led Eli along a cavernous first-floor corridor to a large, disorderly office. Two military policemen, who were already waiting there, regarded him impassively. He was told to remove his clothes, and as soon as he was naked, one of the guards fingered every cavity in his body while the other meticulously placed the items he had taken from his pockets in a small pile with his belt and shoelaces. Eli's inner garments were then returned to him, but all personal effects had to be left behind. A prison clerk finally began processing him. He was issued brown prison garb, fingerprinted and photographed full face and profile, but spared the indignity of having his head shaved. After these preliminaries, a guard motioned him out of the office; he was escorted through a gray-walled main corridor past an iron gate and down to an underground high-security cell block which housed the prison's twenty-eight solitary confinement cubicles. The damp cellar wing was crossed by two narrow passages with seven cells lined on each side. Not far to the right was the dreaded *al-Aadem* (Death Row) and beyond, the *muabed* area reserved for prisoners serving life terms. The second tier, Eli would later learn, contained larger cells and an interrogation room which the prisoners unsparingly described as a torture chamber.

The solitary cubicle assigned to him was an evil-smelling, 3-by-4-foot hole, 18 feet high, which looked more like a medieval dungeon than a modern prison cell. The heavy wooden door, with tiny peephole and small opening to allow the passage of food, sealed almost hermetically, leaving him in semidarkness. Across the room, the concrete was raised slightly for use as a bed. (To cover the stony surface, Eli was later given a thin, torn mattress and three soiled blankets.) An empty gallon can which served as a washbasin stood in one corner, an open toilet in another. There were no windows; air found its way through a ventilating strip above the door. The walls, which had been last whitewashed sometime in the distant past, bore the graffiti scrawled by long-forgotten inmates. Among the inscriptions, Eli noticed a number of crudely drawn hammers and sickles, swastikas and Stars of David.[3]

The daily routine in solitary followed a grim and purposefully erratic pattern—part of a systematic attempt to cut inmates loose from time as a pillar of sanity. Long before it was light, the prisoners were awakened by shouts and curses, and after washing with icy water poured sparingly into their basins, the faithful prepared for prayer. Not long after they answered the call of the muezzin, a bowl of jasmin tea with spices was silently passed through the food trap in the door. Then came a long, uninterrupted wait, terminated only in the middle of the day by another meal—a round loaf of dark bread, soup and *burgul* (porridge made from the roasted grains of wheat), all spooned together on a tin plate.[4] It took Eli only days to learn about hunger. A part of the bread, he found, had to be hoarded to eat with the watery soup served as the evening meal, unless one wanted to awaken with hunger pangs during the night.

While the jailers were thus trying to control his behavior with food, Eli made enormous efforts to maintain his integrity.

Forbidden to speak, read, write or exercise, he merely stood waiting for the guard to look through the peephole or conduct the three daily searches or head counts. One of his few distractions was to use the same spyhole from the inside to observe the duty prisoner, who slept on a mattress in the middle of the corridor, go about his chores. Like every inmate confined to solitary, Eli soon realized how many details one can see if there is nothing to do but look. Emancipated from the pressure of time, he had the first opportunity in many years to think over and digest all that he had seen, learned and done in a lifetime. He began reviewing his past, remembering books he had read and movies he had seen, reciting poetry, humming quietly. He was just beginning to tire of such a mental diet when the ordeal began.

Eli had most probably lost count of the days since he was placed in solitary, with only the periods of interrogation to provide an erratic calendar. In the afternoon on the last day of January, as he was sitting in a corner of his cell, he heard the clatter of footsteps outside, then the staccato sound of a bugle and the rolling of a single drum. The eight businessmen who had been found guilty of opposing the new measures of Socialization only four weeks earlier were being led to the gallows.

A few days later, shortly after noon, Eli heard the guard making his way along the corridor toward his cell. In a matter of seconds the duty prisoner was standing at attention. There was a clatter of bolts. He swung the door back and motioned him to follow. The guard shoved and pushed Eli all the way to the nearby interrogation room, where, in the presence of Suidani and the military prosecutor, he was ordered to correct and elaborate on previously recorded data. As the weeks passed, the interrogations lengthened. At first, they were held twice a day for two hours at a time, but soon there were three and even four sessions, sometimes lasting as long as seven hours without food or water. At the beginning of each period, the interrogators, who were relieved every two hours, would place the stenographic records of the previous sessions before Eli and demand that he sign them. A barrage of questions followed. When he dozed off from exhaustion, they would shake him awake with screams accompanied by curses and obscenities. At some sessions, different measures were applied to help him remember: Fingers were jammed up his nostrils, a fist was thrown into his mouth, his lips were stretched sideways, and tobacco was rubbed into his eyes. His teeth were pulled and his fingernails crushed and torn, and he was kicked and lashed and beaten with bamboo rods until his blood flowed. His feet were laced with birch branches until they were a mass of bruises, pins were inserted into his fingertips, and burning cigarettes were ground out on his back. He was made to stay on his knees or stand at attention with hands tied behind his back until his senses dimmed, and at times, a car tire was placed over his shoulders, immobilizing his arms and allowing him to be rolled about the room or down the stairs while being pummeled by the guards. When all these tactics failed, metal clips protruding from a power joint were attached to his tongue and sexual organs, and the *harka* (electric shock) treatment was applied amid constant threats that he would die like a dog. Shattered and faint, he had to be dragged back to his cell after every session. But Eli refused to show fright and, as Suidani himself confessed, told them "only what he thought fit to say."[5] That was when his interrogators decided to try psychological torture. Their target was not his body but his will. They first attempted to make Eli lose hope, telling him that Israel had repeatedly blocked his release by turning down an offer to exchange agents. The threat to hang him also became a favorite theme, and they actually subjected him to a mock execution and a game of Russian roulette.

Such treatment was not reserved for the interrogation sessions. During his walks to and from the torture room, Eli found himself staggering under blows from the kurbash, a short leaden whip made from a bull's tail which was carried by every guard. When he attempted to rest in his cell, water was thrown on the floor, and he was forced to stand for long periods. After weeks of unrelenting ordeal, his will to live finally gave out, and he attempted to commit suicide by cutting his wrists with a nail. Put before he had lost sufficient blood, a guard happened to peer into his cell. Eli was attended by the prison doctor and returned to solitary confinement.[6]

On a weekday night, after a long day of interrogation, he was awakened by a commotion in the nearby corridor. Lieutenant Colonel Abd al-Muein Hakimi, who occupied a cell in the neighboring Death-Row, was being taken before a firing squad amid shouts and curses. Minutes later, Eli heard a volley of shots. Within less than an hour, Hakimi's second cousin, Farhan Attassi, a thirty-seven-year-old Syrian-born naturalized American, who had been sentenced to death for espionage in behalf of the United States, was dragged out of his cell, driven to Marjeh Square and publicly hanged.

Both executions were the culmination of a CIA plan to obtain information from Syrian sources on a new missile and antiaircraft gun the Soviets had supplied the Syrian Navy, which Eli had seen thwarted by the Second Bureau while he was still free. In the winter of 1964 Attassi, a Brooklyn resident and father of two, who handled the distribution of American television films in Syria, was requested by Walter Snowdon, the second secretary of the U.S. Embassy in Damascus, to get details of the weapons from Hakimi. Attassi was given $7,500, part of which he offered to his cousin for the effort. The lieutenant colonel delegated the assignment to a loyal subordinate who promised to gather the information but instead reported the incident to his superiors. The Second Bureau was alerted and supplied the officer with false data and eleven shells, which Hakimi handed over to Attassi for Snowdon. Counterespionage agents arrested the two cousins and declared Snowdon *persona non grata*, ordering him and his secretary, Martha Sherer, to leave the country.

The trial of the two CIA operatives was brief. Attassi did not hesitate to denounce his interrogators' brutality, accusing them of having "tortured me with electricity as soon as I was arrested." He claimed that he had been savagely beaten, brainwashed and starved. U.S. officials were not allowed to see him in jail, he was denied legal counsel, and only selected portions of his secret trial were televised for propaganda reasons. The authorities at once launched a hate campaign against what Information Minister Mashur Zaitun called an "American policy of sabotage and espionage in Syria." Attassi and Hakim's close relationship with a former president and a high Baath official did not save them from the noose.[7] Their deaths, which the Syrians labeled a warning "to all agents of imperialism, capitalism and Zionism," brought the number of executed spies and traitors since Eli's arrest to thirteen and were an ominous example of what he could expect from his captors.

In spite of their open hatred of the Israelis, many of the guards came to respect Eli for his exploits and defiant stand. His courage won him the privilege of being called a *shater* (brave one) and, as soon as the interrogation ended, a transfer from solitary confinement.[8] The new cell located on the ground floor was also isolated but had the additional comforts of an iron bed and a straw mattress; in addition, the burden of darkness was lifted. By comparison, the arrangement seemed a paradise, and his normal zest for living slowly returned. Regulations allowed him 15 Syrian pounds a month, which the white-haired Circassian warden, Sergeant Major Hussein Azzat, personally made certain that he received. From this sum he was now able to pay the 30 piasters required for a haircut or a shave by the prison barber. The six cigarettes to which he was entitled daily served to bribe the guards, who usually reciprocated with a copy of *Mujlat al-Jundi*, the armed forces weekly, permission to listen to the afternoon *Hebrew Hour* over the Voice of Damascus or the chance to borrow one of the Hebrew books from the library which bore the marks of other Israeli prisoners. He was occasionally allowed to wash his clothes, though under heavy guard, and was later even granted an afternoon solitary *tnafus* (walk), unlike the other inmates who were allowed out only in the morning.

Eli's official status came to be termed "most unusual." He

did not enjoy the privileges of some political prisoners, who could have their food delivered from a nearby bazaar and prostitutes in their cells, but neither was he forced to work at hard labor on a nearby road or runway of the al-Mazza Air Force Base.[9] Eli adhered to the mold of the penal routine with the same imperturbability with which he had performed his mission. He was affable to the guards, but ever the professional, he spoke little and never mentioned politics, Israel, agents or espionage. Like all foreigners who had passed through al-Mazza in the last twenty years, he was at the mercy of his jailers. "All the Arabs are good," the veteran guard, Toufak Toufak, would reassure him. "If they weren't you would by now be in heaven."

Contrary to al-Mazza regulations, the authorities allowed Eli to be interviewed by the press. Simat Maaruf, Damascus correspondent of Beirut's *al-Asbua al-Arabif* was given permission to visit him in order to counteract anti-Baath accusations published in Lebanese newspapers. Eli refused to talk about his exploits and remarked quietly, "I told the interrogators everything I know. I have nothing to add." When asked whether he had worked for the Israelis under duress, he answered, "No. No pressure," and explained, "I worked for Israeli intelligence only to secure the future of my wife, my three children and my mother. Only for them did I agree to undertake such a dangerous mission." But as if to reassure his superiors, he emphatically reiterated: "I did not betray them! I did not betray Israel!"[10]

The French Maîtres

For all their dark thoughts about Syrian justice, Israeli officials had not neglected to ensure that Eli would be adequately represented in the event that he was brought to trial. Unexpectedly, it was on this front that the rescue campaign was showing some signs of progress. Five days after Suidani had sent his telegram to Levi Eshkol, the director general of the Israeli Ministry for Foreign Affairs instructed Ambassador Eytan to recommend a French law firm that would agree to defend Eli in the Syrian courts. Jerusalem wanted an experienced counsel who could effectively represent the interests of the Cohen family. But above all, it was considered vital that the attorneys command the respect of the Syrians. The first secretary of the embassy in Paris, Yosef Hadass, made a painstaking inquiry among his contacts in the capital's legal community and proposed five prominent local lawyers. Eytan and his advisers selected Batonnier Paul Arrighi, the prestigious former president of the French Bar Association, renowned for his combativeness in the courtroom, who enlisted the aid of Maître Jacques Mercier, a well-known Resistance figure and paratrooper in the Free French Forces, who had represented many freedom fighters of the Front de Libération Nationale during the Algerian War of Independence. Both were considered *personae gratae* by the Arabs, and Jerusalem readily approved the embassy's choice.

In a number of lengthy conferences held in Arrighi's office, the *maîtres* were briefed by Eytan and Hadass. The attorneys' next move was to seek an audience with the Syrian ambassador to the Quai d'Orsay, Dr. Sami al-Jundi. The status both men enjoyed brought a prompt, affirmative response. Ambassador al-Jundi was courteous but pleaded ignorance to more than hearsay of the affair. He would, he promised, forward their request to represent Cohen to Damascus and notify them of the decision as soon as he received word from Foreign Minister Ibrahim Makhus.

Dr. al-Jundi was far from detached over the fate of Eli Cohen. The ambassador's career had, in fact, been markedly influenced by the émigré from Argentina, whose machinations had helped bring about his political exile to Paris, thus earning the ambassador's undying enmity. Al-Jundi found himself in an ideal situation for revenge on his adversary, now exposed as an Israeli spy. While blithely encouraging the French attorneys with empty promises, he set out to interfere in every way possible with their efforts to see Eli. Damascus, however, reacted differently. The director general of the Foreign Ministry, Asad al-Khanji, instructed al-Jundi to extend the necessary visas to the two lawyers. Within twenty-four hours, an embassy attaché called the law firm with encouraging news: "The government will be happy to do everything in its power to help Monsieurs Mercier and Arrighi in their task to defend Eli Cohen."[1] On the basis of this apparently heartening message, Mercier prepared to leave for Damascus.

On the afternoon of January 31 Maître Mercier checked into the Orient Palace Hotel, where a room had been reserved. The French attorney was told that all interviews had been scheduled for the following morning.

Secretary-general to the presidency, Maamun al-Atassi, appeared apprehensive when he greeted Maître Mercier in his chamber at the Muhajerin Palace, shortly before 11 A.M. Atassi was extremely cordial and seemed to make every attempt to cooperate. His duties, he explained, merely called for him to inquire of the *maître*'s proposals and pass them on to the minister, "so that His Excellency may be in a better position to help when he meets with you."

In the course of their conversation, Atassi told Mercier that in the past week the ministry had been besieged with hundreds of letters and telegrams from around the world appealing for a fair trial. The secretary-general did not try to hide his admiration for Israel's ability to recruit international assistance at such short notice. As a graduate of the École Supérieure d'Administration in Paris he was well schooled in the power of public opinion. The *maître* stood up to leave. While showing him to the door, Atassi promised to arrange an audience with his minister for early in the afternoon.

Mercier returned to the palace after a quick lunch at the hotel and was ushered into the plush, tapestry-walled office of the minister of presidential affairs, Walid Taleb, at precisely 1 P.M. Atassi was standing by. Mercier repeated his request to see Eli and defend him before a Syrian court. Taleb assured the *maître* that he wanted to do everything he could to cooperate, but since the police were still investigating, Mercier must understand it would be impossible to see Cohen just yet. However, the moment the investigation was completed, and the dossier referred to the *parquet* and military interrogating judge, Mercier would certainly be able to visit his client. Taleb remarked that special permission was required by law to see a prisoner, but, he added, "I assure you, *cher maître*, it is a mere formality." Mercier would, of course, be able to plead the case as soon as the Syrian Bar Association granted him permission to plead in court. Naturally, Cohen would be notified of this visit and of the attorney's desire to defend him. In fact, Mercier must immediately write a note to the prisoner. It would be delivered at once. In the meantime, Taleb suggested, there was no point remaining in Damascus. Mercier would do best to return to Paris, and Atassi would cable to inform him when the authorities were ready to prosecute.[2] Taleb was most convincing. Mercier left reassured that he had succeeded in his mission, and that he could certainly follow Taleb's advice.

Before departing, Mercier approached a number of law firms, seeking the services of a local attorney to aid him in the case, but met with polite rebuffs. The *maître* was not surprised. Rumors abounded about the affair—rumors so various that it was difficult to extract the facts from the body of fiction. The only common reaction in almost every conversation was the grudging respect Eli's deeds had won in the eyes of the Syrians. Yet when the *maître* tried to contact government officials who might be of help, he received guarded replies. All were hesitant to continue the discussion at the very mention of the name Eli Cohen.[3]

On February 2, Mercier flew to Paris believing the situation was well in hand. Two days later, he wrote Taleb reviewing their meeting and called Atassi to inquire when the police investigation would be completed. Both the minister and the secretary-general never replied. Toward the end of the month, Lebanese sources notified the law firm that the trial was about to begin. The attorneys questioned Syrian officials in Paris without satisfaction. Ambassador al-Jundi could not be reached, and an embassy spokesman had no comment. Mercier decided he could wait no longer and returned to Damascus to survey the situation.

The Presidential Palace was almost deserted at 5:30 P.M. that Saturday, February 27. Atassi welcomed Maître Mercier in his office with the same amicable greetings. Both men observed the formality of small talk until Mercier felt the social amenities had been satisfied. He then brought up the subject of Eli's investigation. Atassi expressed surprise at the *maître*'s concern. The prisoner's interrogation was still continuing, he insisted. Mercier had been promised he would be notified when it ended. "Nothing has changed as far as the assurances given you are concerned. You will see the accused and will defend him."[4]

Mercier had no choice but to believe the secretary-general. He was ready to leave on Sunday afternoon when a routine check with one of the Arab attorneys he had met on his first visit revealed that "the trial of the Israeli had already started."

The news stunned Mercier. He attempted to verify the information and, after more calls, found that the case had been brought before a military tribunal—Mercier had hoped for a civil trial—and was being held at an unspecified location behind closed doors. Infuriated, Mercier phoned Atassi. In spite of the late hour, he was able to reach the secretary-general, who expressed dismay at the report. He would *certainly* investigate —at once. And if the trial had started, he, for one, had not been informed. But the *maître* must not be concerned. This misunderstanding, if one should actually exist, would be resolved.[5] When Mercier called again an hour later, as instructed, Atassi was in conference. The *maître* tried to reach him later in the afternoon, but the secretary-general was still in a meeting. Walid Taleb had just left the capital. Other Syrian officials knew nothing of the matter. Mercier tried to notify his office but was told the lines were out of order; neither could a call to Beirut be completed.

The *maître* was determined not to desert his client before making one last effort to see Taleb or Atassi. He spent the evening by the phone, trying to reach either of the Syrians. Late that night, Atassi finally answered. His tone carried no hint of the new developments. He was about to get in touch with the *maître* to notify him that *"Monsieur le ministre* would be honored to receive you the following day." The experiences Mercier had so far had made him wary, if not pessimistic. Yet at least he had one more chance to protest.

On Monday morning March 1, Mercier was summoned to the Palace of Guests. At ten thirty an usher escorted him into a study, where he was greeted by Walid Taleb with Atassi at his side. Barely controlling himself throughout the seemingly endless amenities, Mercier objected violently to the treatment he had received. In carefully couched terms, he alluded to the lies and deceptions he had encountered. Why had the minister and his secretary been so studiously avoiding him? Why could he not call his office in Paris? Taleb patiently allowed Mercier to finish his list of grievances. Except to note that he had been a victim of misunderstandings, the minister dodged the questions. Instead, he offered reassurances. He was happy to inform the *maître* that his request to see the prisoner had *just* been granted. Moreover: "You will be able to visit your client today." The minister then smiled benignly, Mercier later recalled, as if to say, "You see, you have misjudged us."

A moment of silence was permitted to allow Mercier to feel relief and exhilaration over the unexpected turn of events. When Walid Taleb saw the expected response, he continued: "The government is now contemplating the possibility of allowing you to attend the trial as an observer. Monsieur Atassi will gladly interpret the proceedings." Anticipating an objection, Taleb added quickly, "Acting as counsel for the defense is out of the question." Mercier would be allowed to sit in court, if he so desired, but only during sessions previously approved by the military tribunal. He could either accept the government's invitation or leave the country. These were the terms, and further discussions would not benefit either party.

The *maître* later recognized that he had been left with even less choice than Walid Taleb implied. Mercier told the minister that he could not agree to these terms without consulting his client. He would have to explain to Cohen the details of "this situation in which defense rights have been deliberately ignored," and only then would he be able to make a decision. The minister nodded impatiently and signaled that the interview had neared conclusion by giving Atassi instructions about the meeting with the defendant. The *maître* would have to wait in his hotel for Atassi to call with details.

Atassi phoned at 1:30 P.M. The court-martial had unanimously decided to deny the request for a meeting with the prisoner.[6] No one would be authorized to see him at this time. The decision was final. There would be no appeal. Mercier remained silent. There was nothing to be gained by objections. The conversation concluded with cool *au revoirs*. The *maître* was left speechless, phone in hand. He decided to leave for Paris at once.

On March 3, Mercier wrote Taleb from Beirut protesting the treatment he had received at the hands of Syrian officials. Back in Paris, he briefed Ambassador Eytan and, together with Ar-

righi, drafted a formal protest to Damascus "against the procedures . . . which constitute a defiance of moral law."[7]

In the early afternoon of March 6, 1965, one week after Eli's
trial had opened in Damascus, Walter Eytan and his first secretary, Yosef Hadass, hurriedly entered the somber embassy
building on Avenue Wagram and went directly to a conference
room where the military attaché and the embassy's security
officer were already waiting. Eytan smiled amiably at Nadia and
Eli's oldest brother, Rafael, who stood by a window, talking in
low voices.

Nadia had arrived in Paris the day before with her brother-in-
law, Sofie and Iris. (Shaul had remained at home in the care of
Eli's mother.) The trip to the French capital had not been
endorsed without reservations. Nadia initially encountered opposition from the Mosad's liaison officer, but after she had
explained to officials at headquarters that she could no longer
bear to stay home without trying to intervene personally, the
memune finally approved the flight to Paris. The embassy had
then been instructed to take every step to make her feel
welcome.

Eytan shook Nadia's hand firmly and invited her to sit at
the table. As the ambassador was about to open the meeting, a
secretary, apologizing for the interruption, ushered two Frenchmen into the room. Nadia and Rafael then met Maître Mercier
and Batonnier Arrighi for the first time.

In his cordial and reassuring manner, Ambassador Eytan
began to recount the diplomatic interventions made in Eli's
behalf. The entire operation, he told Nadia, was being personally directed by Foreign Minister Golda Meir. The Muhajerin Palace
was subsequently swamped with calls and telegrams from
throughout the world, urging that Eli be given a fair trial.
Admittedly, the Hafez administration had ignored these pleas
until now, but further assistance from European and South
American countries was still being sought. "We have not lost faith
in this approach," Eytan summed up. "You can rest assured we
will try to enlist the aid of every friend we have to save Eli."

Maître Mercier, who had returned from his second visit to Damascus only forty-eight hours earlier, continued on a positive note. There was hope to be found in a growing split between the civilian and military factions of the Baath Party over Eli's fate. As a result, the *maître* sensed a favorable climate in Syrian political circles. "The struggle within the Baath indicates that I may be able to play one group against the other." Mercier concluded, "I am almost certain that I can save Eli."[8]

Nadia had sat through the conference listening silently. When she finally spoke, it was in a measured but taut voice. While awaiting the outcome of events in Syria, she had followed the Mosad's instructions to the letter, but she could sit quietly no longer. The ambassador surely understood what it meant to hear hate propaganda day in and day out over Damascus radio and television. She had brought Sofie and Iris with her to Paris so that all three might attempt to convince the Syrian ambassador to let them see Eli. "And if there is a heart in these people," Nadia said, "they will listen and allow us to join our beloved."

Hadass, knowing she would meet only with frustration, attempted to change her mind by repeating in detail the efforts now being made to influence Damascus. Nadia was resolute. As his wife, she argued, it was her right to plead for Eli's life with the Syrians. Eytan impatiently interrupted. "Let her go," he snapped, turning to Hadass. "We must try anything to save him." Addressing Nadia, he explained that she would be entirely on her own in dealing with the Syrians; intermediaries would only hinder her. All he could offer was a hearty *behatzlacha* (good luck).

The following morning Nadia told Rafael she had made up her mind to see the Syrian ambassador that same afternoon. He suggested she call first and inquire about a visa. Nadia was skeptical. She feared to alert the embassy about her intentions but suddenly reconsidered and asked the hotel operator for the embassy. A feminine voice answered, and Nadia inquired in her Iraqi Arabic about visa arrangements. She was abruptly transferred to a clerk in the Consular Department. When he heard the name Cohen there was a pause, then a click. Nadia called again, this time requesting to speak with Ambassador al-Jundi. She was switched to a member of his staff. The second response was no more polite. As soon as the aide learned who she was, he slammed down the receiver. Despite the rebuff, Nadia tried to . contact the embassy once more. By now, though, the switchboard had been alerted, and the call was disconnected at the mere sound of a woman's voice.

Nadia sat stunned, staring at the phone. Rafael said nothing. She then asked him whether she should call al-Jundi's private residence, whose unlisted number had been supplied by the Israeli embassy. Unwilling to discourage her, Rafael nodded. But there, too, Nadia was unsuccessful. Sofie saw her mother's agony and whispered, embracing her, "Why don't you let me talk to .this man who is keeping Father away? I am sure that he will listen to me." Nadia could barely conceal her tears as she sent Sofie to play with Iris.

Rafael offered no objections when Nadia insisted that she would still attempt to confront Ambassador al-Jundi with the children. He accompanied his sister-in-law and the two little girls to the lobby, put them in a taxi and gave the driver an address in the Sixteenth Arrondissement. A while later, the cab halted at 22 Boulevard Souchet in front of the Syrian embassy. Nadia led her daughters toward the gray stone building and forcefully rang the bell. A *portier* peered through a portholelike window. Hesitantly, he opened a small door in the massive wooden gate and eyed Nadia bleakly as she expressed the wish "to see His Excellency Ambassador al-Jundi." Without a word, the man left her standing outside and went for someone who could help.

After what seemed an eternity, a stocky, well-dressed official appeared and asked Nadia her name and business. She began by explaining that she wanted a visa to visit her husband in Syria. "I am Nadia Cohen," she finally blurted. "I respectfully demand to see the ambassador about my husband, who is imprisoned in Damascus." The Syrian interrupted curtly. Almost incoherent with rage, he shouted in a mixture of French and

Arabic: *"Allez-vous-en! Imshi!"* (Leave! Get out!) a barrage of abuse followed. Nadia recoiled but did not betray her emotions. Before she could plead with him further, the door was shut in her face. She rang again, but the porter had vanished.[9] As she stood there sobbing, a curious crowd surrounded her. Nadia looked up and saw the Syrian officials staring at her coldly from behind drawn curtains.

A group of Parisian newspapermen filed into a room at the Hôtel Astor, where a press conference had been called by the Israeli embassy. Nadia, Rafael and the girls were already seated, waiting. The plea to the assembled reporters was brief. Nadia had sought to meet with Syrian diplomats in Paris, but they would not even consent to talk. She had also approached various international organizations without results. "I don't know if Eli was a spy or not," Nadia said, "and I don't care. All I am trying to do is save his life." Tremulously she entreated them to appeal for world support to prevent the Syrians from killing her husband.

Most of the newsmen questioned her sympathetically. One direct query, though, took her aback. It was obvious, the reporter noted, that if the wife of an Israeli operative of such standing had been brought to Paris to face the press, the government must feel it has no chance to save him. Does she blame the Israelis for their failure? Nadia's eyes blazed defiance. "My government did more than any other would have done for one of its agents."[10]

When the press conference ended, some journalists promised to do their best to publicize her story. Nadia remained behind until the last newspaperman left. "There is nothing more we can do here," she told Rafael. "We are returning home."

Two weeks after the attorneys had protested to President Hafez, a member of Mercier's legal team, Maître Jean Talandier, was sent to Damascus to try his hand with the Syrians. Walid Taleb received Talandier on March 20. The minister listened to the attorney's presentation without interruption. Talandier argued that according to the special decree of January 7, a verdict of the military court would have to be approved by the president of the republic. He requested that Maître Mercier or Arrighi be received by President Hafez before he made the final decision. Taleb tried to evade the issue. The trial was not yet over, he insisted. In fact, it was nowhere near completion. Maître Talandier would have to wait until sentence was passed.

That same evening Talandier had his baptism in Syrian politics when he was startled by a radio report directly contradicting Taleb's statements. Radio Damascus announced on its late news program that the last session of the Cohen trial had taken place the day before and a taped version would be televised shortly. Ignoring the hour, Talandier called Atassi at home and demanded an explanation. Atassi feigned astonishment. The *maître* could surely not be concerned after today's conversation with Minister Walid Taleb. "The broadcast is merely meant to satisfy public opinion," Atassi said. While a court session had been taped and would be televised, it certainly did not indicate the trial itself had ended. Talandier was assured that no decision would be made by President Hafez before he consulted with one or all of the French attorneys.[11]

Somewhat confused, Talandier rushed to Paris. On the basis of his report, Arrighi and Mercier confirmed by telegram their request for an audience with President Hafez and anxiously awaited an answer. None was forthcoming.

When the team of *maîtres* realized that their efforts were at a standstill, they decided to seek the aid of the International Commission for the Rights of Man. Mercier was dispatched to Geneva to protest Damascus' legal abuses and request that the organization intervene on Eli's behalf. The commission assigned Maître Adrien Wolters, a Brussels attorney who headed the Belgian League, to handle the case. Wolters was briefed by the French lawyers and prepared to leave for the Syrian capital.

The *maître* arrived in Damascus on Sunday evening, March 14, and immediately contacted Batonnier Sabah al-Rikabi, the president of the Syrian Bar Association. As Wolters carried powerful credentials—in addition to being secretary-general of the Belgian League, he spoke for the French chapter and represented the international organization—Rikabi agreed to see him at once. The *batonnier* listened politely to his plea and offered to call Justice Minister Hussein Muhana immediately. The minister was evasive at first but finally agreed to a meeting the following day at eleven.

Monday morning Rikabi accompanied Wolters to the ministry, where Muhana received him. The minister, who did not speak French, told the *maître* through an interpreter that he had no power over the case and could not interfere in the proceedings of a court-martial. Special military tribunals, he explained, fell under the jurisdiction of the Ministry of Defense. Wolters expressed the wish to see Defense Minister Mamduh Jaber and was promised that Muhana would recommend a hearing.[12] The audience ended as abruptly as it had begun.

A Tuesday appointment with Jaber was canceled at the last moment, and Wolters had to wait another day before the minister could see him. Jaber told the *maître* plainly that he would not interfere with the workings of a special tribunal which had been appointed by the president of the republic. He suggested that Wolters direct his requests to the president of the court, Lieutenant Colonel Salah Dalli. But when Wolters sought an introduction from the minister, Jaber flatly refused.[13]

Still undeterred, the *maître* asked Rikabi to drive him to General Staff Headquarters, where the court was in session. With the *batonnier*'s aid, he requested an audience but was turned down without an explanation. Dalli nevertheless agreed to talk to Rikabi. A half hour later the *batonnier* emerged with a negative answer to all of Wolters' demands.[14]

An audience with President Hafez appeared pointless, and Maître Wolters left Damascus having achieved even less than his two colleagues. In view of the failure of his interventions, the French attorneys drafted a cable to Hafez on March 23, but as with all other appeals, their renewed pleas to aid Eli remained unanswered.

22
Trial Onstage

The Mosad, like the French *maîtres*, had been unable to pierce the shroud of secrecy surrounding Eli's trial. For the past month, ever since department heads were told about the capture, they had feared the worst. There was a measure of relief at headquarters, therefore, when, on February 28, Radio Damascus had announced that "the Israeli spy Eliahu Cohen will be brought today before a special military tribunal." Although the time and location had not been specified, Tel Aviv at least knew that Eli was still alive.

The Syrian morning press was no more revealing. The Damascus papers carried little about the trial, while provincial newspapers merely ran short news items. The Lebanese press, however, particularly the independent *al-Hayat*, the pro-Nasser *al Muharrer* and the Baath organ *al-Ahrar*, printed more detailed stories. From these sources it was learned that in addition to Eli the authorities would try 6 major defendants—Sheik Majid al-Ard, Georges Seif, Maazi Zaher ad-Din, Ibn-Salim al-Masr, Nasser a-Din Manes and Ahmad Hatem al-Katub—and 30 accomplices, including 9 women, indicted from among the 500 persons investigated by the police and the Second Bureau. The court martial was to be conducted *in camera*; local as well as foreign journalists were conveniently excluded.[1] There was still no indication where the trial would be held, and only a privileged few were privy to the site. In a later bulletin, the Ministry of

368 The Shattered Silence

Information promised that it would periodically release accounts of the court session to national radio and television. Intelligence analysts in Tel Aviv concluded that the Syrians were planning a staged trial, not only to prove Eli's guilt but to vindicate the Establishment. The Hafez administration was considered unable to withstand the open controversy that might result from the public disclosure of Eli's contacts in the government and the Army.

Late in the morning on the last day of February, Eli was transferred under heavy guard from Sigin al-Kala, where he had been held for the past few days, to an annex of the General Staff Headquarters. To ensure strict secrecy, massive security measures had been taken at both ends of the route and along the road leading to Abu Rummaneh. It was shortly after noon when the military motorcade halted in front of the building where a claque of officers had gathered for a glimpse of the Israeli spy. An armed detail quickly encircled one of the trucks. As the back door was lowered, the prisoner, who sat on the floor manacled hand and foot, was ordered to jump out.

An escort with fixed bayonets led Eli into the building. Guards were posted in the hallways leading to the courtroom, at the head of each stairway and at every door. (A large office had been converted for the occasion and furnished with a collapsible prisoners' dock, several benches and a long, heavy mahogany table with six chairs raised on a dais.) The sterile surroundings were not entirely unfamiliar. Eli had spent many hours surveying the complex and had often been guided through its corridors as a guest of high-ranking officers bidding for his favor.

The room stirred as he entered, wedged between military policemen. Members of the court staff watched the defendant take his place in the dock. Minutes later, the uniformed personnel came to attention as the judges filed in. The six officers who composed the military tribunal wore dark khaki dress uniforms gleaming with rows of medals and ranged in rank from captain to colonel. The president of the court, Colonel Salah Dalli, a sturdy, ruddy-faced figure with black, burning eyes, aquiline nose and an Arab-cut mustache, sat on a thronelike chair with his associates on each side. No prosecutor or defense attorney was present, merely a small staff of aides.* Two of the judges Eli faced, the colonels Dalli and Hatoum, had, ironically, called him their friend. Both officers were confidants of President Hafez and had been appointed to the bench as his personal representatives. Through them, the president intended to control the trial and prevent the disclosure of data which could incriminate the regime. Dalli was to guide the proceedings in a way that would minimize the importance of Eli's accomplishments and counter anti-Baath propaganda. But, above all, he was to see that no names of important officials were mentioned and make certain that his own involvement with the defendant and that of his wife, Hatoum and Hafez was kept hidden.

Waiting for the proceedings to begin, Eli sat on a bench, his back rigid, chin thrust out. Behind him, two burly, impassive Syrian soldiers stood watch. The dock was a small rectangular platform, 6 feet by 10, enclosed by a spiked wooden railing raised to a level which bisected Eli across the chest. The accused wore a double-breasted woolen suit with a white shirt and striped tie. He was closely shaven, his hair neatly trimmed. To the television viewer, his appearance was marred only by a tic which frequently flickered across his drawn face. The cameras concealed the missing teeth and fingernails by showing him in full figure or profile.[2] (Nadia and her two daughters followed the trial on a television set the Mosad had supplied. Four radios lent by neighbors also allowed the family to monitor major Arab stations. At the western edge of Bat Yam, in Shechunat Amidar, Eli's mother, his two sisters and five brothers, with their husbands and wives, also kept a constant vigil for news from Damascus.)

* Syrian civil and military court practices follow the French pattern. The prosecutor usually restrains himself, while the president of the court conducts most of the interrogation. In the Cohen trial, Colonel Dalli also officially assumed the role of prosecutor.

The president pounded his gavel. The trial opened as a court assistant came forward to read the charges. Eli was not asked to confess his guilt. Colonel Dalli simply said: *Ma esmak?* [Your name?] "

Eli answered softly, stating his full Hebrew name. He hesitated for a moment, then, in a clear tone, said: "Mr. President, I would like an attorney."

In the silence that followed, the six officers appeared transfixed by the request. Colonel Dalli looked bewilderedly at his colleagues. Then, suddenly furious, he demanded, "What? A lawyer? "

"Yes, if it is possible." Eli's reply took no notice of the colonel's anger.

Dalli regained his composure and remarked dryly, as if reading from a prepared statement. "Owing to the fact that the charge is espionage, the tribunal rejects this request. Actually, Cohen, you already have a defender. And what a noisy one! The entire sold-out Lebanese press is at your service."[3]

Eli sat down wearily. His resignation made it apparent that he had not expected to be granted counsel. In a later session, he would make another formal plea for a defense attorney, providing the president with one more opportunity to berate him: "Are we going to grant this spy a lawyer? This man who has managed to indicate to the Israelis, with such exactness, the emplacement of our guns and tanks along the border? Who else, if not he, is responsible for the precise shelling of our positions . . . ? "[4]

For the remainder of the first day, Eli was asked to give the court a full account of his life. He spoke quietly and carefully, as if to miss no point or exaggerate any. Although some details were omitted or modified to avoid divulging activities unknown to the Syrians, his testimony was reasonably complete. He related the story of his youth in Egypt, but did not mention his complicity in the Marzouk-Azar espionage affair. He disclosed certain basic facts about his recruitment and training, yet would not elaborate; nor did he furnish much information concerning his change of identity in Buenos Aires or his contacts in Europe.

The people he incriminated were those he believed had already been arrested. He refrained from supplying particulars about his mission in Syria, as he had done during his interrogation, and offered the tribunal only what intelligence circles term "burned" data (data that are known or can be readily obtained by investigation).

The prosecution tried to portray Eli as having led a licentious life in Syria. Witnesses who testified in quick succession, as though reading from prepared statements, described him as operating in a demimonde of cabarets and seedy cafés. With infuriating calm, Eli refuted their testimony; his remarks were clear and direct. There was a brooding power in the simplicity of his speech. He leaned forward, made few gestures and spoke reflectively—almost as though thinking aloud—like a teacher instructing students. It was done dramatically and effectively. Sometimes he sat sphinxlike and became animated only when his turn came to speak in defense of the others on trial. When given documentary evidence to check, he read it as if the pages dealt with some banal problem which did not concern him. There was not the least trace of a squint or a raised eyebrow.

Whenever the opportunity arose, Colonel Dalli patronizingly lectured Eli and the other defendants. He made no attempt at reason or justice. Exhibiting a fanatic religiosity and rabid nationalism, he refused to conduct the inquiry in the usual method of a court of law. But while the president's handling of the trial appeared most arbitrary to non-Arabs, his behavior met with enthusiastic approval within Syria. And that, of course, was the audience of prime importance to him. Dalli used his oratorical gifts to full advantage as he intimidated the defendants. The richness of Arabic, a scholar of the culture once noted, has an almost bewitching effect on those for whom it is the native language; the colonel was successful in casting an eloquent spell. Baath circles were filled with praise for his handling of these "devilish spies and villainous traitors who had endangered our country's security."[5]

Overreaction was the president's most consistent response.

When Eli answered a question in low tones, the colonel would jump from his chair and roar, "Raise your voice, *ya* Cohen, so everyone can hear you." Then, sarcastically, he added, "Where do you think you are, in school?"

Eli passively complied. On one occasion, however, he rebelled when after three hours of uninterrupted questioning he snapped, "I want a glass of water and a chair," and would not continue until they granted his request. Only once, though, did a note of disdain enter his testimony. When asked if his superiors had been satisfied with his work, Eli casually replied, "Yes, Mr. President, they were pleased . . . because I did a very fine job."[6] His voice rang with irony. Some of the spectators chuckled. The president of the court lost his grim look for a moment and smiled faintly.

Colonel Dalli's approach at times seemed entirely irrelevant to the court's determination of guilt or innocence. Still, Eli responded as though each question deserved serious consideration. When describing the training he underwent in Tel Aviv, Eli revealed that he had received instruction in the Koran. The president's face reddened.

Dalli: Why did you study our religion?
Cohen: I was given an identity card which listed [me] as a Moslem.
Dalli: And all this so you could be a good Jew, so you could be a good spy?

There was laughter in court. Eli continued his explanation unruffled.

Cohen: I was told the Moslem religion was more adaptable to my personality than Christianity, which . . . is more complicated.
Dalli: So you have exploited Islam in order to become a spy. You have used our religion to pass as a Moslem and to enter Syria, our country, with greater ease. May your soul be cursed!

The president no longer attempted to maintain his composure.

Dalli: Your superiors in Israel have forgotten that when [the Jews] tried to exploit the Moslem religion, they were hanged. Are you forgetting history? ... [*Then, somewhat more softly*] Do you know the Talmud?

Cohen: No, I do not, Mr. President.

Dalli: Didn't they teach you the Talmud?

Cohen: No, *abadan* [not at all].

Dalli: And the Bible, at least you know the Bible?

Cohen: Yes, Mr. President.

Dalli: We all know the Bible ... but I don't understand why you ignore the Talmud. ... Are these the new instructions for Zionists?

Cohen: I don't know, Mr. President.

A note of resignation in Eli's voice invoked a bitter rebuke from the bench.

Dalli: *Yachre b'tkum!* [May your home be ruined]

There was no response. The president pursued other matters for a while but soon returned to religion.

Dalli: ... It is not enough to say *Allah akbar* to become a Moslem.

Cohen: I know, Mr. President.

Dalli: You Jews, you have the Talmud ... but you ignore faith. You are a lost [people]. You have strayed from the right path because you ignored the true religion. The day will come when we will get rid of you [unfaithful] once and for all, and in the great Arab fatherland there will not be left even one spy, not one foreign agent .... All those like you, who have accepted the Talmud and not the Koran, their fate will be the same. They will be exterminated. We will finish with you all in one blow. Not otherwise. *Insh'Allah* [with the aid of God].[7]

Colonel Dalli could not resist trying his hand where Suidani and his interrogators had failed. By not so subtle intimidation, he attempted to pressure Eli into revealing the name of an

Israeli agent Tel Aviv had asked him to locate when their radio communications had failed. As Eli had often done before, he pleaded total ignorance.[8] Dalli responded with more harassment but could not uncover in the courtroom what Colonel Suidani had been unable to pry from Eli in the dungeons of the Second Bureau.

At the beginning of March, shortly before adjourning for the anniversary of the revolution, the military tribunal produced an expert to identify the espionage devices found in Eli's apartment. The incriminating evidence was exhibited on a table placed in front of the president's chair. Dalli motioned to one of the guards who led the accused from the dock to acknowledge possession of the equipment. Eli took each item in his hand and admitted ownership by nodding affirmatively.

During this tedious process, Eli appeared drowsy and inattentive. The tribunal watched impassively. A sudden movement of the prisoner's hand brought Dalli up sharply. He leaned forward and grabbed Eli's wrist before his fingers could reach the mouth, twisting it until two cyanide capsules fell to the table. Dalli flushed and shouted, "That's enough, that's enough. Don't make us lose our time, ya Cohen. All this belonged to you, didn't it? "

"Yes, Mr. President."[9] Eli answered as if the incident had never occurred.

As the trial progressed, Colonel Dalli lapsed frequently into diatribes against the "agents and traitors who have sold their souls to the Devil, Zionism and imperialism." But his most scathing barbs were reserved for the accused Syrians.

Maazi ad-Din's claim that he never knew Kamal Amin Taabet was an agent set the stage for one of Dalli's most dramatic television performances. Since the court had already established that the lieutenant had seen a code sheet in Eli's apartment, Dalli poured on the sarcasm.

Dalli: You didn't suspect him at all? By Allah, this is incredible! You never even had the slightest suspicion? The fact that the accused lived in luxury and . . . spent money freely, gave receptions, arranged orgies for you and your friends, all this never intrigued you? Oh, Allah, preserve us! Didn't it ever astonish you that he spent a fortune on an apartment of which he only used one room? Tell me? By Allah . . . what stupidity!

Maazi: I didn't suspect anything, Mr. President.

Dalli: Not really?

Maazi: No. But, Mr. President [*hesitating*], I would like to make a confession.

Dalli: Yes, yes, Maazi. Tell us. You are here for that purpose. Speak up.

Maazi: I don't think I have any gift for observation, Mr. President.[10]

Colonel Dalli threw up his hands defeatedly and closed the session.

When the court turned to the complicity of Georges Seif and Majid al-Ard, the two men made every effort to minimize their dealings with Eli. Both contended they had been deceived by Kamal Amin Taabet, who had involved them in an Isareli plot. Dalli, oddly enough, accepted many of their explanations. In some cases, though, for no obvious reason, he insisted they were lying.

The sheik's friendship with Rademacher and Cohen particularly irritated the colonel. When asked how he had brought the two together, al-Ard attempted to belittle his role in the meeting. The president succumbed to his frustration by lashing out at him.

Dalli: Why did you always have contact with spies, Majid?

Al-Ard: But, Mr. President, how could I know they were spies?

Dalli: Be quiet, criminal! It is I who asks the questions.

Eli would not help al-Ard deny facts already confirmed by the police. But the sheik, in spite of the evidence against him, stubbornly held to his story. Al-Ard's claim that he was "the victim of unjust accusations" inflamed Dalli and brought the violent rejoinder "Remain quiet, *canaille!* You'll get your justice."

Whenever the president cross-examined Eli about al-Ard's involvement, the sheik would interject, accusing the Israeli of perjury and demanding a retraction. At one point, while the Rademacher episode was being aired, Eli recounted his meeting with the former Nazi official. Al-Ard suddenly exclaimed, "You are lying, Cohen! You are dreaming!"

Colonel Dalli came to his feet and, pointing a finger at the sheik, bellowed, "So he is imagining, ah, Majid?

Al-Ard: But, Mr. President . . . [*imploring*] no, no, no!
Dalli: You had better admit that you took Cohen to Rosello.
Al-Ard: No. Everything is a lie, Mr. President.
Dalli: Now listen, liar, you had better respect the tribunal you
            stand before.

The president's admonition made the sheik realize that his pleas of innocence were too absurd even for this court.

Al-Ard (meekly): I don't know anything, Mr. President, I
            think you are mistaken, I really don't know, Mr. Presi-
            dent.
Dalli (mimicking): So you really didn't know that Rosello was
            a spy?
Al-Ard: I didn't know it, Mr. President. I really didn't know it.
            I swear I didn't.[11]

These exchanges were not damaging to the sheik in any legal sense. Dalli made no attempt to demonstrate conclusively that al-Ard was a willing agent, nor did he try to show that his acts were as devastating as Eli's.

Most of the witnesses called before the court had been innocently acquainted with Eli and other defendants. Airline stewardesses, secretaries, matrons and prostitutes were interrogated along with storekeepers, café proprietors, minor government officials and low-ranking Army officers. The procession was climaxed by the appearance of Ahmad Suidani.

The president did not harangue the colonel but solicitously questioned him about the pretrial inquiry. Suidani dwelt at length on the achievements of his counterespionage apparatus in

reconstructing the activities of the accused. Yet even the intelligence chief was embarrassed when asked just how Cohen had
been able to operate in Syria as an Israeli agent for such a long
time. "The investigation of Kamal Amin Taabet's contacts,"
explained Suidani, "had been an extremely difficult one . . . he
was very careful . . . and had large amounts of money at his
disposal and quite a number of people to help him."

Angered by his evasiveness, Dalli insisted on specifics. Suidani
resorted to Arabic rhetoric, complete with raised hands and
florid language. "Israel, Mr. President, is Satan, and Eli Cohen
his emissary. And who am I, a simple person, to fight Satan?"[12]

The formal notice that the Cohen trial had ended was broadcast by Radio Damascus on March 19, at 7 P.M. The fact that
the court held additional sessions was kept hidden.[13] Forty-three
days later, the tribunal met to formulate a decision. It was not
until May 8, however, that the verdict was finally made public.

The Baath in Turmoil

As weeks passed after the trial with no word of a decision, speculation abounded in Syria about the reasons behind the delay. Within the Baath there was talk of conspiracy and treachery. Rumors spread that Eli had been exchanged. Some even whispered that he had been secretly shot to prevent further revelations. The tensions fostered by doubt and mistrust were heightened by the prospect of the upcoming Eighth International Congress of the party. The Syrian National Command clearly saw that to limit the damage resulting from criticism over the Cohen affair, the government's handling of the case would have to satisfy sister parties in the region.

A potentially devastating intraparty battle over the espionage episode, which was still raging in the Baath, had begun almost immediately after it was learned that Kamal Amin Taabet had been arrested as a spy—an Israeli agent was operating in the midst of the party's highest echelons. When the first repercussions were felt, the moderates in control had achieved a temporary reconciliation of almost all factions by arguing that the party's very survival depended on finding a way out of the crisis. By a rare unanimous vote, a policy decision was temporarily delayed while party members waited impatiently for an estimate of the political and military damage the Israeli operative had caused. Daily reports flowed from Suidani's desk to

Hafez, his ministers and the Baath hierarchy. As the results of the interrogation slowly came to light, it became apparent that the situation was more critical than anyone had anticipated. Each day prominent officers and politicians were being implicated; the affair was beginning to bring the government to its knees.

The momentary truce in the Baath ended when the civilians and the military split over what measures should be taken against Cohen. The civilians, who feared the effect of Arab public opinion, were divided into two camps. Secretary-General Michel Aflak and his supporters, who tended to be more cautious, proposed that a trial be avoided altogether. They argued that even if secret proceedings were held, classified material that would discredit the government might be disclosed. The most practical solution, they insisted, was to leave Cohen in prison until the matter was forgotten and then to determine his fate.

Bitar and his followers pressed for a staged trial in a civil court, with the prosecution asking only those questions necessary to prove that the defendant had violated Syrian security laws. The government would make certain that merely enough information was revealed to ensure a long prison term. Cohen's testimony would be classified "most secret" and restricted to members of the Regional Command loyal to the present administration. All details of the case were to be withheld not only from the public but from the rank and file. The National (inter-Arab) Command would also be excluded to prevent leakage to the enemies of the party.

The military strongly disagreed with the proposals to suppress the affair, yet were divided over a course of action. The moderates, headed by General Hafez, favored a perfunctory court-martial to be held *in camera,* with the charges reduced to military espionage. Cohen would be sentenced to death and summarily shot. The hard liners, led by General Salah Jadid, supported a public tribunal conducted according to military regulations, with the decree of January 7 as the basis for the proceedings. They proposed that Cohen be questioned closely. "He must be made to reveal everything he knows," said Jadid,

"and let the heads that would fall fall." Such a course, the chief
of staff hoped, would humiliate the Hafez administration and
become a pretext for a coup.[1] Jadid's hard liners, however,
were relatively few. Because Syrian law prescribed incarceration
as a preventive measure for mere suspicion of opposition, the
general's sympathizers were not overly forceful in presenting
their case.

Near the middle of February, Aflak's civilian faction eventually agreed to compromise with Hafez and his officers. To offset
any accusation that the government was soft on its enemies, the
public hanging of the two CIA agents was ordered on the
twenty-first. Several days later, the five judges loyal to Hafez,
including Dalli and Hatoum, were appointed to the special
military tribunal.

Although the president of the court-martial manipulated the
trial and controlled the television sessions, the disclosure of
some of Eli's activities and contacts could not be prevented. He
incriminated high party officials in the anti-Hafez camp, to the
embarrassment of their followers, but refrained from implica-
ting Hafez's confidants. The uncensored accounts of his mission
which were published by the Lebanese press gladdened the
hearts of Baath opponents and supplied them with ammunition
for a campaign against the party; the Syrians had handed them
unanticipated grist for their propaganda mills.

President Nasser, always alert for grounds to discredit his
revolutionary competitor, ordered an all-out political offensive
to exploit the affair. Ever since Syria's secession from the UAR,
Nasser had been anxious to show that his rivals in Damascus
were incapable of leading the Arab world. He had always called
the Baath quixotic in its approach to revolutionary Socialism,
but could now finally claim that the party was even unable to
deal with its own problems, much less serve as a model for other
Arab nations. Cairo hurled accusations of corruption and in-
efficiency at the Hafez administration, urging the Syrian masses
to revolt. Leading the barrage was Muhammad Hassanein Hei-

kal, editor of the daily *al Ahram*. His Friday columns, regarded as unofficial UAR policy statements, lashed out at the Baath hierarchy. When Damascus countered by alleging that the Cairo press had disclosed vital secrets of the Syrian Air Force, Egyptian propagandists used the Cohen affair as a natural rejoinder. "What secrets do they think we have made known? " asked the political commentator of the Voice of the Arabs. "What is there still to be revealed about Syria? After all, almost everything has been told by Cohen."[2]

Lebanon, Jordan, Kuwait and Saudi Arabia added to the humiliation. Their mass media described Eli as "the master Zionist agent" and "the wizard spy." Iraq, sometimes Syria's foe, sometimes its friend, was now siding with Nasser. Like Egypt, the Iraqis used Eli's accomplishments to belittle Syria's ability to cope with international security. Baath adversaries in Baghdad scored Damascus' claims that the apprehension of the Israeli agent was a victory for its espionage apparatus and described Suidani's Second Bureau as inept in protecting the country from Zionist intrusions. "If counterintelligence operations were as sound as the Baath regime boasts," asserted Radio Baghdad, "how did Cohen achieve such influence? . . . He was a close friend of most, if not all, Cabinet members. He had risen to the highest ranks in the Baath—proof of the corruption in the party—and its members had attended wild affairs at Cohen's apartment. These orgies were also frequented by top military and government officials. . . . Where were the counterespionage operatives for which Syria claims victory? Were they at the orgies, too? "[3]

The Baath used every medium available to counter the virulent attacks. Radio Damascus lashed out at the party's enemies whenever the opportunity arose, while *al-Baath* chided its critics. The major weapon, however, was the trial itself. Colonel Dalli had been ordered to elicit testimony from Eli that would directly contradict anti-Baath propaganda and imply that he had done little to undermine Syrian security. In one instance, during the second taped session, the defendant was questioned about his intimacy with the military leadership.

Dalli:	Radio Baghdad claims that Colonel Salim Hatoum was in your circle of friends. Is that true, Cohen?
Cohen:	This is the first time I have seen Colonel Hatoum, Mr. President.
Dalli:	Then they must be insane in Baghdad?
Cohen:	Without a doubt. [*hesitant*] They must be *provocateurs.*
Dalli:	*Al-Hayat* also pretends that all our officers are your friends. This is an outrage!
Cohen:	(*indignantly*) But, Mr. President, I knew only four officers. [4]

Colonel Dalli attempted to turn the court-martial into a platform to denigrate the reports of the Arab press by publicly ridiculing its editors. But whatever hopes the Baath may have had of silencing its enemies were short-lived. Syria's Arab brethren, led by Egypt, continued to blast the Hafez regime and intensified their attacks after the trial had ended by hinting or openly charging that the delayed verdict was a ruse to cover up a secret agreement with the Israelis for an exchange of spies. In this troubled climate, party members prepared for the International Congress which would become an unwilling jury to determine the fate of Eli Cohen.

Early in February the Baath had mailed notices calling for a formal session of the congress in April. The circular inviting representatives from Lebanon, Iraq, Jordan and Syria stated that the congress was being held to resolve doctrinal and organizational matters. But the inquiries received from sister party members since Eli's capture soon made it obvious to the planning committee that the congress would have to discuss the Cohen episode thoroughly and examine its effect on Baath rule in Syria. The outcome of other issues might very well hinge upon the way the affair was handled.

The congress met in a deeply uncertain atmosphere on the morning of April 7, at Baath headquarters in Damascus. But the infiltration of an Israeli agent into the party's highest ranks was not its only profound problem. The political direction of the Baath had collapsed into total confusion and its contest with Egypt for Arab leadership had so far proved a losing battle. At each turn, the force of Nasser's dynamic personality and innate political cunning had thwarted Syrian plans for hegemony. The scholarly theoretician Aflak, who had successfully dealt with the Nasserites in Syria, was unable or incapable of matching the effect of Nasser's pan-Arab overtures and securing the influence of the Baath in the region. The vacillation and ineptitude of the prudent, unemotional Aflak created an ideal climate for a younger and more ambitious party member to seize the reins of power. It was a development that would play a large role in the outcome of the Cohen affair.

The opening sessions were held secretly within the confines of security-checked rooms. After working units had been created, party leaders began shuttling from one faction to another, probing for possible alliances over the various issues, but no one doubted that the party's stand toward Israel remained the essential problem. Pointed questions were also being asked about the real significance of the Cohen case, forcing Syrian spokesmen to offer more than just official explanations. As the congress progressed, an almost unanimous demand was voiced that Eli and his collaborators be dealt with in a way that would silence Baath opponents once and for all.

The revolutionary aims of the Baath came under careful scrutiny in committees of the congress. Disgruntlement with the "old liners"—the legitimists of Aflak and the moderate officers of Hafez—was endemic among both civilian and military left-wing factions. Leftist officers showed their disenchantment and got ready to press for a sweeping reorganization. To counteract a growing threat from a group of rightists and Fascists conspiring to take control of the party and recast it in a more conservative mold, the leftists gathered around the influential militant Munif Razzaz, a man Eli knew only vaguely. A forty-six-year-old physician and native-born Syrian, Razzaz had spent much of his career in Jordan and had been arrested there for his Baath activities. He was amnestied by King Hussein and released from a Jordanian prison only six weeks before the congress opened. His imprisonment had earned him the badge of martyrdom.

384 The Shattered Silence

Discreetly but forcefully, Razzaz criticized the failures of the theoreticians and moderates whom he considered too short-sighted to grasp the extent of the party's chaotic condition. Razzaz argued that the major difficulties could be eliminated only by change of guard and presented the congress with elaborate measures to reform the party, the last of which did not bode well for Eli. The most emotional plank in his platform was to throw down the gauntlet to Nasser; he would force the Egyptian president to come from behind "the screen of contradictory statements" and take a definite position on Israel—either seek peace or join the Baath and its "progressive" allies in a "direct confrontation with the Jews."

Aflak ultimately recognized the critical position in which the party found itself and admitted his impotence to cope with the crisis. Considering the Baath above his self-interest, he voluntarily stepped down, urging his comrades to elect Munif Razzaz as his successor. By the end of April, as the congress prepared to adjourn, Razzaz established a concordat with Hafez. The agreement was not a compromise. In return for backing his renomination as president of the republic and commander in chief, Hafez agreed to support the installment of Razzaz as secretary-general, and to adopt a more radical orientation to the country's policies.[5]

The Socialist aims of Munif Razzaz were not inconsistent with revolutionary means; he favored a policy of cooperation with the Communists and planned to nationalize Syria's economy even further. His approach to the problems of the party and Syria was three-pronged: opposition to Egypt's "dictatorial Socialism"; the propagation of Baath ideology throughout the region; and an ultramilitant policy toward Israel. Razzaz was a pragmatic man, but not without passion. Like his Moslem brothers, he believed in paradise and the martyrdom that would ensure it. He understood the nuances of Arab sentiment and was willing to exploit the emotions of his people. These characteristics made him a dangerous political figure. With such a man in power, the fate of Eli Cohen was sealed. There could be no compromise with Israel.

On May 8 Colonel Dalli called a press conference to announce the verdict. Before pronouncing sentence, the president of the court read a tersely worded statement.

> My Arab brothers, Syrian citizens. This special tribunal has heard for a period of two months about the diabolical deeds of the Israeli spy, Eliahu Cohen, who has passed himself as a wealthy Moslem under the name of Kamal Amin Taabet. The facts unearthed during the trial spoke against him; the accused hardly tried to contradict them. Therefore, I will read the sentence issued by this special tribunal from the stenographic transcript of the court-martial.[6]

Dalli carefully arranged his papers, using the pause to dramatize the decision Arab reporters had gathered to hear.

> Having heard the facts and evidence presented to this tribunal, and
> Having had our convictions reinforced by these testimonies,
> The court finds that the accused Eliahu ben Shaul Cohen, who has been known under the alias Kamal Amin Taabet, has penetrated the security zone called "Elaal," a military area restricted to civilians, in order to collect information that could aid the enemy.
> Because penetration without authorization into a military zone is punishable by death, according to Paragraphs 158 and 159 of the Military Code, and
> Because obtaining military information which could aid the enemy and which must remain secret to ensure the security of the state is punishable by death, according to Paragraphs 271, 272 and 274 of the Military Code,
> In view of these aforementioned paragraphs of the Military Code,
> And in view of the Constitutional Ordinance Number 6 of January 7, 1965, amended by Constitutional Ordinance Number 33 of February 9, 1965,
> This tribunal declares the accused Eliahu ben Shaul Cohen, age forty, of Tel Aviv, Bat-Yam Street, in occupied Palestine, guilty of all these accusations.
> This tribunal sentences him to be executed by hanging.
> The judgment was given in his presence and must be con-

firmed by the President of the Council of the Presidency.

The verdict was issued today, the first of May, 1965, in Damascus, and read publicly.

Signed, Colonel Salah Dalli
President of the Special Military Tribunal[7]

Eli and his six collaborators were notified of their sentences in their cells. The confirmation of President Hafez was still needed, but there would be no appeal. Maazi-ad-Din and Sheik al-Ard received death penalties, which were later commuted to five and ten years at hard labor respectively. Georges Seif was sentenced to five years in prison, while the three other members of the spy ring were given terms of from three to six months. The remaining twenty-eight defendants, including the nine women, were found not guilty and freed.[8]

24
Last Efforts

Nadia heard the announcement of the death sentence on the Saturday evening six o'clock newscast from Damascus. Stricken by dread, she stared vacantly at the radio before suddenly collapsing to the floor. In the weeks since the trial had ended, Nadia had waited tensely for word of the outcome. She had retained a measure of optimism even after the Syrians in Paris refused to see her. There was a possibility, she felt, that Eli would be sentenced to a long prison term, but eventually exchanged. "In my heart," she later said, "I always hoped he would be freed and returned to us."[1]

But now even after the judgment she secretly feared had been handed down, some faith still remained and was encouraged by relatives and loyal friends: there were bound to be postponements; President Hafez might not approve the sentence. "What else could we do but believe?" Maurice would recall. "We lived with the hope that a miracle might occur."[2]

The bulletin disclosing the verdict in the Cohen case was monitored by the BBC and immediately rebroadcast. At 10:30 P.M. Greenwich Mean Time, a half hour after the Syrian commentator had aired the court's decision, the story was repeated on the Paris station Radio Europe No. 1. Walter Eytan heard the news while visiting friends in Montparnasse. He summoned his aides to the embassy by phone and left hurriedly for Avenue

Wagram, pondering what could still be done that late in the evening.

Eytan tried without success to contact Premier Pompidou and Foreign Minister Couve de Murville, who were spending the weekend in the country. Hadass, in turn, called Faure and Mendès-France, but neither could be reached. When several other statesmen did not answer the phone, it became apparent that any further efforts to forestall the execution would have to wait until morning. The following day, upon Eytan's request, the Quai d'Orsay approached the Lebanese ambassador and asked him to relay to the Syrians the Foreign Ministry's hopes that a civilized solution would be found to the problem. The envoy reluctantly complied.[3]

In Jerusalem, the Ministry of Foreign Affairs, like its representatives in Paris, still attempted to sway the Syrians through diplomatic channels and fired off cables to Washington, Buenos Aires, London and Bonn, stressing both the need for more intervention and the urgency of the matter. Ambassador Abraham Harman once more prodded Philips Talbot, but the reluctant Assistant Secretary had only good advice to offer: The French alone could bring sufficient influence to bear in such a delicate situation. The Bonn government was similarly unresponsive. A recent break in relations with many of the Arab states over Germany's recognition of Israel had made its intercession impossible.

In England, Israel's chargé d'affaires again sought out Labour Party leaders. Victor Feather, the general secretary of the Trades Union Congress, called the Syrian chargé d'affaires in London and appealed for clemency, arguing that "such an act would greatly increase the respect of progressive nations everywhere for the Syrian Republic." The envoy's angry reply indicated that his government could never grant clemency "to a man who had jeopardized the security of Syria and caused the death and suffering of many of its nationals."[4] Ambassador Gershon Avner personally solicited the intervention of Canadian Prime Minister John G. Diefenbaker, who wrote to Damascus, "because I was shocked by the verdict . . . I felt that this was a matter that deserved being looked into."[5] Ehud Avriel approached the Holy See for the second time, and Israeli diplomats in African and South American nations plied every friend for strongly worded messages of protest. A new wave of calls and telegrams was soon flooding the Muhajerin Palace.

When Mercier and Arrighi received word of the sentence, they concluded that the only course open was to appeal directly for commutation. Time was running out; Arrighi proposed that Mercier make another trip to Damascus. In April the *maître* had been in the Syrian capital twice. On the first of these visits he had informed Atassi and Taleb that the Israelis had granted him bargaining powers. He held a list of ten Syrians convicted of espionage whom they were ready to exchange for Eli. Jerusalem was also prepared to include money, medical supplies and agricultural equipment for a total value of a half million dollars. Taleb summarily rejected the offer. "We do not recognize the State of Israel," he said coldly, "and therefore no such transaction can be made."[6]

Unmoved by the minister's rebuff, Mercier arranged to see Colonel Ahmad Suidani. The chief of military intelligence received him at his office in the General Staff building.

There were no formal courtesies this time. Suidani, who had been dressed down like a private at the trial, was still bristling over the Cohen affair. "Who are you anyway?" he snapped at the *maître*. "Haven't you too been sent by Israeli intelligence to spy on us?" Mercier was taken aback. He replied evenly that he was not accustomed to spying when carrying out the duties of his profession and reminded Suidani that he had defended many a lonely man in even stranger circumstances. And some of his clients had been the colonel's own Arab brothers. Since the Syrians were making a travesty of their laws by not observing the most rudimentary principles of justice, the *maître* continued, he had no alternative but to offer an exchange of prisoners.

Suidani glanced at the list Mercier handed him and remarked cynically, "Why should we make this exchange? After all, Israel does not execute spies." Yet, at one point, the *maître* remembered, the colonel faltered. His voice softer, Suidani sounded him out on the extent to which Israel might go in applying pressure for Cohen's release. "If you act unjustly," the attorney warned, "the Israelis will pursue you without end. They will not forgive any of you. They never forget an act of injustice." Suidani merely laughed, but the *maître* was aware of a trace of concern.

When Atassi greeted Mercier on May 11, three days after sentence had been passed, the secretary-general said simply that he did not know what, if anything, might be done to save the prisoner's life. He could only promise to call the *maître* within a few days and tell him whether he would be permitted to make a formal plea. Mercier waited twelve hours near the phone. On the fourteenth at four, the *maître* was notified that he would be able to request commutation. An audience with President Hafez had been tentatively scheduled for May 22 or 23. There was no need, Atassi advised, for him to wait in Damascus until that time.[8]

Helpless to act further, Mercier returned to Paris via Beirut, where he learned that the Lebanese press had mounted a propaganda campaign accusing the Syrians of having already bartered Cohen. The same charges were being echoed by Cairo's Voice of the Arabs and Radio Baghdad—accusations which were undoubtedly helping unite the Baath membership behind Hafez and Razzaz. Gloom descended on Mercier. "My heart told me," he later recalled, "that the situation was growing worse."[9]

Although Mercier's proposal to Suidani and Taleb had been turned down, the Mosad continued to explore the possibility of obtaining Eli's release in exchange for prisoners and goods. In Tel Aviv, Knesset member Sneh tried desperately to arrange an exchange; the replies he received from the diplomatic representatives of two Socialist countries "were quite polite but negative" in essence. Meanwhile, Moshe Bentsur, Israel's envoy to Switzerland, requested the International Commission of Jurists—an organization well known for its investigations of legal injustices—to act as intermediary. Secretary-General Séan MacBride was at first reluctant because the commission never intervened in cases of espionage but finally agreed "on a humanitarian and confidential basis, to arrange for Cohen's exchange for some prisoners held by the Israeli authorities." The commission's reports about legal practices in Syria, however, had been critical, and Arab representatives in Geneva would not listen to MacBride's offer. One of the difficulties, the secretary-general later explained, was that no prisoner of Eli's stature was being held by the Israelis.[10]

Somewhat later, a staff member of the Israeli military attaché's office in Paris met with a liaison of the French Documentation and Counterespionage Service (SDECE) and asked that the intelligence agency act as intermediary with the Second Bureau. (The SDECE and the Second Bureau maintained a close relationship, which dated back to French rule in the Levant.) A reserve colonel, who had lived in Damascus for many years, was married to a Syrian and possessed the indispensable qualification of having once been an intimate of President Hafez, was given free rein to oversee the negotiations. The colonel was instructed to offer Damascus ten Arab spies, including three Syrians, a quarter of a million dollars, medical supplies, ambulances, tractors and bulldozers for Eli. As a token of goodwill, the Israelis anonymously deposited $250,000 in a Swiss bank account and issued a check, leaving the recipient's name blank.

With his bargaining power established, the colonel spent the first week of May in Damascus, using his influence to contact government officials. It was a frustrating task. Taleb and Suidani would not see him, nor would any one else in authority give serious consideration to his proposition. The office of the president flatly refused to grant him an audience. General Hafez apparently preferred to avoid a confrontation with a French emissary, rather than have a negative reply on record.[11] The colonel returned to Paris emptyhanded.

The Mosad, nevertheless, pressed in the same direction, this time using a more circuitous approach. With the aid of a second

French intelligence officer, who was well connected with Syrian military attachés in Europe, a concession was made: The spies, money and equipment would be turned over for the assurance that Eli's life would be spared. Syrian representatives in Switzerland studied the idea carefully. A tentative agreement was discussed through the French intermediary, and a check for $5,000 eventually changed hands during the secret talks. But predictably, Damascus declined to recognize the negotiations, and the matter was dropped. The Syrian officer who had accepted the advance payment later was to go into "voluntary exile" in Switzerland, using the funds to start a new life.[12]

As the Mosad was trying to arrange a settlement with the Syrians, high-ranking officials of the Ministry of Defense and officers of the General Staff were favoring stronger measures. A split, in fact, had occurred within the defense community over which steps should be taken to save Eli. The moderates backed the diplomatic approach employed by the Foreign Ministry, while the activists called for direct action. Past experience proved, they asserted, that it was futile to attempt any accommodation with the Syrians, particularly at a time of political insecurity. They proposed that the special forces unit of the paratrooper brigade be sent into Syria to capture hostages and bring them to Israel. Combined with the offer of convicted spies and the psychological shock of the kidnapping itself, they contended, the captives would give Israel the leverage needed to force the Syrians to negotiate in earnest.[13]

Those who argued in favor of such tactics had a number of precedents to add weight to their view. An elite unit, Yechida 101, the General Staff's arm for special commando and intelligence missions which was later absorbed into the paratroopers, had performed similar infiltration operations in the past. Meir Har-Zion, its slight, self-effacing leader, was thoroughly familiar with the terrain on both sides of the border. He had led forays on many occasions into Egypt, Jordan and Syria to take hostages which were exchanged for Israeli soldiers or intelligence agents. Israel, the activists pointed out, had never been successful in retrieving men held by the Arabs until such punitive measures were undertaken.

A decade before, a young paratroop sergeant, Yitzhak Gibli, was found to be missing after his unit returned from a foray inside Jordan. When Modiin determined he was in enemy hands, legionnaires captured by counterespionage agents of the Shin Beth were offered in exchange. The Jordanians refused, and Har-Zion's commandos penetrated as far as Hebron in search of hostages. Village chiefs and minor functionaries were taken to Israel and later exchanged for Gibli.

During the same year, Sergeant Uri Ilan and four comrades were apprehended in Syria while on an intelligence mission. Damascus categorically denied their existence. A team recruited from the ranks of Yechida 101 moved deep into Syrian territory, captured a jeep with four privates, a sergeant and their Circassian officer. The moment Damascus learned of the operation, preparations were made through the MAC for the return of the four soldiers and the body of Ilan, who had committed suicide to avoid breaking under torture.

Despite these successes, opponents of such a plan claimed that attempts to kidnap Arabs had never been made over an espionage case. If force were used, a dangerous precedent might well be set. And the Eli Cohen affair was not just another espionage episode. Given the instability of the Syrian government and the critically watchful eye of the Arab world, it was not likely that military action would be accepted passively. Eshkol decided there was no alternative but to rely on diplomatic probes.

The aggressive policy of the Baath toward Israel, coupled with the disclosure of the death sentence, had heightened tensions along the border. Fearing reprisals, Lieutenant General Salah Jadid ordered the commander of the southern front, General Fahd al-Shaer, to keep his troops on a blue alert until the Cohen affair was settled. Reinforcements, tanks and heavy artillery were sent to the lines, and al-Shaer braced for the worst.

Ever since the beginning of the year, the situation along the northern frontier had deteriorated swiftly as the armistice line became the scene of numerous clashes. UNTSO observers registered hundreds of complaints: Israel police boats were fired upon, *kibbutzim* were intermittently shelled, units of the green-bereted Mishmar Hagvul were ambushed, and patrol tracks constantly mined. When Syrian positions in the heights employed recoilless antitank guns and mortars against the Israelis, Zahal used tanks and heavy machine guns to silence the artillery. By mid-March the first clash over the Arab water diversion project had occurred; as the Syrians started preliminary work to divert the Baniyas and Hasbani rivers, Zahal retaliated, attacking the emplacements above Dan and the village of Daka; bulldozers were destroyed and drivers killed on both sides. Shortly afterward, work was halted until Syria could demand protection from Arab premiers scheduled to confer in Cairo later in the spring.

Apart from frequent clashes between the two armies, there was a sudden outbreak of guerrilla warfare along the border. Al-Assifa sabotage teams, which had been systematically infiltrating the area since the beginning of the year, stepped up operations, bombing installations of Israel's National Water Carrier, derailing trains, mining roads, ambushing vehicles, dynamiting houses and burning crops in Jewish settlements. Although they crossed into Israel mainly from Jordan and Lebanon, the intelligence Eli had supplied indicated that Syria was the source, mobilizer, training ground, principal supplier and main political patron of the organization. The Second Bureau manipulated these terrorist activities to justify "the people's war of liberation" to which the new Syrian leadership was committed. "The traditional war, based on superiority in the equality of arms, will lead us nowhere," Colonel Suidani later explained. "Therefore, we have no choice but to launch a war of liberation. Algeria will serve as our model—as will Vietnam."

The Hafez administration openly identified with the Palestine Liberation Organization, the General Command of al-Fatah and its military arm, al-Assifa. The Baath regime claimed credit for their activities, published their "war communiqués" in the government-controlled press and broadcast their feats. Syria defiantly rejected the criticism of other Arab states for its support of the movement and chided its neighbors for their lack of courage. "Every drop of blood that is spilled on the soil of Palestine," boasted Radio Damascus, "brings us more honor than all the utterances outside those borders."[14]

The influence these explosive conditions on the frontier line might have on the Cohen case greatly concerned the Eshkol government. Golda Meir discussed the skirmishes with the ambassadors of the United States, Britain, France and the USSR. She then summoned General Odd Bull, informed him of "the serious situation created by the shooting" and warned that if the attacks continued, Damascus would have to accept the consequences.[15]

The senior delegates of Israel and Syria filed their routine complaints with the Mixed Armistice Commission, and UNTSO's apparatus went into action. The investigations that followed were little more than a farce. In every case, UN observers first brought about a cease-fire; then each observation post along the border filed its findings with the control centers in Tiberias and Kuneitra. Teams of Blue Berets visited the sites in conflict, questioned the combatants and cross-examined civilian eyewitnesses. The information was referred to the MAC chairman, who prepared his own report and relayed it to UNTSO's chief of staff, General Odd Bull. The unperturbed Norwegian added his recommendations and forwarded the dossier to Secretary-General U Thant.

The reports were received at United Nations Headquarters in New York with weary resignation. Department heads carefully read and discussed them, and experts included their own interpretations. The documents were then translated into the three official languages, circulated among the delegations and filed in the massive archives. Syrian Ambassador George Thome requested an urgent meeting of the Security Council to consider "the latest aggression committed by Israel," while Michael Comay lodged his own similarly worded complaint.[16] When the incident finally came before the council, they each denied responsibility for the skirmishes, and the case was closed.

Whether coincidental or not, the bellicose statements of Syrian officials intensified in the weeks following the announcement of Eli's sentence. The campaign of threats by members of the Cabinet against the territorial integrity at the political independence of Israel continued uninterruptedly. At a parade in Aleppo marking the twentieth anniversary of the French evacuation, President Hafez harangued the crowds on the need to wipe Israel off the face of the earth. "The liberation of Palestine," he shouted in his usual blood-and-thunder oratory, "requires that we mobilize all Arab energies on the largest scale." His verbose deputy premier, Nur ad-Din al-Atassi, enraged by President Bourguiba's recommendation of negotiations with Israel and Tunisia's establishment of diplomatic relations with West Germany, urged his Arab brothers to apply economic sanctions against Bonn, recognize East Germany and expel Bourguiba from the Arab League.

Minister of Defense Mamduh Jaber, infuriated by Israel's bombardment of the Arab water project, asked the United Arab Military Command to attack Zahal's artillery. Lieutenant General Ali Ali Amer refused to consider the Syrian request. Other Baath demands also met with a cool reception from Arab heads of state, who warned Hafez to refrain from provoking the Jews. Nasser urged momentary moderation, "until we can carry out our ultimate goal and liberate Palestine," but Baath leaders persisted in calling for joint action against Israel. At a Damascus rally, Hafez mocked his Egyptian counterpart, "the self-proclaimed pioneer of Arab nationalism," and gibed: "What is he waiting for? I went to the first Arab summit eighteen months ago under the impression that the conference would lay down plans for the liberation of Palestine. Instead, we were faced with a plan to divert the Jordan waters. Now we are told that even this is impossible. Is this the mark of a successful leader? "

Tel Aviv was left impassive by Syria's call to war. During the last session of the Knesset before the forthcoming elections, Prime Minister Eshkol presented his blueprint for a settlement in the Middle East. Proposing direct negotiations with the Arabs, he explained that peace must be made "with Israel as it is. . . . Any Arab who proclaims his fear of aggression on our part," Eshkol concluded, "is only the victim of propaganda—if he is not one of those who, in the Talmudic phrase, know the truth and seek to rebel against it."

The warfare along the border and the Baath plea for united Arab action against Israel worried the French attorneys. The militant climate, they feared, did not bode well for a compromise over Eli. Maître Mercier, back in Paris from a week of futile interventions, cabled Atassı on the morning of May 17, reminding him of his pledge to arrange a meeting with Hafez. As a further precaution, the attorney sent a telegram to the president asking to be received on a "mission of mercy." Both wires urged an immediate reply.[17] The maîtres were still waiting for an answer in the evening when the phone rang at Arrighi's home. The batonnier was surprised to hear Hadass' voice. "The Syrians have cheated you," the first secretary blurted. An announcement that the execution would be carried out at dawn had been read on the last news program from Damascus and rebroadcast by Radio Paris. Hadass suggested that the attorney call the Vatican. Despite the late hour, Arrighi was able to contact Cardinal Cicognani's office and request that the Vatican make a last appeal.[18] At the same time, Mercier was trying to reach the Presidential Palace in Damascus. When he finally did get through, at 8 A.M., it was too late.

25
Spectacle on Marjeh Square

Monday had dawned over Damascus in an atmosphere of danger. The Hafez administration, which was well aware of the furor Eli's death sentence had caused in Israel and knew that pressure was being exerted on Eshkol and his Cabinet to respond forcefully, feared that Zahal might institute a border action on the day of the execution or retaliate afterward. Against this contingency, the General Staff had placed all units attached to the Southern Command on a red alert. To forestall a possible rescue operation, part of the Damascus Garrison had been ordered deployed. Infantry, artillery and armor moved into strategic positions throughout the capital. Yet despite the reassuring precautions, Damascus had been swept by wild rumors: Israeli saboteurs had mined the site chosen for the event; intelligence teams aided by paratroopers had infiltrated the city and would assault the prison; an airborne commando unit would land in the city, free the prisoner and fly him out of Syria in a helicopter. Government officials, Baath leaders and Army officers, while not panicky, were alarmed enough to remain in their offices waiting anxiously for the end.

It was already Tuesday, May 18, when a black police limousine halted before the iron gate of the al-Mazza Prison. A warm breeze had slowly spent itself, leaving a stillness and a coolness in the air. The morning mists were beginning to drift in, weighing down the feathery grass that surrounded the compound. Two military policemen, hunched in their capes, cautiously approached the car from both sides. Their routine check was brief. They were about to return the identification papers, when a plainclothesman, sitting in the front, said in a low voice: "We have brought the rabbi." The two guards peered inside the car, trying to catch a glimpse of the Jewish *hacham,* then motioned the driver to proceed into the prison courtyard.

One of the detectives helped the old man from the limousine and led him up the steps through long corridors to the second floor. A glass door opened, and Rabbi Nissim Andbo was unceremoniously escorted into the warden's office. The scene was later described by a Syrian newsman: "Lieutenant Naim [the warden] nodded cooly and informed the rabbi that 'the sentence of death against the spy Cohen will be carried out within the hour.' Though the old Jew knew, he paled at the words and started praying."[1]

Rabbi Andbo had been notified of the execution earlier in the evening. Shortly before 10 P.M., the director general of the Interior Ministry had called the sergeant in charge of the police detachment in the *haret* and ordered him to bring the "unofficial representative" of the Damascus Jewish community, a merchant living in the ghetto, to the ministry at once. The sergeant summoned the liaison to his office at the police station and personally drove him to the ministry.

The acting interior minister, Abd al-Krim Jundi, received the "unofficial representative" in his study. The Jewish leader, who later fled to Beirut, recalled that, without preliminaries, Jundi informed him in the greatest secrecy that Eli Cohen would be hanged at four o'clock the next morning. The minister warned him to say nothing of the impending execution to anyone, "not even your wife." He was to tell Rabbi Andbo only that he would be called upon to accompany a condemned man to the gallows and give him religious consolation in his last hour. He would also have to arrange for the ghetto undertaker to collect the body. "And remember," Jundi added, "any demonstration of sympathy for Cohen among your people will be dealt with severely."[2]

The minister's curt reminder was unnecessary. The liaison knew perfectly well that no Jew living in Damascus would dare protest or show his true feelings, much less voice support for an Israeli agent. Only once, a year earlier, did the community react with anger against the government, following an incident which had capped a period of severe repression. The 300 families left in the Jewish Quarter were suffering from police harassment and serious economic hardships when, on February 17, 1964, two young brothers, Joseph and Isaac Hasbani, were attacked by a Moslem thug as they returned from school. Joseph was stabbed through the heart and fell dead in the street; Isaac, who came to his aid, was badly wounded. The murder threw the community into deep mourning. But the news that the assailant had been released without charges touched off a storm of indignation. The atmosphere of furious despair that enveloped the community prompted the leadership to act swiftly. A peaceful protest was organized, turning the funeral of the victim into one of the largest Jewish gatherings Damascus had witnessed in years. Several hundred Jews marched in silent anger, accompanying the coffin to the local cemetery, despite a police ban on such demonstrations.[3] This act of defiance proved disastrous. Police pressure increased, and arbitrary arrests became commonplace. The Hafez administration staged a number of anti-Zionist trials, charging the accused with "attempted illegal exit," "Zionist leanings" and "espionage for Israel."

Since Eli Cohen had been apprehended, the conditions under which the Damascus Jewry lived had taken an even more dangerous turn for the worse. All Jews were now restricted to the closely guarded *haret*. A government decree limited travel to a radius of two and a half miles from home; no one was permitted to go from one section of the city to another without a special police "Circulation Permit." The economic situation thus gradually worsened until many families were living in near total poverty.[4] The community was terrified by the possible outcome of the Cohen case and feared that whatever the results, there would be an intensification of the persecution.

It was well past 11 P.M. when the "unofficial representative" was provided with a pass and sent back to the ghetto. As instructed, he first notified the undertaker and then went to see Rabbi Andbo, to whom he related everything, in spite of the minister's warning. The rabbi listened quietly and only expressed the hope that he would be adequate to this terrible moment.

While the two were still talking, a police car arrived for Rabbi Andbo. The exchange between the detectives and the *hacham* awakened the rabbi's wife. When she appeared alarmed, the plainclothesmen politely reassured her and promised to "return your husband safely within hours."

Rabbi Andbo had been in the warden's office less than a half hour before the prison doctor arrived, accompanied by Colonel Dalli. Within minutes, they were all on their way to Death Row, where Eli was waiting. Earlier in the afternoon, the warden had seen him in his cell, during what seemed to be a routine inspection. Lieutenant Naim issued an array of instructions, replete with curses, and bellowed orders to the guards. Before leaving, he told the prisoner to shower and shave, adding, "You will be moved later tonight." Eli was probably puzzled by the decision. Transfers from one prison to another were generally conducted in the early-morning hours. Moreover, it seemed unlikely that the Syrians would transport a dangerous political prisoner to the remote Tadmor penitentiary in order to execute him. Public hangings were usually held in Marjeh (Martyrs') Square, while death by firing squad was carried out at al-Mazza. Regulations also prohibited executions on Tuesdays (visitors' day) and Fridays (the Moslem day of rest). Yet Eli knew from experience that rules had little relevance for the unpredictable Syrians. His doubts were finally dispelled when the guard in charge of the lower cell block told him at dinner that he would be allowed to see a rabbi later in the evening. At eleven, the same guard brought him a gray suit (the one he had worn the day of his arrest) and ordered him to remove his red prison clothes.

When the officials arrived, Eli was calm. The heavy wooden door swung open, and Colonel Dalli entered the dismal cell, followed by Lieutenant Naim and *Rakib* Azzat. Rabbi Andbo remained behind in the corridor. "The prisoner was standing in the middle of the cell," a reporter of *Mujlat al-Jundi*, the Syrian Army weekly, wrote of the confrontation. "He had no doubt heard the shuffle of footsteps . . . . He was a dark, squarely built man with a strong face, brown, frightened eyes and a stubborn line to his mouth . . . . Colonel Dalli began reading the verdict from a paper in his hand. He spoke quietly but quickly. The prisoner listened, standing with legs spread a little apart, a slight smile on his face. He lowered his head and shifted his position now and then."

Dalli stepped aside as soon as he had finished, and Rabbi Andbo was permitted to spend a few minutes with the condemned man. No one left the cell; praying would have to be conducted in front of the curious onlookers. The rabbi attempted a few words but was overcome by his emotions. In a trembling voice the white-haired octogenation mumbled in Arabic, "It is a decree from heaven, *ya ibni* [my son]. You must accept it with love." Eli nodded silently. The rabbi then asked him to repeat the *Vidui*—confession recited by a person about to be executed. (According to the tenets of Judaism, he prayed with Eli, not for him.) *"El Shadai, mehal li al kol avonotai* . . . " Rabbi Andbo chanted softly in Hebrew. "Almighty God, forgive me for all my sins and transgressions," Eli repeated, "from the day of my birth until this hour. May my soul rest in paradise with the saints who sacrificed themselves to consecrate Thy name and for Thy people Israel. May my body rest in peace in the grave and rise up to its fate in the resurrection that comes at the end of all the days of the world."

The warden stepped forward. There would be no time for the *Shema,* the second prayer said by the dying. The Syrians were anxious to get Eli out of al-Mazza. "With a last glance at his cell," reported *Mujlat al-Jundi,* Eli "buttoned his coat and said, 'I am ready.' A sergeant, holding a pair of handcuffs, came forward. The prisoner put his hands behind his back resignedly . . . . The five armed soldiers who had waited in the corridor surrounded him. The rabbi walked with him, and the officers followed . . . . The detail, preceded by two blue uniformed guards, started down the corridor slowly."[5]

The procession made its way up the stairs and into a patio where a sentinel opened the iron gate. As the group entered the courtyard, an officer of the Second Bureau signed the release form. Outside, the night air had cleared; the mists had rolled away with dramatic speed. At the wheel of a military van, its motor idling, sat a corporal, a submachine gun resting between his legs. Two soldiers jumped onto the back of the truck and sat on a wooden bench, their weapons pointed at the prisoner. Eli climbed in, followed by the other two guards. The sergeant in charge took his seat in the cab next to the driver.

Four red-capped soldiers had meanwhile slid into a glistening black Moskwich, their Samoval submachine guns ready. A military police escort had joined the limousine as it sped away, sirens wailing and warning lights flashing, along the eight-mile road to Damascus. The special unit alerted Army and police checkpoints and inspected the soldiers strategically located along the route. Regular infantry patrolled the highway in pairs, each within sight of the other; sentries were posted on and under every bridge; additional guards reinforced vulnerable points. Its mission completed, the detachment roared back to al-Mazza.

A squad of military police on motorcycles encircled the truck carrying Eli. A flotilla of vehicles, including Land Rovers and Soviet-built armored cars, moved into position in front of and behind the van. As the commanding officer gave the signal to pull out, the task force left the prison yard and headed south along the narrow al-Mazza dirt road and onto the Kuneitra-Damascus highway.

Although the Syrian military had anticipated trouble, no unforeseen incidents delayed the convoy. Tight security extended into the center of the capital, which was deserted and silent at 3 A.M. The motorcade entered Sael Aliah al-Jabri Street and halted at the corner of Jamhuriya in front of the three-story L-shaped Central Police Station. The van transporting Eli stopped at a side entrance in the back alley. One of the soldiers pushed the prisoner onto the pavement. Guards seized him as soon as he got to his feet. Walking in front of the headlights, he looked pale but, outwardly at least, composed.

The police had taken the building virtually *modus militari*. Every available man was on duty in the area; detectives, as well as uniformed patrolmen, were posted at every exit, in the lobbies and corridors. Eli was hurried up the stairs to the second floor and ushered into an office. The room was of adequate size, but filled to capacity with police and Army officers, it seemed much smaller. A captain pointed to a chair before a wooden desk. Someone forced Eli to sit and placed paper and pencil in front of him. Another officer said that he could write a last letter and promised it would be delivered.

The sea of faces staring at Eli added to his confusion. As he prepared to write, he was startled by eyes he had come to know well. Directly in front of him, leaning against the wall, was Colonel Ahmad Suidani. Suidani was far from pleased with the assignment to supervise the execution proceedings. For the last several weeks he had been in the Soviet Union at the invitation of the GRU, enjoying the finest Moscow could offer. But on Sunday a telephone call from President Hafez had cut short his trip. The president had decided the hanging should take place without delay, before additional pressures could be brought to bear by the hard liners in the Baath. Some factions were plotting to use the Cohen affair as a pretext for a coup, and Hafez told Suidani that he must return at once to prevent a take-over.

Eli tried to concentrate on writing the letter to his wife. He appealed to Nadia to look after their children and keep in close contact with his family. "You ought to remarry," he added, "so that the children will not remain fatherless . . . . I can only ask you not to waste your time in weeping and mourning for bygones and always look forward to the future." Closing with kisses to all and a final shalom, he set down the date and signed his full name.[6] He then transcribed the Arabic letter into French, hoping that Nadia would receive at least one copy in his own hand.

After the captain had read the letter, Rabbi Andbo was escorted in; Eli was now permitted the second prayer. The rabbi's eyes filled with tears as he began to recite the *Shema.* "Hear, O Israel . . . . " The rabbi hesitated. Reporters in the room thought that he had forgotten the words. Eli took the old man's hands in his and continued, *"Beyadha efkod ruhi . . . . "* They then recited together: "Into Thy hand I will entrust my soul. Thou hast redeemed me, O God of Truth."

Eli was motioned to rise. An armed detail led him down the steps and into the street. There the six members of the military court fell into line behind him. Eli walked the last few hundred feet to the gallows with a firm step and head high.

The Chuhada, or Marjeh Square, which connects the legendary Saruja Suq, its minarets and Arab domes of vanished grandeur, with the modern, bustling center of town, looked like an occupied city. The Army had frozen an area for two miles around, and the plaza teemed with heavily armed soldiers whom Colonel Suidani directed from an open Land Rover on nearby Victory Avenue. No potential trouble spot lacked its contingent. Secret servicemen, in Arab and European attire, milled with the crowds in front of the New Ommayad Hotel, while uniformed police were stationed on rooftops and balconies, in backyards, alleyways and city sewers. On the asphalt path cutting through the small square-shaped flower garden near the monument which commemorates the completion of the telegraph line to Mecca, the Army had erected a wooden scaffold and a human fence of steel-helmeted troops of the elite Commando Battalion formed a double cordon around it.

Damascus had risen early for the event. As a result of the midnight newscast which announced the time and site of the hanging, more than 10,000 Arabs crowded the square. A steady murmur of impatience, broken by shouted threats, emanated from the multitude that pushed and shoved to secure ringside locations. Just as soldiers bordering the packed throng attempted to establish some kind of control, a sudden hush came over the square. Caught in the glare of two powerful floodlights, the procession was sighted filing down Barada Street toward the gallows. Curses and cries of condemnation pierced the silence when the mob identified the figure of the Israeli agent.

Eli and the military detail reached the edge of the platform and were ordered to halt not far from a group of fifty local and foreign correspondents from Eastern Europe and neighboring Arab countries. (The press had been invited to attend by the minister of information, Mashur Zaytun, "so you can report to your readers that justice has been done.") Colonel Dalli approached the prisoner and haughtily demanded the traditional "Do you have anything to say?" The question, in this case, was more than a formality. Damascus radio and television were recording every moment for the 9 A.M. news program. Eli began to speak, his voice surprisingly firm. "I am sorry for what I have done," he said, and added quickly, "I confirm all my previous confessions." There was a short pause before he continued more slowly: "During my work as an intelligence agent for Israel I had no other accomplices but the five Arabs who were tried and sentenced with me." Eli then looked questioningly at Colonel Dalli, as if to indicate that he was finished. The president of the court did have a last question. Were there any funds in or outside Syria which he would like transferred? "I have nothing!" Eli replied brusquely.[7]

The executioner took the prisoner by the arm and led him up the steps onto the wooden scaffold. Colonel Dalli appeared disheartened as he watched the two men approach the gallows. He had hoped that Eli would break in the final moments. The sight of the hated Israeli cowering before the hangman would have been a scene for the crowd and the television audience to remember and could have helped erase the grudging respect many felt for his extraordinary exploits. But the colonel's adversary was determined to die with dignity for the very same reason Dalli wished for the opposite. Eli had been sabotaging Syrian plans for almost four years and seemed resolved to carry out his mission to the end.

Khaled Abu Salim, the executioner, who held the noble title *mualem* (master artist), stood next to the condemned man in the center of the platform. Compared with the lean, erect Eli, the round-faced Abu Salim, noose in hand, an enormous mustache and ample belly swelling his gray business suit, did not improve the Syrian image. At a sign from Dalli, the *mualem* turned to the prisoner. Eli refused the black hood, and he proceeded to perform his duties swiftly and with expertise. From the time he tied the rope and until Eli was dead, the slow-moving clock registered only 90 seconds. At 3:55 A.M. the first Israeli citizen executed in Syria as an agent was officially pronounced dead.[8] Attached to the white sheet covering the body which swayed from the rope, a poster carried the entire verdict printed in letters large enough for all to read.

The night ended the way it began—gray red—its pale light matching the gloom of the occasion. As the chill of dawn settled into the day, new droves of onlookers moved past the gallows, while the soldiers paced back and forth keeping a watchful eye on their countrymen. A group of Druzes, who had arrived late for the hanging, performed a macabre sword dance. At 10 A.M., six hours after the execution, the corpse was cut down and taken to a pathological clinic. Still unsatiated, the crowds dispersed reluctantly with ugly muttering and scowling.

Throughout the morning, Radio Damascus continued to describe the hanging, and Syrian television showed films of the proceedings to the accompaniment of Sousa marches. Later in the day, officers of the Second Bureau and Internal Security Services agents oversaw the funeral service at the old Jewish cemetery, southeast of the *haret,* where only Rabbi Andbo and a minyan of Jews prayed in sorrow.

Book Five
Epilogue

Syria

After the execution, the Jews of Syria huddled even closer together in fear of reprisals. Oppressed and in dire need, the community had dwindled to less than 3,500 (about 2,000 in Damascus, 1,000 in Aleppo and the remainder in Kamishlieh). There was little, short of genocide, the Syrians could do to worsen their plight. Yet when a more militant left-wing faction of the Baath came to power, the new administration published a series of decrees that heightened the desperation of the Jews residing in the *haret*.

The Damascus Jewish community was now confronted with new restrictions resembling those imposed by the Third Reich. Identity cards were stamped in red with the word *Yahud* (Jew), reminiscent of the red *J* the Nazis had printed on all the documents issued to Jews. Travel curbs were tightened, and those caught venturing outside the quarter received sentences of ten days' imprisonment on charges of "illegal loitering." After the police detail in the ghetto was strengthened so that it could keep strict surveillance over the population, both the old and the young were required to report to the local station several times each month. Whenever border clashes with the Israelis intensified, political police and counterespionage agents swarmed into the ghetto, subjecting residents to repeated questioning. The Second Bureau even attempted to use the Jews as scapegoats in espionage trials in order to cover military blunders, but as it was widely known that all their movements were being closely watched, intelligence officers realized that such accusations would never stand in a court of law or even a military tribunal and gave up the idea. Periodically, however, arbitrary arrests were made in the *haret*. Those apprehended would later tell of beatings, ice water showers and electric shock treatments.

The community's Talmud Torah and the two secular schools for boys and girls were closed and the teachers fired. The little property some Jews had managed to retain was seized, and those who were still in the employ of Syrian firms were summarily dismissed. These families lived for a time on funds provided by the community, but this source of income was also cut off when the government expropriated the balance in the communal bank account. To remain alive, they sold what was left of their personal belongings.[1] Those with no means of support survived with the help of generous Christian Arabs. When identified, the benefactors were ousted from the Army and relieved of government positions. Those who dared complain to Bishop Hakim, the head of the Greek Orthodox Church headquartered in Beirut, were arrested and held without trial.[2]

The harassment in the *haret* reached its peak when houses left empty by fleeing Jews were turned over to Palestinian refugees. Burning with resentment which had built up over the years and incited by the harsh anti-Jewish stand of the Baath, the frustrated refugees tormented and humiliated their neighbors at every turn. A Jew walking in the street, day or night, risked being cursed, spat upon or beaten, often within sight of the authorities. A gang led by a thug named al-Zura extorted protection money from many but offered no security to those who paid. Young girls had to be kept indoors after several were kidnapped by Arab youths, raped and either forcefully converted to Islam or murdered. The police conveniently looked the other way whenever the Palestinians terrorized the ghetto; even demonstrators who occasionally stormed the quarter destroying property and killing Jews went unpunished.

Conditions in Aleppo resembled those in the capital, but the situation in Kamishlieh reached unprecedented dimensions after the Six-Day War, when a pogrom was unleashed and men, women and children were murdered in cold blood. The few hundred who survived the onslaught were deprived of all source of income and placed under perpetual house arrest. A decree allowing them outside once every month to purchase food caused many deaths from starvation. Only aid from merciful Christian neighbors saved the community from certain extinction. Religious services were also banned, and the synagogue was turned into a stable. The holy relics were then burned in the public square while the congregation, guarded by soldiers with bayonets, was compelled to watch.[3]

An investigation by the International Red Cross, brought about at the insistence of the World Jewish Congress, did not achieve any results. A committee from Geneva was guided through the Jewish Quarter by political police detectives, while the Palestinians, who had been warned of the visit, maintained an appearance of peace. The Jews understood that any complaint would bring swift reprisals. A number of them, nevertheless, did tell the Red Cross representatives of their difficulties and were promptly arrested and imprisoned without trial. [4]

During the next four years, conditions in the Syrian *harets* remained unchanged. The third wave of persecution continued in the lull after the last war between Israel and the Arabs. This time, however, there was no relief through expulsion. The doors of emigration had been permanently closed, and those left in the ancient communities were forced to live as aliens in their own land. Only a scattered few managed to escape with the aid of false papers and make their way to Israel via Europe. But the heavy reprisals against their families finally brought illegal immigration to a halt.

After the execution, the Second Bureau presented General Hafez with an estimate of the political and military damage Eli had caused. Since prominent officers and Baath leaders were implicated and the affair threatened to bring the government to its knees, a wave of transfers and demotions engulfed the administration and the armed forces. Another immediate consequence of the Cohen Affair was an intensification of the power struggle within the Baath. The conflict between the moderates and the extremists grew steadily. The leftist faction exploded the case to attack the rightists and increase their demands for further reform. Fearing a take-over, President Hafez ousted Premier Yussuf Zuayyen, spokesman for the civilian left-wingers, in September, 1965, and replaced him with the more moderate Salah al-Bitar. Two months later, the nominal head of the leftist militants in the armed forces, Chief of Staff Lieutenant General Salah Jadid, was forced to resign. His followers were transferred to less sensitive posts; Colonel Suidani was replaced at the head of the Second Bureau by Lieutenant Colonel Azziz Maaruf.

Backed by Hafez and the right wing of the party, Bitar attempted to assert civilian authority over the Army, but the rivalry among the top leadership, both civilian and military, eventually turned into an ideological struggle, with the radical left wing that supported Jadid outbidding all other groups in their zealous approach to Socialism. By mid-December the leftist hard liners had tried to stage a court rebellion; they were outvoted and ousted.

In the chilly dawn of February 23, 1966, infantry units loyal to Jadid and Suidani, backed by a tank column of the 70th Armored Brigade, laid siege to strategic buildings in the capital while the commandos of Colonel Salim Hatoum surrounded the presidential residence on Abu Rummaneh Boulevard and awaited the order to attack. As soon as the assault began, Hafez's mother, his wife and three children took refuge under a white flag in the home of a foreign diplomat living nearby. The general was slightly wounded during the commandos' assault on his home, but continued battling Hatoum's men for four hours. Only after most of the 100 red-turbaned Bedouins of his presidential guard had been killed by mortar and bazooka fire did Hafez abandon resistance. Using a passageway, he slipped into the Palace of Guests, changed into civilian clothes and fled from the quarter.[5]

After combing the country for the missing General Hafez, Maaruf found him still hiding in the capital. The ex-president was arrested, indicted for high treason and court-martialed on March 29. Hafez stood before the military tribunal along with a number of his collaborators in the same room and dock used for Eli's trial only a year earlier. To his right sat Colonel Salah Dalli, the judge who had sent Eli to the gallows, this time much less outspoken than he had been when presiding from the dais. The proceedings were brief. Hafez and Dalli were sentenced to life imprisonment and remanded to al-Mazza Prison.

In June, 1967, when the Army proved incapable of blocking the advance of Zahal, which had overrun the Golan Heights and was fighting within 50 kilometers of Damascus, the neo-Baathite administration granted amnesty to all but a handful of its political opponents and appealed to the exiles to return home and join the jihad. Hafez took advantage of the decree but, still mistrustful of the leftist Baathites, crossed into Lebanon within hours.[6] He was granted political asylum and settled in Beirut, yet in defiance of the code of sanctuary the general continued plotting. A year later, in July, 1968, nationalists and Socialists of the old National (inter-Arab) Command in exile set aside their differences and in true Middle Eastern tradition united with their former enemies to create a National Progressive Front against the radical faction entrenched at home. Hundreds of exiled officers in Europe and throughout the region joined the front which based its headquarters in Lebanon. While the future tactics of this coalition were being worked out, a coup in Iraq brought to power General Ahmad Hassan al-Bakr and the moderate faction of the Baath. Hafez and his supporters, whose political activities had incurred the wrath of Damascus officials and the uneasiness of the Lebanese authorities, moved to Baghdad, where they created a government in exile under the auspices of the new Iraqi regime.[7] Awaiting the proper political moment to declare an interparty war, the exiles organized and trained a cadre of guerrilla units for the invasion of Syria.

Major General Salah Jadid, whose extremist policies had been responsible for Eli's summary execution, had emerged as the strong man behind the plot. A fiery Marxist-Leninist with pro-Chinese leanings (he boasted of having memorized all the sayings of Chairman Mao Tse-tung), Jadid was supported by the left-wing hard liners who firmly believed that he was the only man to "purify the revolution of March, 1963" and rid the party of elements that had been deviating from the proper revolutionary path. In a swift move, the leftist majority in the National Revolutionary Council voted Jadid its president and elected him secretary-general of the Baath. His civilian allies included Nureddin Atassi, a husky physician, the son of a famed Suuni family, who was named to the honorary office of head of state; Yussuf Zuayyen, also a Suuni, who had practiced orthopedic surgery in Algiers before becoming Hafez's minister of agrarian reform, received the premiership. The Alawi foreign minister, Ibrahim Makhus, a former general practitioner, retained his post, and all the remaining Cabinet positions were filled by Jadid's supporters. The neo-Baathites at once initiated a radical program. They activated an antireactionary campaign, patterned economic and military planning after East European nations, implemented a drastic nationalization program and enforced hurriedly passed land reforms. They allowed Communist Party leader Khaled Bakdash to return from exile, organize the workers into a people's militia and proceed to help the Russians tighten their grip on the country.[8]

The new regime initiated a purge of right-wing elements, among them aging bourgeois statesmen who had been out of office since before 1958. Former conservative politicians, tribal chiefs, Moslem Brotherhood leaders, rightist Nasserites and even Socialists were tried and sentenced to long prison terms. The fate of moderate Baath leaders who had been arrested on the night of the coup was not much better. Aflak and Bitar faced the bitter irony of sharing the same cell with their rival Razzaz, who had deposed them only a few months earlier. The neo-Baathites accused them of moderation in economic, inter-Arab and international policies. They were forced to resign and after short terms in prison were driven to the Lebanese border and forcibly exiled.[9]

Changes effected in the armed forces were as far-reaching as the political shake-up. Continual purges deprived the Army of its few remaining competent officers, leaving it almost void of leadership. Hundreds of officers sought asylum in Iraq, Jordan, Lebanon and Egypt. But General Jadid's ally, Colonel Suidani was generously rewarded for his loyalty. Ahmad Suidani became chief of staff with the rank of brigadier and later major general. His ultimate fate, though, would be better than that of those he had forced out of power. After the collapse of the Syrian Army in the Six-Day War, the leadership found in him an easy scapegoat. He was sent on an extended visit to Communist China and while there was transferred to a lesser position and replaced by Major General Mustafa Tlas.[10]

Although a rightist Baathite, Salim Hatoum emerged from the power struggle unscathed. He was given command of the special forces and promoted to brigadier. With mounting trepidation, Hatoum watched the neo-Socialist civilian-military Baath taking over the party machinery and plunging Syria deeper into the sphere of the Soviet bloc. Being the only nonleftist among the high-ranking officers, he had no allies in the new military hierarchy. His closeness to President Hafez had made Jadid a prime antagonist and Suidani a major opponent. The new minister of defense, Lieutenant General Hafez Assad, had always been his personal friend, yet finally remained loyal to Jadid. Hatoum thus began plotting rebellion against the neo-Baathites with fellow officers in the Air Force, the armored "coup brigade" and counterespionage services. But the Second Bureau, which had the officialdom under surveillance, smashed the conspiracy before it could take final shape. Hatoum was arrested and sent to al-Mazza. Yet no sooner did security relax than a mass prison break took place, and the leaders of the plot were able to flee. Hatoum regained control of his commando units and launched the coup before dawn on September 8.

The regime's newly created militia, the Blue Guards, thwarted the insurrection. The rebels nevertheless managed to take Jadid and Atassi prisoners and exchange them for Hatoum's freedom and that of his officers. "We decided to withdraw— temporarily—to Jordan," Hatoum later explained. In Amman he and his staff were lodged in luxurious suites at the Philadelphia Hotel, where they proceeded to hurl charges at the neo-Baathites.[11] But ultimately a patriot, Hatoum took advantage of the wartime amnesty and returned to fight the Israelis. He was arrested upon arrival at the Damascus International Airport and whisked to al-Mazza. A court-martial held at the end of hostilities sentenced him to death; he was executed by firing squad in the prison courtyard on June 26, 1967.[13]

The political instability of the neo-Baathite regime affected another of the personalities who had marked Eli's mission in Syria. A year after the Six-Day War, on July 19, 1968, Syria's ambassador to Paris, Dr. Sami al-Jundi, was relieved of his duties and recalled to Damascus. Al-Jundi was reprimanded for having written a book on the Palestinian problem without approval of the Foreign Ministry; he was also accused of having made unauthorized contacts with Israeli Foreign Minister Abba Eban during the war. He was arrested, tried and imprisoned for three months and three weeks. Following his release on November 1, he left clandestinely for Beirut and later settled in Paris.

The terms of Eli's collaborators, Lieutenant Maazi ad-Din and Georges Seif, were administratively extended and they continued serving in the Tadmor penitentiary. Sheik Majid al-Ard, unable to withstand the harsh treatment at the desert prison, committed suicide in January, 1969.[14]

Israel

Nadia and Eli's brother Rafael had watched the execution on the first news program from Damascus. Throughout the proceedings, Nadia kept tight control over her emotions, displaying the same restraint that had awed all those who had seen her during the last two weeks. Only when the camera showed her husband's face did she break into quiet sobs. Her composure shattered as Abu Salim placed the noose around Eli's neck; she sprang screaming from the sofa, smashed the screen with her fists, and fainted.

Nadia's brother and sister-in-law had left the apartment at midnight, after Eli's mother, who had been caring for the children, collapsed when she heard the Radio Damascus broadcast announcing that the sentence would be carried out in the morning. Seized by an uncontrollable rage, she threw the radio to the floor and, before her sons could contain her, broke all the windows in the apartment. One of the daughters took her home to Ramat Yosef while Sofie, Iris and Shaul were sent to stay with relatives and neighbors.

Later in the day, after Kol Israel broke its five-month silence with the disclosure of the hanging, friends and neighbors, who had gathered outside the Cohen apartment, were kept away by security agents. At noon the officer who had been the Mosad's contact with the family arrived with the official notification of Eli's death. He found Nadia under a doctor's care after a suicide attempt.[1] (For the next three days, she would often lapse into a state of delirium, shrieking and crying out for her husband's return.) The liaison had to convey the condolences of the *memune* to Rafael.

That evening the head chaplain of Zahal, Brigadier Shlomo Goren, came to Bat Yam to lead the family in the ritual of tearing their clothes in mourning. The house was then opened to all those who wished to express sympathy. Rabbi Goren conducted the maariv (evening) services, and prayed quietly with the mourners. As he began reciting the kaddish in Aramaic, the mother, widow and two sisters suddenly collapsed in grief and had to be helped from the room. Rafael could barely repeat the sanctification prayer said for the dead by the male nearest of kin; he merely managed to utter in a choked voice: "The Lord hath given, the Lord hath taken away. Blessed be the name of the Lord." The ceremony ended with eulogies delivered by the leading rabbi of Bat Yam and the *rishon lezion,* Israel's chief rabbi, Ytzhak Nissim, who had ordered earlier in the day that special prayers for the repose of Eli's soul be said in every synagogue after the reading of the Torah.[2]

On Wednesday, following a continuous stream of dignitaries, a four-man delegation of the Foreign Affairs and Security Committee, headed by Chairman David Hacohen, visited Nadia on behalf of their fellow Knesset members. Senior government officials offered their respects in hundreds of letters and telegrams. Among the first to wire Nadia was President Zalman Shazar. "Eli's life and death will be an example of sacrifice and dedication to his country for generations to come," the president wrote. "Perhaps in this, you, his mother and his children will find a slight consolation and encouragement." Premier Eshkol, on his part, attempted to ease at least one of Nadia's burdens. "We will take upon ourselves the care of the family," he promised. "But there are many things for which there is no monetary conpensations."[3]

Even though Nadia's financial needs were provided for by a pension from the Ministry of Defense, the period following Eli's death would be one of great trial. She continued wearing black after the traditional year of mourning, rarely left the apartment—shopping and other errands were done by understanding neighbors—and only occasionally attended dedications and commemorative ceremonies.* She later decided to return to work and found employment as a waitress in a café Eli's brothers owned on the outskirts of Ramat Gan. Her free time was spent with the children, who had become her life. She raised them to venerate their father's heroism but seemed determined to prevent Shaul from following his father's example. "The important thing," she said about the boy, "is that he return to his wife every evening and never be an agent." Eli's final wish, though, would go unheeded. Remarriage was inconceivable. "How can I think of it? " Nadia remarked. "For me Eli is still here."

The children had not been stricken as sharply by the tragedy. Iris and Shaul were too young to understand, and Sofie continued to fantasize that Eli was still alive. As her fifth birthday approached, she rehearsed the songs she would sing at the party and told her friends, "My father promised to come home and bring me many presents." She eventually accepted the fact of Eli's death. When Nadia once told the two younger children that "the good Lord who sits in heaven" had taken their father away, Sofie spoke up angrily: "Mother, this is not true. They hanged him."[4]

The day after the execution, as Prime Minister Eshkol mounted the dais at Ramat Hasharon to address the crowds celebrating the village's fortieth anniversary, he seemed to be struggling vainly to suppress his anger. The press, which had been expecting the usual political speech, instead witnessed one of the premier's rare displays of passion. Putting aside the prepared text, he spoke of Eli instead. The trial, he began heatedly, had

*Haifa named a new park in Kirat Shprinzak-Ramat Shaul after Eli; Lydda gave his name to a main street in a new quarter, while Bat Yam also dedicated a thoroughfare in Ramat Hanassi to his memory, commissioned a statue to be placed in a nearby plaza and renamed a synagogue, in Ramat Yosef, Beit Eliahu. The government planted a forest in his honor. Zahal was urged to accord him the rank of *sgan aluf* (lieutenant colonel) posthumously, and the Mosad recommended that he be given the Hero of Israel commendation, the country's highest military medal.

been a flagrant miscarriage of justice. "Eli Cohen was deprived of the most elementary rights accorded by every civilized country to a man as a human being. He was executed on the basis of a political sentence which had nothing to do with justice." Eshkol was visibly moved as he continued: "Eli Cohen bore his fate nobly and serenely. He died a hero's death . . . the victim of internal intrigues and a struggle between Syria and other Arab states." A denunciation by the then-private citizen David Ben-Gurion was equally furious. "A most despicable act," he thundered in Ashdod. "It was done by the greatest enemy among our neighbors."[5]

Foreign Minister Golda Meir was shocked and outraged by the court proceedings. Eli had been sentenced "without an opportunity for legal defense, in defiance of the most elementary precepts of justice," a Foreign Ministry spokesman declared in her name. "In no enlightened country, has a foreigner been executed in peacetime on charges of espionage."[6] On the floor of the Knesset, Israel Galili, leader of the Ahdut Avodah Party, described the act as a "contemptible barbarity." His colleague, Baruch Arditti, from the opposition Herut-Liberalim bloc, demanded retribution and proposed legislation making the death sentence for espionage mandatory—not only in time of war. The bill was defeated.[7]

While anti-Syrian rallies were held in Lydda, Beersheba and a number of other cities, Ben-Gurion led a protest march of Egyptian Jews from Jaffa to Bat Yam. The Israeli press, for once united behind an issue, damned Damascus for its perversion of justice and mockery of mercy. Eli's death, the right-wing *Herut* editorialized, had been caused by "a fanatical hatred of Israel in which they [the Syrians] vie with their colleagues in the Arab league and try to exceed everyone else." The liberal *Haboker* charged that Syria had treated Eli "with the cruelty characteristic of that . . . country's regime." The Jerusalem *Post* described such conduct as barbarous, even by Syrian standards of justice, adding, "And these are not high." Echoing the government stand, the organ of the ruling Mapai Party, *Davar,* threatened Damascus that it would have to "pay the price for its shameful behavior."[8]

The Israeli Bar Association denounced the behavior of the Syrians to all juridical bodies in the world. In Paris, Mercier, Arrighi and Talandier, who had found the events of the last few months beyond their experience, spoke out of anger and frustration they felt at "the affront to justice and rights of man made by Damascus in preventing the defense of a man facing trial," in a full report to the president of the French Bar.[9] The *batonnier de l'ordre* publicly admonished the Syrians and granted the attorneys special permission to divulge the contents of their last letter of protest to Ambassador al-Jundi and President Hafez.

In further statements to the press, Mercier and Arrighi described the agony of Eli's last days: "No man . . . no matter what the crimes he was accused of might have been . . . has faced the supreme instant of his execution in such solitude . . . . Israel was ready to do everything in her power for Cohen. We have never known another nation . . . to make such efforts to save a human's life . . . . But Eli Cohen did not know that his family, his friends and his country did all they could to save him. He went to the gallows feeling he had been abandoned." It was an infamous deed, the attorneys concluded, "of which the Syrians will never exonerate themselves."[10] The office of President Hafez was deluged with letters and telegrams condemning the hanging.

The Baath was quick to lash back at its critics with a Radio Damascus editorial entitled *After Cohen.* The "routine" execution of a dangerous agent, went the Hafez administration retort, had been carried out to safeguard the national interest and to set an example for all agents planted in Arab lands. "Cohen is gone, but many others like him are scattered throughout the Arab world, hiding in their lairs and operating without fear, far from the hands of justice." The commentator raked the foreign powers and financial interests which had intervened to rescue the many like Cohen from well-deserved hanging. "Syria's actions are not to the liking of the United States and Zionism," the announcer added, "nor are they acceptable to Arab countries which use the affair to seed uncertainty about Syria's policies. Our regime . . . should not be the target of whispers . . . . Those who have spread rumors about Cohen being smuggled out of Damascus and exchanged for Syrian citizens imprisoned in Occupied Palestine are worthy of being the targets of such accusations."[11]

When anti-Baath attacks intensified, the Syrians—undisturbed by any inconsistency—attempted to minimize the consequences of Eli's actions, charging that the stories about his accomplishments had been fabricated by the United States Central Intelligence Agency in revenge for the exposure of the American espionage ring earlier that year. Foreign Minister Makhus was angry enough to lodge a complaint with the Lebanese authorities about "the campaign of lies" waged by its press and the disclosure of material damaging to the Syrian armed forces. Damascus even threatened to try *in absentia,* the editors of *al-Hayat, al-Muharrer* and *al-Shia* if Beirut failed to take action. To counteract the hostility of the Arab press, Hafez hastened to reassure his countrymen: "No lies or pressures will alter our policy toward spies. For Syria there will be one verdict for all Cohens."[12]

Israeli officials wasted no time in requesting MAC Chairman Eric Spaare to find out what had happened to Eli's corpse. Damascus evasively replied that Cohen had been attended by a rabbi and buried in the Jewish cemetery. A note with this information received by Israel's senior delegate, Major Zvi Shpan, mentioned nothing about a transfer of the body.

Despite the obvious rebuff, Israel continued to seek repatriation of the corpse. Golda Meir asked Lieutenant General Odd Bull to intervene, but even his prestige carried little weight with the Syrians. On May 20 Damascus notified Sparre that the government had decided against returning the corpse, as Syrian law prohibited the removal of bodies from the country after burial.

The intractableness of the Syrians did not discourage Israel Calev, director of the Department of Armistice Affairs. Damascus had usually acquiesced in such matters, though only after prolonged negotiations. The Syrians had reacted with similar intransigence before sending the remains of the CIA agent to his wife in the United States. Another cause for optimism was that two months earlier, Israel had released the bodies of two Syrian fedayeen killed in action. Calev felt certain that Damascus would ultimately compromise, but his superiors at the Foreign Affairs Ministry, who believed that pressure from international organizations and friendly governments might encourage the Syrians to change their minds more quickly, proceeded to solicit the aid of the Red Cross and Human Rights Commission in Geneva.[13]

Ambassador Eytan had meanwhile persuaded the Quai d'Orsay to negotiate with Damascus, but the efforts of Foreign Minister Couve de Murville proved futile. In desperation, Nadia had a cable sent from Paris to Rabbi Andbo.[14] She received no answer. The bluntness with which the Syrians had rejected these interventions only strengthened an already-widespread rumor that the Hafez administration was anxious to prevent an autopsy that would uncover evidence of torture.

As soon as it became apparent that diplomacy had failed, Israel was said to have attempted what some Mosad officials believed would be a more effective method of retrieving the body. On the night of June 21, four men carrying shovels slipped into the Jewish cemetery in Damascus and started opening a grave near the southwestern wall. After exhuming the casket, they carried it to the road and, with the aid of a fifth accomplice, placed the wooden box on a small truck and drove off in the direction of Beirut. A few miles from the Syrian-Lebanese frontier post, the four men removed the body from the coffin and set out toward the border on foot; they planned to rendezvous with the truck on the other side.

As the macabre procession skirted the village of Zabdanieh, a dog was attracted by the odor of the decomposing corpse. The barking roused its master, who was sleeping near his flock. The shepherd, expecting a reward for discovering what he thought was a band of smugglers, alerted a passing Syrian patrol. The moment the border guards were spotted the four men started to run. When the distance between them and their pursuers narrowed, they were forced to abandon the body and fled into Lebanon. The soldiers were astounded to find a month-old corpse and brought it to the Zabdanieh police station. Unable to solve the mystery, a village judge promply notified Damascus. An examination revealed the marks left by a noose. Counterespionage officials were told about the body and identified it as that of Eli Cohen. The Second Bureau arrested Rabbi Andbo and the cemetery keeper but had to release them for lack of evidence.[15] The Syrian government drew a veil of silence around the incident. The story was leaked to the Egyptian press, but the Syrians and the Israelis remained tight-lipped.

In the succeeding months, Major Zvi Shpan periodically pleaded for the return of Eli's body and the seven compatriots still held in Syrian prisons. His requests and those of the International Red Cross were ignored by the administrations which succeeded that of General Hafez. At the conclusion of the Six-Day War, in June, 1967, the Israelis held 591 Syrians; Damascus had only one injured flyer, the bodies of two others and that of a civilian who had died in prison. Jerusalem agreed to exchange the prisoners for the wounded and the dead but insisted on the return of Eli's corpse. Yet Syria still would not surrender the body. The Israelis stalled until Modiin received word that the pilot's life was in danger. Only then did they accept the terms laid down by Damascus.[16] A year later, after two Syrian pilots had mistakenly landed their jets in the Galilee, the Israelis again sought to retrieve Eli's remains by using them to bargain, but Damascus categorically refused.

Bibliography

SELECT BIBLIOGRAPHY

Only few biographical studies of Eliahu Ben Shaul Cohen have been published to date. With the exception of the work by Ben Dan (pseudonym of Yishayahu Ben Porat and Uri Dan), *The Spy from Israel*(London, Valentine, Mitchell, 1969; also Zurich, Ferenczy Verlag, 1967; Paris, Fayard, 1968, and Tel Aviv, Massada, 1968), which contains some original material, the rest are padded compilations of newspaper accounts. The work of Jacques Rabin and Jacques Ovadia, *Elie Cohen, l'Espion de Damas* (Paris, Flammarion, 1967), gives a romantic view of Cohen's life and deeds; yet for all its hero worship, the book contains some hard facts about the operative's early life in Alexandria. Eli Ben Hanan's *Eli Cohen, ha-Ish Shelanu be-Damesek* (Our Man in Damascus) (Tel Aviv, E.D.M., 1967; an edited English edition has been published by Tel Aviv, E.D.M., 1967; New York, Crown and Popular Library, 1971), is a highly fictionalized version of the story carried by the press shortly after Cohen's capture; the author himself acknowledges that "the dialogs and some of the names have been changed to complete the picture." Finally, A. Hagai's *Eli Cohen, ha-Gibor ha-Israeli be-Damesek* (The Israeli Hero in Damascus) (Tel Aviv, Gevura, n.d.), is a quasi-fictional account "to which much has been added from the imagination." A number of authors have included the Eli Cohen Affair in their general works on espionage. In *The Silent Warriors* (New York, Macmillan, 1969), Joshua Tadmor wrote a chapter entitled "Eli Cohen, Spy in Damascus," pp.155-76; Arieh Hashavia's *Rigul* (Espionage) (Tel Aviv, Ledori, n.d.) gives a short version of the case in "Eli Cohen ve-Eile she-Kadmu Lo"; *Maalot Lochamim* (Best Fighters) (Tel Aviv, Hadar, 1960), edited by Moshe Ben Shaul, contains a chapter by Gavriel Strassman: "Kamal Amin Taabet—Eli Cohen," pp. 276-84; and an article by Dan Willis, "The Jew Who Played Arab," originally published in *True* magazine (New York, June, 1968), is reprinted in *The Spies,* Robert G. Deindorfer, ed. (New York, 1970), pp. 60-74.

Articles on the subject published in the world's press have added little to the knowledge of the man, both with fact and, more important, a dispassionate appraisal of his exploits. By far the best, though, are "Damesek Koret le-Tel-Aviv" (Damascus Calling Tel-Aviv), by Dr. Michel Bar Zohar, *Haaret* (weekly supplement), Nos. 51, 52, and 53, September 8, 15 and 22, 1967 (reprinted in *Midstream*, Vol. 14, No. 9, November, 1968), and "La Vie Double d'Elie Cohen," by Eric Rouleau, *Le Monde*, May 23, 1965 (reprinted in *Atlas,* July-August, 1965, and the *Jewish Digest*, December, 1965). Among other articles which make interesting reading are "Kamel Tabet s'appelait Elie Cohen," by Edouard H. Saab, *Jeune Afrique*, No. 223, March 14, 1965, and "Eli Cohen Velcher Iz Geshtorben Oif der Tlieh in Damesek," by Shmuel Aizban, *Der Tog Morgen Jurnal*, June 14, 1970.

For the bare and unvarnished facts the authors have thus resorted to primary sources such as documents, radio and television tapes and transcripts, letters and interviews conducted both by them and their delegates or published in the Arab, Israeli and French press.

As a wide variety of subjects are covered in the book in only broad brushstrokes, the following list of works consulted and noted is by no means exhaustive in any section.

ESPIONAGE

Allison, Colonel Ind, *A History of Modern Espionage*. London, Hodder and Stoughton, 1965.

Alon, Ygal, "Maavak ha-Haapala" (The Immigration Struggle) in *Kovetz Tzava u-Milchama be-Israel u-ba-Amim,* pp. 822-30.

Atlas, Yehuda, *Ad Amud ha-Tliah* (To the Gallows: Exploits of the Underground in Iraq). Tel Aviv, Maarachot, 1969.

Avnery, Aryeh, *Lotz, ha-Meragel al ha-Sus* (The Spy on Horseback). Tel Aviv, I. Gutman, 1968.

Avneri, Uri, *Israel Without Zionists: A Plea for Peace in the Middle East.* New York, Macmillan, 1968.

Bar-Zohar, Michel, *The Hunt for German Scientists.* London, Hawthorn, 1967 (also New York, Avon, 1970. Originally published by Fayard, Paris, 1965).

———, *Iser Harel.* Tel Aviv, Yedioth Ahronoth Press, 1971. See also "Alilot Sherutei ha-Bitachou," also in *Yedioth Ahronoth-7 Yamim,* Tel Aviv.

Bayne, E. A., *Israel's Affair.* American Universities Field Staff, Southwest Asia Series, Vol. X, Nos. 3, 4, 5 and 6 (Israel), Hanover, New York, May, 1961.

Ben Dan (pseud: of Uri Dan and Yishayahu Ben Porat), *Poker d'espions a Tel-Aviv et au Caire.* Paris, Fayard, 1970.

The Cairo Trial, Committee for the Defense of the Accused in the Cairo Trial. Jerusalem, 1955.

Cohen-Sidon, Shlomo, *Drama be-Alexandria.* Tel Aviv, Sgial, 1965.

Daniel, G., *Sherut ha-Bitachon ve-Tzaid ha-Meraglim be-Israel* (The Security Service and the Spy Hunt in Israel). Tel Aviv, Yifat, 1968.

Dekel, Efraim, *Benetivei ha-Bricha* (In the Path of the Bricha). Tel Aviv, Maarachot, 1958.

———, *Shai: The Exploits of Hagana Intelligence.* New York, Yoseloff, 1959.

Derogy, Jacques, *La Loi du retour.* Paris, Fayard, 1958.

Dubkin, Eliahu, *Ha-Aliah ve-ha-Hatzala bi-Shnot ha-Shoa* (Immigration and Rescue in the Years of the Holocaust). Jerusalem, Reuven Mas, 1947.

Eytan, Steve (pseud.), *L'Oeil de Tel-Aviv.* Paris, Edition Speciale, 1970.

"Giborei ha-Esek ha-Bish" (The Heroes of the Affair). *Haolam Haze,* No. 1607, June 19, 1968, p. 19.

Gilead, Zerubavel, ed., *Magen ba-Seter* (Secret Defense: Operations of the Palestine Underground). Jerusalem, Jewish Agency, 1949.

Habas, Bracha, *Portzei ha-Shearim* (The Story of Aliah "B"). Tel Aviv, Maarachot, 1957.

Hasin, Eliyahu, and Horowitz, Dan, *Ha-Parasha* (The Affair). Tel Aviv, Am Hassefer, 1961.

Heiman, Leo, "Dr. Marzouk ve-Haveraiv," in *Maalot Lochamim,* edited by Moshe Ben Shaul. Tel Avai, Hadar, 1966, pp. 268-75.

"Hitpatrut ha-Memune." *Haolam Haze,* No. 1334, April 3, 1963.

Kimche, John and David, *The Secret Roads.* New York, Farrar, Straus and Cudahy, 1955.

Larteguy, Jean, "Israel's Intelligence Service," reprinted from *Les Murrailles d'Israel.* New York, Jewish Press, March 27, 1970.

"The Lavon Affair 1954-64. What Really Happened." *Jewish Observer and Middle East Review,* Vol. 13, No. 51, December 18, 1964.

Levit, Yishayahu, *Milchemet ha-Tzlalim. Rigul Aravi be-Israel* (War of Shadows: Arab Espionage in Israel). Tel Aviv, Moked, 1969.

Lotz, Wolfgang, *Shlichut be-Kahir* (Mission in Cairo). Tel Aviv, Shikmona, 1970.

Mader, Julius, *Who's Who in the CIA.* East Berlin, Mader, 1968.

Mardor, Meir, *Shlichut Aluma* (Secret Mission). Tel Aviv, Maarachot, 1957. Also published as *Haganah.* New York, American Library, 1964.

"Parshat Aleksis." *Haolam Haze,* Nos. 1385 and 1386, March 23 and April 1, 1964; a disguished but most accurate account of the Cairo espionage case. See also *Haolam Haze,* No.1608, June 26, 1968.

Penkovskiy, Oleg, *The Penkovskiy Papers*. New York, Doubleday, 1965.
Sager, Peter, *Kairo und Moskau in Arabien*. Paris, Soi, 1967.
Sansom, Major A. W., *I Spied Spies*. London, Harrap, 1965.
Shaker, F., *L'Agent du Caire*. Paris, Edition Speciale, 1970.
Shmulewitz, Mattityahu, *Beyamim Adumin* (Bloody Days). Tel Aviv, Elisha Printing Press, 1949.
Slotzki, Yehuda, *History of the Haganah*. Jerusalem, Sifria Zionit, 1954.
Story of Zionist Espionage in Egypt. Cairo, Ministry of Foreign Affairs, n.d.
Tadmor, Joshua, *The Silent Warriors*. New York, Macmillan, 1969.
Thayer, George, *The War Business*. New York, Simon and Schuster, 1969.
"Tlia Bimkom Pegisha," (A Hanging Instead of a Meeting). *Haolam Haze*, No. 1425, December 30, 1964.
Toldot ha-Haganah (History of the Haganah). Jerusalem, Sifria Zionit, 1969, 2 vols.
Tully, Andrew, *CIA: The Inside Story*. New York, Morrow, 1962.
Wise, David, and Ross, Thomas B., *The Espionage Establishment*. New York, Random House, 1967.
Yona, Amnon, *Le-Lo Ikvot* (Without Footprints). Tel Aviv, Maarachot, 1957.

MINORITIES

Egyptian Refugee Students in Israel. Jerusalem, World Union of Jewish Students, n.d.
Jews in Arab Countries During the Middle East Crisis (mimeo). London, Institute of Jewish Affairs, World Jewish Congress, June, 1967.
Jews in Arab Countries Since the End of the Six-Day War (mimeo). London, Institute of Jewish Affairs, World Jewish Congress, August, 1967.
Karlikow, Abraham S., "Jews in Arab Countries," in the *American Jewish Year Book, 1968*, Vol. 69. Reprint by American Jewish Committee, New York, 1969.
Landshut, Siegfried, *Jewish Communities in the Moslem Countries of the Middle East*. London, 1950.
Lestchinsky, Jacob, *Jews in Moslem Lands*. Jewish Affairs, Vol. 1, No. 6, April 15, 1946.
Rabinowitz, Rabbi L., *Soldiers from Judaea*. London, Victor Gollancz, 1944.
Robinson, Dr. Nehemiah, *The Arab Countries of the Near East and Their Jewish Communities*. New York, Institute of Jewish Affairs, World Jewish Congress, 1951.
———, *The Recent Anti-Jewish Persecution in Egypt*. New York, Institute of Jewish Affairs, World Jewish Congress, November, 1954.
———, *Egypt in September, 1957*. (mimeo). New York, Institute of Jewish Affairs, World Jewish Congress, September 30, 1957.
———, *Jews in Moslem Lands: A Quarter Century of Decline* (mimeo). New York, Institute of Jewish Affairs, World Jewish Congress, 1959.
The Treatment of Jews in Egypt and Iraq. New York, World Jewish Congress, December, 1948.

NAZIS

Bar-Zohar, Dr. Michel, *The Avengers*. New York, Hawthorn, 1970. Also Tel Aviv, Levin-Epstein, 1969.
Eisenberg, Dennis, *The Re-Emergence of Fascism*. New York, A. S. Barnes, 1967.
Engelman, Bernt, *The Weapons Merchants*. New York, Crown, 1968.
Hausner, Gideon, *Justice in Jerusalem*. New York, Harper & Row, 1966.

Hilberg, Paul, *The Destruction of the European Jews.* Chicago, Quadrangle Books, 1963.
Kempner, Robert M. W., *Eichmann und Komplizen.* Zurich, Europa Verlag, 1961.
Paneth, Philip, *Eichmann, Technician of Death.* New York, Robert Speller, 1960.
Pearlman, Moshe, *The Capture and Trial of Adolf Eichmann.* New York, Simon and Schuster, 1963.
Poliakov, Leon, *Harvest of Hate.* Syracuse, New York, Syracuse University Press, 1954.
Reitlinger, Gerald, *SS: Alibi of a Nation, 1922-45.* New York, Viking, 1957.
Schechtman, Joseph B., *The Mufti and the Führer.* New York, Yoseloff, 1965.
Sidap, Irving, and Grinberg, Harold I., *Behind the Egyptian Sphinx.* New York, 1960. Also Tel Aviv, Tamar, n.d.
Tetens, T. H., *The New Germany and the Old Nazis.* London, Secker and Warburg, 1962.
Wiesenthal, Simon, *Ich Jagte Eichmann.* Gütersloh, Sigbert Mohn Verlag, 1961.
——, *The Murderers Among Us.* New York, McGraw-Hill, 1967.

SOVIET AND CHINESE PENETRATION

Demchenko, P., *Siriskaia Republica na strazhe sroei Nezavisimosti.* Moscow, 1957.
Gataullin, M., *Siriia.* Moscow, 1956.
Hinton, Harold C., *Communist China in World Politics.* Boston, Houghton Mifflin, 1966.
Humbarach, Arslan, "Chou's Mediterranean Tour." *Far Eastern Economic Review,* January 23, 1964, 9. 154.
Laqueur, Walter, *The Soviet Union and the Middle East.* New York, Praeger, 1959.
Sikor, S. "V Solnechonoi Sirii" (In Sunny Syria). Moscow, 1957.
"Siriia," *Ezhegoduik Bolshoi; Sovietskoi Entziklopedii 1957,* p. 398.
Sultanov, F., *Sovremennaia Siriia.* Moscow, 1958.
Velie, Lester, *Countdown in the Holy Land.* New York, Funk and Wagnalls, 1969.

GENERAL

Abu Jaber, Kamel S., *The Arab Ba'th Socialist Party.* Syracuse, New York, Syracuse University Press, 1966.
Arab Socialist Baath Party, *Al-Nizam al-Dakhili* (The Internal Rules Manual). Damascus, 1963.
Beeri, Eliezer, *Army Officers in Arab Politics and Society.* Jerusalem, Israel University Press, 1969.
Bar-Yaacon, Missim, *The Israel-Syrian Armistice, 1949-66.* Jerusalem, Magnes Press, 1967.
Ben Dan (pseud. of Yishayahu Ben Porat and Uri Dan), *Embargo. Mirage neged Mig* (Mirage Against Mig). Ramat Gan, Massada, 1968. Also Paris, Laffont, 1967.
Ben-Gurion, David, *Devarim ke-Havayatam* (Things as They Are). Tel Aviv, Am Hassefer, 1965.
Benjamin, Leo, *Martyrs in Cairo: The Trial of the Assassins.* New York, 1953.
Borisov, J., *Palestine Underground.* New York, Judea, 1947.
Carlson, John Ray, *Cairo to Damascus.* New York, Knopf, 1951.
Frank, Gerold, *The Deed.* New York, Simon and Schuster, 1963.
Golan, Aviezer, *Ha-Mizrach ha-Tichon: Suria* (The Middle East: Syria). Pamphlet No. 5. Tel Aviv, Zahal General Staff Publications, Ministry of Defense, n.d. (1970).
Hameiri, Yehezkel, *Prisoners of Hate.* Jerusalem, Keter Books, 1969.
Harkabi, General (Res.) Yehoshafat, *Fatah ba-Estrategia ha-Aravit* (Fatah and Arab Strategy). Tel Aviv, Maarachot, 1969.

Hurewitz, J. C., *Middle East Politics: The Military Dimension.* New York, Praeger Council on Foreign Relations, 1969.

Husaini, Ishak Mussa, *Al-Ikhwan al-Muslimin* (The Moslem Brotherhood). Beirut, 1964.

Joundi, Sami, *Le drame Palestinien.* Paris, Fayard, 1969. Also Munich, Bechtle Verlag, 1968.

Kerr, Malcolm, *The Arab Cold War 1958-64.* London, Oxford University Press, 1965.

Kimche, David, and Bavly, Dan, *Sufat Ha-Esh* (The Fire Storm). Tel Aviv, Am Hassefer, 1969.

Mansdield, Peter, *Nasser's Egypt.* London, Penguin, 1965.

Margalit, Dan, *Tzanchanim ba-Kele ha-Suri* (Paratroopers in Syrian Prisons). Tel Aviv, Moked, 1968.

Nevada, J. B., *Olei Hagardom* (Those Who Mounted the Gallows). Tel Aviv, Shiloach, 1952.

Porat, Dr. Eliahu, *Know Your Neighbors: Syria.* Tel Aviv, Yavneh, 1962.

Saab, Edouard, *La Syrie ou la Revolution dans la Rancoeur.* Paris, Julliard, 1968.

Safdi, Mataa, *Al-Hizb al-Baath* (The Baath Party). Beirut, 1964.

Seale, Patrick, *The Struggle for Syria (1945-58).* New York, Oxford University Press, 1965. Epilogue by Itamar Rabinowitz on Syria 1961-63 in Hebrew edition. Tel Aviv, Maarachot, 1968.

Stern, Michael, *Farouk.* New York, Bantam Books, 1965.

Syria. U.S. Army Handbook. Washington, D.C., Government Printing Office, 1965.

Torrey, Gordon H., *Syrian Politics and the Military 1945-58.* Columbus, Ohio, Ohio State University Press, 1963.

Van Horn, Major General Carl, *Soldiering for Peace.* New York, David McKay, 1966.

Vernier, Bernard, *Armée et politique au moyen-orient.* Paris, Payot, 1966.

Yaari, Ehud, *Fatah.* Tel Aviv, Levin-Epstein, 1970.

Yitzhaky, Shimshon, *Be-Einei Ha-Aravim* (In Arab Eyes). Tel Aviv, Maarachot, 1969.

PERIODICALS

UNITED STATES: *New York Times; Newsweek; The Middle East Journal; Israel Horizons.*

ENGLAND: *The Times; Jewish Chronicle; Jewish Observer and Middle East Review; World Today.*

FRANCE: *Le Monde; La Terre Retrouvé; Orient.*

GERMANY: *Orient.*

SWITZERLAND: *Neue Züricher Zeitung.*

ISRAEL: *Haaretz; Maariv. Yamim Veleilot; Yedioth Ahronoth. 7 Yamim; Bamahane; Haolam Haze; New Outlook; Middle East Record.*

LEBANON: *Al-Hayat; Al-Nahar; Al-Ahrar; Al-Muharrer; Orient; Chronology of Arab Politics; Arab Political Documents, 1961 to 1965.*

EGYPT: *Al-Ahram; Egyptian Gazette; Al-Asbua al-Arabi.*

SYRIA: *Al-Baath; Mujlat al-Jundi.*

Reference Notes

CHAPTER 1

1. Interviews of Colonel Ahmad Suidani with Simat Maaruf in *Al-Asuba al-Arabi*, Beirut, May 19, 1965 (hereafter cited as Suidani Interview).

2. Interview of Jacques Lacoste (hereafter J.L.) with H.T.M., Damascus, May 12, 1966, and interview of Major Adam Tawara (hereafter cited as Tawara Interview) in *Al-Safaa*, Beirut, May 19, 1965.

3. Suidani Interview, *Al-Asbua al-Arabi*, May 19, 1965.

4. *Ibid.* Taabet had already transmitted a message concerning a Second Bureau plan to form a Palestine Commando Brigade under Syrian command. See Ben Dan, p. 182.

5. Accounts of the raid given by Suidani in *Al-Asbua al-Arabi*, May 19, 1965 and Tawara, *Al-Safaa*, May 19, 1965 are identical. Also Jacques Lacoste's Report No. 4, "Eli Cohen—Arrest and Interrogation" (hereafter cited as J.L., Report No. 3), pp. 1-4.

6. Interviews with Major General Amin al-Hafez (cited hereafter as Hafez Interview) in *Al-Asbua al-Arabi*, May 19, 1965; and *Al-Taliaa*, Damascus, January 17, 1966.

7. *Al-Asbua al-Arabi*, May 19, 1965.

8. Ammon Kapeliuk, "A Stunning Espionage Trial," in *Al-Hamishmar*, Tel Aviv, May 19, 1965. Also in interview of Zwy Aldouby (cited hereafter as Z.A.) with S.H.M., Tel Aviv, February 24, 1970. Details of Suidani's attempt to feed the Mosad misinformation are given in *Al-Safaa*, May 19, 1965.

9. *Al-Asbua al-Arabi*, May 19, 1965.

CHAPTER II

1. Rabin and Ovadia p. 232. Interview of Z.A. with Nadia Cohen, Tel Aviv.

2. *Laisha*, Tel Aviv, April 28, 1970.

3. Interview of Dan Margalit with Maurice Cohen, *Haaretz*, Tel Aviv, May 19, 1965.

4. Interview of Z.A. with Baruch Mizrachi, Paris, March 1, 1970.

5. Interview of Zvi Algat, with David Crudo in Maariv-Yamim Veleilot *(weekly supplement)*, Tel Aviv, May 28, 1965.

6. Letter of Alexander Cohen, London, August 3, 1967. On school years, letter of Moshe Sachs, Tel Aviv, June 1, 1970.

7. Interview of Bruria Avidan-Brir with Sofia Cohen, *Laisha*, April 28, 1970.

8. Interview of Yadin Dudai with Avraham Cohen, *Bamahane*, Tel Aviv, June 18, 1965.

9. Laisha, April 28, 1970. Also Maariv, May 28, 1965; letter of Rabbi Moshe Ventura, Tel Aviv, June 15, 1970.

10. Z.A. interview with Baruch Mizrachi, Paris, March 1, 1970.

11. *Ibid.* See also Sansom, pp. 185-88.

12. Frank, p. 186. See also London, *The Economist*, May 8, 1951; Robinson, *Arab Countries of the Near East*, p. 71, and Cohen-Sidon, p. 24-26. For the Jewish Community in Egypt during World War II, see Lestchinsky, pp. 14-26, and *Jewish Events*, No. 4-5, July-September, 1945, pp. 14-17.

13. Sansom, p. 177.

14. Borisov, pp. 40-53; Sansom, pp. 166-82. Also see Frank, *The Deed*, Benjamin, *Martyrs in Cairo*, Nedava, *Those Who Mounted the Gallows*, and *Freedom Fighters of Israel*.

15. Cohen-Sidon, p. 36. Also Z.A. interviews with Alex Siton, New York, April 16, 1966, and Y.N., Tel Aviv, February 14, 1970.

16. "Our activities in Maccabi and the Halutz," memorandum written at the author's request by Caesar Levi, Rome, October 7, 1968. Also *Lamerchav*, Tel Aviv, May 19, 1965. *Maariv*, May 28, 1965 and *Bamahane*, June 18, 1965.

17. Cohen-Sidon, pp. 51-56; *Haaretz*, May 19, 1965.

CHAPTER III

1. Letter of Murad Semach, Haifa, June 1, 1970.
2. Z.A. interview with Baruch Mizrachi, Paris, March 1, 1970. See also Sansom, p. 205.
3. Letter of Alexander Cohen, London, August 3, 1967.
4. *Ibid.* On Moslem Brotherhood see "The Muslim Brethren in Egypt," by Frank Rosenthal, *Muslim World*, Hartford, October, 1947; "The Muslim Brotherhood," MEA, New York, Vol. 5, No. 12, December, 1954, pp. 377-85; and Carlson, pp. 78-92. See also Ishak Mussa Husaini, *The Moslem Brotherhood.*
5. Letter of Murad Semach, Haifa, June 1, 1970.
6. *Ibid.*, and letter of Moshe Sachs, Tel Aviv, June 1, 1970. Also Cohen-Sidon, pp. 57-61, and *Egyptian Refugee Students in Israel.*
7. Z.A. interview with Baruch Mizrachi, Paris, March 1, 1970. On Egyptian Jewry before and during the 1948 war, see Zeltzer, pp. 27-31; *The Treatment of Jews in Egypt and Iraq*, pp. 9-12; and "The Situation in Moslem Countries," *Current Events in Jewish Life*, 2d Series, No. 1, January-February, 1949, p. 3. Also *Al-Ahram, Le Monde, Neue Züricher Zeitung* and New York *Times* between November 2, 1947, and September 29, 1948.
8. Letter of Alexander Cohen, London, August 3, 1967.
9. *Laisha*, April 28, 1970.
10. Z.A. interview with Baruch Mizrachi, Paris, March 1, 1970. Cohen-Sidon, p. 77. See also Sansom, pp. 249-58; Robinson, *Anti-Jewish Persecution in Egypt*, pp. 1-2; Landschut, pp. 53-59; *Dvar Hashavua*, Tel Aviv, April 15, 1954; *Evidances*, Paris, November, 1954; and *Jewish Chronicle*, February 11, 1955.
11. *Bamahane*, June 18, 1965.

12. Letters of Moshe Sachs, Tel Aviv, July 6, 1970, and Murad Semach, Haifa, June 1, 1970.
13. Rabin and Ovadia, p. 29.
14. Letters of Murad Semach, Haifa, July 6, 1970.
15. Steve Eitan, pp. 17-26; Rabinowitz, pp. 33-35. Tadmor, pp. 30-33; Cohen-Sidon, pp. 39-45; Kimche, pp. 49, 59-66; Habas, pp. 29-36; and Dubkin, pp. 18-27. See also Dekel, *In the Path of the Brieha*; Derogy, *La Loi du Retour;* and Gilead, *Secret Defense.*
16. Z.A. interview with J.R., Tel Aviv, February 10, 1970; and with A.D., Tel Aviv, February 13, 1970. Also Rabin and Ovadia, p. 34; Ben Dan, p. 15. See *The Immigration Struggle*, by Yigal Alon.
17. *Ibid.*; Z.A. interview with Baruch Mizrachi, Paris, March 1, 1970.
18. Interview of Zvi Algat with Dr. A. Morris in *Maariv-Yamin Veleilot* (weekly supplement), May 28, 1965.
19. *Al Tahrir*, Cairo, December 21, 1954; Tadmor, p. 30; and *The Story of Zionist Espionage in Egypt* (hereafter cited as Zionist Espionage), p. 15. On early intelligence gathering in Egypt, see also *Shai*, by Efraim Dekel. *History of the Haganah*, by Yehuda Slotzki.
20. *Al Tahrir*, December 21, 1954 and *Al Akhbar*, December 24, 1954; also Steve Eytan, pp. 92-93; Zionist Espionage, pp. 29-39; *Yedioth Ahronoth*, December 13, 1964; and "Max Bennet. Note of the Government of Iraq to the Supreme Military Tribunal," quoted in *Jewish Observer and Middle East Review*, London, January 14, 1955. See also *To the Gallows*, by Yehuda Atlas.
21. *Al Tahrir*, December 21, 1954, and Z.A. interview, Los Angeles, February 25, 1971.
22. Z.A. interview, Los Angeles, February 25, 1971.
23. *Al Tahrir*, December 21, 1954; Zionist Espionage, p. 13; and *Egyptian Gazette*, Cairo, December 14, 16, and 17, 1954.

24. Z.A. interview, Los Angeles, February 25, 1971; Steve Eytan, pp. 92-93. Azar testimony at trial in *Jewish Observer and Middle East Review*.

CHAPTER IV

1. Hasin and Horowitz, p. 53.
2. *Ibid.*, pp. 11-32; Avneri; pp. 101-22; Steve Eytan, pp. 98-99. See also Bayne, *Israel's Affair* and Ben-Gurion, *Things as They Are*.
3. Steve Eytan, p. 91.
4. Gibli's refusal to assume responsibility for the operations in Egypt and his efforts to blame the minister of defense for giving the orders to initiate them triggered the Lavon Affair, Israel's *cause célèbre*. When, six years later, Lavon demanded to be cleared of any responsibility for the "security mishap," the investigation led to a feud between him and Ben-Gurion which would rock the country until late in 1964. Lavon eventually retired from public life; Gibli was exiled to the post of military attaché in London and finally left the Army in January, 1961.
5. "The Third Man," by A. B. (memorandum prepared at the authors' request), pp. 1-4. See also Steve Eytan, pp. 93-94. Bayne, p. 11; Hasin and Horowitz, pp. 85-86, 239; Zionist Espionage, p. 11, *Al Tharir*, December 21, 1954, and *Haolam Haze*.
6. Hasin and Horowitz, pp. 55. Steve Eytan, p. 94.
7. Interview, Los Angeles, February 25, 1971; *Al Tahrir*, December 21, 1954.
8. *Al-Ahram* and *al-Gumhuriya*, July 3 to 25, 1954. *Al-Tahrir*, December 21, 1954. Zionist Espionage, pp. 9-11, and *The Cairo Trial*, p. 3. See also "The Alexis Affair," *Haolam Haze*, Nos. 1385 and 1386, March 23 and April 1, 1964, and No. 1608, June 26, 1968—a disguised but accurate account of the case.
9. Interview, Los Angeles, February 25, 1971, and Zionist Espionage, p. 11.

10. *Ibid.* Also "The Cairo Trial" by Felix Harari, *Yedioth Ahronoth,* December 13, 1964.
11. Bar Zohar, "Damascus Calling Tel Aviv," *Haaretz* (weekly supplement), September 8, 1967, p. 7; and *Maariv-Yahim Veleilot*, May 28, 1965, p. 3. Eli's testimony in the first televised session of the court-martial (hereafter cited as Transcript No. 1 February 28, 1965, p. 9; also *Al-Hayat*, March 2, 1965.
12. Zionist Espionage, p. 13.
13. *Ibid.* Also *Jewish Observer*.
14. *Ibid.* On Ninio's suicide attempt see, "A Hanging Instead of a Meeting," *Haolam Haze*, No. 1425, December 30, 1964. *Yedioth Ahronoth,* December 13, 1964, and *Jewish Observer*, December 17, 1954. Victorine later claimed that Eliahu Armand Carmona, a clerk at the commercial firm in Heliopolis, had committed suicide because his daughter lived in Israel and he feared the authorities would suspect him of collaboration with the Zionists.
15. Interview, Los Angeles, February 25, 1971. Zionist Record, p. 37; and *Jewish Observer*, December 24, 1954.
16. "The Third Man," by A. B. (memorandum), pp. 4-11. Avri was tried in 1959 *in camera* by a military court in Jerusalem and sentenced to twelve years imprisonment on a security breach involving another mission in Germany. Azar was later commissioned a lieutenant in Zahal, Marzouk received the rank of second lieutenant, and Levi, Nathenson and Dassa became sergeants. They all were finally released in 1968 as part of an exchange of prisoners.
17. *Bamahane*, July 18, 1965; *Haaretz*, September 8, 1967. *Maariv-Yamim Veleilot*, May 28, 1965. Also *France Observateur*, Paris, June 16, 1955; and *Jewish Observer and Middle East Review*, October 15 and December 10, 1954.
18. Preliminary investigations in *Al-Ahram*, October 7 through 12, 1955, and Zionist Espionage, p. 23. Ninio's second suicide attempt in *Haolam Haze*, December

30, 1964, and "Record of Sessions, Special Military Tribunal, Case Against Thirteen Zionist Spies," Cairo Parquet (hereafter cited as Stenographic Record), 9. 379. Record), p. 379.

19. *Al-Ahram,* October and December 12, 1954; Radio Cairo, December 13, 1954. Zionist Record, pp. 25-26 and NBC interview with Interior Minister Zakharieh Muhieddin (transcript), New York, December 13, 1954. Also "Observations of the Public Prosecutor" (indictment), Cairo Parquet, November, 1954; excerpts in *Jewish Observer,* November 12 and December 3 and 31, 1954.

20. *Jewish Observer,* No. 52, December 24, 1954, p. 3-4; New York *Times,* December 22, 1954; and Zionist Espionage, p. 18 & 37; Cohen-Sidon, p. 67; and *Jewish Observer,* February 4, 1955.

21. Stenographic Record; "The Roger Baldwin Reports" (confidential), January 8, 10 and 12, 1955; "The Cairo Espionage Trial-Confidential Report," by MP Maurice Orbach, December 19, 1954; Correspondence of Maurice Orbach about the Cairo trial (letters), December 21, 1954, through February 10, 1955; Orbach eyewitness account, *Jewish Chronicle,* February 4, 1955, "Le Compte Rendu du Proces," *La Terre Retrouvé,* Vol. 24, No. 7, January 1, 1955; interview of Jacques Calmy with Maître Dreyfus-Schmitt, *La Terre Retrouvé,* February 15, 1954. See also New York *Times,* December 12 through 20, 1954; *Manchester Guardian,* December 23, 1954; and *Jewish Observer,* November 19, 1954, through January 14, 1955.

22. While Cairo was preparing the trial, Israeli authorities brought to court 14 teenagers from the Gaza secondary school, captured in February near Ashkelon; they all were sentenced to five years imprisonment for espionage in behalf of Egypt.

23. Cohen-Sidon, pp. 63-67; New York *Times,* February 1, 1955; *Al-Ahram,* February 6, 1955; *Manchester Guardian,* February 8, 1955; *Time,* New York, February 14,

1955, *Jewish Observer,* February 4, 1955; and *Maariv,* November 30, 1955.

24. Z.A. interview with Baruch Mizrachi, Paris, March 1, 1970.

25. *Ibid.* See also Karlikow, pp. 6-9, and Edward Wakin, *A Lonely Minority,* and "The Copts of Egypt," *MEA,* Washington, Vol. 12, No. 7, August-September, 1961, pp. 198-208.

26. Eli's testimony in Transcript No. 1, February 28, 1965, p. 23; also *Al-Hayat,* March 2, 1965, and *Bamahane,* July 18, 1965.

27. Letter of Eli to Alexander Cohen, Tel Aviv, May 28, 1959.

CHAPTER V

1. Eli's testimony in Transcript No. 1, February 28, 1965, pp. 24-25.

2. *Laisha,* April 28, 1970. Also *Maariv,* May 19, 1965.

3. *Ibid.* and *Haaretz,* May 19, 1965.

4. *Bamahane,* June 18, 1965.

5. In "Eli Cohen, The Life and Death of a Hero," by Arieh Avnery and Yichezkel Adiram, *Yedioth Ahronoth,* May 19, 1965.

6. Eli's testimony in Transcript No. 1, February 28, 1965, p. 25.

7. *Yedioth Ahronoth,* May 19, 1965.

8. *Ibid.,* and Z.A. interview with S.T., Tel Aviv, February 11, 1970; and Y.R., Ramat Gan, February 13, 1970.

9. *Laisha,* April 28, 1970.

10. On Nadia Cohen see Adam Sidon's interview in *Laisha,* May 25, 1965.

11. Z.A. interview with Nadia Cohen, Tel Aviv, February 26, 1970. Also *Haolam Haze,* No. 1446, May 26, 1965.

12. Eli's testimony in Transcript No. 1, February 28, 1965, pp. 28-29.

13. *Ibid.,* p. 30.

14. *Ibid.,* pp. 31-32.

15. Interview of François Voisin with Nadia Cohen. *France Soir,* March 12, 1965.

CHAPTER VI

1. Z.A. interview. Tel Aviv, February 8, 1970.

2. Eli's testimony in Transcript No. 1, February 28, 1965, p. 34.

3. *Ibid.*, and Ben Dan, p. 43-44.

4. Quoted in Rabin-Ovadia, p. 222.

5. *Ibid.*, pp. 218-19.

6. Quoted in Tadmor, p. 186; see also Steve Eytan, pp. 27-32.

7. Eli's testimony in Transcript No. 1, February 28, 1965, p. 35-36. Also *Al-Hayat*, March 2, 1965.

8. *Ibid.*

9. *Laisha*, April 28, 1970.

CHAPTER VII

1. Eli's testimony in Transcript No. 1, February 28, 1965, pp. 36-39.

2. Interview of Miguel Angel Roig (hereafter cited as M.A.R.) with Trinidad Rodriguez, Buenos Aires, July 12, 1966.

3. Z.A. interview with Mari Cruz Echeverria, Buenos Aires, March 16, 1968.

4. M.A.R. interviews with Juanita Echeverria, Buenos Aires, March 19 and 23, 1968.

5. *Gente*, Buenos Aires, August 12, 1965, p. 35.

6. *Ibid.*, p. 36.

7. *Ibid.*, p.37.

8. Letter to *Al-Hayat*, March 23, 1965, and *Yedioth Ahronoth*, May 18, 1965. Also *Gente*, August 12, 1965.

9. *Gente*, August 12, 1965, p. 35.

10. *Ibid.*, p. 36.

11. M.A.R. interview, Buenos Aires, July 12, 1966, and *Gente*, August 12, 1965, p. 37.

12. Eli's testimony in Transcript No. 1, February 28, 1965, p. 42.

CHAPTER VIII

1. "Notes sur le deroulement du coup d'Etat en Syrie," September 28-29, 1961. *Journal d'Egypte*, September 30, 1961, and *Orient*, Paris, Vol. 5, No. 19, 3ème Trimestre, pp. 177-95; "The Break-Up of the UAR," in *Middle East Record*, 1961, pp. 605-14. "The Break-Up of the United Arab Republic," by Patrick Seale, *The World Today*, Vol. 17, No. 11, November, 1961, pp. 471-79; *The Atlantic*, Vol. 209, No. 1, January, 1962, pp. 19 and 23; *The Reporter*, Vol. 25, November 26, 1961, pp. 29-31; *New Outlook*, Tel Aviv, Vol. 4, No. 8, October 11, 1961, pp. 33-36; *Israel Horizons*, New York, Vol. 9, No. 5, November, 1961, pp. 12-14 and 30. See also *What Happened in Syria?* by Muhammad Hassaneim Haykal Kutub Qawmiyyah, Cairo, 1962; *We Wanted A Union but They Gave Us a Plantation*, by Halil Kallas, Matboat al-Jamhuriyah, Damascus, 1962.

2. Z.A. interview with Nadia Cohen, Tel Aviv, February 26, 1970.

3. Eli's testimony in Transcript No. 1, February 28, 1965, pp. 44-46.

4. *Ibid.*, p. 49.

5. *Ibid.*, p. 52.

6. *Ibid.*, p. 53, and *Al-Asbua al-Arabi*, May 19, 1965.

7. Eli's testimony in Transcript No. 1, February 28, 1965, pp. 58-61.

8. Z.A. interview with M.R., United Nations, New York, January 18, 1969. *Al-Nahar* and *Al-Hayat*, March 2 through March 19, 1965. J.L. interview with H.T.M, Damascus, May 12, 1966.

9. Eli's testimony in Transcript No. 1, February 28, 1965, pp. 62-65.

10. Bill O'Donnell (cited hereafter as B.O.) interview with H.H.R., Beirut, June 3, 1968.

11. Eli's testimony in Transcript, No. 1, pp. 66-72.

CHAPTER IX

1. Series of articles by Sofie Reynolds in Maariv, June 1, through 5, 1965.

2. On Eli's relations with Sheik Majid al-Ard: J.L. interview with H.T.M., Damascus, May 12, 1966; and A.J., Damascus, May 17, 1966.

3. Ben Dan, p. 101.

4. Eli's testimony in Transcript No. 1, February 28, 1965, pp. 96-98; and J.L.'s Report No. 1, "Eli Cohen—Contacts on Collaborators" (hereafter cited as Report No. 1), p. 1.

5. Suidani Interview in *Al-Asbua al-Arabi,* May 19, 1965,

6. J.L., Report No. 1, p. 5.

7. *Ibid.,* p. 6-8. Also Z.A. interview with R.D., Zurich, March 2, 1970.

8. B.O. interview with B.C. Beirut, June 16, 1968. Also *Al Hayat* and *Al Nahar,* March 21, 1965.

9. *Al Asbua al Arabi,* May 19, 1965.

10. J.L., Report No. 1, pp. 9-13.

11. Eli's testimony in Transcript No. 1, February 28, 1965, pp. 101-3; *Al Asbua al-Arabi;* and J.L. Report No. 1, p. 14.

12. J.L. Report No. 1, p. 16-18.

13. Ben Dan, p. 104-5.

CHAPTER X

1. Paneth, p. 239; *Al-Nahar* and *Al-Gumhuriya,* April 15, 1961; *An-Nasr,* Damascus, April 11, 1961. Jerusalem *Times* (Jordan), April 24, 1961; *Akher Saa,* March 15, 1961. *Eichmann dans le miroir d'Israel,* Al-Taawon, Cairo, 1961, p. 12.

2. Eli's testimony in televised session no. 3 (hereafter cited as Transcript No. 3), March 19, 1965.

3. Z.A. interview, Munich, March 4, 1970.

4. Poliakov, p. 43-47; Hilberg, p. 81.

5. Hilberg, p. 78-112; Reitlinger, p. 236; Kempner, pp. 133-78; Hausner, pp. 1-5; Pearlman, pp. 443-90 and 581-82.

6. Letter of F. R. Bienenfeld to Dr. M. L. Perlzweig, New York, March 24, 1952. FRB/5/165B, World Jewish Congress. Also Franz Rademacher, World Jewish Congress Dossier. Correspondence between February 9, 1949, and March 24, 1952.

7. Request for Judicial Investigation by an Examining Magistrate. District court of Nuremberg-Fürth 10 JS 2464-67/48, Nuremberg, September 15, 1948.

8. Franz Rademacher. *Urteil des Schwurgerichts beim Landgericht Nürnberg-Fürth,* March 17, 1952. Also New York *Times,* March 18, 1952; Aufbau, New York, January 25 through April 18, 1952.

9. Tetens, pp. 45-48, 180-89; Letters of Carlos Estevez, Ministry of Foreign Affairs, Madrid, March 14, 1970; and Letter of consul general, José Balenchana, Marseilles, February 6, 1970.

10. Eli's testimony in Transcript No. 3, March 16, 1965, pp. 123-37.

11. Ben Dan, p. 155.

12. *Ibid.,* pp. 155-56.

CHAPTER XI

1. Radio Damascus, March 8, 1962.

2. *Haaretz,* March 5, 1962.

3. *Bamahane,* Vol. 14, No. 28, March 13, 1962.

4. Ben Dan, p. 108.

5. *Al-Baath,* March 9 and 10, 1962.

6. J.L.'s Report No. 2, "Eli Cohen—His Assignments' (hereafter cited as Report No. 2)., p. 3.

7. *Haaretz,* March 12, 1962.

8. *Haaretz* and Maariv, March 15, 1962, and *Barmahane, Vol. 14, No. 28, March 13, 1962.*

9. Von Horn, pp. 275-84.

10. Z.A. interviews, Tel Aviv, March 11 through 16, 1970, and *Bamahane,* March 13, 1962.

11. *Bamahane,* March 13, 1962, and February 11, 1969.

12. *Ibid.,* and March 27, 1962. Also *Haolam Haze,* No. 1280, March 12, 1962; interview with the commander of the Golani Sayeret, *Bamahane,* Vol. 14, No. 30, March 27, 1962; stenographic account of the interrogation of Hussein Ahmad Yechia, *Bamahane,* Vol. 14, No. 28, March 13, 1962; and Harel, *Tzlash,* Moked, Tel Aviv, n.d., pp. 208-20.

13. Interview with General Meir Zorea, *Bamahane,* March 27, 1962.

14. *Haaretz,* March 18, 1962.

15. *Bamahane*, March 27, 1962.
16. J.L., Report No. 2, pp. 2-4; and Ben Dan, p. 129.

CHAPTER XII

1. J.L., Report No. 2, pp. 19-21; "La Republique arabe syrienne à la lumière du coup d'état du 28 Mars, 1962," *Orient*, Paris, Vol. 6, No. 21, 1ère Trimestre, 1962, pp.11-17; and J.L. Report No. 2, pp. 5-9.
2. *Saab*, pp. 109-11; *Beeri*, p. 146; *Bamahane*, No. 31, April 3, 1962, p. 3-4. *Newsweek*, Vol. 59, April 9, 1962, p. 49. *The Economist*, Vol. 203, April 7, 1962, p. 15.; *New Outlook*, Vol. 5, No. 4, May, 1962, pp. 21-25; J.L., Report No. 2, pp. 11-12; Beeri., p. 146-47; and Rabinowitz, pp. 269-71.
3. *Al-Hayat*, April 15, 1962.
4. J.L. Report No. 2, pp. 13-16; Beeri, pp. 146-47; Rabinowitz, pp. 269-71.
5. *Newsweek*, Vol. 59, April 16, 1962, and *Economist* Vol. 203, pp.156-57, April 14, 1962, and April 21, 1962, p. 239.
6. *Jewish Observer and Middle East Review*, April 6, 1962.
7. *Al Nahar*, April 1, 1962, and Ben Dan, p. 124.
8. *Jewish Observer and Middle East Review*, April 6, 1962.
9. *Ibid.*, and *Bamahane*, No. 32, May 6, 1962.
10. *Ibid.*, and *Al-Hayat*, April 2 through 6, 1962.
11. J.L. Report No. 2, pp. 11-15.
12. Beeri, pp. 147-48 and 340-41.

CHAPTER XIII

1. On debriefing: Eli's testimony in Transcript No. 1, February 28, 1965, Z.A. interviews, Tel Aviv, February 10 and 11, 1970.
2. *Abu Jaber*, pp. 63-66; and "Damascus Calling Tel Aviv," by Michel Bar-Zohar, *Midstream*, Vol. 14, No. 9, November, 1968 (hereafter cited as Bar-Zohar, Damascus), pp. 43-44.
3. New York *Times*, September 13,

1962; *Haaretz*, September 17 and 18, 1962. See also *Times*, Vol. 80, September 21, 1962, p. 30, and *Newsweek*, Vol. 60, September 10, 1962, p. 59.
4. Eli's testimony in fourth televised session (hereafter cited as Transcript No. 4), March 19, 1965, pp. 23-27; also Beeri, pp. 148-49.
5. Seif's testimony in Transcript No. 4, pp. 29-31.
6. *Jewish Chronicle*, March 18, 1966, and J.L. Report No. 2, p. 24.
7. *Ibid.*; J.L. interview with H.T.M. Damascus, May 12, 1966; and *Haaretz*, May 19, 1965.
8. Eli's relationship with Aflak and Bitar is dealt with extensively in J.L.'s "Eli Cohen—Activities in the Baath" (hereafter cited as Report No. 3), pp. 7-21. Also "Profile of Michel Aflak," *Middle East and Maghreb Topics*, UK Foreign Office, London, November, 1969; *Newsweek*, Vol. 61, April 15, 1963, p. 50; "Documents on the Coup d'État in Syria," *Middle Eastern Affairs*, Vol. 14, No. 4, April 4, 1963, pp. 108-12; "Documents sur les revolutions d'Irak et de Syrie," *Orient*, Vol. 7, No. 25, 1ère Trimestre, 1963, pp. 177-90, and No. 34, pp. 181-82.
9. J.L. Report No. 3, pp. 31-34.
10. Beeri, pp 149-53 and 339. Saab, pp. 111-13, Kerr, pp. 58-61; Al Jundi, pp. 138-39; Abu Jaber, pp. 68-69; *Al Hayat*, March 9 and 14, 1963. *Arab Political Documents 1963, p. 77;* Le Monde, *March 21, 1963; New Republic*, Vol. 148, March 23, 1963, pp. 7-8.
11. J.L. Report No. 3, pp. 27-29.
12. *Minutes of the Unity Talks*, Muassassat al-Ahram, Cairo, 1963. See also Riad Taha, *Minutes of the Unity Talks*, Dar al-Kifah, Beirut, 1963; Saab, pp. 116-29; *Orient*, Vol. 7, No. 26 2eme Trimestre, 1963, pp. 7-14 and 105-50. *The Nation*, Vol. 196, May 4, 1963, pp. 375-76 and 384. *Jewish Observer and Middle East Review*, series of five articles, July 5 through August 12, 1963. The Federal Pact of April 17,

Ministry of Foreign Affairs, Tel Aviv (restricted).

13. J.L. Report No. 3, pp. 35-37; *Abu Jaber*, pp. 69 and 71; *Al-Jundi*, p. 139. *Al-Baath*, March 15 to 21, 1963; Radio Damascus, March 22, 1963.

14. Beeri, pp. 154-55. *Al-Hayat*, June 26 and 28, 1963; and *Al-Ahrar*, Beirut, June 27, 1963. *Al Baath*, July 8, 1963.

15. New York *Times*, July 23, 1964; Beeri, pp. 155-60 and 339.

16. J.L. Report No. 3, pp. 42-54, and Abu Jaber, pp. 73-74.

17. Beeri, pp. 155-56; Saab, pp. 130-31; *Al Hayat*, July 19, 1963. *Time*, May 1, 1963.

18. Abu Jaber, pp. 72-74; *Time*, July 26, 1963.

19. J.L. Report No. 3, pp. 42-54.

CHAPTER XIV

1. Eli's first visit in televised session No. 3 (hereafter cited as Transcript No. 3), pp. 96-97; second tour in J.L. Report No. 3, pp. 57-61. Also *Al Nahar*, May 19, 1965.

2. Z.A. interviews with Israel military personnel in Kuneitra, in February, 1970, and with M.D., Haifa.

3. J.L. Report No. 3, pp. 83-85; and Z.H. interviews in Kuneitra, February, 1970.

4. Ben Dan, p. 133.

5. Sentence of special military tribunal, Damascus, in *Al Naher* and *Al Safaa*, May 9, 1965.

6. J.L. Report No. 3, pp. 79-81; *Haolam Haze*. April 6, 1966.

7. J.L. Report No. 3, pp. 81-83; *Al Ahrar*, May 21, 1965.

8. *Al Nahar*, May 19, 1965.

9. Eli's testimony in Transcript No. 4, March 19, 1965, pp. 10-19. Also J.L. Report No. 3, pp. 23-31.

10. Bar Zohar, *The Hunt for German Scientists*, pp. 197-217 and 224-25; Avneri, pp. 13-16; Eisenberg, pp. 13-17; Also *Der Spiegel*, No. 53, 1963; *Stern*, April 23, 1964; *Candide*, Paris, No. 239, November 22, 1965, pp. 17-18; and *Saturday Evening Post*, July 13 and 20, 1963.

11. "German Scientists in Egypt," by Fred Udall (manuscript), pp. 15-26; see also Wolfgang, Lotz, *Mission in Cairo*.

12. Avnery, pp. 64-77, Tadmor, pp. 129-52.

13. Avnery, p. 64; Steve Eytan, pp. 31-32; Ben Dan, *Poker d'Espion*, pp. 96-162; Levit, pp. 250-53.

14. Interview of Aryeh Avnery with Iser Harel, p. 132; Steve Eytan, pp. 27-32; Tadmor, pp. 129-52; *Haolam Haze*, No. 1334, April 3, 1963. See also Michel Bar Zohar, *Iser Harel*.

15. Steve Eytan, pp. 33-37.

16. Interview of Joshua Tadmor with Meir Amit, in *Lamerchav*, 1965, and of Eytan Haber in *Yedioth Ahronoth*, September 6, 1968.

CHAPTER XV

1. Wiesenthal, *Ich Jagte Eichmann*, pp. 134-56; Carlson, pp. 401-3; Bar Zohar, *The Avengers*, p. 149. *Le Monde Juif*, Paris, No. 4, December, 1946, pp. 4-5.

2. Wiesenthal, *Ich Jagte Eichmann*, pp. 135-42.

3. Carlson, pp. 392-406.

4. Sidar and Grinberg, p. 94.

5. J.L. interview with H.T.M., Damascus, May 12, 1966.

6. Wiesenthal, *The Murderers Among Us*, pp. 78-95; *Ich Jagte Eichmann*, pp. 185-86 and 194-201; Carlson, pp. 434-35; Tetens, p. 203; Bar Zohar, *The Avengers*, pp. 114-23. See also *Revue*, Nos. 10, 11, 12, March 7, 14 and 21, 1953; and *Prevent W.W. III*, No. 41, January–February, 1952, pp. 13-15.

7. Bar Zohar, *The Avengers*, pp. 145-46.

8. Wiesenthal, *The Murderers Among Us*, pp. 301-8.

9. Bar Zohar, *The Avengers*, pp. 241-42; and *Ich Jagte Eichmann*, p. 246; *Revue*, No. 10, 11 and 12, March 7, 14 and 21, 1953. See also Alan Levy, *Wanted Nazi Criminals at Large*, Berkely, New York, 1962, and Joseph B. Schechtman, *The Mufti and the Führer*.

10. Eli's testimony and al-Ard's testimony in Transcript No. 4, March 19, 1965, pp. 139-215; Thayer, pp. 138-39.

11. Engelman, pp. 111-27; Thayer p. 138.

12. Lestchinsky, pp. 16-17; Nehemiah Robinson, *Jews in Moslem Lands*, pp. 14-15.

13. On Heyden: L.C. Report No. 2, p. 48; on Israeli prisoner: Hameiri, p. 50.

14. *A Secret Syrian Document Reveals,* Zahal Spokesman Office, Ministry of Defense, Tel Aviv, n.d.; *Congress Weekly, Vol* 24, April 8, 1957, pp. 5-7; *La Terre Retrouvé,* May 15, 1957, p. 7, and *Jewish Observer,* August 9, 1957, p. 7.

15. Ben Dan, p. 160.

16. Testimony of Eli and Seif in Transcript No. 4, March 19, 1965, pp. 111-14; J.L. Report No. 3, pp. 39-40.

17. Testimony of Maazi in Transcript No. 4, March 19, 1965, pp. 115-27.

CHAPTER XVI

1. *Laisha,* April 26, 1966, and April 28, 1970.

2. Bar Zohar, *Damascus,* pp. 46-48.

3. Eli's testimony in Transcript No. 4, March 19, 1965, pp. 23-26; L.C. Report No. 3, pp. 42-43; A.M.R. interview with J.L.C., Buenos Aires, July 15, 1966.

4. *Abu Jaber,* pp. 86-88; Beeri, pp. 199-201.

5. *Al Baath* and *Al Nahar,* January 8 and 24, 1964.

6. Demchenko, pp. 15-19; Gataullin, pp. 18-19; Sikov, pp. 12-15; *Sirii,* pp. 395-99; Sultanov, pp. 157-60; Laqueur, *The Soviet Union and the Middle East,* pp. 197-98, 216-22, and 247-61.

7. Laqueur, *The Soviet Union and the Middle East,* pp. 153 and 264-75; *Communism and Nationalism in the Middle East,* pp. 263-7.

8. Hinton, pp. 181-5; *China Quarterly,* No. 18, April–June, 1964, pp. 182-83; *For Eastern Economic Revue,* January 23, 1964, pp. 154 ff.

9. Eli's testimony in Transcript No. 4, March 19, 1965, pp. 43-45. L.C. Report No. 2, pp. 39-40. See also Ben Dan, pp. 159-60.

10. J.L. Report No. 3, pp. 69-72; also L.C. "Indications on the Second Session Held *in Camera*," and Bar Zohar, *Damascus,* p. 46.

11. Eli's testimony in Transcript No. 4, March 19, 1965, pp. 67-68. L.C. Report No. 3, p. 16; interview of J.L. with A.K.R., Damascus, May 27, 1966. See also Bar Zohar, *Damascus,* pp. 47-48.

CHAPTER XVII

1. J.L. Report No. 3, p. 15, and interview with K.K.H., Aleppo, May 23, 1966. See also *Abu Jaber,* pp. 89-91.

2. J.L. interview with K.K.H. Aleppo, May 23, 1966; and with H.T.M., Damascus, May 12, 1966. Also Beeri, pp. 157-59; Saab, pp. 169, 237-38; Golan, pp. 35-36; *Abu Jaber,* pp. 71-72; *Al Akhbar,* Cairo, April 8, 1964, *Al-Jarida,* Beirut, April 15, 1964; *Al Hayat,* April 25, 1964; and *Al Baath,* April 27, 1964.

3. On Hatoum's promotion, J.L. Report No. 3, p. 115; also *Time,* May 1, 1964.

4. Yaari, p. 31.

5. *Ibid.,* pp. 15-25; Yitzhaki, p. 38; Harkabi, pp. 24-25; Kimche and Bawly, pp. 9-22; *Arab World,* New York, May, 1969, pp. 16-23; *Arab Journal,* New York, Vol. 2, No. 3, summer, 1965, pp. 3-7; *Diskussion,* Vol. 6, No. 17, 1965, pp. 10-12; *Al Nahar* (supplement), February, 1968.

6. Interview of Ghareeb Edmund with Yassir Arafat, *Arab World,* New York, May, 1969, pp. 26-28; Yaari, pp. 10-21; Yitzraki, pp. 46-47; Kimche and Bawly, pp. 9-18; *Haolam Haze,* No. 1599, September 13, 1969; *Akhbar Saa,* Cairo, April 24, 1968; and *Al-Mussawar,* May 24, 1968.

7. Yaari, pp. 39-40; Yitzhaky, pp. 34-35; and *Al Ziyad,* Beirut, August 12, 1965.

8. *Al Baath,* November through December 31, 1964.

9. *Al Aharrar*, May 19, 1965.

10. J.L. Report No. 3, pp. 135.

11. J.L. Report No. 3, pp. 137-9; interview with H.T.M., Damascus, May 16, 1966; *Al-Ahran,* May 19, 1965.

12. Ben Dan, p. 178.

13. *Laisha*, April 26, 1966; Bar Zohar, *Damascus*, pp. 46-48.

14. *Ibid.*

15. The Mosad would unofficially deny that Eli had been advised to marry Saliha if Abu Mahmud's pressure intensified.

16. *Bamahane*, July 18, 1965.

17. Ben Dan, *Mirage Against Migs*, pp. 79-80; *Haaretz*, November 14, 1964.

18. J.L. Report No. 3, pp. 50-51. See also New York *Times*. On events at the beginning of 1965, see Saab, pp. 208-29. On nationalizations, see New York *Times*, December 12, 1964, and *Time*, January 22, 1965.

CHAPTER XVIII

1. *Al-Muharrer*, May 21, 1965; *Al-Safaa*, May 19, 1965.

2. Levit, pp. 76-77.

3. *Middle East Record, 1961*, pp. 602-4.

4. Beeri, p. 165; Saab, p. 230, *Haaretz*, No. 23, March 15, 1968; *Al-Jarida*, August 3, 1965; and L.C. "Akid Ahmad Suidani."

5. Bar Zohar, *Damascus* p. 48.

6. *Al-Hayat*, May 19, 1965.

7. *Al-Hayat*, Al-Safaa and *Al Hamishmar*, May 19, and 20, 1965.

CHAPTER XIX

1. February 25, 1965.

2. *Al-Hamishmar*, *Le Monde*, and New York *Times*, February 25, 1965; and Radio Damascus, January 24, 1965.

3. Z.A. interviews, Tel "Aviv, February 15 through 23, 1970.

4. *Ibid.*

5. *Ibid.*, and New York, September 3, 1968; and Washington, March 27, 1967.

6. *Yedioth Ahronoth*, May 21, 1965.

7. Letter of Dr. Bruno Pietermann, December 31, 1969; *Yedioth Ahronoth*, May 21, 1965. *Gente*, Buenos Aires, August 21, 1965.

8. "Eli Cohen. Dossier I Spionnagesaak E.C. 65/05/4/10," Archives Camille Huysmans, Antwerp, Belgium.

9. *Yedioth Ahronoth*, May 21, 1965.

10. B.O. interviews in London, July 15, 1969, through March 12, 1970.

11. *Yedioth Ahronoth*, May 21, 1965.

12. Letter of Linus Pauling, October 10, 1969; Z.A. interviews, Washington, March 17, 1967.

13. Z.A. interviews at the United Nations, July through September 17, 1968.

14. *Gente*, August 12, 1965; letter of the Ministry of Foreign Affairs, Buenos Aires, March 23, 1970.

15. *La Prensa*, February 28, 1965; and *Gente*, August 12, 1965.

16. Letter of Eugene Descamps, October 9, 1969; *Yedioth Ahronoth*, May 21, 1965. See also Ben Dan, p. 202.

CHAPTER XX

1. Hafez interview in *Al-Asbua al-Arabi*, May 19, 1965.

2. *Al-Hayat*, May 19, 1965.

3. On al-Mazza Prison see Hameiri, pp. 22, 44, 63 and 74; also series in *Yedioth Ahronoth*, March 17-22, 1966; Margalit, pp. 44 and 159-65.

4. Margalit, pp. 45-62, and Hameiri, p. 29.

5. J.L. Report No. 1, pp. 39-46.

6. *Ibid.*, p. 72. Also interview with H.T.M., Damascus, May 12 and 14, 1966.

7. *Newsweek*, March 14, 1965; and *L'Observateur Juif du Moyen Orient et de L'Afrique*, Paris, March 5, 1965.

8. Sofie Reynolds in *Maariv*, June 1, 1965.

9. J.L. Report No. 1, pp. 13-19; and interview with M.A.S., Damascus, July 18, 1966.

10. *Al-Asbua al-Arabi*, May 19, 1965.

CHAPTER XXI

1. Z.A. interview in Paris, March 2, 1970.

2. Letter of Maître Jacques Mercier to Walid Taaleb, Beirut, March 13, 1965 (hereafter cited as Letter A) and Letter of Batonnier Paul Arrighi and Maître Jacques Mercier to General Amin al-Hafez, Paris, May 24, 1965 (hereafter cited as Letter B).

3. Interview of Edwin Eytan with Maître Jacques Mercier in *Yedioth Ahronoth,* May 19, 1965 (hereafter cited as Interview A) and May 21, 1965 (hereafter cited as Interview B); Inter of Uri'Dan with Maître Mercier in *Maari,* May 19, 1965 (hereafter cited as interview C), and May 21, 1965 (hereafter cited as Interview D).

4. Letter A, May 24, 1965.

5. *Ibid.*

6. *Ibid.*

7. *Ibid.,* and letter of Maître Mercier to Walid Taleb, Beirut, March 3, 1965 (hereafter cited as Letter C).

8. Interview A.

9. Interview of Adam Sidon with Nadia Cohen, *Laisha,* May 25, 1965; and Interview of Bruria Avidan with Sofia Cohen, *Laisha,* April 20, 1970.

10. *France-Soir,* March 7, 1965.

11. Letter B; and letter to Z.A., December 31, 1969.

12. Report of Maître Adrian Wolters, Brussels, March 19, 1965 (hereafter cited as Report A).

13. *Ibid.*

14. *Ibid.,* and letter to Z.A., Brussels, October 30, 1969.

CHAPTER XXII

1. *Al-Hayat, Al-Muharrer, Al-Ahrar* and *Al-Baath,* March 2, 1965.

2. Description by author was made after viewing tape of the first televised session of the court-martial.

3. Transcript No. 1, February 28, 1965, pp. 1-20; also *Al-Hayat,* March 2, 1965.

4. *Ibid.*

5. *Al-Baath,* March 2, 1965

6. Transcript No. 1, February 28, 1965, pp. 21-25.

7. *Ibid.*

8. Transcript No. 3. March 16, 1965, pp. 37-52.

9. *Al-Hayat,* March 19, 1965.

10. Transcript No. 3, March 16, 1965, pp. 48-53.

11. Transcript No. 4, March 19, 1965, pp. 78-92.

12. *Al-Hayat,* March 19, 1965.

13. *Al-Ahrar,* March 20, 1965.

CHAPTER XXIII

1. J.L. Report No. 1, pp. 9-11.

2. *Al-Ahram,* March 17, 1965.

3. Radio Baghdad, and *Al-Gumhuriya* (Baghdad), March 16, 1965.

4. Transcript No. 3, March 16, 1965, pp. 61-2.

5. *L'Observatore du Moyen Orient et de l'Afrique,* May 19, 1965.

6. *Al-Baath,* May 9, 1965, and *Al-Hayat,* May 9, 1965.

7. *Ibid.* and *Al-Nahar,* May 9, 1965.

8. *Al-Hayat,* May 9, 1965.

CHAPTER XXIV

1. Nadia Cohen interview in *Laisha,* April 26, 1966.

2. *Haaretz,* May 19, 1965.

3. Ben Dan, p. 203; also J.L. and Z.A. interviews, Paris, March 2, 1970, and *Le Monde,* May 20, 1965.

4. Letter of Victor Feather, London, December 1, 1969.

5. Letter of John G. Diefenbacker, Ottawa, September 19, 1969.

6. Interview A and B; *Le Monde,* May 22, 1965.

7. Interview A and B.

8. Letter B, May 24, 1965.

9. *Jewish Chronicle,* May 21, 1965.

10. Letter of Sean MacBride, October 2, 1969.

11. *Times*, London, May 30, 1965.
12. *L'Observateur du Moyen Orient et de l'Afrique*, May 28, 1965.
13. *Maariv*, May 23, 1965.
14. Radio Damascus, January 3, 1965.
15. *Haaretz*, May 19, 1965.
16. *Haaretz*, May 21, 1965.
17. Letter B.
18. Ben Dan, pp. 204-5.

CHAPTER XXV

1. Special supplement inserted in *Yaish al-Saab* and *Mujlat al-Jundi*, Damascus, May 28, 1965 (hereafter cited as Supplement).
2. B.O. interviews, Beirut, January 12, 1968.
3. *Jewish Chronicle*, February 21, 1964.
4. Supplement, May 28, 1965.
5. *Ibid.*
6. *Ibid.* Also letter in *Al-Hayat,* May 19, 1965; *Yedioth Ahronoth,* May 19, 1965.
7. *Al-Hayat*, May 19, 1965; Radio Damascus, May 19, 1965.
8. Description made by authors after viewing tape of execution. Also *Al-Hayat, Al-Nahar, Amman al-Massa* and *Yedioth Ahronoth*, May 18, 1965.

EPILOGUE (SYRIA)

1. *Maariv*, January 17, 1969.
2. *Ibid.*
3. *Ibid.*
4. Karlikov, pp. 13-14; *Jews in Arab Countries During the Six Day War*, June, 1967; *Jews in Arab Countries Since the Six Day War*, August, 1967; *Jerusalem Post*, October 28, 1968; *Yedioth Ahronoth-7*

Yamim, No. 331, May 15, 1970, pp. 5-8.
5. Beeri, pp. 164-5; Abu Jaber, XI-XIII; Rabinowitz, pp. 269-71; Saab, pp. 224-50.
6. *Ibid.; Haaretz*, April 16, 1968.
7. *Ibid.; Al-Hayat*, August 21, 1969.
8. Saab, pp. 234-5; Beeri, pp. 159-62.
9. *L'Express*, Paris, No. 774, April 18, 1966.
10. *Haaretz*, No. 23, March 15, 1968.
11. *Jewish Observer*, September 23, 1966.
12. Beeri, p. 169; *Moscow Times*, July 27, 1968.
13. *Le Monde*, February 16-17, 1969; *Jewish Observer*, July 19, 1968.
14. *Haolam Haze*, January 8, 1969.

ISRAEL

1. *Maariv*, May 19, 1965.
2. *Davar*, Tel Aviv, May 19, 20 and 21, 1965.
3. *Haaretz*, May 21 and 23, 1965.
4. *Laisha*, April 26, 1966.
5. Davar, May 20, 1965.
6. *Haaretz*, May 19, 1965.
7. *Ibid.*
8. *Herut, Haboker, Jerusalem Post* and *Davar*, May 19, 1965.
9. *Jewish Chronicle*, May 21, 1965.
10. Interview C and D.
11. Radio Damascus, May 21, 1965.
12. *Al-Baath*, May 20, 1965.
13. *Haaretz*, May 20 and 21, 1965.
14. *Maariv*, May 21, 1965.
15. *Al-Akhbar*, July 3, 1965.
16. *Yedioth Ahronoth-7 Yamin,* June 12, 1968.

Index

447